L · I · V · Y

DATE DUE

DEMCO 38-296

Also by Gary B. Miles

Virgil's "Georgics": A New Interpretation

L · I · V · Y

RECONSTRUCTING EARLY ROME

GARY B. MILES

Cornell University Press

Ithaca and London

First published 1995 by Cornell University Press.
First printing, Cornell Paperbacks, 1997.

Library of Congress Cataloging-in-Publication Data

Miles, Gary B.
    Livy : reconstructing early Rome / Gary B. Miles.
       p. cm.
    Includes bibliographical references and index.
    ISBN 0-8014-3060-7 (cloth: alk. paper)
    ISBN 0-8014-8426-X (pbk.: alk. paper)
    1. Rome—History. 2. Rome—Historiography. 3. Livy. Ab urbe condita. 4. Livy—Criticism and interpretation—History.
I. Title.
DG207.L583M5   1995
937—dc20
                           94-43821

Printed in the United States of America

♾ The paper in this book meets the minimum requirements of the American National Standard for Information Sciences—Permanence of Paper for Printed Library Materials, ANSI Z39.48-1984.

Cloth printing   10 9 8 7 6 5 4 3 2 1

Paperback printing   10 9 8 7 6 5 4 3 2 1

For Penny,
my prose for your poetry,
and
for Peggy,
of course

————————————

Contents

Acknowledgments

This book is the product of work done intermittently over a decade. During this time I have enjoyed support from several institutions and individuals. The generous sabbatical program of the University of California and research grants awarded by the Academic Senate of the University of California, Santa Cruz, have been indispensable, as was a National Endowment for the Humanities Fellowship, which allowed me to devote all of 1986 to research on this project. I am indebted to Michael Cowan, David Konstan, and T. J. Luce for supporting my application for that fellowship. David Konstan, in addition, read some of the earlier material in this book, as well as some false starts, and offered criticisms with a wonderful blend of perceptiveness and tact. T. J. Luce and Kate Toll read the entire manuscript with a sympathetic care for which I cannot express adequate thanks. The editor and other readers for Cornell University Press have also provided much valued guidance. I am especially indebted to Daniel Selden, who read several of the later chapters in various stages, made suggestions that helped me rethink and recast important parts of my arguments, and urged me to gather them into a single volume. Without his insight and encouragement, this book would not exist. Others who have kindly taken the trouble to read and criticize drafts of one or another of the chapters in the book are the late Archibald W. Allen, Robert McMahon, and my friends and colleagues at the University of California, Santa Cruz: Karen Bassi, Norman O. Brown, Mary-Kay Gamel, Charles Hedrick, Sharon James, and Helene Moglen. The editorial skills of my wife, Peggy Miles, have contributed to the clarity and coherence of my arguments in many places. Jennifer Wheat and Lauren Woll rendered valuable assistance in proofreading. I am especially grateful as well for Marian Shotwell's excellent copyediting.

I owe a different sort of thanks to the early morning crew at Queens, Ernie Tanaka, my friends in the HLSA and the BSSA, and especially Gary Silberstein, all of whom helped me keep things in perspective while I was working on this book.

Earlier versions of Chapters 2, 3, and 5 were published, respectively, as "The Cycle of Roman History in Livy's First Pentad," *American Journal of*

Philology 107 (1986): 1–33; "*Maiores, Conditores,* and Livy's Perspective on the Past," *Transactions of the American Philological Association* 118 (1988): 185–208; and "The First Roman Marriage and the Theft of the Sabine Women," in *Innovations of Antiquity,* ed. Ralph Hexter and Daniel Selden (New York: Routledge), pp. 161–96. I am grateful for permission to reuse that material here.

G. B. M.

Abbreviations

Abbreviations used for ancient authors and works are generally those listed in the *Oxford Classical Dictionary*. The following works are also abbreviated.

ANRW   *Aufstieg und Niedergang der römischen Welt*. Edited by Hildegard Temporini and W. Haase. New York: de Gruyter, 1972–.

BMCRE   H. Mattingly, *Coins of the Roman Empire in the British Museum*. London: Trustees of the British Museum, 1965.

CIL   *Corpus Inscriptionum Latinarum*.

FGH   *Die Fragmente der griechischen Historiker*. Edited by Felix Jacoby. Berlin and Leiden: E. J. Brill, 1961.

HRR   *Historicorum Romanorum Reliquiae*. Edited by H. Peter. 2 vols. Stuttgart: Teubner, 1967.

IG   *Inscriptiones Graecae*.

ILS   *Inscriptiones Latinae Selectae*. Edited by H. Dessau. Rept. Chicago: Ares, 1979.

LSJ⁹   Henry George Liddell, Robert Scott, and Henry Stuart Jones, eds. *Greek-English Lexicon*. 9th ed. Oxford: Clarendon Press, 1961.

Ogilvie   R. M. Ogilvie. *A Commentary on Livy: Books 1–5*. Oxford: Oxford University Press, 1970.

RE   *Paulys Real-Encyclopädie der classischen Altertumswissenschaft*.

Introduction

Two distinct schools have set the tone for modern scholarship on Livy. Each has its own virtues, but each has also imposed its own limitations on subsequent Livian scholarship. The first, in order of time and influence, is *Quellenforschung*, the effort to identify the literary sources Livy used and to describe how he used them.[1] Because their principal tack has been the identification and reconstruction of Livy's sources, the practitioners of Quellenforschung have generally sought to explain his narrative, and, in particular, apparent inconsistencies or anomalies in it, in terms of those sources. This effort has discouraged them (and others influenced by them) from attempting to understand Livy's narrative in terms of its own dynamics and has led to a perception of Livy as a historian of indifferent, if not outright inferior, talents—one who chose his sources more or less randomly and who, once having chosen them, followed them mechanically. Such a perception has of course further discouraged critics from looking to Livy for interesting ideas of his own, particularly in the area of historiography, where his supposedly arbitrary and mechanical reliance on his sources would seem to preclude the possibility of his having possessed any coherent historiographic principles.

There is a further limitation to Quellenforschung. Insofar as it is concerned with Livy's relation to sources that no longer survive, it necessarily operates in terms of comparisons and contrasts on a rather gross level.[2] It cannot effectively take into account the elaborations, condensations, and changes of diction that accompany any rewriting of a source, even at the level of paraphrase. Consequently, Quellenforschung itself cannot address the extent to which such changes may have been coherent and systematic

---

1. For a more detailed, and more impassioned, critique of Quellenforschung and its impact on appreciation of Livy, see T. J. Luce, *Livy: The Composition of His History* (Princeton: Princeton University Press, 1977), pp. xv–xxvii; for a more general review and critique of the prevailing modern view about the historical tradition of early Rome (of which Livy's narrative is a part), see also T. J. Cornell, "The Formation of the Historical Tradition of Early Rome," in *Past Perspectives: Studies in Greek and Roman Historical Writing*, ed. I. S. Moxon, J. D. Smart, and A. J. Woodman (Cambridge: Cambridge University Press, 1986), pp. 67–86.

2. This is especially true of the early books, less true of the period for which Livy relies heavily on Polybius.

1

and may have resulted in significant changes of emphasis and meaning between Livy's narrative and its source at any particular point.

The second group of Livian critics addresses this deficiency, although their perspective has its own limitations. This group constitutes what, for want of a generally accepted name, I will call the rhetorical-thematic school of interpretation. Its most influential and prolific practitioner has been Erich Burck.[3] Scholars of this orientation have sought to demonstrate Livy's literary originality and excellence. They have concentrated their attention chiefly on two closely related areas: structure and theme. Structure concerns, specifically, the effective units or episodes within Livy's narrative and the artistry with which those episodes are constructed and integrated with one another. The structural approach is essentially formal and rhetorical. The thematic approach concerns central or controlling ideas that provide the unifying focus for individual episodes or the underlying common element for an entire book or part of one. The two approaches, although different in their central emphases, often overlap considerably.

Their practitioners, especially Burck, have often found it useful to contrast the organization of a particular episode or section of Livy's narrative with parallel narratives in other authors (most frequently, of course, Dionysius of Halicarnassus). Although the use of such comparisons regularly confirms the distinctiveness of Livy's handling of particular material, it has rarely led to a direct challenge to the conclusions reached through Quellenforschung. The reasons for this are essentially twofold. The first is simply that Quellenforschung and rhetorical-thematic analysis deal with very different kinds of evidence and reasoning and focus on very different questions: Quellenforschung, on Livy's sources and analytical methodology (or lack of it); rhetorical-thematic analysis, on both the finer questions of style that Quellenforschung cannot address and thematic questions that have been outside

---

3. The first and most influential of Burck's many studies of Livy is *Die Erzählungskunst des T. Livius*, a revision of the *Habilitationsschrift* that he presented to the University of Münster in 1931. It was republished with a new foreword in 1964 by Weidmann, Berlin and Zurich. Most recently, Burck has published a broad-ranging literary history of Livy's narrative, *Das Geschichtswerk des Titus Livius*, Bibliothek der klassischen Altertumswissenschaften, n.s. 2, vol. 87 (Heidelberg: Carl Winter, 1992). A good sense of the kind of work done by Burck's successors is available in *Livius: Werk und Rezeption: Festschrift für Erich Burck zum 80. Geburtstag*, ed. Eckard Lefèvre and Eckard Olshausen (Munich: C. H. Beck, 1983). Burck himself was extending the more narrowly focused concerns with structure that Kurt Witte pioneered in his "Über die Form der Darstellung in Livius' Geschichtswerk," *Rheinisches Museum* 65 (1910): 270–305, 359–419, repr. separately (Darmstadt: Wissenschaftliche Buchgesellschaft, 1969).

the interest of Quellenforschung. There simply has been very little common ground on which the two schools might confront each other.

A second reason that rhetorical-thematic analysis has not led to a general reopening of the questions apparently closed by Quellenforschung has to do with certain limitations of the rhetorical-thematic school itself. This school has generally argued for Livy's originality in matters of style and rhetorical organization, while conceding his lack of originality in the area of content.[4] Perhaps because he was viewed as a typically derivative Roman (inferior to the Greek historians just as Roman poets were at one time regarded as inferior to their Greek predecessors) or because Quellenforschung seemed to have precluded the possibility of conceptual originality in this particular author or because Augustus' program of reform seemed to necessitate the uncritical taking of sides rather than the critical examination of them, even the most sympathetic of Livy's critics have generally tended to interpret his narrative by identifying which among established Roman views are reflected in it. They ask: Does he subscribe to Stoic notions of fate? Are his sentiments Republican or Augustan? Which of the several circumstances traditionally thought responsible for the decline of Rome does he emphasize? How are traditional Roman virtues (*moderatio, constantia, pietas,* for example) exemplified in his narrative? This line of approach has proven to be highly productive, but it has not challenged the perception of Livy as an essentially unoriginal, derivative author. His narrative remains for most of his critics a selective, but otherwise more or less straightforward, compendium of traditional Roman stories, values, and attitudes, artful at its best, but a compendium nonetheless—scarcely a place to look for original ideas about the nature of history and historical inquiry or to explore the ideological complexities, paradoxes, and contradictions that one might expect to find in times of such extraordinary turbulence, disjuncture, and change as the period of transition from Roman Republic to Roman Empire.[5]

4. Burck makes this concession explicit on p. 34 of "Zum Rombild des Livius," *Der altsprachliche Unterricht* 3 (1957): 34–75: "Livy clearly had no strong philosophical gift and disposition that would have led him from the actual course of Roman history to general discussions of basic historical, political, or social problems and would have induced him to form a judgment of principle regarding the historical forces, possibilities, and missions of Rome. As is well known, general remarks on the phenomena of politics and power are almost totally lacking, as well as any methodological reflections on the analysis of his materials that . . . go beyond reporting the historical facts to seek to establish their fundamental significance and importance."

5. Perhaps it is my own bias, but I find too few scholarly discussions of Livy that regard him either as independent enough to transcend conventional Roman ideas or as complex enough to reflect contradictions within Roman ideology itself. An example of the former is

In 1977, T. J. Luce mounted a sustained challenge to Quellenforschung, an attempt to refute its depressing conclusions about Livy's history and to open the way for serious consideration of him as a historian. Even in Luce, however, we can feel the ponderous weight of traditional scholarship in the substantial ground that he is willing to concede to Livy's critics and in the modesty of the claims that he seeks to substantiate on behalf of Livy's narrative:

> Livy was an uneven writer, capable of great care and great carelessness in almost the same stroke of the pen. . . . Nor will it be claimed that he was one of the leading intellects of the ancient world. Livy was not a deep thinker; but he was intelligent and ought to be treated as a thinking adult who had ideas concerning the subject he chose to write about. . . . Although for most matters of fact and for many of interpretation he had to follow what his sources reported and although he did not possess the (mostly modern) critical tools to evaluate, select, and combine their various elements to form a version essentially of his own making, he was nevertheless still free to omit, expand, abridge, and change sources over long stretches; hence, it will be argued, he was able to impose a design and structure of his own on the larger units of his history. In this respect, I believe, he was in control of his sources, rather than an immovable victim caught in their toils. The structure, however, was not one of great complexity. . . . The traditional view . . . that Livy's chief contribution to his history was in the adaptation of individual scenes and episodes is probably true.[6]

Perhaps the most influential aspect of Luce's argument, certainly the one that received the most consistent praise from his reviewers, has been his rebuttal of scholars who had characterized Livy's narrative as lacking the most basic historiographic elements. As one reviewer observed, "[Luce's] brave aim is to vindicate Livy from the charges of Collingwood and Syme and other critics . . . that Livy was unable to interpret historical phenomena or visualize historical change. This book is the first to come to grips with these criticisms."[7] In particular, Luce refuted R. G. Collingwood's conclusion

---

Joseph B. Solodow, "Livy and the Story of Horatius, 1:24–26," *Transactions of the American Philological Association* 109 (1979): 251–68; of the latter, Patricia Klindienst Joplin, "Ritual Work on Human Flesh: Livy's Lucretia and the Rape of the Body Politic," *Helios* 17 (1990): 51–70.

6. Luce, p. xxvi.

7. P. G. Walsh, review of *Livy: The Composition of His History*, by T. J. Luce, *Phoenix* 32 (1978): 271. George Houston, in his review of the book in *Classical Philology* 75 (1980): 73–77, also acknowledges the originality and significance of Luce's thesis, while offering a more qualified assessment of its success.

that Livy had no sense of historical change, a conclusion that Collingwood had advanced on the grounds that Livy presented Rome as full-blown from its inception.[8] Luce demonstrates, to the contrary, that Livy presents Roman character and institutions as developing by a process of "accretion."[9] In this and in other ways, Luce sought to open Livy's narrative to serious inquiry about a larger range of issues, especially historiographic, than had concerned previous critics. Luce's avowedly, although modestly, controversial work was met with mixed reviews. Although most of them were enthusiastic, praising its usefulness and originality, few scholars have as yet taken up Luce's invitation to look for complexity and originality in Livy's historiography and in his conceptualization of Roman history.[10]

My goal here is partly to respond to Luce's invitation. I do so principally in two ways: by approaching Livy with questions about his historiography and ideology that have received little attention to date and by viewing Livy's narrative from new theoretical and methodological perspectives. The chapters that follow suggest how these two approaches can lead to progressive refinement in analysis, working from themes that are developed systematically in the narrative to implicit contradictions that reflect larger, ideological dilemmas. Although Chapters 1 to 3 focus primarily on historiography and Chapters 4 and 5 on ideology, my underlying purpose is to demonstrate that both of these subjects are in fact inextricably interwoven in Livy's narrative and, together, express his particular relationship to his society and its dominant ideologies.

Chapter 1 lays out and supports the basic assumptions on which arguments in the subsequent chapters depend. Underlying its own argument are two theoretical assumptions. The first is that interpreting a text involves in part a process of decoding it, of identifying meaning not only in specific statements but also in various kinds of rhetorical gestures. The second is that this activity in turn involves continual interaction between reader and text as the reader negotiates the text, seeking to find meaning in it, that is, to supply meaning to it. I apply these methodologies, first, to identify the

---

8. R. G. Collingwood, *The Idea of History* (Oxford: Clarendon Press, 1946).

9. Luce, chap. 7, pp. 230–97, and p. 239 for the idea of "accretion" in particular.

10. In addition to Walsh and Houston, cited in note 7 above, see for a favorable review Paul Jal in *Latomus* 39 (1980): 230–34. The review of John Briscoe, *Journal of Roman Studies* 68 (1978): 227–28, however, is highly critical. One work that does approach Livy from a radically new perspective, although coming out of a different philosophical tradition from Luce's, is Michel Serres' *Rome: Le livre des fondations* (Paris: Éditions Grasset & Fasquelle, 1983), trans. Felicia McCarren under the title *Rome: The Book of Foundations* (Stanford: Stanford University Press, 1991).

analytic categories that Livy himself employs to discriminate among different kinds of evidence and, then, to illuminate the ways in which he actually employs those categories in constructing his history—an investigation that leads to reassessment of the fundamental question, what is the object of this historian's narrative? My answer is that Livy makes quite clear his awareness of the limitations of the available evidence as a means for reconstructing the past that lies behind it. His narrative is organized so as to direct attention away from the idea of Roman tradition as something permeable, through which the historian may penetrate to a prior reality, toward the idea of tradition as something opaque and impenetrable and therefore itself the ultimate object of the author's reconstruction, analysis, and interpretation.

Chapters 2 and 3 focus more directly on Livy as an active interpreter and reinventor of tradition. Methodologically they are the most conservative, lying essentially within the tradition of New Criticism as it has been diffused and modified over the past several decades. What is new here, or at least atypical in the context of Livian scholarship, is that I apply this critical approach directly to historiographic issues, and, in particular, to the question of whether Livy's narrative is informed by a coherent concept of historical time. I originally took up this question after rereading an article in which my former mentor, Adam Parry, explicated the conception of time and evolution in Thucydides' archaeology.[11] In Chapter 2 I offer one answer to this question as it applies to Livy, and I further refine and develop that answer in Chapter 3. As a kind of by-product, both chapters indicate that Livy's historiography at its most fundamental levels is informed by and expresses an active engagement with the ideologies of his own age.

Chapters 4 and 5 directly address the subject of political and cultural ideology in Livy's narrative. My approach in Chapter 4, although not itself Marxian, was inspired by the combination of semiotic and Marxian analysis in Fredric Jameson's *Political Unconscious: Narrative as a Socially Symbolic Act*. Particularly valuable to me were his demonstrations of the ways in which deep narrative structures may express ideological dilemmas that are ultimately rooted in the social and political structures of societies themselves.[12] Chapter 4 is concerned with such dilemmas in Livy's story of Romulus. Chapter 5 employs perspectives from anthropology as heuristic devices to help expose and focus attention on another set of ideological dilemmas. Here, comparison

---

11. Adam Parry, "Thucydides' Historical Perspective," *Yale Classical Studies* 72 (1972): 47–61.

12. Fredric Jameson, *The Political Unconscious: Narrative as a Socially Symbolic Act* (Ithaca, N.Y.: Cornell University Press, 1981).

between Livy's narrative and those of several other ancient authors is central and serves not only to suggest how deeply rooted those dilemmas were in Roman ideology but also to develop, through explicit contrast, a theme common to the preceding chapters: how exceptionally persistent Livy was in confronting and engaging problems of methodology and ideology.

I was initially inclined to let my arguments speak for themselves and to forego a direct survey of the methodologies underlying them. I was concerned that such a survey might seem pretentious to those familiar with a body of theory that is now widely used outside the study of Livy, or, equally, that it might evoke the prejudices of those in the field who continue to regard the application of modern critical theory to ancient texts as artificial and inappropriate. In the end I decided that it would be better to take those risks in hopes that doing so would contribute to a clearer understanding of my own critical assumptions, would help explain the rationale for this book's organization, and might be of value to those who share my interest in discovering new ways of approaching Livy's narrative.

My criticisms of the Quellenforschung and rhetorical-thematic traditions notwithstanding, it will be clear to any student of Livy that my own work relies very heavily on, indeed would be unthinkable without, the achievements of the scholars who have preceded me. If I have been able to spy out any new possibilities here, it is because of my vantage point on the shoulders of such giants as R. M. Ogilvie in the Quellenforschung tradition and Erich Burck in the rhetorical-thematic school, and because of the invaluable syntheses of P. G. Walsh, the magisterial overview of Ronald Syme, and the pioneering work of David Packard, whose concordance to Livy has been invaluable.

Chapter 1

History and Memory
in Livy's Narrative

That identities and memories change over time tends to be obscured by the fact that we too often refer to both as if they had the status of material objects—memory as something to be retrieved; identity as something that can be lost as well as found. . . . Memories and identities are not fixed things, but representations or constructions of reality, subjective rather than objective phenomena. . . . And "memory work" is, like any other kind of physical or mental labor, embedded in complex class, gender and power relations that determine what is remembered (or forgotten), by whom, and for what end.

John R. Gillis, introduction to *Commemorations:*
The Politics of National Identity

Examples of Livy's shortcomings as a systematic, analytical evaluator of historical evidence and of his often arbitrary treatment of questions of historical fact are familiar to all students of his narrative. Modern scholars have traditionally responded to such examples by understanding them in terms of "Livy's" own character and disposition, seeing them as consequences of and evidence for his carelessness as a historian, for his personal lack of interest in methodological rigor and even in narrative consistency. Insofar as scholars have directed attention toward the personal failings of "Livy" as a historian, they have also contributed to the negative evaluation of his work that remains influential in modern scholarship. It is not my purpose here to refute such essentially circumstantial and speculative arguments about Livy's personal disposition or the specific circumstances of his narrative's

All translations are my own. For Livy books 1–5 I have followed the text of R. M. Ogilvie, *Titi Livi Ab Urbe Condita,* vol. 1 (Oxford: Clarendon Press, rpt. 1979), unless otherwise noted.

8

composition. These arguments have often served a purpose.[1] While they can find support in professions of uncertainty and indifference in the author's own text, their effect, nonetheless, has been to divert attention from the text itself, from consideration of how lack of methodological clarity or authorial professions of disinterest function in their immediate contexts, how they influence the ways in which readers must negotiate the text and its arguments. Analysis of what Livy says in his preface and of his practice in the narrative reveals that he uses the traditional apparatus of historical analysis available to him in new ways and to new effect. To appreciate the extent to which his methods and their results were unconventional, it will be necessary first to look briefly at the historiographic tradition within which Livy operated, second to examine the ways in which he evokes that tradition, third to look at his actual practice, and, finally, to consider its implications, both political and historiographic.

I

The great historians who preceded Livy focused primarily on events that happened either within their own lifetimes or within the lifetimes of their informants; events, that is, for which they could rely heavily on their own firsthand observations and, more often, on the eyewitness accounts of others: Herodotus on the Persian wars, Thucydides the Peloponnesian wars, Polybius the Punic and Macedonian wars. Those same authors played a decisive role in defining history as a literary genre that is centrally concerned with the historian's unique claim to reconstruct as true, as accurate, or as reliable an account of past events as possible.

Just as these Greek historians defined the genre of history with its distinctive claims to "truth," so they established the standards, the essential terms, by which claims to historical truthfulness were to be measured. When they took up questions about the past and how to evaluate evidence for it, their theoretical discussions reflected a long-standing tradition in Greek thought that was especially well suited to their more particular interests in the immediate past:[2] the principle that direct, firsthand observation, autopsy,

---

1. E.g., T. J. Luce, "The Dating of Livy's First Decade," *Transactions of the American Philological Association* 71 (1965): 209–40.

2. Thus Polybius (12.28a) says that the difference between a history based on the author's own participation in or direct, personal observation of the events that he narrates and history based on hearsay is greater than the difference between real buildings and painted images of them.

was the most reliable basis on which to reconstruct a record of events.[3] Indeed, the very term that came to identify the narratives of past events based on critical assessment of evidence, *historia,* is derived from the Indo-European root **weid,* "to see."[4]

By the time of Polybius, the problem of weighting different kinds of direct and indirect testimony had been developed at some length. Kenneth Sacks has observed that Polybius' theoretical analysis ordered the ways of gathering evidence into a clear hierarchy: "with one's eyes, by actually witnessing events; with one's ears, by interviewing witnesses; and again with one's ears, by reading written accounts" (27.1–4). "Ancients 'heard' memoirs, as all reading was done aloud. This last approach to collecting information . . . is the least accurate."[5] Although Polybius placed sight at the top of his hierarchy, he recognized, as had Thucydides before him (1.22.2–3), that even direct observation could be unreliable if biased or uncritical (Polyb. 12.4d, 24). The corrective to such shortcomings for Polybius lay in practical personal experience of warfare and politics. Such experience alone prepared one to be an informed and critical interpreter of evidence (Polyb. 12.25e–g, l, 27a, 28a). This final and ultimate standard for historical criticism is directly related to Polybius' own understanding of the special function of history, to educate generals and statesmen, but it is also

3. Bruno Snell surveys the history of this idea chiefly in the Greek archaic literary and philosophical tradition in "Human Knowledge and Divine Knowledge among the Early Greeks," in *The Discovery of the Mind,* trans. T. G. Rosenmeyer (New York: Dover, 1982), pp. 136–52.

4. See H. Frisk, *Griechisches etymologisches Wörterbuch* (Heidelberg: Carl Winter, 1973), vol. 1, pp. 740–41 s.v. ἵστωρ. I am aware, of course, that the primary sense of *historia* is related to the juridical concept of inquiry or investigation (see Gerald A. Press, *The Development of the Idea of History in Antiquity* [Montreal: McGill-Queens University Press, 1982], pp. 23–34) and even more specifically to the juridical concept of arbitration (see Gregory Nagy, *Pindar's Homer* [Baltimore: Johns Hopkins University Press, 1990], pp. 250–73). The root idea of seeing, however, lies behind the predilection for firsthand knowledge, personal confrontation and interrogation of witnesses, and direct examination of material evidence, all of which are essential to the juridical concepts of inquiry, investigation, and arbitration.

5. Kenneth Sacks, *Polybius on the Writing of History,* Classical Studies 24 (Berkeley: University of California Press, 1981), pp. 49–50, with reference to Kendrick W. Pritchett, *Dionysius of Halicarnassus: On Thucydides* (Berkeley: University of California Press, 1975), pp. 67–68, on reading as an oral activity in antiquity. On written documents as the least reliable sources, see also Polyb. 12.25i. Other major discussions of Polybius' theory include F. W. Walbank, *Polybius* (Berkeley: University of California Press, 1972), esp. pp. 43–58 and 66–74; Charles Fornara, *The Nature of History in Ancient Greece and Rome* (Berkeley: University of California Press, 1983), esp. pp. 112–16.

very closely associated by him with the idea of direct observation.[6] At 12.25g he develops the position that personal experience in warfare and politics is essential for the historian, on the grounds that lack of such experience leads to the arbitrary inclusion and omission of details. He illustrates this claim by observing that Timaeus, as a result of his lack of personal experience, often makes this error (i.e., arbitrarily including or omitting detail in his historical accounts), because he doesn't rely on the evidence of his own eyes, *dia tēn aorasian*. Thus, even though Polybius is aware that direct observation has its limitations, it remains for him the superior kind of historical testimony. Oral evidence, hearsay, and what one "hears" from written documents remain at the bottom of Polybius' list as less reliable sources of information about the past (12.25i, 27a, and 28a).

Not all of Livy's predecessors, of course, confined themselves to recent history. Among the Greeks there were the logographers and Atthidographers, many of whom dealt with foundations, *ktiseis*, in the remote past of legend and myth. Ephorus, the author of the first universal history, began his narrative with the legendary invasion of the Peloponnese by the Heraclidae. In Italy the elder Cato and such early historians as Fabius Pictor and Cincius Alimentus went back to the origins of Rome. But the latter, according to Dionysius of Halicarnassus, treated early history in a very summary way (*kephalaiōdōs*, Dion. Hal. 1.6.2), concentrating instead on contemporary events that they could record "accurately because of their experience," *dia tēn empeirian akribōs* (1.6.2). The fragmentary nature of those works makes conclusions about their theory and methodology highly speculative. Such indirect evidence as we have suggests that the long-established, deeply rooted, elemental distinction between seeing and hearing in ancient historiography was essentially unaltered by the emergence of historians who dealt with the remote past, and that it remained one of the two essential standards inherited by Livy for judging historical sources.[7] The reliance on the dichotomy set up by Polybius (especially given his methodological self-consciousness and his active engagement with the theory and practice of his predecessors) certainly suggests that it continued to provide the essential theoretical framework within which ancient historians operated.

---

6. For modern discussion see especially Sacks, chaps. 2 (pp. 21–95), 4 (pp. 122–70), and especially 6 (pp. 171–86); and Walbank, *Polybius,* chap. 3 ("Pragmatike historia"), pp. 66–96.

7. The other was freedom from personal bias. See Fornara, pp. 99–104; and T. J. Luce, "Ancient Views on the Causes of Bias in Historical Writing," *Classical Philology* 84 (1989): 16–31.

Livy's Greek contemporary, Dionysius of Halicarnassus, is not unaware of the problems of writing about Rome's early history. Methodologically he justifies his own efforts on the grounds that no "accurate history," *akribēs historia*, of Rome existed in Greek, only brief epitomes (1.5.4). In referring to his own practice, Dionysius claims that he based his narrative on

τὰ μὲν παρὰ τῶν λογιωτάτων ἀνδρῶν, οἷς εἰς ὁμιλίαν ἦλθον, διδαχῇ παραλαβών, τὰ δ' ἐκ τῶν ἱστοριῶν ἀναλεξάμενος, ἅς οἱ πρὸς αὐτῶν ἐπαινούμενοι Ῥωμαίων συνέγραψαν. (1.7.3)

what, on the one hand, I have learned orally from the most learned men with whom I have come into contact, and, on the other hand, what I have read from the histories written by those whom the Romans approve.

Here Dionysius seems to be trying, with some difficulty, to adapt the traditional distinction between hearing and seeing to his particular circumstances. He contrasts what he has learned by hearing (*paralabōn*) with what he was able to read (*analexamenos*). In both cases his sources of evidence are indirect, and he seeks to ameliorate that limitation in two ways. Regarding what he has heard, he emphasizes that he has heard it at first hand, and that he has heard it from "the most learned men," *logiōtatōn*. This same appeal to authority seems to be the best he can do in the face of previous written narratives that are not those of eyewitnesses: he has selected those of "approved," *epainoumenoi*, authors. He does not, however, attempt to identify what makes an informant "learned" or on what basis an author comes to be "approved." Nonetheless, Dionysius explicitly dissociates himself from those who base their narratives on "random oral reports," *tōn epitychontōn akousmatōn* (1.4.2).[8]

The absence of any real methodological alternative to the established dichotomy between hearing and seeing created problems for Livy as well, inasmuch as he chose to treat the history of early Rome in much more than cursory fashion. By the prevailing, indeed by virtually the only explicit, standard of his age and tradition, Livy could not hope to reconstruct a reliable account of this remote period of Roman history. His decision to treat that remote past at some length raises at least two questions within the context of ancient historiography. The first has to do with the basis on which Livy would rest history's unique claim to accuracy and reliability,

8. For discussion of other aspects of Dionysius' methodology, see Emilio Gabba, *Dionysius and the History of Archaic Rome,* Sather Classical Lectures 56 (Berkeley: University of California Press, 1991), pp. 60–92.

that is, by what standards would he discriminate among his sources? The second question follows from the first: since he could not hope to achieve a fully accurate or reliable record of the past by traditional historiographic standards, on what basis could he rest his claim for the value of his work? Explicitly or implicitly, Herodotus, Thucydides, and Polybius had established historical recurrence, the inevitable similarity, if not identity, of patterns of events in the future to those in the past as the principal source of history's appeal and value.[9] While there might be disagreement over whether recognition of patterns in past events enabled one to plan for the future in such a way as to alter its course, there was undoubted agreement that it did make possible a fuller and more precise comprehension of present events and their likely consequences.[10]

Among Livy's Roman predecessors the idea of history's utilitarian value had been refined and reinforced by the example of Polybius, a native didactic tendency, and perhaps also by Greek rhetorical teaching.[11] But any sense of utility based upon analogy between past and present events depends on the accuracy with which the past has been reconstructed. Polybius makes this explicit: "Past events make us particularly attentive to the future, if in each case one investigates the past truthfully," συνεφίστησι γὰρ τὰ προγεγονότα πρὸς τὸ μέλλον ἡμᾶς οἰκείως, ἐάν τις ὑπὲρ ἑκάστων ἀληθινῶς ἱστορῇ τὰ παρεληλυθότα (12.25e–6). To write a history about a past

9. On the essential similarity of Herodotus and Thucydides in this regard I find Virginia Hunter, *Past and Process in Herodotus and Thucydides* (Princeton: Princeton University Press, 1982), especially useful. For Polybius, see 12.25b.

10. The ambiguity as to whether a knowledge of history enhances control of the future or merely enables recognition of familiar patterns is most close to the surface in Thucydides; see, for example, his famous remarks about recurrence at 1.22.4; his account of the plague (2.47–54), especially 2.48 (and see A. M. Parry's excellent discussion in "The Language of Thucydides' Description of the Plague," *Bulletin of the Institute of Classical Studies* 16 [1969]: 106–8); and his description of *stasis* at Corcyra (3.70–84.1). Polybius introduces his work by endorsing the view of "all" historians that "the most reliable education and training for political affairs is the learning of history," ἀληθινωτάτην μὲν εἶναι παιδείαν καὶ γυμνασίαν πρὸς τὰς πολιτικὰς πράξεις τὴν ἐκ τῆς ἱστορίας μάθησιν (1.1.2), although he perhaps qualifies that optimistic view of history's practical usefulness when he goes on to observe that "the most manifest and only teacher of the ability to bear fortune's vicissitudes nobly is being reminded of others' reversals," ἐναργεστάτην δὲ καὶ μόνην διδάσκαλον τοῦ δύνασθαι τὰς τῆς τύχης μεταβολὰς γενναίως ὑποφέρειν τὴν τῶν ἀλλοτρίων περιπετειῶν ὑπόμνησιν.

11. For a clear survey of the idea of utilitarian history, its evolution and sources in antiquity, see Fornara, pp. 109–20, although I do not find all of his conclusions persuasive. For a survey of relevant Latin sources for the idea, see A. D. Leeman, *Orationis Ratio* (Amsterdam: Adolf M. Hakkert, 1963), vol. 1, pp. 67–88.

that could not, by contemporary standards, be accurately reconstructed strains both the traditional definition of history as a literary genre and the basis for its claim to offer a useful perspective upon the present. Such an undertaking, therefore, demands either that history rest its claim to the reader's attention on some basis other than utility or that the relationship between utility and the accuracy of historical reconstruction be somehow recast.

In his preface Livy addresses these problems directly and explicitly, but only briefly and partially. The positions that he sketches in the preface are elaborated, modified, and more fully integrated implicitly in the subsequent course of the narrative itself. The result, as we shall see, is a historiography that evolves during the course of the narrative as the narrator confronts successive problems, a historiography that is particularly well suited to the author's specific social and political circumstances, and that issues, finally, in a distinctive conception of the proper object of history and of the historian's role.

II

In the opening sentence of his preface Livy identifies two standards by which he expects his narrative to be judged. One is its accuracy. The other is its style, an aspect of historical narrative that distinguished it from such nonliterary products as *commentarii* and that was regarded as essential to history's capacity to persuade and give pleasure:

> Facturusne operae pretium sim si a primordio urbis res populi Romani perscripserim nec satis scio nec, si sciam, dicere ausim, quippe qui cum ueterem tum uolgatam esse rem uideam, dum noui semper scriptores aut in rebus certius aliquid allaturos se aut scribendi arte rudem uetustatem superaturos credunt. (pref. 1–3)

> Whether it would be worthwhile if I should write the affairs of the Roman people continuously from the very beginnings of the city, I don't really know. Even if I should know, I would not dare to say, inasmuch as I see that the subject is an old and a common one, while new writers one after another believe either that they will have something more reliable to add in their facts or that by their skill in writing they will surpass crude antiquity.[12]

12. On the idea that one of history's distinctive functions is to produce pleasure in its readers, see Fornara, pp. 120–34. On Roman views of history as a *munus oratoris* that must be persuasive and give pleasure, see also Leeman, pp. 168–97.

In this introductory statement Livy evokes the standards of accuracy and pleasure only to cast doubt upon his ability to be successful on those terms. Nonetheless, he goes on to identify them as the particular virtues of his work, but he does so in such a way as to give to each his own, subtly distinctive meaning. He returns to the idea of pleasure after first calling attention to the antiquity of his subject (the story of Rome from its origins) and his expectation that such remote history will be of little interest to the majority of his readers—impatient as they are for an account of their own troubled age. It is at this point that he reintroduces the idea of pleasure, offering the very remoteness of his subject, its apparent irrelevance to the present, as the distinctive basis for its capacity to please: it provides a distraction from present ills, which may be titillating but are nonetheless distressing to contemplate. Content, then, not style, will be the source of pleasure in Livy's history, but content here has the capacity to please, and to do so, paradoxically, precisely because it concerns events that are remote rather than contemporary.[13]

The second section of the preface (usually printed in modern editions as the second of two paragraphs) focuses on the closely related subjects of usefulness and accuracy. This section leads to a clear and dramatic affirmation of the usefulness of Livy's undertaking in terms that are entirely consistent with established historiographic notions:

> Hoc illud est praecipue in cognitione rerum salubre ac frugiferum, omnis te exempli documenta in inlustri posita monumento intueri; inde tibi tuaeque rei publicae quod imitere capias, inde foedum inceptu foedum exitu quod uites. (pref. 10)

> This is what is especially beneficial and fruitful in the study of affairs, that you look to models of every kind as though set in an illustrious monument. From there you may choose for yourself and your state what to imitate and what, shameful in both its inception and outcome, to avoid.[14]

Livy has set this statement, however, in a new relationship to the problem of historical accuracy, one that suggests a somewhat modified basis for historical utility and the possibility of a new kind of utility itself.

---

13. For further elaboration of the interrelations between pleasure and historical subject matter in Livy's preface, see John Moles, "Livy's Preface." *Proceedings of the Cambridge Philological Society* 39 (1993): 141–168.

14. On the difficulties of translating *in inlustri posita monumento,* see Ogilvie, ad loc., p. 28.

In the sentences leading up to this assertion of his work's utility, Livy addresses the question of accuracy and the special problems that it entails for the study of the remote past:

> Quae ante conditam condendamue urbem poeticis magis decora fabulis quam incorruptis rerum gestarum monumentis traduntur, ea nec adfirmare nec refellere in animo est. Datur haec uenia antiquitati ut miscendo humana diuinis primordia urbium augustiora faciat; et si cui populo licere oportet consecrare origines suas et ad deos referre auctores, ea belli gloria est populo Romano ut cum suum conditorisque sui parentem Martem potissimum ferat, tam et hoc gentes humanae patiantur aequo animo quam imperium patiuntur. Sed haec et his similia utcumque animaduersa aut existimata erunt haud in magno equidem ponam discrimine. (pref. 6–7)

> As for those things that are handed down from before the city was founded or was planned, things more in keeping with poetic fictions than with the reliable monuments of deeds, these I intend neither to affirm nor to refute. This concession is made to antiquity, namely, that the mingling of the human and the divine may make the beginnings of cities more venerable. And if it is appropriate that any people be allowed to treat its origins as sacred and to trace them to divine agents, such is the military glory of the Roman people that especially when they report that Mars is their own parent and the parent of their founder, the peoples of the world accept this also with equanimity, just as they accept Roman rule. But as for these and things similar to them, I at any rate will not make an issue of them, whatever attention or judgment they attract.[15]

Several aspects of this passage deserve close attention. First is the introduction here of the familiar discrimination between oral and visual evidence that is expressed in the contrast between *fabulae* and *monumenta*. *Fabula*, based on the IE root **fa-*, "to talk," in its most limited sense means "talk" or "conversation" but most often has clearly pejorative associations: "fiction,"

---

15. J. Poucet, "Temps mythique et temps historique: Les origines et les premiers siècles de Rome," *Gerion* 5 (1987): 69–85, esp. pp. 76–78 and 85, locates Livy's skepticism here in relation to the larger traditions of Roman and Greek historiography. For his more general argument (with which I am not here concerned) that Livy did not support the notion of divine intervention in human affairs and in Roman destiny in particular, see I. Kajanto, *God and Fate in Livy*, Annales Universitatis Turkensis 64 (Turku: Turun Yliopiston Kustantama, 1957), esp. pp. 42–53. To his survey of opposing views (esp. p. 10) should be added M. Rambaud, "Une défaillance du rationalisme chez Tite-Live?" *Information littéraire* 7 (1975): 21–30.

"nonsense," "myth," or "legend," as well as "drama" or "pretence." It is in turn the root of *fabulosus,* "legendary," "incredible," "unhistorical."[16]

Monumentum, by contrast, is based on IE **men-,* "to think," plus the causative suffix **-yo,* plus *-mentum,* an expanded form of the suffix *-men,* and so means, at base, "something that makes one think." In Livy, as in other authors, *monumentum* refers so often to specific, concrete objects that the very few occasions when it does not do so can be taken as metaphors.[17] Often *monumenta* refers to objects that were created intentionally to serve as memorials: "monuments," tombs, temples, and the like. A second major subcategory in the word's usage is constituted by physical things, objects, and places that may not have been intentionally created as memorials but nonetheless serve that function: the remains of walls and trenches that recall great wars, for example, or, equally often, simply the place where something dramatic and memorable occurred.[18] A further distinctive subcategory of usage comprises written documents.[19]

In this context what distinguishes the written from spoken word and, similarly, what the basis is for the preference of the visible thing over the spoken tradition are suggested by Livy's characterization of *monumenta* as *incorrupta,* "uncorrupted," literally, "undamaged" or "unbroken." The essential attribute of *monumenta,* whether written or not, is that they are themselves direct survivals from the past for which they provide evidence: they represent an unbroken link with the past, a part of the past that is still available for direct, personal inspection. By implicit contrast, oral tradition, *fama, fabula,* is *corrupta,* that is, composed of a series of independent repetitions, of retellings, each separated from the last. Inasmuch as its path is marked by a succession of ruptures, it can guarantee no continuity between present and past. To the extent, then, that Livy can base his narrative on *incorrupta*

16. See *Oxford Latin Dictionary,* s.vv. "fabula," "fabulosus." See also Ogilvie who observes that *"fabula* for Livy means a story to which he attaches little belief," p. 675.

17. E.g., in Camillus' speech at 5.52.1, where "These great monuments of worshipped and neglected divinity," *Haec culti neglectique numinis tanta monumenta,* seem to refer generally to the consequences of the Romans' worship or neglect of their gods, although those consequences had been made visible in the successive growth, destruction, and recovery of the city.

18. Walls and trenches: e.g., 10.15.5, 45.27.11; places: e.g., 1.48.7, 6.20.12, 26.41.11 (Trebia, Trasumennus, Cannae), 5.30.2 (the city of Rome itself).

19. E.g., 2.33.9, 6.1.2, 6.29.9, 7.21.6, 8.11.16, 29.37.7, 38.57.8, 39.37.16. The range of phenomena (including written texts and histories) encompassed in the term *monumentum* as used by Livy is well within the limits of conventional Roman thought: see T. P. Wiseman, "Monuments and the Roman Annalists," in *Past Perspectives: Studies in Greek and Roman Historical Writing,* ed. I. S. Moxon, J. D. Smart, and A. J. Woodman (Cambridge: Cambridge University Press, 1986), p. 89 and n. 13 there.

monumenta, he can make some claim to the precision, accuracy, carefulness, and truthfulness that lie at the heart of history's traditional claim and obligation to be useful, to provide a reliable model for the extrapolation of present events by analogy with the past. So far, then, Livy has acknowledged ideas about the nature and role of history that were well established in the historiographic and rhetorical traditions of his age, and has attempted to adapt them to the specific subject matter of his own historical narrative.

Other aspects of this passage hint at a departure from historiographic tradition. Even though Livy acknowledges the utter unreliability of the earliest period of Roman history, for which *fabulae* provide the only evidence, he not only expresses his intention of including that period within his narrative but gives two reasons for doing so. The first is that stories about the divine origins of states are commonly accepted because they lend dignity to their subjects. His illustration of this point, the story of Romulus' descent from Mars, suggests a second reason for inclusion of unverifiable traditions about the remote past. According to Livy, this story has a certain kind of validity. It expresses something about how the Romans choose to view and represent themselves; something, moreover, that is in some sense both true and verifiable in the present, namely, Rome's overwhelming superiority in warfare. Thus, in addition to history's traditional concern with the past as a succession of specific patterns that can provide a model for the present ("what to imitate and what, shameful in both its inception and outcome, to avoid," *quod imitere capias, inde foedum inceptu foedum exitu quod uites,* to use Livy's own words), Livy's preface suggests another subject for his narrative, the collective identity of the Roman people, a subject that depends less upon what actually happened in the past than upon how the past has been remembered. The discussion of Rome's early history and of Mars, brief and dismissive as it is, may be read as an elaboration of Livy's affirmation at the outset of his preface: "I will take pleasure nonetheless in the fact that to the best of my ability I too have given thought to the memory of the deeds of the leading people on earth," *iuuabit tamen rerum gestarum memoriae principis terrarum populi pro uirili parte et ipsum consuluisse* (pref. 3). Note that Livy here anticipates pleasure from giving thought not to the Romans' actual deeds but to "the memory" of their deeds—a subtle distinction perhaps, but possibly not insignificant, as the later reflection on Mars and his meaning suggests.[20]

---

20. Contrast Moles, p. 148, who regards the contrast between *fabulae* and *monumenta* in Livy's preface as an unqualified token of Livy's commitment to history that "will be true . . .

Still, in Livy's preface it is the traditional conception of history as a source of useful analogies that receives the most emphasis and to which the greatest significance and value are attached. Livy professes to indulge the fantastic stories that intermingle human and divine only for the earliest period of Roman history (a period for which there simply is no other evidence) and promises thereafter to focus on the paradigmatic *uita, mores, uiri, artes,* by which Rome grew great at home and abroad—attributes, presumably, for which he can rely upon the evidence of *monumenta.* From the very outset of the narrative, however, the characters of these spheres of history (oral tradition and material evidence, early myth and later exempla), their relationship to each other, and their relative value prove to be very much more complicated and problematic than they initially appear to be in the preface. Ultimately, it is the problem not of constructing an accurate, "truthful" record of past events but rather of revealing the character of the historical tradition itself, the collective memory of the Roman people, and so, their identity, that becomes the persistent focus of Livy's narrative.

Let us examine several narrative passages in which Livy calls attention, both explicitly and indirectly, to his performance as a historian, to the ways in which he does and does not evaluate the evidence available to him, and to the ways in which he communicates his judgments about historical evidence to the reader. We shall see that rhetorical gestures asserting the narrator's authority and methodological integrity do not hold up to close or systematic scrutiny. Rather, their failure, whatever it may suggest about "Livy's" character, constitutes a consistent pattern that is significant within the context of the narrative itself. At one level, the narrator's conspicuous and repeated difficulties constitute, paradoxically, a proof of his integrity, evidence that he does not make a greater claim to certainty and factual reliability than the historical tradition will bear. In an age when the systematic appropriation of the past in the interests of political programs was especially blatant, the author's own avowed inability to resolve questions of facticity reinforces his claim that factual certainty is impossible, while at the same time removing him from the field of potential competitors for control over the past—a position that is consistent with the emphatically deferential stance that Livy assumes in his preface. Another effect of the narrator's conspicuous and repeated failure to control the rhetoric of factual analysis and source criticism is to divert the reader's attention from questions of historical facticity

---

in the most basic sense: factually true." It is the purpose of this chapter in part to argue that such a reading, while questionable for the preface, fails to consider how Livy's historiographic goals and expectations evolve in the course of his narrative.

to other, more rewarding sources of intelligibility and meaning in the narrative.

III

Livy begins with a period of Roman history for which, we have been informed in the preface, there are no reliable records. The rhetoric of the opening narrative recalls that judgment and is shaped so as to incorporate its implications into the actual narration. In fact, the distinctive rhetoric of this opening narrative can be read on more than one level and performs more than one function. On one level, it offers familiar kinds of reassurances about the narrator's conscientiousness and critical discernment as an interpreter of his sources. The narrative opens with a series of rhetorical gestures that confirm the narrator's awareness of the unreliability of the tradition within which he is writing and that call attention to his own discrimination.

The very first sentence begins a report in indirect statement that is governed by the assertion *satis constat,* "there is sufficient agreement," a statement that implies an awareness of disagreement within the tradition.[21] The subsequent indirect discourse serves to mark the narrator's own reserve about material that he reports, not on his own authority but rather on that of this "sufficient agreement." This use of indirect discourse to mark authorial reserve and distance is apparently confirmed when the narrator switches to direct discourse in order to identify a "real" place associated with the tradition, a place that exists and is known in the narrator's own time. Not

---

21. Here I expand upon the idea of "shifters," changes between first- and third-person narrators that express different attitudes toward material reported in a historical narrative. The seminal formulation of this concept is Roland Barthes, "Le discours de l'histoire," *Social Science Information* 6 (1967): 65–75, reprinted several times, recently in Roland Barthes, *The Rustle of Language,* trans. R. Howard (New York: Hill and Wang, 1986), pp. 127–40. The use of indirect discourse makes possible a similar distinction between third-person narrator and other third-person authorities whom the narrator may invoke ("This happened" vs. "They say that this happened"). In Latin and Greek the use of extended indirect discourse may serve both to keep the implied change of perspective vividly before the reader's attention and to define precisely its extent, as though parts of the text were printed in italics, the rest in the usual roman face. For further references to the theoretical literature on the concept of "shifters" and for examples of its application to analysis of an ancient historian, see Carolyn Dewald, "Narrative Surface and Authorial Voice in Herodotus' *Histories,*" *Arethusa* 20 (1987): 147–74, and John Marincola, "Herodotian Narrative and the Narrator's Presence," *Arethusa* 20 (1987): 121–45. I have found both of these articles particularly helpful in suggesting ways of interpreting the narrator's voice and its significance in Livy's history.

long after this, the narrator once again interrupts his report of legendary events in indirect discourse to assert directly that "from this point on the *fama* is double," *Duplex inde fama est* (1.1.6). This assertion presumably constitutes an authorial acknowledgment that there is no longer "sufficient agreement" about the tradition, and indicates his determination, in the service of disinterested objectivity, to provide his readers an account of both variants within the tradition, since there is no objective basis for discriminating between them. Thus in the opening few sentences of his narrative the narrator has, through a series of rhetorical gestures, offered tokens of his own awareness as a historian of the nature of his sources, of his forthrightness in acknowledging their limitations, of his conscientiousness in discriminating between unreliable tradition and reliable fact, and of his disinterested honesty in reporting all variants when there is no reliable basis for preferring one version over the others. And he has done all this in terms that seem to locate him squarely within a dominant historiographic tradition.

This is readily apparent when we compare the opening of Livy's narrative with the introduction to Herodotus' *Histories*. Similarities of outline suggest the extent to which Livy worked within established historiographic tradition and to which his readers would have found the rhetorical gestures of his opening narrative familiar. A more detailed comparison will reveal how distinctive Livy's use of that tradition actually is. Herodotus begins with a brief paragraph, corresponding to Livy's preface, in which he identifies himself and his reasons for writing his history (Hdt. pref.). This is followed by several paragraphs summarizing the "prehistory" of the Persian wars, the legendary traditions about the earliest conflicts between Greeks and Eastern peoples (Hdt. 1.1–5). These traditions are introduced only to be dismissed as unreliable and beyond confirmation (1.5). Herodotus contrasts them with the more recent events that he identifies as the starting point for his own narrative:

> Ταῦτα μέν νυν Πέρσαι τε καὶ Φοίνικες λέγουσι. ἐγὼ δὲ περὶ μὲν τούτων οὐκ ἔρχομαι ἐρέων ὡς οὕτως ἢ ἄλλως κως ταῦτα ἐγένετο, τὸν δὲ οἶδα αὐτὸς πρῶτον ὑπάρξαντα ἀδίκων ἔργων ἐς τοὺς Ἕλληνας, τοῦτον σημήνας προβήσομαι ἐς τὸ πρόσω τοῦ λόγου. (1.5.3)

> Now, this is what both the Persians and the Phoenicians say. For my own part, I am not going to say about these things that they happened this way or some other way. But first indicating the one whom I myself know to have initiated the injustices toward the Hellenes, I will continue on to the rest of the account.

Up to this point in the narrative, the Persians' and Phoenicians' respective versions of events have been reported consistently and exclusively in indirect discourse; and, conversely, indirect discourse has been used only to report their views. There are only three departures from indirect discourse, each of which is an editorial aside that is clearly parenthetical to the events reported in indirect discourse and implies nothing about their validity: Argos was preeminent among Greek states when the Persians were alleged to have gone there (1.1.2); the unnamed Greeks who supposedly abducted Europa "would have been," *eiēsan . . . an*, Cretans—if the story were true (1.2.1); the Persians date the beginning of hostilities between themselves and the Greeks to the Greek invasion of Troy, because they regard Asia as theirs and separate from Europe (1.4.4). When Herodotus summarizes the Persians' point of view, he again employs indirect discourse: "So the Persians say it came about that . . . ," *Houtō men Persai legousi . . .* (1.5.1). After the general summation quoted above, the author turns to his own version, which he presents in direct discourse.

The argument of the passage just surveyed is organized around three overlapping contrasts. The first is explicit. This is the contrast between what is said and what is known on the basis of firsthand experience and inquiry. And since firsthand knowing is expressed here by a verb that also means "to see," the contrast is also between what is said and what, as the result of firsthand experience or inquiry, has been in some sense seen (*oida*). The second contrast is implicit. It is between a more distant past about which there is and can be no agreement—because all the investigator has is one set of unverifiable and obviously biased assertions to oppose to another—and a more recent past about which some kind of agreement can be reached, because it is (somehow) more accessible to direct perception and so can be known. These two substantive contrasts are underscored, in turn, by a third, which is a consistent rhetorical contrast: Herodotus reserves indirect discourse for oral tradition, which he characterizes as both inconsistent and unreliable, and direct discourse for what he claims to know with certainty. These contrasts, between things that can be known and things that are merely reported, between things about which there is or can be agreement and things about which there is not, between things that are reported on the author's own authority in direct statement and things that are attributed to others in indirect statement, all have their parallels in Livy's narrative. Before looking at significant differences between the deployment of these elements in Livy and Herodotus, let us consider briefly the implications of such parallels for Livy's reader.

Because the principles according to which Livy organizes the very opening of his narrative were familiar to ancient readers of histories—as they are familiar to us—because their meanings and functions are apparently self-evident, it is easy to take them at face value, to assume that the messages that they send about the author and his text are reliable, or at least that they fairly represent the author's intentions even if they cannot guarantee his perfect realization of them. From this point of view it is unnecessary for the reader to interrupt his or her attention to the clear line of the narrative in order to examine these rhetorical gestures critically: after all, we know what they mean. The real test of the author's capacities as a historian will be his actual narrative. This the reader will judge in the first instance according to its intelligibility and its coherence. Readers who want to attempt a more systematic evaluation of the narrative's reliability will make an independent assessment of the narrator's sources and his use of them, their own assessment of the kinds of choices that the narrator could have made and did actually make. Such readers, of course, will be influenced by the narrator's characterizations of his methodology and by the specific evidences of it that he gives, but will not be limited by them. But barring such independent analysis, the function of the historiographic gestures in Livy's opening narrative is to reassure the reader about its integrity.

If, however, we examine critically the analytic categories and rhetorical gestures with which Livy introduces his narrative, we are confronted by unexpected problems of interpretation, problems that defy easy solution and whose impenetrability undermines faith in the narrative as a reliable or even intelligible guide to historical facticity, to different levels of historical plausibility, and even to the historiographic tradition upon which determinations of facticity and plausibility are based. That is, if examined closely and critically, the elements of historiographic analysis that offer themselves as tokens of the narrative's reliability actually discourage attention to questions of historiographic methodology and to the values of facticity and reliability in whose name that methodology is employed.

Let us then look more closely and more critically at the ways in which the narrator of Livy's history puts his methodological principles into practice. The sentences in the opening narrative are numbered for easy and clear reference, and indirect discourse is in italics.

(1) Iam primum omnium satis constat *Troia capta in ceteros saeuitum esse Troianos, duobus, Aeneae Antenorique, et uetusti iure hospitii et quia pacis reddendaeque Helenae semper auctores fuerant, omne ius belli Achiuos abstinuisse.* (1.1.1)

(1) Now first of all it is sufficiently agreed *that after the capture of Troy the Achaeans took out their anger against the other Trojans but refrained from exercising the right of war against two, Aeneas and Antenor, both because of a long-established right of hospitality and because those two had always been advocates for peace and the surrender of Helen.*[22]

The narrative is introduced with a kind of paradox. We have recently been informed that the subject of this portion of the narrative is more closely related to a poetic fiction than to an "uncorrupted" record of fact, that it is, indeed, beyond the author's powers of proof or refutation. Yet here we are being told that there is "sufficient agreement" about the version of the story that we are about to read. How can this be? On reflection, the paradox provokes several questions: By whom is it agreed? On what basis did they, or indeed could they, reach agreement? And what is the standard for sufficiency? These are exactly the kinds of questions that are entailed in a critical examination of a tradition. The assertion that "it is sufficiently agreed" is an acknowledgment that the past has been the subject of some kind of reflection and some degree of consensus, but it acknowledges that fact only to circumvent a discussion of it. To put it another way, while the assertion raises the question of how an appropriate historiographic consensus is reached, it precludes any examination of the question, any investigation of how in actuality, to what degree, and on what basis consensus was achieved in this particular case and why the narrator chose to accept it.

Perhaps we can avoid those questions by taking *satis constat* as the virtual equivalent of "it is *generally* accepted," as some translators have done.[23] But that only substitutes another set of closely related questions for the first. Does the narrator here refer to "general agreement" as a measure for the tradition's *reliability,* as sufficient justification for believing it, or at least for repeating it? Or is he calling attention to the essentially uncritical nature of that authority and the consequent *un*reliability of a tradition that has been

22. This passage and others like it that I will discuss below seem to fit the category of indirect discourse in Livy that Konrad Gries, "Livy's Use of Dramatic Speech," *American Journal of Philology* 70 (1949) calls "condensed combinations," p. 124. However, Gries is principally concerned with indirect discourse that paraphrases speakers who have a specific identity (even if only vaguely defined): "the confused expression of public sentiment, a resumé of discussion in the senate or a summary of thoughts uttered by the same person or persons at various times," p. 124. Greis does not discuss Livy 1.1.1ff. following or other passages like it. Neither does André Lambert, *Die indirekte Rede als künstlerisches Stilmittel des Livius* (Diss. Zürich, 1946).

23. E.g., Aubrey de Sélincourt, trans., *Livy: The Early History of Rome* (Baltimore: Penguin, 1973), p. 34 and passim.

passed down on no more authority than "general agreement"? Does *satis constat* express a simple acceptance of the tradition, or does it also express an element of reserve? It is best, perhaps, simply to acknowledge the ambiguity of the phrase's value and to take it as an expression of the narrator's own ambivalence toward his material. But if the author himself is ambivalent, then the distinction between "sufficient" and "insufficient" agreement (or between "general agreement" and "lack of agreement") appears not to be significant after all—an empty gesture—for, whatever the degree of consensus, the author remains ambivalent, undecided about its value. One might conclude, hopefully without being too arch, that the translation of *satis* as "general" is not *sufficient* to resolve the historiographic questions raised here. On the surface, this may seem no more than the kind of tactful detachment that the author's statement in the preface has warned us to expect. However, its practical effect is to tell the reader: "Just accept the fact of this consensus; don't ask about it or its value; I, the narrator, am not really interested in such questions, and I am not going to provide you with the information that you would need to pursue them."[24]

This message is reiterated in a very different way by the unusual alternation of direct and indirect discourse that characterizes the opening narrative. The passage begins with the sentence quoted above and continues as follows:

(2) *casibus deinde uariis Antenorem cum multitudine Enetum, qui seditione ex Paphlagonia pulsi et sedes et ducem rege Pylaemene ad Troiam amisso quaerebant, uenisse in intimum maris Hadriatici sinum, Euganeisque qui inter mare Alpesque incolebant pulsis Enetos Troianosque eas tenuisse terras.* (3) Et in quem primum egressi sunt locum Troia uocatur pagoque inde Troiano nomen est: gens uniuersa Veneti appellati. (1.1.2–3)

(2) *That then by various misfortunes Antenor reached the innermost recess of the Adriatic Sea along with a multitude of Eneti who had been driven from Paphlagonia by an uprising and were seeking a place to settle and a leader, since their king, Pylaemene, had perished at Troy; that the Eneti and Trojans drove out the Euganei who dwelt between the sea and the Alps and settled this territory.* (3) In addition,

---

24. Contrast, for example, Dionysius, who justifies a lengthy review of evidence pertaining to the date of Rome's foundation with the assertion that he "did not think it appropriate" (*ou gar exioun*), like Polybius, "only to assert" (*tosouto monon eipein*) that he believes Rome to have been built on a certain date, but that he wanted to "present" (*exenegkein*) his "reasonings" (*epilogismous*) so that they would be "accountable" (*euthynous*) to whoever wanted to examine them (1.74.2–3). I am not here arguing that Dionysius' narrative is therefore a truer history. My point rather is simply that he bases his claim of reliability on a different rhetorical strategy than Livy's.

the place where they first disembarked is called Troy and the region is called Trojan: the entire people are called the Veneti.

The narrative continues in indirect discourse, governed by the initial, problematic *satis constat*. Both the controlling verb, *constat,* and the normal use of indirect discourse to distinguish the reported views or words of others from one's own encourage the assumption that indirect discourse here signifies the author's or narrator's own suspension of judgment about the story that he is reporting: his refusal to report it in direct speech expresses a refusal to take responsibility for its truth or reliability.

However, when the narrative comes to name the place where, as "it is sufficiently agreed," Antenor and his followers settled, the construction shifts to direct discourse. This shift may easily be explained as a reflection of the fact that the narrator is moving from a report of an uncertain tradition to the naming of a real place, from *fabula* to *monumentum*. The shift from indirect to direct discourse signals a shift from an unreliable oral tradition from which the narrator seeks to distance himself (and the reader as well) to a certainty based on visible evidence that the narrator is willing to report on his own authority. But the situation is in fact somewhat more complicated, for the direct report about the current name of the place and people includes a report of the actual disembarkation of Antenor and his followers as though it were part of the larger reality being reported here, and indeed as an important part of that reality, since it explains the contemporary names: "the place where they first disembarked is called . . ." We cannot explain this apparent anomaly away on the grounds that Antenor's arrival on the shores of the Adriatic is simply the first bit of reliable information in the tradition, because that arrival has just been reported in indirect discourse in the preceding sentence, a sign presumably that it is an unreliable part of the tradition—although one about which "it is sufficiently agreed."

Another tack is to explain this apparent anomaly away by arguing that the main point of the direct discourse here is to acknowledge the reality of the places and their names and that the inclusion within the direct discourse of reference to the disembarkation of Antenor and his followers was purely inadvertent. But this act of explaining away is predicated upon the reader's first having considered the possibility that the narrator endorses the arrival of Antenor as an actual event. Otherwise, there would have been nothing to explain away. Indeed, the context encourages acceptance of the disembarkation as a real event. How else to understand identification of a territory in the innermost recess (*intimum . . . sinum*) of the Adriatic with the remote Troy, if not by the arrival of Trojans there at some time in the past? But if this is a reliable part of the tradition, why did the author report it in indirect discourse in the preceding sentence? What does it mean to report an event alternately in direct and indirect discourse? What does the contrast between direct and indirect discourse signify? To remove such questions by assuming that the report of Antenor's disembarkation in direct discourse was an unintentional slip, or merely insignificant, is on some level or another to have attempted to make sense of it and to have failed. It is to have acknowledged a discrepancy between our expectations about the rhetorical function of indirect statement here and its actual use.

This same kind of discrepancy is reiterated, in more direct and less easily avoidable terms, in the next three sentences, which again move from indirect to direct statement:

> (4) *Aenean ab simile clade domo profugum sed ad maiora rerum initia ducentibus fatis, primo in Macedoniam uenisse, inde in Siciliam quaerentem sedes delatum, ab Sicilia classe ad Laurentem agrum tenuisse.* (5) Troia et huic loco nomen est. (6) Ibi egressi Troiani, ut quibus ab immenso prope errore nihil praeter arma et naues superesset, cum praedam ex agris agerent, Latinus rex Aboriginesque qui tum ea tenebant loca ad arcendam uim aduenarum armati ex urbe atque agris concurrunt. (1.1.4–6)

> (4) *That Aeneas, a fugitive from his home because of a similar slaughter but destined by the fates to greater beginnings, at first arrived in Macedonia, that he then was carried to Sicily in search of a place to settle, that from Sicily he held his course for the territory of Laurentum.* (5) Troy is the name for this place, too. (6) There the Trojans disembarked, and while they were driving booty from the fields (inasmuch as nothing was left to them from their almost endless wanderings except their weapons and their ships), Latinus, the king, and the Aborigines who then occupied those places, armed in defense against the violence of the foreigners, come running from the city and fields.

Here, after a sentence of indirect discourse reporting the wanderings of Aeneas (4), the narrator reverts to direct discourse (5). As before, this shift marks a turn from reporting the problematic oral tradition to a *monumentum*, identification of a real place: "Troy is the name for this place, too." The brevity and simplicity of the statement further reinforce the sense that it conveys straightforward, unproblematic information.

The next sentence (6) is far more complex. It begins with a nominative phrase, literally, "There, the Trojans having disembarked," *Ibi egressi Troiani,* as though it were going to continue in direct discourse (which in fact it does), and as though the Trojans were going to be its subject (which turns out not to be the case). So, one's first impression—that the Trojans will be the subject of a statement in direct discourse—would lead one to believe that the author is now accepting responsibility for the following account of their actions, as though it were as reliable as the name of the place where tradition says that they were supposed to have landed. But a couple of lines later, we learn that "the Trojans, having disembarked," are not the subject of the main sentence after all but rather of a subordinate clause, "while they were driving booty from the fields," *cum praedam ex agris agerent*. This kind of proleptic construction, in which the subject of a subordinate clause is announced before the subordinating conjunction that formally introduces the clause itself, is not at all unusual in Latin. Nonetheless, a sentence in direct statement followed by a sentence beginning in the nominative, "There, the Trojans having disembarked," creates the initial impression that the Trojans, and their arrival, are now going to be the subject of a sentence in direct statement; that is, their arrival is a reliable fact for which the narrator takes responsibility. This initial impression is particularly strong in this case because the lapse between the naming of the subject—the Trojans—and the subordinate clause of which they turn out to be the subject is unusually long and because such prolepsis was regularly used in classical Latin to introduce someone or something that will be the subject both of an intervening subordinate clause and of the main sentence that follows that clause.

The sense that the arrival of the Trojans is now being treated as a reliable event, like the name of the place where they were supposed by tradition to have landed, is reinforced by the simple circumstance that the subordinate clause of which they are the subject is part of a larger statement in direct discourse. The reader is confronted with exactly the same kinds of questions and uncertainties as those raised in sentence 3 above, only now perhaps more insistently, inasmuch as the impression that the arrival of the Trojans is a reliable event has been reinforced by the method of its introduction at the beginning of the sentence.

The task of distinguishing between what are supposed to be taken as reliable and unreliable aspects of the tradition—or, alternatively, of identifying some consistent rationale for the choice of direct or indirect discourse—is further complicated in the remainder of the sentence and the announcement of its true subjects, King Latinus and the Aborigines. Here the narrator reports confidently in direct discourse that Latinus and his subjects went out to oppose the violence of the foreigners. But on what possible grounds can the narrator be more confident about this aspect of tradition than about the part, which he reports in indirect discourse, according to which "from Sicily [Aeneas] held his course for the territory of Laurentum," *ab Sicilia classe ad Laurentem agrum tenuisse?* If we can be confident that Latinus and his followers went out to oppose the Trojans, then we must be equally confident that the Trojans had in fact arrived in Laurentum to begin with.

It might be possible to make a case for a coherent and consistent deployment of indirect and direct discourse by arguing that a significant distinction is made between the tradition of Aeneas' departure from Troy, his arrival first in Macedonia and then in Sicily, and his subsequent departure from there for Latium, all reported in indirect discourse, and so uncertain events, and his arrival in Latium and his encounter with the Latins and the Aborigines, reported in direct discourse, thus certain events. But this strategy will not work, for, as we have seen, only a few sentences earlier the narrator first reported the arrival of Antenor on the coast of the Adriatic in indirect discourse and then in the very next sentence reported it again in direct discourse.

In any event, in the next sentence the narrator seems to deny any point to an effort to discriminate different levels of reliability in the preceding passage when he states: "From this point on the *fama* is double," *Duplex inde fama est* (1.1.6). The emphasis here is on *duplex,* that is, what changes at this point is that the *fama* becomes double; it has been *fama* all along. From this perspective there seems little point in trying to find a rationale for distinguishing the force of direct from that of indirect discourse in this narrative: it is all, after all, just *fama.*

The apparent hopelessness of finding a consistent rationale for the disposition of direct and indirect discourse in the narrative seems to be confirmed in the final sentences devoted to Aeneas' arrival and settlement in Latium. The narrative reverts to indirect discourse to report the alternative versions of the *duplex fama,* that Aeneas defeated the Latins and then made a marriage alliance with their leader, or that he and Latinus came to terms without fighting and confirmed their agreement with a marriage alliance. The narrator then reports: "This matter without doubt confirmed the Trojans' hope at last for an end of wandering with a lasting and fixed home," *Ea res utique Troianis spem adfirmat tandem stabili certaque sede finiendi erroris* (1.1.10). Several short and simple statements, also in direct discourse, follow, reporting the founding of a town, its naming, and the birth of a son. Here the shift to direct discourse seems to perform two functions. The first is dramatic, to reemphasize through its own simple directness the Trojans' final release from the demanding and disorienting struggles of their wandering. The second function seems to be to mark the return from a divided to a unified tradition, a use of direct discourse so far unprecedented in the narrative.

From this point on, in fact, direct discourse is the prevailing mode of the narrative—a circumstance that raises questions yet again about the significance of direct and indirect discourse in the narrative and about the various elements of the tradition that are reported in one or the other of these modes. The author's preface, after all, has led us to believe that the entire tradition "before the city was founded or planned" was unreliable, not just the part of it that pertained to Aeneas' travels and his final settlement in Latium. It may be tempting to seek refuge in conjectures about Livy's carelessness or lack of consistency as an author: he got bored with indirect discourse, gave it up as too cumbersome, felt that he had already made his point. But such attempts at explanation constitute an effort to explain what is otherwise a rhetorical anomaly; they acknowledge that the text does not make sense by itself; they represent the reader's admission of defeat in his or her efforts to discover a logic in the text. And that, as I have said before, is exactly my point. Taken literally, the text introduces a kind of rhetoric that implies distinctions between more and less reliable elements of tradition but that on examination provides no ready indication of what exactly those distinctions might be or on what basis they might have been made.

This anomaly will perhaps be easier to appreciate if we return briefly to consider differences between the passages just discussed and the analogous passages in Herodotus' *Histories* discussed earlier. These differences are easily summarized. Herodotus' narrative, as we saw, was based on three congruent and reinforcing contrasts: oral vs. visual evidence (i.e., what has been said vs. what Herodotus himself knows, "has seen"); unreliable tradition vs. reliable knowledge (i.e., conflicting oral reports vs. what Herodotus can report with authority); indirect vs. direct statement (i.e., what Herodotus reports on the authority of others vs. what he is prepared to report on his own authority). In Livy's narrative the same three principles of analysis and organization are evoked: unreliable *fabula* vs. reliable *monumenta*; what is "sufficiently or generally agreed" vs., implicitly, what is not; indirect vs. direct discourse. But in Livy's narrative these three principles are not congruent, mutually reinforcing. Rather, they seem to be inconsistently applied and to work against each other: it is the least reliable part of the tradition about which the narrator reports "sufficient or general agreement"; *fabula* and *monumenta* are both included within direct discourse, and both are embraced retrospectively by the overarching category of *fama: duplex inde fama est.*

Livy's introductory narrative seems to work against itself in its presentation of tradition in an additional way. As noted above, the narrator describes the alternatives embraced by the *duplex fama*. Although both are reported in indirect discourse, they are not given equal weight. The first alternative is reported tersely: "Some pass on that Latinus was defeated in battle, made peace with Aeneas, and then formed a marriage alliance with him," *Alii proelio uictum Latinum pacem cum Aenea, deinde adfinitatem iunxisse tradunt* (1.1.6). The second alternative is developed much more dramatically and at greater length: we see the two sides already drawn up for battle, the signal for battle about to be sounded, Latinus advancing through the front ranks, calling Aeneas to a parley, learning his story (in some detail), offering alliance, the striking of the truce, and more, leading finally to the marriage of Aeneas and Latinus' daughter.

Of the two accounts offered at this point in Livy's narrative, the second is clearly more emphatic than the first: it is longer, richer in circumstantial detail, more vivid. Its status is further enhanced by its position in the narrative. As the second and final alternative, it to some extent displaces the first alternative; it has in a sense the last word. Its favored status is the more conspicuous if we reflect how easy it would have been to reverse the order of the alternatives or to amplify the first, shorter alternative (a description of the forces on each side, their relative strength, then the course of the battle, the final defeat, the surrender, the terms of the peace, and so on) and abbreviate the second ("Before the two armies engaged, however, their leaders met and agreed to make peace and to confirm it through a marriage alliance"). Here, then, relative position and length form a consistent pattern of emphasis that clearly privileges one of the two alternatives reported.

Yet according to the author's own judgment in the preface, there can, of course, be no objective basis for favoring one version over the other. Having stated clearly that he has no intention either "to refute or to affirm" an unreliable tradition, the narrator has nonetheless conspicuously favored one variant within the tradition over another. Thus the actual character of the narrative is conspicuously inconsistent with the spirit, if not the letter, of the principles articulated by Livy in his preface. If we look for some objective basis in historical evidence or in the nature of the sources to explain the narrator's choice of emphasis, we can find none. On this level, too, then, the rhetorical organization of the narrative is not only inconsistent with the characterization of the tradition that Livy here reports; it is also not made comprehensible in terms of any standards of historical reliability. Thus Livy discourages the reader from seeking actively to evaluate his narrative objectively, in terms of historical reliability.

IV

The implications of the opening narrative are even broader once we recognize that the same kinds of historiographic confusions apparent there recur later in the narrative, where it has passed beyond the pre-foundation stage that the preface had specified as particularly unreliable. As a consequence, it is difficult to determine exactly when uncertainty is supposed to give way to likelihood. On the one hand, Livy abandons indirect discourse as the narrative's dominant mode well before the narrative reaches Romulus and Remus, let alone Romulus' initial founding of the city. On the other hand, the narrator's practice of calling into question not just the reliability of the tradition that he must follow but the reliability both of his own critical methodology and of the narrative itself persists beyond the opening sentences of indirect discourse, beyond the initial founding of the city by Romulus, and in fact recurs intermittently throughout the narrative. Let us take a close look at several passages that present some of the same difficulties of interpretation as the opening narrative.

The kind of obscure and confusing alternation of direct and indirect discourse noted in the opening narrative recurs, for example, in Livy's account of Tullia and her behavior after her father's assassination:

> Ipse [Servius] prope exsanguis, cum semianimis regio comitatu domum se reciperet, ab iis qui missi ab Tarquinio fugientem consecuti erant interficitur. Creditur, quia non abhorret a cetero scelere, admonitu Tulliae id factum. Carpento certe, id quod satis constat, in forum inuecta nec reuerita coetum uirorum euocauit uirum e curia regemque prima appellauit. . . . cum se domum reciperet . . . restitit pauidus atque inhibuit frenos is qui iumenta agebat iacentemque dominae Seruium trucidatum ostendit. (1.48.4–6)

> [Servius] himself was almost dead. While returning home only half-alive with a royal attendant, he is killed by those whom Tarquinius had sent after him as he fled. It is believed (since she did not shrink back from the rest of the crime) that this was done at Tullia's urging. For certain, as is sufficiently agreed, she rode into the Forum in a carriage and, undismayed by the gathering of men, called her husband out from the Senate house and was the first to address him as king. . . . While she was returning home, . . . the man who was driving her carriage-team came to a stop in terror, checked the reins, and pointed out to his mistress Servius lying there slaughtered.

The alternation of direct and indirect discourse here is noteworthy. The narrative reports as a simple fact, in direct discourse, that Servius was murdered (1.48.4), then continues: "It is believed," *creditur,* that Tullia was responsible for ordering his murder, a belief that is encouraged "because she did not shrink back from the rest of the crime," *quia non abhorret a cetero scelere.* In any event, the narrative goes on (in direct discourse), she certainly did ride into the Forum to salute her husband as king, "a fact about which there is sufficient [or general] agreement," *id quod satis constat.* On the way home her driver "stopped" the carriage and "pointed out" that their way was blocked by Servius' body (*restitit . . . ostendit*). Hereafter, the rhetoric of the narrative becomes somewhat more complex (italics mark indirect discourse):

> Foedum inhumanumque inde traditur scelus monumentoque locus est— Sceleratum uicum uocant—quo *amens, agitantibus furiis sororis ac uiri, Tullia per patris corpus carpentum egisse fertur.* (1.48.7)
>
> At this point tradition reports a foul and inhuman crime, and the place is a monument to it—they call it the Street of Crime—where *the maddened Tullia, driven by the furies of her sister and husband, is said to have driven her carriage over her father's body.*

Reviewing the whole episode from our starting point, we meet a wide array of rhetorical gestures that imply discrimination among differing levels of reliability within the tradition. Here, as above, I use italics to highlight the contrast between parts of the narrative reported by Livy in his own voice and parts that he attributes to the authority of others. Servius "*is* killed," *interficitur;* but "it is *believed* [that it was done on Tullia's authority]," *creditur;* "tradition *reports* [a foul crime]," *traditur;* but "the place *is*," *est;* "they *call* it," *uocant;* the driver actually "*stopped*" and "*pointed out*," *restitit . . . ostendit;* but "Tullia . . . *is said* [to have driven over her father's body]," *Tullia . . . fertur.*

In fact, with only one exception (which I shall discuss presently) the narrative offers no objective basis for thus distinguishing between more or less plausible aspects of the tradition. The narrative offers no better reason to believe those aspects of the story that are presented as simple, unproblematic facts (that Servius was killed, that Tullia rode into the Forum and saluted her husband as king, that her driver stopped and pointed out her father's body on the road) than it does to believe other elements from which the narrator distances himself through explicit attribution to report or tradition and through indirect discourse (that Tullia was responsible for her father's murder, that she ordered her servant to drive over her father's body).

Paradoxically, the one element of the tradition for which there is some sort of objective verification is presented not as a fact but as a report. This is Tullia's alleged order to drive over her father's body—a part of the tradition for which there is some visible testimony, a *monumentum,* the street, still surviving, where this crime was supposed to have taken place and whose association with the event is preserved in its name. By contrast, the narrator sanctions the report of Tullia's arrival in the Forum after her father's murder, a report for which he offers no independent evidence, by attributing it to a sufficient or general consensus (*satis constat*). In other words, the narrator's decisions whether to report elements of the tradition on his own authority or to attribute them to a general consensus—or to anonymous (and therefore presumably unauthoritative) report—seem to be completely unrelated to the nature of the evidence and in particular to the distinction between *fama* and *monumentum* that he made in his preface and that he evokes here. Once again, rhetorical strategies that seem on the surface to suggest different levels of historical reliability and authorial discrimination lead only to confusion and paradox if taken literally.

The kind of arbitrary discrimination between variants within tradition that was noted in the initial narrative also recurs subsequently. The two versions of Remus' murder provide an early example. Livy's first account of this murder follows directly on an account of the twins' search for omens that would settle the question of who should give his name to the new city, and in fact is a direct consequence of that dispute:

> Priori Remo augurium uenisse fertur, sex uoltures; iamque nuntiato augurio cum duplex numerus Romulo se ostendisset, utrumque regem sua multitudo consalutauerat: tempore illi praecepto, at hi numero auium regnum trahebant. Inde cum altercatione congressi certamine irarum ad caedem uertuntur; ibi in turba ictus Remus cecidit. (1.7.1–2)

> It is said that a sign appeared first to Remus, six vultures. The sign had just been announced when double that number appeared to Romulus. Each man's own following had saluted him as king: the former claimed the kingship because of priority in time; the latter because of the number of birds. This led to an altercation between the assembled parties. The conflict turned from expressions of anger to slaughter. Thereupon, amidst the mob, Remus was struck down.

So far the story seems quite straightforward. At this point, however, the narrator introduces, quite without preparation, a second version of Remus' death:

> Volgatior fama est ludibrio fratris Remum nouos transiluisse muros; inde ab irato Romulo, cum uerbis quoque increpitans adiecisset, "Sic deinde, quicumque alius transiliet moenia mea," interfectum. (1.7.2)

The more common story is that, in mockery of his brother, Remus jumped over his walls. This enraged Romulus, who killed him, taunting him as he did so with the words "So perish, then, whoever else will jump over my walls."

It is difficult to determine from the narrative what the exact status of this variant is. It is presented to us as a *fama,* a story, not something that the narrator is prepared to report on his own authority, not something, presumably, in which we should place much confidence. This interpretation, however, is somewhat complicated by the characterization of the *fama* as "more common," *uolgatior.* On the one hand, "more common" indicates "more widespread, more frequent," and this could be construed as a positive measure of reliability—especially when no other measures of reliability are apparent.[25] On the other hand, of course, simple currency or popularity provides no guarantee of reliability. And, indeed, in Livy's narrative *uolgata* often modifies *fama* in contexts that suggest its unreliability.[26] In a way we are here confronted with the same sort of ambiguity with which *satis constat* introduces the entire narrative: Is consensus or currency a useful measure of a tradition's reliability? But whatever logical analysis may suggest, the second version of Remus' death, like the second version of Aeneas' accommodation with Latinus, is clearly the more memorable. Even though there is no apparent basis for favoring it, it is in fact privileged over the first alternative: it is longer, more dramatic, more detailed, more vivid, more troubling in its implications, and so more likely to engage the reader's attention. As he did in the story of Aeneas' encounter with Latinus, Livy has again favored one traditional variant over another without any decisive basis for judging their relative facticity.

Perhaps the most striking example of the apparently arbitrary privileging of one traditional variant over another occurs in the two passages that explain the origins of the Lacus Curtius in the Forum Romanum. They fall into

25. See 25.17.4, the only other passage in Livy where *uolgatior* appears, as here, modifying *fama,* and apparently with no derogatory sense. Compare also *insignitius* at 7.6.6. At 2.32.2–3 Livy reports that the plebeians withdrew to the Sacred Mount and then adds: "This account is the more common [*frequentior*],"—that is, compared to that for which Piso is the authority, that they withdrew to the Aventine. Here, frequency of a report seems to be adduced as evidence for its reliability.

26. See 45.10.5, where Rhodian speakers appeal to Roman officials to acquaint themselves with the real state of affairs at Rhodes, and then "to report back to Rome what they had discovered for themselves, not indiscriminate rumor," *comperta per se, non uolgata fama Roma referre.* Cf. also, for example, 3.40.13, 35.31.5 and 11, 42.42.9, and 26.19.7, where *uolgata fama* is associated with stories that are false, misleading, or outright fantastic.

a now familiar pattern in which the narrative undercuts its own credibility by introducing an unexpected and favored variant *after* having given an apparently straightforward and unproblematic account.[27] What makes the Lacus Curtius example especially striking is the distance that separates the two versions of the story. The story is first reported at 1.12–13.5. According to this version, the Lacus Curtius is named after the Sabine Mettius Curtius. During the climactic battle between Sabines and Romans after the Roman theft of the Sabine women, Curtius' horse was spooked and galloped off into a treacherous swamp, carrying its helpless rider along. Roman and Sabine alike were distracted by Curtius' plight. Encouraged by the gestures and shouts of his fellow Sabines, Curtius took courage and was able to make his way back out of the swamp to safety. Although the Romans ultimately won the battle, Curtius' misadventure and his determined self-rescue remained one of the battle's highlights and were commemorated in the name of the place where he and his horse finally emerged from the swamp. The story is presented as straightforward and unproblematic, with not the least hint that there might be an alternative, let alone better-known, account for the place-name. In fact, the reader is allowed to accept the story as an authoritative account, *the* explanation for the place-name Lacus Curtius, for more than six books.

Not until book 7 (6.3–5) are we given any reason to suspect that the history of the name is problematic. Now, for the first time and without any prior warning, we are presented with a quite different *aetion* for the name. We learn that the Lacus Curtius was a great hole in the Forum that had opened up mysteriously after an earthquake. All attempts to fill it with earth were unsuccessful. When priests were consulted, they said that the hole would be sealed only when the Romans had made an offering of what was the chief source of their strength. It was left to a young Roman aristocrat, Marcus Curtius, to understand that the priests' words referred to Roman youth, and then to "devote" himself to the gods and ride into the gaping hole. The spot thereafter bore his name, in memory of his heroic self-sacrifice.

---

27. In his discussion of Cossus and the *spolia opima* at 4.20.5–11 Ogilvie notes that "the habit of adding qualifications and doubts after a story is a fixed technique," and refers to 10.5.13, 17.11–12, and 26.5–7 as examples (p. 564). Luce makes the more particular claim that "when the *identity* of magistrates is in doubt, Livy's habit is to note discrepancies when the magistrates are first mentioned; when their *activities* are in question, he appends variants at the end of the narrative unit" ("Dating," pp. 216–17, his emphasis; and see his n. 22 for a list of illustrative passages).

The conclusion of this passage calls attention explicitly to the contradiction between this explanation for the name Lacus Curtius and the derivation of the name from Mettius Curtius' exploit in the battle between the Sabines and the Romans:

> [dicitur] lacumque Curtium non ab antiquo illo T. Tati milite Curtio Mettio sed ab hoc appellatum. (7.6.5)
>
> [It is said] that the Lacus Curtius is named not after that ancient well-known soldier of Titus Tatius, Mettius Curtius, but after this man [Marcus Curtius].

This assertion makes virtually certain that the reader will recall the first *aetion* for the name Lacus Curtius earlier in Livy's own narrative. Even so, nothing thus far in this story of Marcus Curtius has acknowledged directly the apparent contradiction with Livy's own previous narrative or has prepared the reader to cope with it. Readers are left to speculate for themselves about the author's intentions, about his possible carelessness or even indifference to narrative consistency and historiographic responsibility. The one possible clue to the relationship between these two contradictory versions is that the second is presented in indirect discourse, ascribed to an anonymous authority—a suggestion possibly that this is a less reliable variant than the earlier version, which the narrator had reported in direct discourse and without qualification.

In fact, the situation turns out to be rather more complicated than this. To begin with, the second variant concludes, as we have seen, with the explicit affirmation that it and *not* the Mettius Curtius version is the correct one. Still, this affirmation, too, is included within the indirect discourse, and were the passage to stop there, the reader might conclude that the narrator was simply reporting a point of view that he himself did not share. But there are still further complications. The narrator then continues, now in direct discourse, to add his own assessment of the relative reliability of the two versions, and, far from refuting the judgment of the anonymous supporter of the Marcus Curtius version, the narrator actually endorses it, although somewhat equivocally:

> Cura non deesset, si qua ad uerum uia inquirentem ferret; nunc fama rerum standum est, ubi certam derogat uetustas fidem; et lacus nomen ab hac recentiore insignitius fabula est. (7.6.6)
>
> Effort would not be lacking if any route would bring an inquirer to the truth, but as it is, we must stand by the report where antiquity removes

certainty. In addition, the name of the lake is better known from this more recent story.

Although the narrator does here finally subscribe to the view of his anonymous authority, that the Marcus Curtius version is preferable to the Mettius Curtius version, his reasons for doing so are, by his own account, not only indecisive but essentially arbitrary. The one thing that is clear and unequivocal in all this is simply that certainty is impossible.

Still, far from resolving the problem of how to interpret the contradictions within Livy's narrative, this "explanation" of the author's preference for the second version and, tacitly, his justification for including both versions only call attention to the narrative's lack of reliability in matters of historical facticity. To begin with, it raises the question, Why do we the readers learn only now, almost inadvertently, that in fact neither version of the story is reliable? Why weren't we told all this to begin with? Why were we left with the inaccurate impression that the original story about Mettius Curtius was authoritative, or at least undisputed? The most remarkable thing about this passage in its relation to the preceding narrative is that it explicitly reaffirms the narrator's own essential arbitrariness and the narrative's untrustworthiness in matters of historical facticity. This dramatic reaffirmation is especially noteworthy because it occurs as late as it does in the narrative. Consequently, it not only confirms what the author said in his preface about the shortcomings of the historical tradition for pre-foundation Rome, but also demonstrates dramatically that those shortcomings apply to a much longer, indeed an indefinite, period of Roman history.

V

This practical and recurrent demonstration of the author's own inability to present clear and unambiguous judgments about questions of historical fact has important political implications. By suggesting that a factual record of the past cannot be reconstructed with confidence, the author's evident difficulties bring into question any effort to monopolize the past. In particular, they deny to established powers the ability to monopolize the truth by using their authority to determine what is and is not a fact. Such a position was especially relevant to the age of Livy's narrative, for it was an age when the leading contenders in the Roman civil wars, above all Julius Caesar, and then his heir and successor, appealed to the "facts" of the remote past in extraordinarily concerted, systematic, and overt efforts both to secure their own personal preeminence and to support the larger ideologies by which they sought to legitimize their power and authority.[28]

Livy's narrative addresses explicitly two specific examples of attempts by Augustus to use his influence to monopolize historical fact in the service of his own ideological program. In neither case does the narrative directly refute Augustus' claims, but in each case it does undermine them by calling attention to the essential unreliability of the historical tradition. The first passage (1.3.1–3) takes up Augustus' claim to be a descendant of Aeneas, father of the Roman people, and through him a descendant of Venus. This claim was based on Augustus' adoption into the Julian *gens,* which in turn had in recent years emphasized a tradition according to which they traced their name to an ancestral Iulus, the son of Aeneas.[29] It was well established in tradition that Aeneas' son was named Ascanius. Iulus was explained as an alternative name that reflected the child's birth in Troy, or Ilium, as it was also known. At 1.3.1 the narrator introduces uncertainties about this tradition in a way that will by now seem familiar. He begins by identifying Ascanius as the son of Aeneas and his successor as ruler of Latium. He goes on to explain that since this Ascanius was too young to rule at the time of his father's death, his mother, Lavinia, ruled until he was old enough to assume the responsibility himself. So far the narrative and so, implicitly, the tradition seem straightforward. For anyone familiar with the ideology of the Julian *gens,* however, and virtually all of Livy's readers must have been familiar with it, this story presents something of a problem. An Ascanius who is the son of the Italian Lavinia is not easy to reconcile with the foundation story of the Julian *gens.* However, it is only *after* Ascanius has been identified in the narrative as son of Lavinia that the narrator interrupts unexpectedly to acknowledge the existence of an alternative tradition and the difficulty of determining which is true:

> Haud ambigam—quis enim rem tam ueterem pro certo adfirmet?—hicine fuerit Ascanius an maior quam hic, Creusa matre Ilio incolumi natus comesque inde paternae fugae, quem Iulum eundem Iulia gens auctorem nominis sui nuncupat. (1.3.2)

28. Augustus' exploitation of the remote past continues themes that had already been developed into a concerted program by his successor and adoptive father, Julius Caesar. These themes and their exploitation in different media are surveyed fully by Stefan Weinstock, *Divus Julius* (Oxford: Clarendon Press, 1971). See also Paul J. Zanker, *The Power of Images in the Age of Augustus,* trans. Alan Shapiro (Ann Arbor: University of Michigan Press, 1988).

29. See Weinstock, pp. 5–17 and passim.

> I shall not argue the question—for who would affirm as certain a matter
> so old?—whether this one was Ascanius or an older one than this, born
> of the mother Creusa when Ilium was still undefeated and who then was
> the companion of his father's flight, the same Iulus from whom the Julian
> clan declares to be the author of its name.

This appears to be a rather disingenuous assessment of the tradition. Did
Aeneas really have two sons? And if so, what happened to the one born in
Ilium, and how could he have sired the Julian clan, if he, the elder of the
two, was not around to succeed his father? As for the rhetorical question
"Who would affirm as certain a matter so old?" the answer is, of course,
the Julii, who affirmed with confidence that Iulus was the founder of their
clan. By his own easy dismissal of the whole question, the narrator dissociates
himself from the Julii and, by his example, undermines their claim. He
reiterates his indifference as he resumes the narrative: "This Ascanius [not
Iulus!], wherever and from whatever mother born—it is certainly agreed
that he was born from Aeneas," *Is Ascanius, ubicumque et quacumque matre
genitus—certe natum Aenea constat* (1.3.3).

More subtly but no less devastatingly subversive is the "notorious" digression on A. Cornelius Cossus and the *spolia opima*, or "spoils of honor," at
4.20.5–11.[30] Here again we find Livy interrupting the narrative unexpectedly,
ostensibly to correct an important detail in the account that he has just
given of how Cossus had won the *spolia opima* while fighting as a military
tribune under the command of the dictator, Mam. Aemilius. The narrative
had unambiguously identified Aemilius as dictator as early as 4.16.8 and
had thereafter referred to him never by name but only by title. Cossus had
been identified with equal assurance as military tribune at 4.19.1: "There
was at that time among the cavalry a military tribune, A. Cornelius Cossus,"
Erat tum inter equites tribunus militum A. Cornelius Cossus. Only *after* the story
of his winning and dedication of the *spolia opima* has been completed are
we told that Cossus' exact title has been a matter of dispute.

It had, in fact, been an issue of some contemporary significance for Livy's
readers. The historian Dio reports that in 29 B.C.E. M. Licinius Crassus had
claimed the honor of the *spolia opima* for having personally killed the leader
of the Bastarnae in battle while he, Crassus, was commander of the Roman
army in his province of Macedonia (51.24.4). Further, according to Dio,
Octavian had disallowed that claim on the grounds that the *spolia opima* had
in the past, and so could in the future, be awarded only to a commander

---

30. See Ogilvie, p. 563.

who had fought under his own auspices and that Crassus, serving as proconsular legate, did not possess *imperium* in his own right but rather served under Augustus' *imperium*. Historians have concluded, plausibly, that Octavian opposed Crassus' claim because he felt that his own position would be diminished if others were allowed to receive high military honors, a conclusion that is supported by Augustus' close control over the award of triumphs throughout his reign.[31] While Crassus and his claim to deserve the *spolia opima* are not acknowledged directly in Livy's narrative, they are certainly invoked indirectly. The sole evidence cited in the narrative in opposition to the identification of Cossus as a military tribune is attributed explicitly to the authority of Augustus. As with the identification of Ascanius, then, we are once again confronted with a question of historical facticity that has important political and ideological implications for the position and policy of Augustus in the age of Livy and his readers.

The digression on Cossus' position begins with apparent straightforwardness but soon becomes unexpectedly convoluted:

Omnes ante me auctores secutus, A. Cornelium Cossum tribunum militum secunda spolia opima Iouis Feretri templo intulisse exposui; ceterum, praeterquam quod ea rite opima spolia habentur, quae dux duci detraxit nec ducem nouimus nisi cuius auspicio bellum geritur, titulus ipse spoliis inscriptus illos meque arguit consulem ea Cossum cepisse. Hoc ego cum Augustum Caesarem, templorum omnium conditorem ac restitutorem, ingressum aedem Feretri Iouis quam uetustate dilapsam refecit, se ipsum in thorace linteo scriptum legisse audissem, prope sacrilegium ratus sum Cosso spoliorum suorum Caesarem, ipsius templi auctorem, subtrahere testem. Quis ea in re sit error quod tam ueteres annales quodque magistratuum libri, quos linteos in aede repositos Monetae Macer Licinius citat identidem auctores, decimo post demum anno cum T. Quinctio Poeno A. Cornelium Cossum consulem habeant, existimatio communis omnibus est. Nam etiam illud accedit, ne tam clara pugna in eum annum transferri posset, quod imbelle triennium ferme pestilentia inopiaque frugum circa A. Cornelium consulem fuit, adeo ut quidam annales uelut funesti nihil praeter nomina consulum suggerant. Tertius ab consulatu Cossi annus tribunum eum militum consulari potestate habet, eodem anno magistrum

31. See Frances V. Hickson, "Augustus *Triumphator:* Manipulation of the Triumphal Theme in the Political Program of Augustus," *Latomus* 50 (1992): 124–38; Ronald Syme, "Livy and Augustus," *Harvard Studies in Classical Philology* 64 (1959): 44; id., *The Roman Revolution* (Oxford: Oxford University Press, 1967), pp. 404–5; and for further literature see Meyer Reinhold, *From Republic to Principate: An Historical Commentary on Cassius Dio's "Roman History," Books 49–52 (39–29 B.C.)* (Atlanta: Scholars Press, 1988), p. 162.

equitum; quo in imperio alteram insignem edidit pugnam equestrem. Ea libera coniectura est sed, ut ego arbitror, uana.[32] Versare in omnes opiniones licet, cum auctor pugnae, recentibus spoliis in sacra sede positis, Iouem prope ipsum, cui uota erant, Romulumque intuens, haud spernendos falsi tituli testes, se A. Cornelium Cossum consulem scripserit. (4.20.5–11)

Following all the authorities before me, I have stated that A. Cornelius Cossus bore the second "spoils of honor" to the temple of Jupiter Feretrius as a military tribune. But apart from the fact that formally they are called "the spoils of honor" which a leader has taken from a leader and that we only recognize as a leader one under whose own auspices a war is waged, the inscription itself on the spoils argues, against those authorities and me, that Cossus captured them as a consul. When I had heard that Augustus Caesar, the founder and restorer of all temples, on entering the shrine of Jupiter Feretrius (which he restored when it had collapsed from old age), had himself read this very thing written on the linen breastplate, I thought it almost sacrilege to deprive Cossus of Caesar, the founder of the temple itself, as a witness to his spoils. What the error in this matter might be—that such old annals and magistrates' books (the linen ones that are deposited in the shrine of Moneta, and that Licinius Macer cites repeatedly as authorities) do not have A. Cornelius Cossus as consul with T. Quinctius Poenus until ten years later—is anybody's guess. There is, in addition, the following consideration against such a famous battle being transferred to this year, namely, that the three-year period about the time A. Cornelius Cossus was consul was for the most part free from war owing to plague and famine—to such an extent that certain annals, as though casualty lists, include nothing except the names of the consuls. The third year after the consulship of Cossus has him as military tribune with consular power and in this same year, master of the horse. In this command he fought another distinguished cavalry battle. Conjecture here is legitimate, but, in my view, pointless. One opinion is as good as another, although the person responsible for the battle, the one who placed the spoils in the holy shrine while they were still fresh and who virtually looked upon both Jupiter himself, to whom they had been vowed, and Romulus—not witnesses of a false inscription to be taken lightly—wrote that he was Consul A. Cornelius Cossus.

This is a remarkable passage and requires detailed commentary.[33] The passage begins with the narrator's reason, and an apparently strong one at that, for

---

32. I follow the punctuation suggested by H. Dessau, "Livius und Augustus," *Hermes* 41 (1906): 142–51, and adopted by R. M. Ogilvie, ed., *Titi Livi Ab Urbe Condita*, vol. 1 (Oxford: Clarendon Press, 1979). Here, as throughout, I have followed Ogilvie's text. See also his commentary *ad* 4.20.11, p. 567.

33. Not coincidentally, the text presents an unusual number of irregularities. While alterna-

identifying Cossus as military tribune: that is how all of the authorities identify him. Although the very fact of justifying the identification implies some dispute, the unanimity of the authorities, combined with the fact that the narrator has actually identified Cossus as military tribune throughout the foregoing narrative, implies that whatever alternatives may have been suggested have not been persuasive. This proves to be misleading, for the next sentence gives two compelling reasons for rejecting the identification of Cossus as military tribune: the winner of the *spolia opima* must be fighting under his own auspices (which a military tribune certainly would not have been), and the spoils themselves bear an inscription identifying Cossus as consul. The next sentence reports the discovery of the inscription and the unimpeachable character of its discoverer, Augustus. His *pietas,* exemplified by the restoration of the temple of Jupiter Feretrius, provides both the occasion for the inscription's discovery and a guarantee that his report of the inscription is trustworthy.

How are we to take this evidence? Both the nature of the document and the authority of its witness seem to constitute incontrovertible testimony— and yet we read of them in the context of a narrative that has clearly ignored their evidence. Some modern critics have viewed this testimony with skepticism, calling attention to the blatant improbability of Cossus' linen corselet having survived intact to the age of Augustus.[34] Critics of Augustus might find further support for an ironic interpretation of his testimony in the attention to alternative evidence in the immediately follow- ing lines.[35] But the report of Augustus' testimony resists clear and decisive characterization. The ancient magistrates' books, whose authority the narra- tor will acknowledge in the next sentence, are also described as "linen." Moreover, this sentence, which immediately follows the report of Augustus' discovery, begins with disconcerting ambiguity: "What the error in this matter might be . . ." The "matter" in question here turns out, however, not to be Augustus' testimony but rather the evidence of other documents.

---

tive readings affect the interpretation of specific clauses or phrases, I can find no combination of readings that significantly alters the sense or tenor of the passage overall. Ogilvie's text goes about as far as any to simplify and clarify the sense of the passage. Only Jean Bayet, ed., *Tite-Live: Histoire romaine,* vol. 4, Budé series (Paris: Les belles lettres, 1965), ad loc., goes farther: he regards *uersare in omnes opiniones licet* at 4.20.11 as a gloss and would eliminate those words altogether from the text.

34. Syme, "Livy and Augustus," pp. 43–46; Ogilvie, pp. 563, 565; Luce, "Dating," p. 215.

35. Bayet, vol. 4, p. 35 n. 3, remarks: "The flattery is not without irony to judge by the skeptical criticism of what follows." For another reading of the passage, see E. Mensching, "Livius, Cossus und Augustus," *Museum Helveticum* 24 (1967): 12–32.

Literally, the sentence expresses bewilderment as to how a mistake could have made its way into the archival material. In assuming the possibility of an error there, the narrator implicitly confirms his positive assessment of Augustus' testimony.

This affirmation of Augustus notwithstanding, the rhetorical effect of the same sentence is just the opposite: it casts doubt on his testimony. The potential subjunctive of the opening clause, "What the error . . . might be," could be read as holding open the possibility that there might *not* have been an error in the archives after all.[36] This possibility is further supported by the central and longest clauses of the sentence, the two *quod* clauses that call attention to the weight of the evidence against Augustus' testimony: the antiquity, official nature, and trusted authority of the archival material. There is, then, a balance between the authority of the archives and that of Augustus. It is precisely that balance that justifies the author's explicit statement at the end of the sentence that there can be no certain decision between the competing evidence.

At this point, the passage seems to be evenly balanced in its support for each of the two conflicting views and therefore to favor the impossibility of deciding between them. The next two sentences, however, reinforce the value of the archival evidence by expanding upon its internal consistency. In both sentences the narrator reports, as unqualified fact in support of the archives' reliability, information that is apparently derived from the archives themselves: for example, that there was a three-year period of military inactivity. In the second sentence he seems even to take for granted the archives' dating of Cossus' consulship (and thus of his year as military tribune), treating as a given the very matter in question: "The third year after Cossus' consulship," *Tertius ab consulatu Cossi annus.* The cumulative effect, then, is to strengthen the impression of the archives' reliability.

Having thus reinforced the evidence of the archives and those who rely on them against the evidence and authority of Augustus, the author now reiterates, perhaps even to the point of overstatement, that the whole matter is beyond rational analysis, that, in fact, all opinions are open to consideration: "Conjecture here is legitimate, but, in my view, pointless. One opinion is as good as another," *Ea libera coniectura est, sed, ut ego arbitror, uana. Versare in omnes opiniones licet.* Nonetheless, even this apparently confident assertion of uncertainty is qualified, and the entire digression ends not with a summation or a logical conclusion but by counterbalancing the preceding support

---

36. I follow the prevailing reading of the text adopted by Ogilvie and other modern editors, most of whom reject the anomalous *qui si ea in re sit error* of the MSS here.

of the archives' reliability with a reason for trusting the alleged inscription on Cossus' breastplate after all. Thus the last word in this digression is devoted not to reaffirming the essentially insoluble character of the historical problem but rather to qualifying that assertion by reaffirming the alternative that the narrator has himself rejected in his narrative. The whole passage, then, is characterized not just by the alternation and counterbalancing of two competing points of view. Even the conclusion that certainty is impossible seems to be qualified. But while the uncompromising endorsement of Cossus' *pietas* seems to reinforce the value of Augustus' testimony and to give it, in effect, the last word, the fact of the narrator's own identification of Cossus as a military tribune remains. And we are reminded of this fact quite strikingly several paragraphs later, when the narrator, without qualification or explanation, reports a speech in which Cossus, now master of the horse, is identified as the same man who won the *spolia opima* as a military tribune (4.32.4).[37] Not surprisingly, scholars are divided in their interpretation of the force of the passage as a whole. Some read it as a firm endorsement of Augustus' testimony;[38] others, on the contrary, regard the passage as more or less subtly undermining Augustus' testimony.[39]

The apparent inconsistency between persistent identification of Cossus as military tribune in the narrative and the narrator's concluding emphasis on evidence for identifying Cossus as consul in his editorial digression is likewise open to various interpretations. T. J. Luce has offered perhaps the most influential modern explanation for this apparent inconsistency.[40] He sees it as a function of the circumstances in which the text was composed. According to his reconstruction, Livy initially composed and published his first pentad *before* Crassus claimed and Augustus denied him the honor of the *spolia opima* in 29 B.C.E. Livy introduced an acknowledgment of Augustus' testimony into a subsequent, second edition of the pentad. He did not, however, revise the actual narrative of the first edition. Luce tacitly regards the difficulties of revising and reissuing an already published edition of the first pentad as sufficient explanation for the discrepancies between the body of the narrative and a presumably later insertion about Augustus' testimony. R. M. Ogilvie speculates that the insertion was made after Livy had written

---

37. Ogilvie, p. 564, notes further discrepancies between the digression on Augustus' evidence and the narrative proper.

38. E.g., Luce, "Dating," pp. 212–13.

39. E.g., P. G. Walsh, "Livy and Augustus," *Proceedings of the African Classical Association* 4 (1961): 30; Bayet, vol. 4, p. 35 n. 3.

40. "Dating," pp. 209–40.

4.20.5–11 (where Cossus is once again identified as a military tribune when he won the *spolia opima*) and that he then failed to reconcile the rest of the narrative with the new passage, an interpretation that is fully consistent with views of Livy as a careless or indifferent scholar.[41]

Another possibility, consistent with a recurrent aspect of the narrative that we have already noted, is that the author, although he felt obligated to acknowledge Augustus' testimony, did not find it decisive: convinced that there could be no rational basis for deciding one way or the other, he left the identification of Cossus in the narrative unchanged. On this view, then, his decision reflects not carelessness but rather is an acknowledgment that any choice must be arbitrary. Yet another possible explanation is that even though he felt obligated to acknowledge Augustus' testimony and was unwilling to reject it overtly, Livy nonetheless regarded it as spurious: he found a way to signal his disagreement tacitly and indirectly by leaving his identification of Cossus unchanged in the body of his narrative.[42] Not only the careful balancing and alternation of evidence in this passage but also the ambiguity and apparent anomalies that characterize both it and its relation to the larger narrative make it equally impossible either to endorse or to reject any single reading decisively. Each of these readings is available to informed and thoughtful readers, as the variety of interpretations of this passage by modern scholars amply confirms.

Thus the author has succeeded in acknowledging Augustus' personal authority generously and uncompromisingly while at the same time undermining it. This he has accomplished not by direct challenge, that Augustus' testimony is (for whatever reason) false, but rather by suggesting that the different evidence upon which Augustus and "the authorities" base their respective conclusions is equally unimpeachable. Without calling Augustus wrong, the author has nonetheless subverted his claim of authority by suggesting that the evidence simply does not support any certain conclusion. This argument is supported rhetorically in several ways. The ambiguity and lack of clear, explicit logical development at the heart of the author's

41. Pp. 563–64; and id., "Livy, Licinius Macer, and the *Libri Lintei," Journal of Roman Studies* 48 (1958): 40. Ogilvie, p. 564, also characterizes the passage as a "footnote," and Livy's failure to modify his narrative, a sign of his self-confidence. He argues that Livy's "ties with the imperial house were close and personal . . . but he remained politically uncommitted. He could afford to neglect the historical niceties which meant so much to Augustus and so little to himself"—a view that I regard as improbable and to which I shall offer an alternative below. See also Syme, "Livy and Augustus," pp. 44, 47; and Walsh, "Livy and Augustus," p. 36 n. 39.

42. Walsh, "Livy and Augustus"; and see Bayet, vol. 4, p. 35 n. 3.

analytical digression dramatically involve the reader in the difficulties and slipperiness of the evidence and its interpretation. Further, the contrast between the direct, uncomplicated, and apparently confident narrative of Cossus the military tribune and the author's subsequent profession of uncertainty calls attention to the essential arbitrariness of the author's own narrative. This same point is made again in the contrast between the narrator's concluding emphasis on the reliability of the evidence that Cossus was consul and his identification of Cossus as military tribune in the subsequent narrative.

In such ways the narrator's own uncertainty, confusion, and conspicuous arbitrariness serve to dramatize the logic of his argument, that a confident determination of historical fact is beyond reach. By exposing the weakness of his narrative in important matters of fact, by himself submitting, conspicuously, to the limitations of the evidence, Livy deprives Augustus of the power to impose his authority on history more effectively than if Livy had attempted to present himself as an authority—an act that would tacitly have conceded that factual certainty was attainable and would have pitted his own unequal authority against that of the emperor. Finally, it is extremely important for the effectiveness of the narrator's argument here that the combination of his argument against factual certainty and his own exemplification of its consequences is not unique to this immediate situation. We have seen, rather, that this combination conforms to a pattern found throughout Livy's narrative. Its appearance here is only a particular example of an argument that has been made and dramatized before—and that the reader will meet again. This pattern constitutes evidence of authorial good faith, proof that tacit criticism of the emperor and his attempts to appropriate the past is not a case of special pleading by the author but is, rather, consistent with his more general assessment of the historical tradition and the ways in which it may (and may not) properly be used.

The authorial position that I have described was especially well suited to an author in Livy's particular social and political position.[43] The scanty tradition about Livy's personal history identifies his birthplace as Patavium, a community prominent in the remote northeast of Italy. There is reason to believe that Patavium was under Roman control (although with local autonomy) at least from 174 B.C.E.[44] However, it long remained on the

---

43. Walsh, "Livy and Augustus," offers a balanced and nuanced assessment of the political pressures (both formal and informal) that might have come to bear on Augustan writers, but does not consider how a writer's social status might have influenced either attitudes toward him or his own sense of vulnerability.

44. Livy 41.27.

margins of Roman political life. It probably did not receive Latin rights until Pompeius Strabo extended them generally in the Transpadane area of Italy in 89 B.C.E., or receive full citizen rights until Julius Caesar's enfranchisement of the same area by fiat when he invaded Italy in 49 B.C.E.[45] There is no evidence that Livy's family belonged to Patavium's political aristocracy, much less that he had any ties with that of Rome.[46]

He appears, moreover, to have been one of the few Romans outside of Rome's active political aristocracy to have written history at all.[47] It cannot be coincidence or accident that Roman history was largely monopolized by members of Rome's political aristocracy. They had long perpetuated their versions of the past through various formalized oral traditions, through the *elogia* on the busts of distinguished ancestors whose display was their legal prerogative, and more recently through the writing of history. They

45. Joshua Whatmough, *The Foundations of Roman Italy* (New York: Haskell House, 1971), pp. 157–58, 172–75.

46. Scanty as the biographical information about Livy is, it is very difficult to imagine that evidence of a political career or of political affiliations at Rome would have been omitted or lost in the ancient testimonia. This argument from silence is all the stronger, given the probability of Patavium's late admission to Latin status and then to full citizenship.

47. E. Badian, "The Early Historians," in *Latin Historians,* ed. T. A. Dorey (New York: Basic Books, 1966), argues that P. Mucius Scaevola's edition and publication of the *Annales Maximi* (sometime during his pontificate from c. 130 to c. 115 B.C.E.) opened the writing of history to "men of lesser rank" at Rome (p. 15) and that for a time thereafter annalists (as opposed to writers of contemporary history) "are now lesser names: a Vennonius, a Q. Claudius Quadrigarius, a Valerius Antias" (p. 18). The first freedman to write history was Lucius Voltacilius Pitholaus, who wrote biographies of the elder and younger Pompeys and opened a school of rhetoric in 81 B.C.E. (Suet. *Rhet.* 3). It is important to bear in mind, however, that even though the circle of historians was widening, on the whole it remained quite narrow. L. Coelius Antipater had no political career himself but was the brother of a senator and, until he gave up public life, a jurist; Aelius Tubero was another jurist who left politics; Sempronius Asellio served as military tribune under Scipio at Numantia. Valerius Antias has left no record of political activity. Whether his family was related to the patrician Valerii of early Rome is a matter of dispute: see T. J. Cornell, "The Formation of the Historical Tradition of Early Rome," in *Past Perspectives: Studies in Greek and Roman Historical Writing,* ed. I. S. Moxon, J. D. Smart, and A. J. Woodman (Cambridge: Cambridge University Press, 1986), pp. 73, 77–79; and T. P. Wiseman, *Clio's Cosmetics: Three Studies in Greco-Roman Literature* (Leicester: Leicester University Press, 1979), p. 135. In the case of Venonnius and Q. Claudius Quadrigarius the most that we can say with certainty is that there is simply no evidence of aristocratic connection or political activity. The writing of history remained the particular domain of men who held or had held political office at Rome. See also Mark Toher, "Augustus and the Evolution of Roman Historiography," in *Between Republic and Empire: Interpretations of Augustus and His Principate,* ed. Kurt A. Raaflaub and Mark Toher (Berkeley: University of California Press, 1990), p. 150 n. 43.

no doubt claimed a unique and superior qualification to write history on the same grounds as did Polybius, a member of the political aristocracy of his native Megalopolis and Achaea. In an aggressive polemic against the historian Timaeus, Polybius argued at some length that only those with personal experience as leaders in warfare and politics were fully qualified to write history, since the purpose of history is to educate military and political leaders (12.25e–28a).[48] Whatever the merits of this view, it clearly served to justify an aristocratic monopoly on the production of history. As one of the very few Latin authors outside the political aristocracy to write Roman history, Livy threatened this monopoly at Rome; as one who had never held political office, he was open to criticism that he was incompetent to write history.[49]

He was also particularly vulnerable to criticism and attack. About the time of his own death, or perhaps a few years earlier, the works of two Romans, T. Labienus and Cassius Severus, both orators and historians, were officially ordered burned.[50] Labienus committed suicide;[51] Cassius was sent into exile, first to Crete and then, some twelve years later, to Seriphus, a barren rock.[52] Labienus, like Livy, was known for his Pompeian sentiments.[53] Both Labienus and Cassius were known for their rancor and their libelous attacks on "illustrious persons of both sexes, without restraint or distinc-

---

48. Much later Tacitus would argue (*Hist.* 1.1) that the writing of history had declined with the advent of the Principate, partly because of men's passion for flattery, partly because of their hatred of their masters, but first of all because of their "ignorance of public affairs as though [something] foreign," *inscitia rei publicae ut alienae*. See also Section I and note 6 above.

49. We hear the echoes of this aristocratic criticism, I suspect, in such modern judgments as the following: "Livy had little knowledge of Roman institutions. His inexperience in military matters affects his description of battles." *Oxford Classical Dictionary*, 2d ed., s.v. "Livius." Dewald, similarly, suggests that Herodotus' expressed reservations about portions of his narrative may account in part for negative assessments of it by later critics both in antiquity and in modern times (p. 151).

50. Their works were burned in C.E. 12. Livy died either in C.E. 12 or 17, depending on how one interprets the evidence for the date of his birth; the evidence is reviewed by Syme, "Livy and Augustus," pp. 40–42. The sources are confusing as to whether the burnings were undertaken at the direct initiative of Augustus (Dio Cass. 56.27.1; Tac. *Ann.* 1.72.4) or of the Senate (Suet. *Calig.* 16; Tac. *Ann.* 4.21.5).

51. Sen. *Controv.* 10, pref. 7.

52. Tac. *Ann.* 4.21.5.

53. Sen. *Controv.* 10, pref. 5: "His spirit was great for all his faults, both violent in proportion to his talent and one that had not yet set aside Pompeian sentiments in a time of such peace," *Animus inter uitia ingens et ad similitudinem ingenii sui violentus et qui Pompeianos spiritus nondum in tanta pace posuisset.*

tion."[54] An example of this invective is reported by Suetonius (*Vit.* 2): Cassius is said to have claimed that a procurator's grandfather was a cobbler and his mother a baker's daughter who had become a prostitute. Yet such invective seems rather common by the standards of Roman oratory, scarcely adequate in any event to explain the extraordinary and unprecedented punishment that the two authors suffered.[55]

Also at issue, however, was the social status of the two authors. Seneca acknowledges Labienus' talent but says of him: "He was extremely poor; his reputation was extremely bad; he was extremely hated," *summa egestas erat; summa infamia; summum odium* (*Controv.* 10, pref. 4). Tacitus characterizes Cassius as "squalid in his origins, wicked in his life," *sordidae originis, maleficae uitae* (*Ann.* 4.21.5). It is fully consistent with Roman attitudes that the social status of Labienus and Cassius should have a decisive effect on judgments about the propriety of the opinions that they expressed in their writings. Seneca expresses the connection between social status, moral judgment, and social propriety clearly in his characterization of Labienus: "His liberty was so great that it exceeded the name of liberty, so great that, because he savaged ranks and individuals without discrimination, he was called Rabie-

54. Syme, *Roman Revolution*, p. 487, characterizing Cassius; he uses almost exactly the same words of Labienus (p. 486).

55. *Pace* Kurt A. Raaflaub and L. J. Samons II, "Opposition to Augustus," in *Between Republic and Empire: Interpretations of Augustus and His Principate*, ed. Kurt A. Raaflaub and Mark Toher (Berkeley: University of California Press, 1990), pp. 440–41. The young Octavian himself, for example, appears to have been reproached by Antony and others on the grounds that his paternal great-grandfather had been a freedman and rope maker from the district of Thurii, that his paternal grandfather had been a money changer, that his father was called a money changer and *diuisor* (distributor of electoral bribes), that his maternal great-grandmother had been born in Africa and had kept a perfumery and then a bakery shop at Aricia, and that his wife came from Aricia. The charges and their sources are discussed on pp. 12–17 of Kenneth Scott, "The Political Propaganda of 44–30 B.C.," *Memoirs of the American Academy in Rome* 11 (1933): 7–49. The enemies of Antony responded with criticism that he had bestowed the kingdom of Cappadocia upon a man who was descended on his father's side from a family that had fought against Rome and from a mother who was a hetaera (Dio Cass. 49.32.3). In his *Third Philippic* Cicero counters Antony's slurs upon Octavian's ancestry by pointing out that, dressed in the tragic robe and buskins of an actor, the grandfather of Antony's wife used to toss coins to the people from the rostra, that Antony's paternal grandmother, Numitoria, was the daughter of a traitor, and that Antony himself had recognized his children by the daughter of one of his freedmen (Cic. *Phil.* 3.16–18). For the burning of books under Augustus as unprecedented, see Sen. *Controv.* 10, pref. 5–6; Tac. *Ann.* 1.72.4. On attacking political opponents through their women as a common strategy, see also Diana Delia, "Fulvia Reconsidered," in Sarah B. Pomeroy, ed., *Women's History and Ancient History* (Chapel Hill: University of North Carolina Press, 1991), pp. 199, 201.

nus," *Libertas tanta ut libertatis nomen excederet, et, quia passim ordines hominesque laniabat, Rabienus vocaretur (Controv.* 10, pref. 5).[56]

Livy himself was criticized for his *Patauinitas,* i.e., for exhibiting character-istics of his native city, Patavium. It is not clear precisely what this charge referred to. But whether it meant writing like a Patavian or thinking like one, it marked him as an outsider.[57] Even though Labienus and Cassius had not yet suffered their unprecedented fates, that did not mean those fates would have been unimaginable when Livy began the composition of his own history some forty years earlier.[58] At that time the memories of the triumvirs' proscriptions would still have been fresh. The writing of history was not normally a dangerous occupation at Rome, but Livy was not writing in normal times, and he was not a member of the privileged class by whom history was normally written.[59] It would be surprising if either circumstance escaped the notice of an author in his position.

In fact, the very first lines of Livy's preface address the question of the author's status directly, and in a way that seems designed to forestall or deflect criticism:

Facturusne operae pretium sim si a primordio urbis res populi Romani perscripserim nec satis scio nec, si sciam, dicere ausim, quippe qui cum

56. Rabienus (for Labienus) is a play on the Latin *rabies,* meaning "animal savageness or ferocity."

57. The criticism is attributed to Pollio by Quintilian (1.5.56) and refers most directly to Livy's diction, but scholars have generally felt that it should be understood as having broad, sociopolitical connotations as well. See, for example, Ogilvie, p. 5; Syme, *Roman Revolution,* pp. 485–86; id., "Livy and Augustus," p. 76, with additional literature cited there. That Patavium appears for some time to have sided with Antony against Octavian is probably not relevant to an assessment of the social or political implications of *Patauinitas;* Patavium's long reputation as a seat of traditional morality (Pliny *Ep.* 1.14.6; Mart. 11.16.8) might be construed to imply political conservatism in a time of change.

58. Raaflaub and Samons (pp. 439–40) cite the elder Seneca's remarks about Labienus (*Controv.* 8) as implying that Labienus "acted out of some measure of fear" when he declined to read some parts of his history aloud, saying that they would be read after his death. Clearly, the new political order had created a new environment in which historians (and no doubt others) could no longer be certain that the liberality accorded freedom of speech in the late Republic continued to apply. The chilling effect of the new order need not have been commensurate with the actual extent of opposition to Augustus or of his measures to suppress it, both of which Raaflaub and Samons argue were more limited than usually perceived.

59. Syme's characterization of Labienus and Cassius ("neither [of them] possessed the social and material advantages that rendered Pollio secure from reprisals as well as formidable in attack," *Roman Revolution,* p. 486) applies equally to Livy—a judgment echoed by Fornara (p. 74) and Raaflaub and Samons (p. 438).

ueterem tum uolgatam esse rem uideam, dum noui semper scriptores aut in rebus certius aliquid allaturos se aut scribendi arte rudem uetustatem superaturos credunt. Vtcumque erit, . . . si in tanta scriptorum turba mea fama in obscuro sit, nobilitate ac magnitudine eorum me qui nomini officient meo consoler. (pref. 1–3)

Whether it may be worthwhile if I should write the affairs of the Roman people continuously from the very beginnings of the city, I do not really know. Even if I should know, I would not dare to say, inasmuch as I see that the subject is an old and a common one, while new writers one after another believe either that they will have something more reliable to add in their facts or that by their skill in writing they will surpass crude antiquity. However that may be, . . . if, amidst such a mob of writers, my own reputation should be obscure, I would console myself with the *nobilitas* and *magnitudo* of those who will stand in the way of my reputation.

With these opening words the author establishes his personal modesty through his expressed uncertainty about the value of his undertaking, through his professed unwillingness to hazard a judgment on such a matter, and through his acknowledgment of the work and aspirations of other historians. These expressions of modesty, however, are subordinate to and serve the expression of a more specific attitude, that of deference. Both in content and in style, both explicitly and implicitly, the author contrasts himself with those who possess the attributes of *nobilitas* and *magnitudo*. This contrast has clear political implications. While *nobilitas* and *magnitudo* might refer to more or less abstract qualities of his rivals, both words have significant social and political associations that could not be ignored.[60] Even leaving aside the technical sense of *nobilitas,* the word nonetheless clearly designates a class of individuals who are "known," visible, in a society where conspicuous display was a central feature of social and political competition.[61] Similarly, *magnitudo* refers first and foremost not to moral or spiritual qualities but to physical and social stature.[62]

60. Ogilvie, pp. 25–26.

61. I.e., a class of individuals one or more of whose ancestors had held the highest political offices at Rome. The exact extent of "the highest offices" (whether including all curule offices, just the praetorship and above, or just the consulship) is a matter of continuing debate. The evidence and arguments are reviewed succinctly and judiciously by P. A. Brunt, "*Nobilitas* and *Novitas*," *Journal of Roman Studies* 72 (1982): 1–17.

62. See *Oxford Latin Dictionary,* s.v. Elsewhere in Livy *magnitudo* is used virtually always to express physical size or scale, occasionally to indicate importance (as in *rerum gestarum magnitudo,* 39.29.5), or rarely to refer to the public stature of a distinguished individual (9.18.9 of Alexander the Great; 30.13.2 of Syphax; 38.51.14, 54.2, 58.9 of Publius Scipio Africanus). Livy never uses it to indicate moral quality.

Thus while the author's assertion that his own reputation will be obscured by the *nobilitas* and *magnitudo* of others may obviously be read as a compliment, it is open to other possibilities—in part because of what it does *not* say. It does not specifically identify those who will obscure the author's reputation with those who believe that they have "something more accurate" to offer or that they will be distinguished by their eloquence: it does not say that those who will stand in the way of his reputation will write better histories than he. What the author does say, quite literally, is that their *nobilitas* and *magnitudo* will stand in the way of his reputation, a statement that is open to the suggestion of suppression as well as to the idea of literary superiority: their celebrity, political stature, and power will stand in the way of his "name." Read this way, the statement remains one of deference, but it is a deference that acknowledges the social authority and power that his critics undoubtedly had, without explicitly conceding to them a superior competence or excellence as historians or literary craftsmen.

But it is an affirmation, nonetheless, of a readiness not only to defer to those with *nobilitas* and *magnitudo* but to do so with a good will. This explicit statement of deference is reinforced by the tone of the passage. In contrast to those with *nobilitas* and *magnitudo,* the author locates himself among the undifferentiated "mob," *turba,* of undistinguished writers. When he subordinates himself to those who will stand in the way of his own reputation, the subjunctives with which he expresses his own uncertain and tentative aspirations and resolves (*Facturusne sim, perscripserim, sciam, ausim, sit, consoler*) contrast sharply with the direct and affirmative future indicative that expresses the certainty of their preeminence over him (*officient*).[63] The deployment of the rhetoric of factual analysis in Livy's narrative serves the same functions as the author's self-presentation in the preface. While reconfirming his unwillingness and inability to elicit certainty from an unreliable tradition, it reinforces the author's deferential presentation of himself as tentative, uncertain of his own merits, unwilling to challenge those whose *nobilitas* and *magnitudo* give them an *auctoritas* that he cannot claim for himself.

This rhetorical strategy allows the author to challenge his social and political superiors with a degree of safety. It enables him to take a stand on sensitive issues while disclaiming responsibility for doing so. Thus he can present his own uncertainty about the origins of the Julian clan or about the history of the *spolia opima* not as a direct challenge to Augustus but as a consequence of the limitations of the evidence or of his own ability to

---

63. The only time in this passage that Livy expresses one of his own actions or attitudes in the indicative is when he expresses his ignorance: *nec satis scio.*

cope with it effectively. He has made it easy for potentially dangerous critics—not only Augustus but all those who had an interest in preserving a monopoly on the past—to dismiss him. We may detect something of this easy dismissal, I believe, in the allegation that is reported in Tacitus' *Annales*:

> Titus Livius, eloquentiae ac fidei praeclarus in primis, Cn. Pompeium tantis laudibus tulit, ut Pompeianum eum Augustus appellaret; neque id amicitiae eorum offecit. (4.34.4)

> Titus Livy, conspicuous among the first rank for his eloquence and probity, exalted Gnaius Pompey with such praises that Augustus named him "Pompeian"—and this did not stand in the way of their friendship.[64]

It is notable that these words, usually attributed simply to Tacitus' *Annales*, are in fact presented there as part of the self-defense given some thirteen years after Livy's death by his fellow historian, Cremutius Cordus. Cordus, charged with *maiestas* for celebrating Republican heroes in his historical writings, subsequently committed suicide; his writings were burned.[65] His speech argues for a contrast between the toleration of Augustus and the oppression of Tiberius, during whose reign Cordus was accused. But in fact, as we have noted, the last years of Augustus' reign had already seen the burning of books. In any event, Augustus' alleged condescension toward Livy is a *re*action. It is a response to the subversive possibilities of Livy's narrative. If it dismisses these possibilities as unthreatening, ineffectual, it nonetheless acknowledges them—evidence that they were there for those who were prepared to take them seriously; evidence, too, that the ambiguities of the author's self-presentation allowed him to escape the hostility of those whose appropriation of the past he challenged. Modern critics who have dismissed Livy for his historiographic shoddiness have read his narrative in a way that they have, in a sense, been invited or set up to do; but they have read it this way, apparently, without appreciating the value that such a historiographic stance and such authorial self-presentation might have had for an author in Livy's particular social position and in the particular political circumstances of the early Principate.

---

64. The precise interpretation of *fidei* in this passage (whether it refers specifically to Livy's historical accuracy or reliability, to his character more generally, or to his political independence) is a matter of some disagreement. My translation follows that of Fornara, p. 74, who argues that *fidei* here refers principally to Livy's political independence. For further discussion see also E. Koestermann, ed., *Cornelius Tacitus: Annalen* (Heidelberg: Carl Winter, 1965), vol. 2, p. 182.

65. See Suet. *Tib.* 61.3; Dio Cass. 57.24.3.

VI

Much more is at issue here, however, than a rhetorical strategy for self-preservation. In the passages discussed above we can also trace the successive blurring, recasting, and ultimate collapse of the traditional distinction between oral and visual evidence that Livy evoked in his preface as the fundamental distinction upon which the construction of a reliable history depends. In the place of this inadequate methodology we are shown an alternative basis for the construction of Roman history, one that does not use received tradition as evidence from which to reconstruct an accurate and reliable record of the past but presents tradition, rather, as the record of the Romans' own perception of themselves, a record that may be used as the basis for reconstructing and interpreting their identity.

As we have seen, the opening narrative of Livy's history recalls the distinction in his preface between *fabulae* and *monumenta,* the latter in this case comprised of peoples and places that offer physical and visible evidence of the past. On close examination, however, we found that the distinction between these two kinds of evidence is blurred by the ambiguous deployment of direct and indirect discourse. It is blurred in another way as well. On reflection, it becomes apparent that the value of peoples and places as *monumenta* depends itself on speech.[66] A location in the innermost recess of the Adriatic serves as evidence of Antenor's settlement, for example, because "it is called," *uocatur,* Troy, because the "name," *nomen,* of the region is Troy, because all the people there "are called," *appellati,* Veneti. The Trojans' arrival in Laurentine territory appears to be confirmed, because "Troy is the name of this place, too," *Troia et huic loco nomen est.* Except perhaps for the idiosyncratic deployment of direct and indirect discourse, nothing in the narrative at this point calls attention to or develops the potential difficulties raised by this dependence of *monumenta* on oral testimony for their meaning.

Subsequent passages, however, suggest further potential complications in the relation between *fabulae* and *monumenta* and reveal increasing uncertainty about their relative value. An apparent anomaly in the story of Tullia and

66. On the relation between oral and material testimony, I have been particularly influenced by Charles Hedrick, "The Meaning of Material Culture: Herodotus, Thucydides, and Their Sources," in *Nomodeiktes: Greek Studies in Honor of Martin Ostwald,* ed. Ralph R. Rosen and J. Farrell (Ann Arbor: University of Michigan Press, 1993), pp. 17–37, who discusses the complex interrelationships between words and things in the historiography of Herodotus and Thucydides.

the assassination of her father, Servius Tullius, has already been noted. There Livy reports a *monumentum* attesting to the tradition that Tullia actually drove her chariot over her father's dead body: "The place serves as a monument [to the deed]," *monumentoque locus est* (1.48.4). But Livy also makes it clear that the meaning of the *monumentum* itself depends on an oral tradition associated with it ("they call it the Street of Crime," *sceleratum uicum uocant*), and he does not present Tullia's alleged crime as a certainty, reporting it rather as tradition (*fertur,* "it is said"). Here, then, the weight of Livy's emphasis seems to fall less on the authority of visible evidence and more on the oral tradition on which the interpretation of that evidence seems to depend.

At 7.6.3–5, where Livy attempts to judge the relative merits of the two Lacus Curtius *aetia,* the dependence of *monumenta* upon oral tradition and the priority of *fabulae* are affirmed explicitly. In his initial story about the Lacus Curtius and how it got its name Livy reported simply: "They named the monument of this battle . . . the Lacus Curtius," *Monumentum eius pugnae . . . Curtium Lacum appellarunt* (1.13.5). In book 7 he claims rather that "The Lacus Curtius is named not after that ancient well-known soldier of Titus Tatius, Mettius Curtius, but after this man [Marcus Curtius]," *lacumque Curtium non ab antiquo illo T. Tati milite Curtio Mettio sed ab hoc appellatum* (7.6.5). The question of naming becomes decisive:

> Cura non deesset, si qua ad uerum uia inquirentem ferret; nunc fama rerum standum est, ubi certam derogat vetustas fidem; et lacus nomen ab hac recentiore insignitius fabula est. (7.6.6)

> Effort would not be lacking if any route would bring an inquirer to the truth, but as it is, we must stand by the report [*fama*] where antiquity removes certainty. In addition, the name of the lake is better known from this more recent story.

The uncertainty created when a single *monumentum* is associated with conflicting oral traditions reveals just how completely the meaning of the place, the *monumentum,* depends upon the oral tradition that interprets it: the *monumentum* can have no meaning independent of that tradition. In fact, rather than the *monumentum* confirming or refuting the tradition, the currency of the oral tradition becomes the standard by which meaning is assigned to the *monumentum.* Contrary to the principle articulated in the preface, *fabula,* not *monumentum* (what is spoken rather than what can be seen), has emerged here as the decisive criterion for judging historical evidence. This collapse of a historiographically useful distinction between oral and visual evidence recalls the kind of methodological impenetrability and uncertainty that Livy had initially assigned only to the earliest, prehistorical era of Rome's past. Now we find that no amount of effort can assure certainty about a much later period of Roman history, even one from which a visible trace remains.

As the historiographic usefulness of the distinction between *fabulae* and *monumenta* grows progressively more problematic in his narrative, Livy turns at first tentatively, then with apparent confidence, to another potential source of reliable information about the past, written survivals. Livy first evokes them in the passage on the *spolia opima* discussed above, where it is immediately clear that their interpretation may be fraught with uncertainties and difficulties. There each side of the argument about Cossus' official rank when he won the *spolia opima* rests principally on written evidence: the *libri lintei* that support his identity as a military tribune, and the inscription on the breastplate that supports his identity as a consul. While Livy does not evaluate these sources in detail, his discussion, particularly his assessment of the inscription on Cossus' breastplate, does indirectly suggest some of their relative shortcomings. When he suggests, for example, that Cossus would not have falsified his rank on the inscription because Romulus and Jupiter would have been witnesses to his fraud, Livy tacitly acknowledges the possibility that such falsification was in theory possible. When he calls attention to the piety of Augustus, on whose authority he reports the inscription, Livy similarly acknowledges that belief in the inscription rests entirely on faith in Augustus' word. In emphasizing the particular authority of Cossus' inscription—that it derives from the recipient of the *spolia opima* himself—Livy invites speculation about the origins of the alternative record in the *libri lintei,* whether they too were contemporaneous with the event or not.

These tacit complications notwithstanding, Livy introduces his sixth book, the beginning of the second half of Roman history, with an emphatic and confident assertion that written records alone provide a secure basis for reconstruction of the past:

> Quae ab condita urbe Roma ad captam eandem Romani . . . gessere . . . quinque libris exposui, res cum uetustate nimia obscuras, uelut quae magno ex interuallo loci uix cernuntur, tum quod paruae et rarae per eadem tempora litterae fuere, una custodia fidelis memoriae rerum gestarum, et quod, etiam si quae in commentariis pontificum aliisque publicis priuatisque erant monumentis, incensa urbe pleraeque interiere. Clariora deinceps certioraque ab secunda origine . . . urbis gesta domi militiaeque exponentur. (6.1.1–3)

What the Romans did from the time of Rome's foundation to the capture of the same . . . I have set forth in five books, matters that are obscure, due not only to their excessive antiquity—just as things that are scarcely made out from a great distance—but also because throughout those same times writing (the one reliable guardian of the memory of deeds) was little used and uncommon and because even if there were any things in the priests' commentaries and in other public and private records, they mostly perished when the city was burned. More bright and definite are the deeds in peacetime and war that will be presented from this point, the second . . . beginning of the city.

This new assertion of authorial confidence in a narrative based on more reliable, written evidence is, however, subsequently undercut. After recording a victory of Aulus Cornelius over the Samnites in book 8, Livy acknowledges that the identity of the actual *triumphator* is a matter of dispute. He goes on to explain why a choice between the alternatives is impossible:

Vitiatam memoriam funebribus laudibus reor falsisque imaginum titulis, dum familiae ad se quaeque famam rerum gestarum honorumque fallenti mendacio trahunt; inde certe et singulorum gesta et publica monumenta rerum confusa. Nec quisquam aequalis temporibus illis scriptor exstat, quo satis certo auctore stetur. (8.40.4)

Memory has been vitiated, I think, by funeral eulogies and false inscriptions on ancestral busts while with deceitful lies every household claims for itself a reputation for past deeds and offices. As a consequence, it is certain that both the deeds of individuals and public monuments have been thrown into confusion. Nor does there exist any writer contemporary with those times whose authority is sufficiently firm to take a stand on.[67]

But even the hope that written testimony of contemporary witnesses will provide reliable evidence proves to be overoptimistic. For one thing, there is much of importance that the writings of contemporaries omit. Livy relates, for example, that Publius Scipio was chosen, despite his youth, to receive the Idaean Mother at Rome, because his contemporaries judged him to be the best of all good men in the state (29.14.8). He adds, however, that he cannot report exactly what the virtues were that merited such an extraordinary distinction for one so young, because they were not recorded "by the writers closest to the memory of those times," *a proximis memoriae*

---

67. This criticism of aristocratic family traditions closely follows that in Cic. *Brut.* 16.62.

temporum illorum scriptoribus (29.14.9).[68] Further, written sources prove to be hopelessly unreliable in matters of numbers. In discussing Publius Scipio's capture of New Carthage, Livy professes himself at a complete loss to determine the actual number of hostages taken, the size of the Carthaginian garrison, the number of captives, the number of scorpions (rapid-fire catapults), the identity of the generals, the number of captured ships, the amount of gold and silver taken—not because of a dearth of written reports but because of a plethora. In reporting the contrasting views of different authors, he gives no more weight to that of the Greek contemporary and companion of Hannibal, Silenus, than to Valerius Antias, the Roman annalist who wrote more than a century after the event. Rather, he falls back on the essentially arbitrary conclusion that "if it is necessary to agree with some [authorities], the middle [figures] are most plausible," *Si aliquis adsentiri necesse est, media simillima ueri sunt* (26.49.6).[69]

But perhaps most telling is the uncertainty and confusion that surround Livy's efforts to identify the exact circumstances and, in particular, the date of Scipio's death. The evidence is abundant and varied. Livy introduces his discussion of it by asserting: "They pass on many other and contradictory things especially about the end of Scipio's life, his indictment, death, funeral, tomb, so that I am at a loss what rumor [*fama*], what writings [*scriptis*], I should agree with," *Multa alia in Scipionis exitu maxime uitae dieque dicta, morte, funere, sepulcro, in diuersum trahunt, ut cui famae, quibus scriptis adsentiar non habeam* (38.56.1). In this introductory statement Livy places the evidence of *fama* and *scripta* on a par. In fact, the evidence includes unidentified informants, *monumenta* (different tombs and statues that are said to be Scipio's), and the speeches of contemporaries. Immediately after pointing out that there are inconsistencies between speeches by Publius Scipio and Tiberius Gracchus as well as an important omission in Gracchus' speech (his failure to mention Scipio's trial or prosecutor), Livy concludes that "an entirely different tale [*fabula*] must be put together, one that is consistent with Gracchus' speech," *Alia tota serenda fabula est Gracchi orationi conueniens* (38.56.8).

Later, near the end of book 39, Livy returns to the question of the date of Scipio's death. He reports that Polybius, a younger contemporary of Scipio's, and Rutilius, a near contemporary of Polybius (and along with

68. For another example of omission by historians (only in this case historians more removed in time from the event with which Livy is concerned), see 3.23.7.

69. For other examples of Livy's concern about historians' unreliability with regard to numbers, see 36.38.7 and 38.55, discussed below.

him an intimate of the Scipio family), disagree with the much later historian Valerius Antias as to whether Scipio died in what we would identify by modern dating as 183 or 187 B.C.E., respectively. Despite his general disdain for Antias' testimony, Livy does not simply reject him here in favor of Polybius and Rutilius.[70] Rather, he rejects the views of all three historians. In a somewhat complicated argument, he rejects the date of Polybius and Rutilius on the grounds that Scipio could not have lived until 183 B.C.E. because, being registered as *princeps senatus* for the previous two years, he should have appeared (but did not) on official records as *princeps* also for 183. He rejects Antias' date on the grounds that Naevius, the tribune who prosecuted Scipio, is reported in official records (*magistratuum libri*) to have held office in 185 B.C.E., so that Scipio must have been alive then and presumably died very shortly thereafter. Here, then, the apparent authority of state records seems to confirm that even the written reports of contemporary individuals cannot be trusted implicitly. Modern editors point to significant confusions and inconsistencies between the discussions in books 38 and 39 as evidence of Livy's own lack of coherent methodology.[71] My point here is rather that they suggest an awareness of the limitations of contemporary written sources, limitations that make it impossible for Livy to reach a confident conclusion. His last words on the date of Scipio's death are the following: "*So it seems* that he lived during the tribunate of Naevius . . . [and] died, moreover, before the censorship of L. Valerius and M. Porcius," *Ita uixisse in tribunatu Naeuii uidetur, . . . decessisse autem ante L. Valerii et M. Porcii censuram* (39.52.6; my emphasis). What is striking about Livy's references to histories taken as a whole is that he rarely evokes them to assert their authority, rather, almost always, as in the examples discussed above, to discuss their shortcomings.[72]

70. On Antias, see, for example, 26.49.3, 33.10.8.

71. See, for example, Evan T. Sage, trans., *Livy,* Loeb Classical Library, no. 313 (Cambridge, Mass.: Harvard University Press, 1965), vol. 11, pp. 384–85 nn. 3 and 4.

72. One of the very few passages where Livy explicitly accepts the reports of historians without apparent reserve is at 9.18.5: he cites their unanimity to support his catalogue of Alexander the Great's flaws. In other cases his appeal to their authority is typically either lukewarm (e.g., 23.6.8, where he agrees that writers were correct to omit certain unreliable information from their accounts) or is justified by reference to some other standard or authority. At 26.11.10, for example, he reports that while there is irresoluble disagreement among *scriptores* about the route by which Hannibal approached a temple that he subsequently looted, "there is no doubt whatso-ever among writers about the looting of this temple," *Huius populatio templi haud dubia inter scriptores est.* However, he explains this agreement on the grounds that the importance of the leader and the traces (*uestigia*) of such a great army would have made it impossible for the *memoria* of the event to have been confused in a short time. At 38.55.8 he says regarding an amount of

The failure of contemporary literary accounts to provide a secure basis for historical reconstruction constitutes the last in a series of frustrated and deferred expectations for the reader. In the preface we were led to believe that the earliest, pre-foundation history of Rome was utterly unreliable, but that we could expect the subsequent narrative, when the author would no longer have to rely exclusively on *fabula*, to be more secure. Although subsequent passages of the narrative suggest that such an expectation was overly optimistic, it is only with the introduction to book 6 that this is acknowledged explicitly and in retrospect. There we encounter a new assurance that the subsequent narrative will be more reliable, because of a new shift from dependence on oral tradition and *monumenta* to a tradition that is supported specifically by *written monumenta* as well. But even this soon appears to be an illusory and unreliable expectation when the author confronts and acknowledges the limitations of written *monumenta* in book 8 and identifies a more limited and specific kind of written source as the necessary condition for reliable history: the accounts of contemporary writers. This is not, then, to deny completely the value of written testimony, but it does seriously qualify the confident judgment offered in the introduction to book 6. Livy's difficulties here point out that sufficient written *monumenta* do not always exist, and, more devastating, that written *monumenta* themselves may be subject to manipulations and distortions so great as to throw even public *monumenta* into useless confusion. Finally, the suggestion that a still more specific form of written evidence, the testimony of contemporary historians, will provide a basis for certainty also proves to be illusory.

This pattern of raised and compromised expectations is analogous on a large scale to the pattern that we have seen on the smaller scale of individual passages where Livy presents a story with apparent confidence only subsequently to offer an alternative that casts doubt on the reliability of that story. Together these recurrent patterns of defeated expectations

---

money supposed to have been accepted as a bribe that, for his own part, he would "prefer there to be an error on the part of the scribe than a deliberate falsification by the historian," *malim equidem librarii mendum quam mendacium scriptoris esse,* but he explains this preference on the commonsense grounds that it simply seems more likely that the weight of silver given would have been greater than the weight of gold and that 4 million sesterces seems a more plausible amount for the bribe than 24 million. He adds that the smaller number is also supported by the fact that "they say," *tradunt,* that it was the number cited in court. The vague *tradunt* here may, of course, refer to the testimony of historians, but Livy makes himself less clear on this point than on his explicit disinclination to trust the *scriptores.* In general, the evidence of historians is most often evoked by Livy not as authoritative in itself but in order to be confirmed or (more often) rejected by reference to some other standard.

undermine confidence in the narrative's reliability as a factual record of the past with the result that after a time the reader does not know when to trust the narrative, when to expect the introduction of alternative versions or methodological difficulties that will cast doubt on what has been presented as straightforward and unproblematic. In addition, the larger pattern of methodological retrenchments raises broader doubts about whether there can be *any* basis for a factually reliable narrative of the past, whether the hope for methodological certainty may not prove to be a chimera, a mirage receding always into the future.

Thus far we have focused on specific passages, some of which address methodological issues directly, all of which overtly and explicitly call attention to uncertainties about the factual reliability of the tradition that they report. I have argued that the cumulative effect of such passages is to undermine confidence both in the factual reliability of the narrative and in the narrator's ability to identify any sound methodological principles on which any factually reliable narrative could be based. At this point, it is perhaps worth noting that such passages in Livy's narrative may have played a large role in shaping the negative assessment of him as a historian that has developed in modern times, particularly in the late nineteenth and early twentieth centuries, when positivism was the prevailing standard among historians and historiographers. It should now be apparent that modern scholars who have found Livy's narrative most lacking are at least in part simply criticizing him for acknowledging openly the limitations of historiographic principles that were prevalent in antiquity and that others either accepted or criticized less overtly than he did. He is being faulted, in other words, not for actually being less capable than other historians of antiquity but rather for acknowledging more openly the kinds of methodological problems that the historiographic standards of his age entailed—especially when applied to study of the remote past. Taken in context, then, those passages that call attention to traditional standards of historiographical analysis and their limitations appear not so much as expressions of the author's particular incompetence as testaments to his honesty, evidence that he is grappling openly with intractable problems and that he is not claiming a greater accuracy for his narrative than it can support.

VII

Strikingly, many passages that call attention to Livy's inadequacy or that of his sources to make a clear determination of fact nonetheless present equally clear weighting of the narrative toward one or another aspect of received tradition. To say that Livy has failed to develop a fully adequate methodology for determining questions of historical fact, indeed, that he repeatedly calls attention to that failure, does not mean that the choices implicit in such weighting are arbitrary or meaningless. There are yet other standards according to which the narrator's choices of dramatic emphasis are readily intelligible: thematic or ideological standards.[73]

Sometimes the refusal to weight alternatives clearly may itself be ideologically significant. I have already suggested that in discussing the identity of Iulus/Ascanius and Cossus' rank, for example, Livy's failure to decide unambiguously between conflicting versions, indeed his conspicuous display of the obstacles to such decisiveness, has significant political implications. Similarly, the deployment of indirect discourse, even when it is not apparently intelligible in terms of relative historical facticity, may nonetheless support a thematically and ideologically coherent commentary on tradition. The ideological significance of the relation between direct discourse, indirect discourse, and attribution to tradition in Livy's story of Romulus and Remus will be discussed in Chapter 4. Their interrelationships in the story of Tullia also reveal an ideological bias. I have already called attention to how their alternation does not bear an apparent relation to the nature of the historical evidence. If we review the passage once again, however, it will be apparent that Livy here uses indirect discourse consistently to distance himself from those specific parts of the story that concern Tullia's violence to her father: Servius "*is* killed," *interficitur;* but "it is *believed* [that it was done on Tullia's authority]," *creditur;* "tradition *reports* [a foul crime]," *traditur;* but "the place *is*," *est;* "they *call* it," *uocant;* the driver actually "*stopped*" and "*pointed out*", *restitit . . . ostendit;* but "Tullia . . . *is said* [to have driven over her father's body]," *Tullia . . . fertur.* By refusing to report Tullia's alleged crimes against her father in his own voice, on his own authority, Livy implies that they are less creditable than the other aspects of the story. As we have seen, the apparent rationale for this judgment has nothing to do with the nature of the historical evidence. But it is readily intelligible as an assessment of psychological plausibility and as a way of expressing the narrator's moral

73. B. Feichtinger, "*Ad Maiorem Gloriam Romae:* Ideologie und Fiktion in der Historiographie des Livius," *Latomus* 51 (1992): 3–33, argues that Livy's and, indeed, the Roman conception of history generally were essentially different from that of moderns: it was constructed according to a cultural "code" that distinguished myth from reality in somewhat different ways than moderns do; for Livy, as for other Roman historians, the reality of historical *exempla* was secondary to their role in dramatizing an ideologically true picture of Roman identity. See especially pp. 17 and 25–26 of Feichtinger's article.

evaluation of Tullia's reported behavior. The parts of the story that the narrator implies are least reliable are those that strain credulity because they stand in such stark contrast to the kinds of feelings and behavior that we would expect of a child toward a father. Livy's implicit incredulity, his reluctance to report Tullia's violation of her father on his own authority, therefore, constitute a moral judgment, a way of saying that Tullia's reported behavior is difficult to believe not because it is unsupported by evidence but because it is such an outrageous violation of accepted social norms. To say that it is difficult to believe that anyone could act as Tullia did is to offer a measure of how extremely unacceptable her behavior is. Here, then, rhetorical strategies that were first introduced in association with questions of historical facticity are, on close examination, intelligible not in terms of historical evidence but rather in terms of ideology.

Perhaps more obvious is the thematic and ideological relevance of the choices that Livy makes between variant traditions whose relative facticity he presents as indeterminate. In the opening narrative, for example, we noted the greater dramatic emphasis given to the second alternative in the *duplex fama* about Aeneas' arrival in Latium. In its narrative context the second, more detailed passage, describing the peaceful settlement between Aeneas and Latinus, serves two complementary functions. First, it recalls the opening sentence of the narrative and confirms the blameless character of Aeneas, the ancestor of Rome's founder, and his link with the more civilized world of the Greeks. According to the second version of the *duplex fama*, after Aeneas and Evander have advanced to meet each other between their opposed armies and Aeneas has told the story of his search for a new homeland, Latinus offers his right hand in a gesture of welcome and peace, "since he admired the illustriousness both of [Aeneas'] race and of the man himself and admired also his spirit, which was ready either for peace or war," *nobilitatem admiratum gentis uirique et animum uel bello uel paci paratum* (1.1.8). In thus reporting Latinus' assessment of Aeneas, Livy protects Aeneas' reputation for courage (his spirit is ready for war) while confirming other qualities that set him apart from most other Trojans, and indeed from most of the heroes in the Hellenic tradition: his readiness for peace, and implicit in that his sense of fairness and justice. These are precisely the qualities for which, according to the very first sentence of the narrative, Aeneas and Antenor were honored by their Greek enemies. The narrative has been weighted, then, to reinforce a consistent emphasis on one aspect of Aeneas' distinctive excellence—an excellence, moreover, that may be understood as paradigmatic for that of the Romans as a people.

This depiction of Aeneas as heroic, yet just and open to peace, has a complementary function, to demonstrate that Aeneas did not impose himself on the Latins but rather won them over by his personal qualities and tact. Shortly after Aeneas accepts Latinus' offer of peace, the Latins and Trojans find themselves threatened by Turnus and the Rutulians. In the face of this threat, Aeneas, "in order to win over the feelings of the Aborigines and in order that they all be under the same name as well as the same law, gave both peoples the name 'Latins,' " *ut animos Aboriginum sibi conciliaret nec sub eodem iure solum sed etiam nomine omnes essent, Latinos utramque gentem appellauit* (1.2.4). The result of this act was that "then the Aborigines were not second to the Trojans in their enthusiasm and loyalty toward King Aeneas," *nec deinde Aborigines Troianis studio ac fide erga regem Aenean cessere* (1.2.5). Thenceforth the two peoples grow closer to each other day by day (*in dies*). By the time of Aeneas' death, the narrative ceases to make any distinction between them: they respond to his death as one people, who collectively "call him Jupiter Indiges," *Iouem indigetem appellant* (1.2.6).

Thus while there is no perceptible basis for giving greater credence to the version privileged in the narrative of how Aeneas and his followers come to establish themselves in Latium, that version fits in with other elements of the story thematically and ideologically. In this way it is reinforced and in a sense reconfirmed. It achieves a rhetorical force, a kind of validity, not because it has a better basis in fact or in the sources, but because it makes good sense in terms of the narrative context, in which it contributes to a larger, coherent portrayal not only of Aeneas as the ultimate ancestor of the Roman people but also of the process of conciliation by which Rome will incorporate new peoples throughout its history. The opening narrative sequence, then, rewards and so encourages a thematic or ideological interpretation of tradition even as it frustrates and so discourages critical assessment of historical reliability. Thus it constitutes a precedent, establishes an initial orientation or set of practical expectations about the narrative that will follow and about how best to read it.

This perspective on the text is reinforced by Livy's two versions of Remus' murder. There, too, even though Livy is conspicuously ambiguous in his assessment of the variants' relative historicity (as we have seen above), the second version of Remus' death, like the second version of Aeneas' accommodation with Latinus, is the more memorable. Even though there is no apparent basis for favoring it, as we have seen above, it is privileged over the first alternative. While the privileging of this variant is clearly unjustified in terms of the historical evidence, it makes sense thematically or ideologically, as did the privileged story of Aeneas that I have just discussed. It is readily intelligible as the outcome of the shameful conflict, the *foedum certamen*, that began when the twins were first moved to rivalry by that "ancestral evil, the desire to rule," *auitum malum, regni cupido* (1.6.4). And, in a way that the anonymous murder of Remus could not do, his murder by Romulus brings the story of sibling rivalry that began with the twins' grandfather and great-uncle full circle. It suggests that the internecine strife that marks the founding of Rome is not incidental or a historical accident but is rooted in the histories of the city's founders, if not in the dynamics of family and power itself.[74] Thus it also engages speculation among Livy's contemporaries that the recent succession of civil wars expressed inherent and ineradicable flaws in the Roman character itself.[75] Here, as before, the very same rhetorical strategies that raise problems concerning the narrator's standards for historical reliability function coherently in thematic and ideological terms.

Perhaps the most striking example of such a contrast between apparent historiographic inconsistency and ideological coherence is to be found in the two etiological stories that explain the origins of the Lacus Curtius in the Forum Romanum. In this case, separation of the two *aetia* allows Livy to take advantage of the thematic or ideological possibilities of each, even though the inconsistency between them entails a particularly radical undermining of the narrative's authority as a record of historical fact. Interestingly, the report that the Lacus Curtius was named after Mettius Curtius does *not* come immediately after the story of his miraculous reemergence from the swamp. Rather, it is delayed for a paragraph or so and is included in a brief summary of the consequences of the peace at the conclusion of the Roman-Sabine war (1.13.4–8). Specifically, it comes between two accounts of how, in the ensuing union of the two peoples, the seat of power was assigned to Rome and how the Romans, in exchange, honored the Sabines, first by naming the new people "Quirites" after the Sabine Cures (1.13.5) and then by naming the new political divisions of the united people (the *curiae*) after Sabine women (1.13.6–7). In the present context, then, the naming of the Lacus Curtius after a Sabine hero constitutes another example of the Romans' willingness to accommodate their allies' proud sense of identity in the practical interests of consolidating power.

The Marcus Curtius version of the *aetion* is similarly appropriate to its immediate context. It is included in the opening sequence of passages in book 7 as one of several apparently more or less random events that distinguish its

---

74. For fuller development of this argument, see below, Chapter 4.
75. See Hor. *Epod.* 7.17–20.

year: the first election of a "new man" to the consulship, a pestilence and propitiatory *lectisternum,* the introduction of the first scenic *ludi,* and the resumption of the ritual driving of a nail to avert plague. This last introduces the figure of Lucius Manlius Imperiosus, appointed dictator to drive the nail, which in turn leads to the story of Manlius' exceptional severity toward his son (the future Manlius Torquatus) and of his son's even more extraordinary loyalty to his father—a *pietas* that leads him not only to tolerate what others regard as his father's abusive behavior but even to challenge a tribune who seeks to prosecute the elder Manlius for his excessively harsh treatment of the son (7.4–5). Marcus Curtius' story, then, is part of a series of reports or stories that illustrate Roman *pietas,* and in particular forms a clear companion to the story of the younger Manlius, another example of an aristocratic youth who submits to the claims of *pietas* willingly and beyond the call of duty.[76]

Thus, even though their factual basis is in question, thematically and ideologically each of the two *aetia* is consistent with its immediate narrative context and contributes to the elaboration of larger, ideological themes within the narrative: the Mettius Curtius version with the larger idea that the accommodation and assimilation of neighboring peoples were a particular source of Roman strength; the Marcus Curtius version with the larger idea that *pietas* was an essential element of Roman greatness. The narrator's initial lack of candor about the status of the Mettius Curtius story and his equivocation about the Marcus Curtius version enable him to present each version where it is thematically relevant and to allow each its full rhetorical impact before distracting the reader with questions of historicity. Once again, the reader finds it easier and more satisfying to assess the thematic and ideological value of the stories than their historical reliability. The message of this orientation is that ideological relevance and consistency rather than factual reliability serve as the essential criteria by which the narrative has been organized and should be judged.

VIII

My point here is not only that several passages in Livy's narrative call attention conspicuously to his inability to determine the historical truth behind

---

76. In this regard it is also suggestive that of the several variants of this story in Greek and Roman tradition, Livy's seems to be the first to identify Marcus Curtius' act specifically as *devotio,* the act of supreme piety in which an individual offers himself to the gods on behalf

Roman tradition, and that some of those passages further suggest the fundamental inadequacy of traditional historiographic principles for making such a determination. Nor is my point simply the rather obvious one that Livy's narrative, like every other history, is informed by thematic and ideological concerns, and that those concerns are advanced, among other ways, through patterns of selective emphasis. Rather what I regard as particularly significant is the juxtaposition, within each of several passages, of analytical incoherence, on the one hand, and thematic and ideological coherence, on the other. The effective consequence of this juxtaposition for the reader is twofold. In the first place it discourages looking to the narrative for a reconstruction of actual events based on a critical analysis of tradition and other evidence. At the same time, however, we are rewarded for turning our attention elsewhere, not to the facts behind tradition and the ways in which they may be retrieved, but rather toward thematic patterns that contribute to a portrait of Roman identity.

This double and simultaneous pressure is the more pointed because of the paradoxical role played in Livy's narrative by analytic categories and rhetorical techniques that were familiar elements of ancient historiographic tradition.[77] Although first introduced and then repeated by Livy himself in the context of explicit questions about historical facticity, in actuality, as we have seen, these historiographic elements function coherently not in relation to historiographic issues but rather in relation to thematic coherence and ideological point. What we see here is that Livy has evoked traditional techniques of historical analysis only to expropriate them for quite different purposes than those with which they were first associated in his narrative. In this way, his narrative makes clear that whatever his conscious intentions may have been, his effective concern is less with the facts (the *res gestae*) that lie behind Roman tradition than with the tradition itself (*memoria rerum gestarum*). It is to that end that he redirects the techniques and resources of traditional historical analysis. Insofar as *memoria rerum gestarum* is shown to be essentially impenetrable and opaque, it becomes itself the ultimate goal and object of the historian's reconstructive efforts.

---

of the welfare of the state. See J. Poucet, *Recherches sur la légende sabine des origines de Rome,* Recueil de travaux d'histoire et de philologie, ser. 4, fasc. 37 (Kinshasa: Éditions de l'Université Lovanium, 1967), p. 253.

77. For a clear discussion of the ways that a text can act upon a reader, see Stanley Fish, "Literature in the Reader: Affective Stylistics," *New Literary History* 2 (1970): 123–62, repr. in *Reader-Response Criticism,* ed. Jane P. Tompkins (Baltimore: Johns Hopkins University Press, 1980), pp. 70–100.

This focus on Roman memory as an entity of significance in its own right is consistent with the characterization of Romans' memory of the past within the very tradition that Livy presents in his narrative. Throughout the narrative, we see Romans recalling their past, being influenced by it, evoking it to influence others—and deliberately shaping the way in which the past will be remembered by posterity.[78] Examples are ubiquitous.[79] A few should suffice here. The city of Rome begins with memory. Romulus first fortified the Palatine, "where he had himself been raised," *in quo ipse erat educatus* (1.7.3). Camillus, the savior of Rome from the Gauls and its second founder, begins his argument against abandoning the city for the newly conquered Veii by recalling his thoughts when in self-imposed exile: "During my absence, whenever the fatherland came to mind, all these things occurred to me: its hills and plains, the Tiber, the region familiar to my eyes, and this sky under which I had been born and raised," *cum abessem, quotienscumque patria in mentem ueniret, haec omnia occurrebant, colles campique et Tiberis et adsueta oculis regio et hoc caelum sub quo natus educatusque essem* (5.54.3). This passage suggests something of the profound depth of Roman memory and its importance. Even as Camillus consciously recalls his own memories of Rome, his words echo unconsciously the unspoken memory that led Romulus to choose the site for Rome.[80] Camillus identifies this deep, virtually innate memory of the past as the source of his patriotism. Through him memory of the past plays a decisive role, first in saving Rome from conquest by Gauls, and then in saving it from abandonment by its own people.

Elsewhere *memoria* and *pietas* are associated explicitly. When Roman colonists refuse to comply with the draft, Roman officials remind them that their obligations to Rome are the same as those to their parents, "if there is any *pietas*, if there is any *memoria* of their former fatherland," *si ulla pietas,*

---

78. This, in fact, corresponds very closely to the way in which, according to Cornell, "Historical Tradition," Romans generally viewed their historical tradition: not as "an authenticated official record or an objective critical reconstruction; rather, [as] an ideological construct, designed to control, to justify and to inspire," p. 83.

79. The manipulation of memory as an aspect of Roman tradition as Livy presents it has received little attention. M. K. Jaeger, "*Custodia Fidelis Memoriae:* Livy's Story of M. Manlius Capitolinus," *Latomus* 52 (1993): 350–63, discusses one example of it.

80. For a similar apparently unconscious recall of Romulus' thoughts, compare the words with which Horatius kills his sister, "So may any Roman woman perish who will mourn for an enemy," *Sic eat quaecumque Romana lugebit hostem* (1.26.4), with the words that Romulus speaks when he strikes down his brother, "So then [may he perish], whoever else will jump over my walls," *Sic deinde, quicumque alius transiliet moenia mea* (1.7.2).

si memoria antiquae patriae esset (27.9.11). Memory appears as the basis of Roman patriotism and identity in other, less explicit terms as well. Capua, for example, so far seduced Roman soldiers with its pleasures that it "turned their minds from the memory of their fatherland," *animos auertit a memoria patriae* (7.38.5), and led them to consider taking over the city for themselves. Subsequently a group of these rebels, while marching on Rome, encounter a force sent out to oppose them; *memoria patriae* averts a civil war at the last minute by reminding both sides of their common identity: "As soon as [the two armies] came within sight of each other and recognized each other's weapons and standards, memory of the fatherland immediately soothed their angers," *Ubi primum in conspectum uentum est et arma signaque agnouere, extemplo omnibus memoria patriae iras permulsit* (7.40.1).

In addition to showing the critical importance of memory to the Roman identity and its decisive influence on Romans' behavior, Livy's narrative also characterizes Romans as actively, often very self-consciously and deliberately contributing to the collective memory that will shape the behavior and identity of their posterity. We have seen already how in each *aetion* of the Lacus Curtius the naming of the lake serves the purpose of perpetuating a memory of the past that has a particular bearing on Roman identity. Perhaps more striking, in part because explicitly deliberate, is the suicide of Lucretia, who kills herself with the famous words "As for myself, although I absolve myself of wrongdoing, I do not release myself from its punishment; no unchaste woman hereafter will live because of Lucretia's example," *ego me etsi peccato absoluo, supplicio non libero; nec ulla deinde impudica Lucretiae exemplo uiuet* (1.58.10). Livy attributes Romulus' performance of Hercules' rites at the Ara Maxima to a deliberate (and revealing) selectivity, one that perpetuated Hercules' cult and the edifying story behind it even as it condemned to oblivion all other foreign rites then practiced on the Palatine: "Romulus then adopted these rites, out of all the foreign rites the only ones he did adopt, even then a promoter of the immortality begotten of virtue to which his own destiny was leading him," *Haec tum sacra Romulus una ex omnibus peregrina suscepit, iam tum immortalitatis uirtute partae ad quam eum sua fata ducebant fautor* (1.7.15).

The story of Manlius Torquatus' execution of his son for insubordination dramatizes the interplay among different concerns with memory on several different levels at once. When the young Manlius disobeys the orders of Manlius Torquatus, his commander and father, to avoid engagement with the enemy and answers a challenge to single combat, he attributes his behavior to the desire to emulate his father and the victory in single combat for which his father was honored with the cognomen Torquatus. He bears the spoils of his defeated challenger to his father with the following statement: "That all men . . . may justly report that I, Father, am born of your blood, I bear these equestrian spoils taken from a dead enemy who challenged me," *Ut me omnes . . . pater, tuo sanguine ortum uere ferrent, prouocatus equestria haec spolia capta ex hoste caeso porto* (8.7.13).

Paradoxically, Livy attributes this act of emulation to forgetfulness. The young man, he says, acted, "forgetful of his father's command and the consuls' edict," *oblitus . . . imperii patrii consulumque edicti* (8.7.8). It is this aspect of the younger Manlius' behavior that his father also emphasizes, pointing out that it imposes upon him, the father, the harsh necessity that "either I must forget the Republic or myself," *aut rei publicae mihi aut mei obliuiscendum sit* (8.7.17). Concerned above all to preserve the Roman tradition of military discipline, the elder Manlius determines: "We will set a grim example, but one that will in the future benefit the youth," *Triste exemplum sed in posterum salubre iuuentuti erimus* (8.7.17). Livy himself seems to endorse Torquatus' judgment when he sums up the results of his action in words that echo Torquatus' own: "And the orders of Manlius were not only horrifying at the moment but also set a grim example for the future. Nonetheless, the atrocity of the punishment made the troops more obedient to their leader," *Manlianaque imperia non in praesentia modo horrenda sed exempli etiam tristis in posterum essent. Fecit tamen atrocitas poenae oboedientiorem duci militem* (8.7.22–8.1). He adds that here, as we have seen above, loyalty is expressed in terms of memory: it involves choices about which memories to honor, to perpetuate. Different loyalties are motivated by different memories.

Manlius' decision to execute his son, however, involves more than a choice whether to remember his son or the state, difficult as that choice may be. It also involves a kind of correction or editing of memory. Torquatus' brief explanation of his decision concludes with two arguments, one essentially official, the other personal:

> sed cum aut morte tua sancienda sint consulum imperia aut impunitate in perpetuum abroganda, nec te quidem, si quid in te nostri sanguinis est, recusare censeam quin disciplinam militarem culpa tua prolapsam poena restituas—i, lictor, deliga ad palum. (8.7.19)

> But since consular orders must either be sanctioned by your death or repudiated forever because of your impunity and since I do not think that you, at least—if there is any of my blood in you—would refuse to restore by your punishment the military discipline that has lapsed because of your fault—go, lictor; bind him to the stake.

The point that military discipline must be maintained is familiar. Torquatus' expectation that his son will submit willingly to his punishment and in particular the reason that he gives for that judgment are striking and new. When Torquatus says: "If there is any of my blood in you," he echoes the younger Manlius' own words, "That all men . . . may justly report that I, Father, am born of your blood," and offers an implicit correction to his son's perspective. Whereas the son sought to emulate the example of his father's personal heroism, the father suggests that he should be remembered for other virtues. Most immediately apparent, of course, is his uncompromising loyalty to military discipline. But his words suggest another possibility as well. This is, after all, the Manlius whose story was noted briefly above, the one whose own father imposed upon him such harsh discipline that a Roman official contemplated bringing the father to trial. Torquatus' response was to threaten that official with death. In challenging his own son to accept the harsh discipline that he will impose on him and to do so as an expression of solidarity with him, Torquatus recalls his own exemplary *pietas* as a son and suggests that he should be remembered for that before being remembered for his personal heroism.

This kind of editing of memory occurs on a collective as well as an individual level in Livy's narrative. Because their disastrous defeat by the Gauls at the Allia fell on 18 July, the Romans designated it a day of evil omen, named it the Day of the Allia, and forbade public and private business thereafter on that day (6.1.11). During subsequent hostilities, the Latins chose the Allia as the site for a confrontation with Rome, reasoning that Romans, who had marked the Day of the Allia as ill omened, would fear all the more the place itself, "the monument of such a great slaughter," *monumentum tantae cladis* (6.28.6). The Romans choose to focus on a different memory and to interpret the memory of the Allia in a different way:

> Romani contra, ubicumque esset Latinus hostis, satis scire eum esse quem ad Regillum lacum deuictum centum annorum pace obnoxia tenuerint: locum insignem memoria cladis inritaturum se potius ad delendam memoriam dedecoris, quam ut timorem faciat, ne qua terra sit nefasta uictoriae suae. (6.28.7–8)

> The Romans, on the other hand, knew well enough that wherever the Latin enemy was, he was the one that they had defeated at Lake Regillus and had held in peaceful submission for a hundred years, and that a place notable for the memory of a slaughter would rather provoke Romans to destroy the memory of disgrace than cause fear that any land was inauspicious for their victory.

The Romans here counter the Latins' selective memory of the past (memory of the Allia but not of Lake Regillus) by emphasizing an alternative memory of the past (Lake Regillus rather than the Allia), reinterpreting the Allia's significance (its power to inspire rather than terrify the Romans), and displacing the old memory of the Allia with a new one. From this and similar episodes it appears that Roman tradition is not the random product of events but rather is as carefully wrought an artifact as are the institutions that Rome's founders created and passed on to posterity.

Livy places himself and his narrative in the context of the tradition that his narrative perpetuates.[81] In his preface he directs the reader's attention first to a series of questions: "what was the way of life, what was the character, by which men, and what skills in war and peace *imperium* was both created and augmented," *quae uita, qui mores fuerint, per quos uiros quibusque artibus domi militiaeque et partum et auctum imperium sit* (pref. 9); then, to how Roman discipline and morale declined to their present nadir; and, finally, to examples from the past that deserve imitation or censure. His narrative makes it immediately clear that these exempla are to be found in the first instance not through the reconstruction of historical fact but through the interpretation of Roman tradition. While Livy does hold out the hope of a time when there might be a secure basis on which to reconstruct a record of *res gestae,* that time constantly recedes into a more distant and problematic future. In the meantime, his own attention and analytic energies are focused rather on Roman tradition itself. The way of life, the customs, the skills, that he presents are those enshrined in a tradition that contains within itself a record of its own deliberate creation. Livy identifies himself with the legendary creators of Rome who shaped the tradition that is the subject of his history. Or perhaps it might be better to say that Livy helps to create a tradition that provides a precedent for his own interventions and interpretations. Sometimes this identification is overt, as above, when Livy's judgment of the younger Manlius' forgetfulness anticipates that of the elder and when his own assessment of Torquatus' decision confirms Torquatus' determination to set a beneficial example for the future, or again, when Livy endorses the judgment of those who punished Manlius Capitolinus' insurrection by banning the use of his praenomen forever in his clan, paradoxically memorializing Capitolinus as "a man worthy of memory had he not been born in a free state," *uir, nisi in libera ciuitate natus esset, memorabilis* (6.20.14). But Livy's identification with the shapers of Roman tradition is everywhere

---

81. See Jaeger on the story of Manlius Capitolinus, although Jaeger attributes to Livy a greater confidence in the power of writing to fix memory permanently than I think Livy's narrative ultimately supports.

implicit in the parallelism between their deliberate concerns with *memoria* and his own. His narrative perpetuates and creates a vision of Roman tradition that sanctions his own self-conscious attention to tradition and includes him among those who created Rome by creating its memory of itself.

All this is not to say that Livy's critics have been altogether wrong when they castigate him for being careless and indifferent in his analysis of historical evidence. Rather they have in an important sense missed the point of Livy's text; they have been evaluating it by a standard that the text itself not only dismisses but even seeks to discredit, and they have failed to appreciate the positive functions that displays of analytical confusion perform in their immediate contexts and in the larger context of the narrative as a whole. I have sought to demonstrate, rather, that in Livy's narrative analytical confusion performs several coherent functions. Coupled with specific claims about the limitations of available evidence and methodology, it dramatizes and so substantiates those claims. In exposing the impossibility of wresting factual certainty from Roman tradition, it allows Livy to undercut attempts to monopolize the past without confronting directly the aristocracy whose position was served by that monopoly. It serves to reinforce the author's deferential representation of himself in his preface, and, finally, it helps to redirect the reader's attention from questions about the factual truthfulness of Roman tradition to the issue of its formative influence on Roman identity and character. In so doing, it contributes to a redefinition of history and its characteristic usefulness. History in this version remains useful not because it represents accurate reconstructions of past events that can serve as analogies in the present but rather because it perpetuates and interprets the collective memory on which the identity and character of the Roman people depend. This is not the only kind of history, to be sure, but one particularly well suited to a society that regulated itself less by a body of written law than by stories, examples, and wisdom transmitted through a rich array of oral traditions that had only recently begun to be reduced to writing.

Chapter 2

The Cycle of Roman History
in Livy's First Pentad

Modern discussions about cyclical concepts of history in classical antiquity, including far-reaching reassessments of older generalizations, have generally overlooked the Roman historian Livy.[1] Scholarship on Livy himself includes only occasional, passing references to cyclical concepts like the recurring Etruscan "ages," *saecula,* that may have influenced, indirectly, his accounts of specific episodes. These concepts, however, are not presented as central to Livy's understanding of the larger course or pattern of Roman history.[2]

1. Discussions about concepts of time in ancient historiography aside, Jane E. Phillips, "Current Research in Livy's First Decade: 1959–1979," *ANRW* 2.30.2 (1982), pp. 998–1057, provides useful surveys of literature up to 1979 on many aspects of Livy touched on in this chapter. An important collection of essays on the idea of cyclical history, with references to earlier literature, is *History and the Concept of Time,* History and Theory 6 (Middletown, Conn.: Wesleyan University Press, 1966); an extensive review of this idea and relevant scholarship is provided by Virginia Hunter, *Past and Process in Herodotus and Thucydides* (Princeton: Princeton University Press, 1982), esp. chap. 5 ("Cause, Event, and Chronology in Relation to Process"), pp. 176–225, and the section of chap. 6 subtitled "Time, Process, and Explanation," pp. 237–64.

2. Ogilvie, p. 662; Ronald Syme, "Livy and Augustus," *Harvard Studies in Classical Philology* 64 (1959): 54–55; Jean Bayet, *Tite-Live: Histoire romaine,* Budé series (Paris: Les belles lettres, 1959) vol. 5, p. 128; Jean Hubaux, *Rome et Véies: Recherches sur la chronologie légendaire du moyen age romain* (Paris: Les belles lettres, 1958), examines Livy book 5 in detail for evidence of an underlying Roman tradition about a "great year," but he does not connect that concept with a systematic plan and presentation of Roman history on Livy's part. A. J. Woodman has touched upon the idea of cyclical history in Livy in chap. 3 ("Style and Attitude: Sallust and Livy") of his book, *Rhetoric in Classical Historiography* (Portland, Oreg.: Areopagitica Press, 1988). For him the cycle is characterized by a contrast between the pessimism expressed in Livy's preface and the optimistic perspective of books 133–42, in which Livy identifies the battle of Actium as a turning point and then goes on to focus on renewed foreign conquests. Woodman explains this apparent shift in attitude in terms of his conclusion that Livy began work on his narrative during the period of civil wars before the battle of Actium. The subsequent optimism reflects a "revised plan," p. 139, for the narrative that expresses his growing perception of Augustus "as the realization or personification of the ambitions which he [Livy] personally entertained for the Roman state," p. 138. Both here and in subsequent chapters I suggest that Livy's preface is not unambiguously pessimistic and that his narrative implies a somewhat guarded attitude toward Augustus. In this chapter I focus on a different cycle, one that I regard as implicit within the first pentad.

Nevertheless, the notion of historical recurrence is central to Livy's interpretation of the past. This is clear not only from the obvious doublets in his narrative but also from the extent to which his accounts of early history reflect his understanding of more recent events. But mere recurrence does not constitute a cyclical pattern of history. A historical cycle implies a *specific sequence* of recurrent events with a clearly identifiable beginning and end which together determine the course of the cycle and, above all, through which the cycle may be seen to pass more than once.[3]

I would like to put forth two theses concerning the cycle of Roman history. First, I propose, the preface and the narrative of Livy's first pentad together suggest the possibility that Roman identity and greatness may be preserved indefinitely through successive reenactments of a historical cycle that is exemplified in the first half of Roman history. Second, the elaboration of this view of Roman history reflects substantial originality on Livy's part: it involves a systematic selection and reshaping of traditional material and combines that (especially in the central concept of refounding) with a synthesis of preoccupations distinctive to Livy's own age, a synthesis that must have been unprecedented in the literary tradition.

I

Scholars have long observed that Livy's preface offers a distinctive interpretation of the decline that he, along with his contemporaries, perceived as the most important fact of recent Roman history.[4] Livy contrasts the vitality of early Rome with the degenerate, self-destructive Rome of his own age, and he ascribes that contrast to the influence of wealth and a human propensity to succumb to its attractions:

> aut me amor negotii suscepti fallit, aut nulla unquam res publica nec maior nec sanctior nec bonis exemplis ditior fuit, nec in quam ciuitatem tam serae auaritia luxuriaque immigrauerint, nec ubi tantus ac tam diu paupertati ac parsimoniae honos fuerit. Adeo quanto rerum minus, tanto minus cupiditatis erat: nuper diuitiae auaritiam et abundantes uoluptates desiderium

---

3. For clear reflections on how the specific concept of a historical cycle relates to other conceptions of historical recurrence, see Garry Trompf, *The Idea of Historical Recurrence in Western Thought* (Berkeley: University of California Press, 1979); Trompf presents his ideas in brief on pp. 2–3 and elaborates and refines his thoughts on the subject thereafter.

4. Ogilvie, pp. 23–25.

per luxum atque libidinem pereundi perdendique omnia inuexere. (pref. 11–12)

Either love of the task that I have undertaken deceives me or no republic has ever been greater or more pure or richer in good examples, nor have avarice and luxury invaded any state so late, nor one where poverty and frugality were so long held in respect. In fact, the more modest its affairs, the less greed there was. Recently wealth has introduced avarice, and abundant pleasures have introduced a longing to perish and to destroy all things through extravagance and passionate desire.

In admitting the evils of greed and extravagance, Romans have at last been overcome by a typical if not universal human weakness. Romans are different from others only in that they have resisted the general process of corruption longer than any people before them.

This view, that Roman decline was due to the kind of self-indulgent extravagance that the prospect of wealth encourages, was certainly not a new one at Rome,[5] but in the works of Livy's predecessors, most notably Sallust, it had been coupled with a second, related explanation for Roman decline: the idea that domestic tranquillity depended on the fear of an external enemy, *metus hostilis,* and that when once that fear was removed (for Romans, by the destruction of their archrival, Carthage, in 146 B.C.E.) citizens turned their energies to unrestrained and violently destructive rival-

---

5. See Polybius: 18.34–35; 31.25.3–7; 39.1.10, regarding Rome specifically; and cf. 6.57.5–9, more generally; Posidonius, the presumed basis for Diod. 37.2.3; and Sallust *Cat.* 11.4–5, *Hist.* 2.70 (Maurenbrecher). D. C. Earl, *The Political Thought of Sallust* (Amsterdam: Adolf M. Hakkert, 1966), p. 44, assigns the introduction of this idea into the historiographic tradition to "a senatorial tradition of the second century"; T. J. Luce, *Livy: The Composition of His History* (Princeton: Princeton University Press, 1977), p. 273, regards the Gracchan historian Piso (frag. 38 *HRR* = Pliny *HN* 17.244) as a direct influence on Livy and, emphasizing particularly the association of luxury with foreign influence, calls attention to the anti-Hellenism of Cato the Elder (Plut. *Cat. mai.* 22–23) and to Livy's use of "move into," *immigrare,* in pref. 11. Two further surveys of ancient explanations for the decline of the Republic are I. Kajanto, "Notes on Livy's Conception of History," *Arctos* 2 (1958): 55–63, and A. W. Lintott, "Imperial Expansion and Moral Decline in the Roman Republic," *Historia* 21 (1972): 626–38. The tenth of the Twelve Tables, restricting conspicuous display at funerals, and subsequent laws governing conspicuous display of wealth (e.g., the *leges Oppiae* of 215, *Orchia* of 182, *Fannia* of 161, *Antia* of 68 B.C.E.), although they may be understood as efforts to control electioneering and the cultivation of *clientela,* nonetheless suggest a strong disposition to regard luxury, or at least certain aspects of it, as destructive to the community.

ries among themselves.[6] Livy's omission of the *metus hostilis* explanation in his preface is conspicuous for two reasons. First, he calls attention explicitly and emphatically to its companion explanation, *luxuria*.[7] Second, Livy's exclusive emphasis on *luxuria* in the preface is extraordinary because, at least in retrospect, it is apparent that the unifying effect of *metus hostilis* and the internal dissension among Romans when it is removed are, nonetheless, prominent and frequently recurring motifs in Livy's own narrative.[8]

Taken by itself, the preface's emphasis on the deleterious effects of *luxuria* certainly does not seem to anticipate a cyclical view of Roman history; rather, it seems to suggest that Rome has reached a final nadir, from which there can be no recovery. Indeed, Livy asserts that Rome has been reduced to such a point of hopeless chaos that its remedies have become as unendurable as its vices (pref. 9). Anyone familiar with Herodotus and the general view of history that he represents might easily assume on reading the preface that Livy saw Rome as simply the latest in an unending succession of peoples, from the Lydians in Croesus' times on, who had grown soft with their prosperity and had succumbed to younger, poorer, and more energetic peoples on the rise.

Such unqualified pessimism, however, does not represent the whole of what Livy has to say in his preface. When he turns to the past as a welcome escape from the present, among the things that he finds there are examples of human behavior, examples, more specifically, "from which you may choose for yourself and your state what to imitate and what . . . to avoid," *inde tibi tuaeque rei publicae quod imitere capias, inde . . . quod vites* (pref. 10). He introduces the subject of these examples, moreover, by asserting: "This is what is especially beneficial and fruitful in the study of affairs," *Hoc illud est praecipue in cognitione rerum salubre ac frugiferum* (pref. 10). Contemplation of Rome's past, then, may offer more than simply an escape from the present; it may also show how to recover a former excellence, both for oneself and

---

6. This idea is generally thought to have become important in the Roman historiographic tradition owing to the influence of Posidonius (see frag. 112.3–6 *FGH* = Diod. 34.33.3–6); see W. Schur, *Sallust als Historiker* (Stuttgart: W. Kohlhammer, 1934), p. 64. M. Gelzer attributes it to Scipio Nasica in "Nasicas Widerspruch gegen die Zerstörung Karthagos," *Philologus* 40 (1931): 261–99. For the idea as a Hellenistic commonplace, see Ogilvie, pp. 94–95; F. W. Walbank, *A Historical Commentary on Polybius* (Oxford: Clarendon Press, 1979), vol. 1, p. 697. See also the works cited above, in note 5 for further discussion.

7. Ogilvie, pp. 9, 23–25, in fact, regards the combination of the exclusive emphasis on *luxuria* with echoes of Sallustian diction in the preface as constituting a deliberate polemic by Livy against his older contemporary.

8. See 1.19.4; 2.32.6, 39.7, 54.2; 3.9.1; and passim.

for the commonwealth. Such a recovery, of course, is contingent upon a true understanding of the past and upon its lessons' being heeded. It is not a sure thing, and Livy quite pointedly reserves judgment on the matter: it may prove that contemplation of the past serves as no more than a mental refuge from the present, but Livy has at least tentatively raised the possibility that it may have a more constructive value.[9]

II

This possibility is recalled and confirmed by the narrative of the first pentad. Long before we come to Livy's description of the decline experienced in his own day and anticipated in his preface, we learn that Rome had, in fact, experienced and recovered from a similar decline once before. Events described in the narrative of book 5, spanning the period from the siege of Veii through the Gallic sack of Rome, conform to the same principles of decline that Livy uses to explain the ills of his own age in the preface, and, as does the preface, book 5 neglects the *metus hostilis* theory.

This omission in the narrative of book 5 is striking for two reasons. For one, as mentioned, Livy appeals repeatedly to the *metus hostilis* theory throughout his earlier narrative. His failure to evoke *metus hostilis* to explain Rome's decline after the defeat of Veii is the more remarkable because of all the events recorded in the first pentad that period of decline would seem the most likely to invite such explanation. As noted above, proponents of the *metus hostilis* explanation for decline during the late Republic pointed to Rome's final destruction of its archrival, Carthage, as a decisive turning point in Roman fortunes. The defeat of Veii was an obvious choice for a precedent. Veii had been Rome's first archrival; Livy himself sees the war between Rome and Veii as a life-and-death struggle to determine which would survive and which perish (5.1.1).

As in the preface, so here the conspicuous neglect of the *metus hostilis* theory throws into relief other explanations for Rome's decline. Here the emphasis is on two narrative themes that explain Rome's precipitous collapse at the beginning of the fourth century. One, the role of *pietas* that Camillus makes the centerpiece of his argument against abandoning Rome for Veii in book 5, is articulated explicitly: history has shown that Roman fortunes decline when Romans neglect their gods, and prosper when they fulfill the

---

9. For further reflection on the play of ideas here, see above, Chapter 1, Section II, and the last section of Chapter 4, below.

obligations of *pietas*.[10] Because Camillus' speech makes this theme explicit, it has been well acknowledged in Livian scholarship.[11] However, implicit and yet persistent and fully developed in the narrative is a second theme, which in fact complements the explicit emphasis on *pietas*. This complementary theme emphasizes the decisive influence of wealth on Roman morale, generally, and on *pietas,* specifically. Following the defeat of Veii, Livy's narrative focuses on three conditions that contribute to Rome's subsequent defeat by the Gauls: the failure of Roman *pietas,* partisan rivalry and conflict between the orders (which had existed since the inception of the Republic), and the tribunician agitations and popular disfavor that led to the self-imposed exile of Camillus, whom Livy calls the Romans' "only human assistance," *humanam . . . opem, quae una erat,* against the Gauls (5.32.7; cf. 5.33.1). But, as I shall argue more fully below, both the failure of *pietas* and the conflict between patricians and plebeians during this period originate with questions of wealth, whether in the form of taxes, booty, land, or, eventually, the property of Veii. If *metus hostilis* has any role in the course of events leading from the conquest of Veii to the Gallic sack of Rome, it is a minor one, clearly subordinate to the problems created at Rome by wealth or the prospect of it. More specifically, the power of wealth to distract Romans from their essential responsibilities emerges as an explanation for the failure of Roman *pietas,* when it occurs. This emphasis on the role of *luxuria* can be shown not only to be a unifying theme in Livy's narrative of Roman decline after Veii but also to express an original interpretation of that decline: where Livy's narrative can be compared with others', the emphasis on *luxuria* appears repeatedly as the result of his own modification of received tradition.[12]

---

10. 5.52–54. Consider also Livy's observation that "Camillus is said to have moved them, not only with the rest of the speech, but especially with that part that pertained to religious scruples," *Mouisse eos Camillus cum alia oratione, tum ea quae ad religiones pertinebat maxime dicitur* (5.55.1).

11. For elaboration of the relation between Roman *pietas* and Roman success in Livy's narrative, see G. Stübler, *Die Religiosität des Livius,* Tübinger Beiträges zur Altertumswissenschaft 35 (Stuttgart: W. Kohlhammer, 1941), p. 93; and, more recently, D. S. Levene, *Religion in Livy,* Mnemosyne Supplement 127 (Leiden and New York: E. J. Brill, 1993), pp. 174–203.

12. Livy's interpretation of the reason for Roman decline after the defeat of Veii has been variously perceived by scholars. Ogilvie (p. 670) and Stübler (pp. 583–89) both, although in different ways, conclude that Livy regards Roman decline and the demoralization leading to it as penalties for having provoked divine envy; F. Klingner, reviewing Erich Burck's *Erzählungskunst des T. Livius* in *Gnomon* 11 (1939): 583–86, sees the concept of hubris as the controlling idea in this part of Livy's narrative; Hubaux and Bayet (vol. 5, pp. 134–40, 143–55) see Livy

In Livy's narrative, civil disputes about money are associated with Veii even before its capture: they begin with the proposal to make possible an extended siege of the city by introducing pay for military service.[13] This innovation is opposed by the tribunes not only because it is used to justify year-round campaigns but, more important, because it requires taxation of the people.[14] Initial failure to collect this tax leads to disorder among the unpaid troops besieging Veii (5.12.7). A crisis is only narrowly averted by the election of a tribune with consular power who is able to collect the taxes (5.12.13)—and there is speculation that his election was possible because he had previously increased pay for the *equites* (5.12.12). During this same period, the troops' preoccupation with their own material advantage is so great that it undermines their effectiveness. A Roman garrison at Anxur is careless of the town's defense, admitting Volscian traders indiscriminately. When the guard is overpowered and the town taken, however, Roman losses are small, because all except the sick were, like sutlers (*lixae*), engaged in business (*negotiabantur*) in the neighboring territory (5.8.2–4).

The long delay in taking Veii is attributed to the fact that the Roman soldiers devote their entire energy (*tota vis*) to plundering the countryside (5.14.6–7). On the other hand, when some Etruscans plunder Roman territory, a levy of troops to oppose them is prevented by the tribunes. Although an army of volunteers is eventually formed, booty rather than honor or the common defense seems to be their chief concern: they recapture

---

as being influenced by a tradition, preserved in some of Livy's sources, of an obscure fatality linking the destinies of Rome and Veii. None of these explanations is necessarily inconsistent with the general outline of Livy's narrative or with what can reasonably be conjectured about his sources, and it is in any event unlikely that Livy himself would have adhered rigidly to any one schema. My argument here is only that emphasis on the Romans' destructive preoccupation with wealth provides the single most pervasive and fully developed counterpart to their declining piety and general morale. T. J. Luce, "Design and Structure in Livy 5:32–55," *Transactions of the American Philological Association* 102 (1971): 270, 276, observes that Livy gives no explicit reason for Roman behavior at several decisive turning points, and concludes that he offers no explanation for the process of demoralization that culminates in the Romans' defeat by the Gauls. Erich Burck, *Die Erzählungskunst des T. Livius* (Berlin and Zürich: Weidmann, 1964), pp. 118–36, presents an extended analysis of Livy's narrative in book 5 that includes comparisons with the corresponding narratives in Dionysius Halicarnassus and Plutarch, but his focus is on the character and role of Camillus as the figure who unites the two halves of the book.

13. Pay introduced: 4.59.11; greeted with unparalleled joy by plebeians: 4.60.1; opposed by the tribunes on the grounds that it will necessitate a tax: 4.60.3–4; some plebeians persuaded by them: 4.60.5.

14. 5.10.3–10, 11.5, 12.3; and see references to book 4 above, in note 13.

the goods taken by the Etruscans and redistribute them to their rightful owners, but they also find additional spoils from the sale of which they are able to distribute profits among themselves (5.16.2–7).[15] Against this rather unbecoming background one episode stands out in sharp relief. After a serious reversal at Veii, some *equites* offer to equip themselves with horses at their own expense so that they can go to the aid of the Roman troops there; inspired by their example, the plebeians in the city rush to volunteer their services as well. The unexpected nature of such selflessness is reflected in the truly extravagant enthusiasm with which the senators react. After their tears of thankfulness, they vote to reward the volunteers with pay (5.7.5–13).

Veii is characterized as an "extremely rich city," *urbs opulentissima*,[16] and in a version of events unique to Livy, Camillus anticipates trouble over distribution of its booty (5.20.1–4). He refers the question of what to do with the anticipated booty to the Senate. Livy then records two speeches in the ensuing debate, in the course of which Appius warns, unsuccessfully, against "bands of unemployed city-dwellers greedy for pillage," *auidas in direptiones manus otiosorum urbanorum* (5.20.6), and both speakers acknowledge the divisiveness that money brings into a community.[17] When the city is finally captured, however, the booty so exceeds Camillus' expectations that he fears envy toward himself and Rome and offers prayers to avert it (5.21.14–15).[18]

As Arnaldo Momigliano has observed, Camillus' sentiments at Veii "are clearly analogous to, and probably imitated from, the sentiments of Scipio Aemilianus over Carthage."[19] When Scipio surveyed the ruins of Rome's great enemy, he is said to have been moved to tears by the reflection that all nations were destined to pass and that a time would come when Rome

15. Contrast Diod. 14. 116.1–2, where in a similar episode Romans recapture booty from a Tyrrhenian raiding party, as in Livy, but it is the captured arms that the victorious troops distribute among themselves.

16. 5.20.1, 21.17, 22.8. The city's wealth is also emphasized by Plutarch (*Cam.* 2.3), but he adds that at the time of the war with Rome, Veii's power was somewhat in decline (2.4). Note, too, that Livy associates wealth and impiety in his initial characterization of the Veientanes. They were unpopular among other Etruscans, he explains, because they had chosen to be ruled by a king—especially one who "had already been oppressive by virtue of his wealth and arrogance, because he had violently disrupted the solemn games," *grauis iam is antea fuerat opibus superbiaque, quia sollemnia ludorum . . . uiolenter diremisset* (5.1.4–5).

17. Ogilvie, p. 673, regards the whole episode as "an interruption which conflicts sufficiently with the thread of the narrative to show that L. has adopted it from a separate account."

18. For other versions of Camillus' prayer cf. Dion. Hal. 12.20; Zonar. 7.21; Val. Max. 1.5.2; Plut. *Cam.* 5.5–6 is ambiguous.

19. "Camillus and Concord," *Classical Quarterly* 36 (1942): 111–20, esp. pp. 112–13.

itself might be reduced to ruins.[20] But there are two significant differences between the Scipionic tradition and Livy's portrayal of Camillus. First, Camillus' fears are aroused not by the destruction of Veii per se, as Scipio's were by the destruction of Carthage, but by the unexpected richness of the captured city's booty. Second, R. M. Ogilvie has noted that Livy "adds one unusual feature which is absent from the other sources, even Val. Max. and Zonaras who are derived from him. Whereas the others concentrated exclusively on the envy of the gods, Livy associates with it the envy of man. . . . The effect is to focus attention on the theme of *praeda Veientana*, the Veientane booty. Livy eschews a divine in favour of a human explanation for Camillus' career."[21] In other words, it is the Romans' own susceptibility to the attractions of luxury, not divine envy or the immutable laws of history, that will be responsible for Rome's undoing.

Greed and the claims of piety come into open conflict soon after the actual distribution of the Veientane booty. Even Camillus is not completely proof against the compromising atmosphere surrounding Veientane wealth: the triumph that he celebrates for his victory is of unprecedented splendor; during it, he seems to usurp Jupiter's role by riding in a chariot drawn by four white horses (5.23.4–6; cf. 5.28.1). Camillus' momentary excess is only incidental to the course of Roman fate, however. Although his triumph is the occasion for some popular resentment, Livy identifies Camillus' insistence on fulfilling his vow to offer one-tenth of the spoils to Apollo as the major and decisive reason for increasing conflict between him and the people and for his ultimate departure from Rome (5.25.12, 32.8).

Livy is here following a tradition found in other sources, but his handling of detail is unique. In Appian and Plutarch, Camillus makes his vow, then forgets it, and does not remember it until after the booty has been distributed.[22] The subsequent confusion and resentment caused by efforts to call back 10 percent of each person's share is obviously Camillus' own fault. We have seen that Livy, however, seeks to minimize Camillus' responsibility by having him refer the matter to the Senate (5.20.1–3); later it is the pontiffs who make the actual decision to fulfill the vow by calling in a tenth of each individual allotment (5.23.10–11).

20. There are three versions of Scipio's reflections at Carthage: Polyb. 38.21; App. *Pun.* 132 (included in Polyb. 38.22); Diod. 32.24. For discussion of the sources and their meaning, see A. E. Astin, *Scipio Aemilianus* (Oxford: Clarendon Press, 1967), app. 4, pp. 282–87.

21. P. 677.

22. App. *It.* 8; Plut. *Cam.* 7.4, 8.2. Dion. Hal. 13.5 simply says that the tribunes prosecuted Camillus because they hated him; he makes no reference to a vow by Camillus. Diodorus does not mention Camillus.

But more important for the present argument than the fact that Livy clearly seeks to shift blame away from Camillus is the consistent emphasis his version places on the greed of the Roman people generally. Thus Livy is the only one to tell us that "a huge multitude," *ingens multitudo,* came from Rome to camp at Veii in anticipation of booty (5.21.1), that even though the profits from the sale of captives were the only monies deposited in the state treasury, the people were nonetheless resentful at this diminution of their booty (5.22.1), and that they felt no gratitude to Camillus for the generous booty that did fall to them (5.24.4–8). From this point in his narrative to Camillus' exile, Livy develops a picture of Rome embroiled in "multifarious discord," *multiplex seditio* (5.24.4–8), accompanied by "shameful rivalries," *foeda certamina,* and near riots (5.25.1–2) that are due entirely to two causes: dissatisfaction about the distribution of booty and disagreement about whether part of the population should emigrate to Veii. If Camillus is at the center of both controversies, it is because he urges an extreme interpretation of his vow that would include land as well as movable property in determining the tithe due to Apollo (5.25.4–8), and he is a leader in the opposition to proposals for emigration (5.30.1–3).

But, as before, Livy clearly presents these central issues as particularly significant expressions of a more general Roman demoralization caused by a virtual obsession with personal gain. According to his narrative, Camillus was elected to oppose what Livy calls the *largitio* of the tribunes (5.26.1—the word means ambiguously "largesse" or "bribery"); after the capture of Falerii he provoked renewed resentment among his troops when he followed the perfectly correct procedure of handing over to the quaestors everything of value captured in the enemy camp (5.26.8). Nor is Camillus the only focus for disputes about wealth. There is general opposition to the move to Veii among the patricians (5.25.13, 29.1–2). In the widespread dissension on this issue, tribunes who advocate emigration are reelected (5.29.1–2), while those who oppose it are successfully prosecuted and fined by their opponents, despite patrician support (5.29.6–10).[23] Livy makes the pervasive influence of *luxuria* extend even to the kinds of rewards granted for public service during this period of Roman history. Although an agreement is finally reached to pay the tithe to Apollo from the public treasury,[24] a shortage of funds is not made up until Roman matrons voluntarily contribute their

---

23. Ogilvie, p. 692, calls attention to the historical improbability of the episode and its "tendentious" nature.

24. Contrast Plut. *Cam.* 8.2, where the citizens individually contribute their own shares of the tithe.

personal jewelry. In Livy, the Senate votes to honor this admirable selflessness with a reward that reflects the self-importance of the aristocracy and their desire for conspicuous display: matrons are granted the right to appear in four-wheeled chariots at festivals and games, in two-wheeled chariots on other occasions (5.25.8–10).[25]

This corrupting influence of greed and wealth comes inevitably to affect foreign as well as domestic affairs at Rome. Just as earlier Anxur was overrun because of Roman preoccupation with making money, so now conflict over the question of emigration to Veientane territory becomes so distracting that the Roman settlement of Vitella is captured amid the general confusion (5.29.3). "Canvassing," "influence," and "resources" (*ambitio, gratia,* and *opes*) assure that the Fabii, whose improper behavior toward the Gauls at Clusium was "contrary to the law of peoples," *contra ius gentium* (5.36.6, and cf. 36.1), not only escape censure before the Senate,[26] but are even elected to high office by the Roman people.[27] Even as the Gauls approach Rome, the Romans fail to make adequate preparations for an attack (5.37.3, 39.2, 39.4) and fail to take the auspices before engaging the enemy (5.38.1). It is true that Livy does not account explicitly for these failures,[28] but at this point in his narrative, he does not need to: the explanation is clear enough. Since the first proposal to introduce pay for military service, the whole campaign against Veii and the subsequent concern about distribution of its booty and its lands have been accompanied by the increasingly disruptive and distracting influence of what Livy summed up in his preface as *auaritia luxuriaque,* "greed and wealth" (pref. 11). The narrative of book 5 has shown the desire for individual gain in repeated opposition to the claims of both civic duty and piety. We have seen the direct influence of such general demoralization

25. Again, contrast Plut. *Cam.* 8.3, which makes the honor the right to receive funeral eulogies, and the Roman response later in Livy, 5.50.7, to a similar self-sacrifice by Roman matrons after the Gallic sack of Rome (and see my discussion below, in this section of the present Chapter).

26. Ascribed to the influence of *ambitio* (5.36.9), which may suggest corrupt electioneering (Plaut. *Amph.* 76) as well as legitimate canvassing for votes.

27. Ascribed to "influence and resources," *gratia atque opes* (5.36.10). Contrast Plut. *Cam.* 18.2, which does not explain why the Senate refers judgment on the Fabii to the people and which ascribes the favorable treatment of the Fabii to the people's hubris and impiety; Diod. 14.113.6, which reports the intercession of a powerful (*dynatos*) father; Dion. Hal. 13.19, which says without explanation that the Senate delayed making a judgment.

28. Luce, "Design and Structure," pp. 270, 276; contrast Diod. 14.114, which shows the Romans making reasonable preparations for the Gauls' attack and, therefore, presumably losing to them simply because of Gallic superiority; Plut. *Cam.* 13.1 asserts that Roman defeat was the fulfillment of retribution for which Camillus prayed when he was driven into exile.

on Roman military performance in two minor defeats that anticipate the disaster at the Allia: when the Roman soldiers' private commercial interests left Anxur open to attack, and when political division at Rome over the question of emigration distracted attention from the proper defense of Vitella. Roman failings and their consequences at the Allia conform to a pattern that has become familiar in book 5.

If the Romans' demoralization in book 5 confirms Livy's introductory generalization about the corrupting influence of wealth, their subsequent recovery conforms to a second, complementary principle introduced in the preface: "the more modest [Rome's] affairs, the less greed there was," *quanto rerum minus, tanto minus cupiditatis erat* (pref. 12). During the night following their disastrous losses at the Allia, when their fortunes seem most hopeless, the surviving Romans experience a sudden change of heart (5.39.8). Dawn finds them in as desperate straits as ever, but with a new spirit of determination and a new piety. Now honor and obligations to the gods become their first concerns and the real measures of value. Livy illustrates this change of perspective in two episodes that are familiar in general outline from Plutarch. In the first, the *flamen Dialis* and the vestal virgins, "setting aside concern for their own affairs," *omissa rerum suarum cura* (5.40.7), devote their energies to saving what they can of the sacred objects in their care. As they are leaving the city, they come upon a plebeian who is fleeing in a wagon with his wife and children; the plebeian orders his family out to make room for the vestals and their sacred objects (5.40.9–10).[29] In the second episode, Manlius' heroic defense of the Capitol is rewarded by his fellow defenders with a spontaneous offering of their personal rations. Livy emphasizes the contrast between the small monetary value of the offering and its great value as an expression of true self-sacrifice and respect (5.47.7–8).[30]

Other details in Livy's narrative that underscore this change of attitude toward wealth do not have even approximate parallels in the other extant sources. Thus, in contrast to Diodorus, who says that the Romans gathered their most valuable movables onto the Capitol for protection (14.115.4), Livy not only omits mention of Romans' efforts to save their personal wealth; he actually emphasizes Roman determination in the face of their

---

29. Cf. Plut. *Cam.* 21.1, a rare instance where Plutarch, who mentions how the plebeian removed his *chrēmata* from his wagon, as well as his wife and children, notices attitudes toward wealth or material possessions, and Livy does not.

30. Cf. the corresponding account in Plut. *Cam.* 27.5, which does not emphasize the disparity between the monetary and the true value of the offering.

loss.[31] When they are finally driven by starvation to agree to ransom, Roman matrons once again donate their jewelry, not because of an absolute shortage of funds (cf. Plut. *Cam.* 8.3) but in order to make up the necessary amount without having to draw on sacred treasures (5.50.7). After the Romans have recaptured their city, they reward the matrons, not with some privilege connected with the display of wealth, as before, but rather with the right to *laudationes* (5.50.7).

The Romans are still not completely impervious to the attractions of Veii. As they survey the wreckage of their city, their thoughts turn again to the idea of emigration. But when Camillus opposes the renewed proposals for resettlement in Veii, part of his argument rests on the Romans' own change of heart and of fortune. He reminds his fellow citizens that in adversity they had turned back to the gods whom they had neglected before, even hiding the gods' sacred implements "amid the rubble of our own possessions," *in ruina rerum nostrarum* (5.51.9). With the sack of Rome, the roles of Gaul and Roman were reversed. The Romans became strong with their renewed piety and the divine help that it brought (5.51.9), while it was their opponents who were "blind with avarice," *caeci auaritia,* and who this time experienced "terror, flight, and slaughter," *terrorem fugamque et caedem,* not the Romans (5.51.10).

Even if we assume that the correspondences between Livy and Plutarch, who most closely approaches Livy's emphasis on wealth, are due not to Livy's influence on the later writer but instead to reliance on common sources (an assumption I am by no means convinced is justified), even if we concede that most of the themes and many of the details in Livy's account are derived from his sources, it is nonetheless clear that Livy imposed his own shape on that material and gave it his own meaning. By selection, arrangement, modification, and elaboration of received elements, he has made the corrupting influence of wealth and the greed it inspires a significant theme in his narrative of Roman fortunes throughout book 5. It becomes the background against which uncharacteristic Roman impiety and corruption are intelligible: Roman piety and martial spirit revive only after the Romans have seen the destruction of their material wealth and have given up their preoccupation with it.

As a consequence of his innovation, Livy has not only given this episode in Roman history a specific character; he has also given it a special place within the larger plan of his work and within the pattern of Roman history

---

31. The Romans are greatly distressed by the Gauls' calculated policy of destroying selected portions of the city, but their determination to resist is unshaken (5.42.7–8).

conveyed by that plan. This instance of Roman decline, in sharp contrast to the numerous reversals recorded in the preceding narrative, has been made to exemplify the general process of decline sketched in the preface, and thereby to anticipate the decline that Livy perceived in his own age.[32]

III

Recurrent decline, however, is part of a larger pattern. Livy identifies Camillus' double saving of Rome as a refounding. After his death Romulus' troops had saluted him as "god, born of a god, king, and parent of the city of Rome," *deum, deo natum, regem, parentemque urbis Romanae* (1.16.3).[33] There is only one other occasion in the first pentad when Romans honor anyone with a comparable series of titles: After Camillus has driven out the Gauls, *his* troops salute *him* as "Romulus and parent of the fatherland, and second founder of the city," *Romulus ac parens patriae conditorque alter urbis* (5.49.7).[34] Immediately after reporting the unique series of titles awarded to Camillus by his troops, Livy adds: "The city then saved in battle he without doubt saved again in peacetime, when he prevented migration to Veii," *seruatam deinde bello patriam iterum in pace haud dubie seruauit cum prohibuit migrari Veios* (5.49.8). Camillus accomplishes this second salvation of Rome through an impassioned speech urging his fellow citizens to stay and rebuild their ruined city. Shortly after his speech, while the *patres* are still debating their decision, a centurion brings his patrol to a halt in the Forum with the command "Standard bearer, plant your standard; here will be the best place for us to stay," *Signifer, statue signum; hic manebimus optime* (5.55.2). The centurion's words are taken as an omen confirming Camillus' argument. A brief para-

32. Luce, *Livy,* pp. 250–75, argues that the fragments of Livy's later books provide sufficient evidence to conclude that he did, in fact, adhere to the views articulated in the preface when narrating the decline of the Republic in its last two centuries; Kajanto, "Notes," conjectures, although without supporting evidence, that *metus hostilis* may also have had a role in Livy's interpretation of events from 146 B.C.E. on.

33. This action reflects partisan sentiments but remains an indication of Romulus' unique position. For further discussion, see Chapter 4, section I, below.

34. The closest parallel to Camillus' identification with Romulus in Livy is that of A. Cornelius Cossus, who was honored by his troops' "equating him" (*aequantes*) with Romulus (4.20.2), but this identification was more limited than that of Camillus, recognizing only that Cossus was the first commander after Romulus to win the *spolia opima,* and not extending to a whole series of titles as in the case of Camillus. For the few other Romans identified as *conditores* in the first pentad, see below, note 89 and Chapter 3.

graph noting the disorderly haste of the actual rebuilding concludes the book and the pentad. In the introduction to the following book, Livy says that he will now relate the deeds of Rome, "a city reborn from its second beginning as though from its roots, more luxuriant and more fruitful [than before]," *ab secunda origine uelut ab stirpibus laetius feraciusque renatae urbis* (6.1.3).

The passages just surveyed frame and thereby emphasize the speech that brings the fifth book and the entire first pentad to their dramatic end. Camillus' speech is important because it reveals the distinctive elements that link his achievement specifically to the city's original foundation, so that Camillus' salvation of the city also constitutes a refoundation of it. Camillus, after all, was neither the first nor the last Roman hero to save his city from foreign conquest. His speech expresses the two overriding loyalties by which he distinguished himself throughout his career: his loyalty to Rome and his loyalty to Rome's gods.[35] His special status as refounder in Livy depends, finally, on his success in persuading his fellow Romans to share those loyalties.

In so doing, Camillus completes a pattern of specific achievements that associate him simultaneously with the original founders of Rome and with the leading statesman of Livy's own day, Augustus.[36] Camillus' expulsion of the Gauls from Rome is itself sufficient to establish him as a worthy successor to that Romulus by whom the city, according to Livy, was first "founded by force of arms," *conditam ui et armis* (1.19.1).[37] Augustus, likewise, clearly sought to place himself in the first rank of Rome's heroic generals when in 29 B.C.E. he celebrated an extraordinary triple triumph (for victories in

35. Ogilvie, p. 742, observes of the speech: "Its contents recapitulate the contents of the whole book and highlight the great moments of the narrative which L. has already spread before us."

36. Of the many parallels between Camillus, Romulus, and Augustus, the three that I regard as essential to the concept of refoundation have generally been singled out by recent scholars as well, although with inevitable differences of emphasis, supporting detail, or precise formulation. See J. Hellegouarc'h, "Le principat de Camille," *Revue des études latines* 48 (1970): 112–32; Ronald Syme, *The Roman Revolution* (Oxford: Oxford University Press, 1967), pp. 305–6; id., "Livy and Augustus," pp. 48, 55; Mario Mazza, *Storia e ideologia in Tito Livio* (Catania: Bonanno, 1966), pp. 186–91; Giovanni Runchina, "Letteratura e ideologia nell' Età Augustea," *Annali della Facoltà di Magistro dell' Università di Cagliari* n.s. 3 (1978–79): 42. Some critics deny that Camillus should be read as prefiguring Augustus, most notably P. G. Walsh, *Livy: His Historical Aims and Methods* (Cambridge: Cambridge University Press, 1961; repr., 1970), pp. 16–17; id., "Livy and Augustus," *Proceedings of the African Classical Association* 4 (1961): 26–37; H. J. Mette, "Livius und Augustus," *Gymnasium* 68 (1961): 269–85, repr. in *Wege zu Livius,* ed. E. Burck (Darmstadt: Wissenschaftliche Buchgesellschaft, 1967), pp. 156–66; Hans Peterson, "Livy and Augustus," *Transactions of the American Philological Association* 92 (1961): 440.

37. For further parallels between Camillus and Romulus, see Bayet, vol. 5, p. 154.

Dalmatia, Egypt, and at Actium), just as Camillus had celebrated his triumph, with unprecedented splendor.[38]

It is characteristic of Livy's style, as I have tried to demonstrate in analyzing the narrative of decline after Veii, that such themes are not only introduced in their broad outlines but are woven into the very fabric of the narrative, so that they are supported by a consistent pattern of detail. Thus the basic commitment to Rome that Romulus, Camillus, and Augustus all reveal in their defense of the city is also characterized in more subtle and distinctive ways. When Cicero praised Romulus' choice of the site for Rome (*Rep.* 2.3–6), he dwelt at length on the location's practical advantages. Once again, Livy's originality is apparent.[39] In describing Romulus' choice, Livy says nothing about rational calculations. Rather, he singles out Romulus' and Remus' emotional attachment to the site as the decisive factor: "A desire seized Romulus and Remus to found a city in those places where they had been exposed and brought up," *Romulum Remumque cupido cepit in iis locis ubi expositi ubique educati erant urbis condendae* (1.6.3). Later he reminds us that Romulus' choice of site was determined by personal sentiment rather than by considerations of expediency: "He fortified the Palatine first of all, where he himself had been brought up," *Palatium primum, in quo ipse erat educatus, muniit* (1.7.3). At the beginning of book 2 Livy expands on the importance of such emotional attachment to place. He identifies the raising of families and "dearness of the soil itself," *caritas ipsius soli,* as the two conditions essential for the creation of community among Rome's first settlers, inasmuch as each "had brought together their spirits," *animos eorum consociasset* (2.1.5).[40]

Camillus shares a respect for this important aspect of Roman foundation with Augustus as well. When he seeks to persuade his fellow citizens to remain in Rome, Camillus catalogues the practical advantages of the city's location and does so in terms very reminiscent of Cicero (*Rep.* 2.5–11), but he confines himself to a brief survey only a few lines long, and he introduces that survey by recalling his own attachment to the site of Rome: "During my absence, whenever the fatherland came to mind, all these things occurred to me: its hills and plains, the Tiber, the region familiar to my eyes, and

---

38. Cf. Livy 5.23.3–4 on Camillus' triumph, and on Augustus', Dio 51.21; and see below, in this section of the present Chapter and note 52.

39. Noted also by Jacques Heurgon, ed., *Tite-Live: Ab urbe condita liber primus,* 2d ed., Budé series (Paris: Les belles lettres, 1970), p. 40.

40. On further development of this theme in Livy, see Jane E. Phillips, "Livy and the Beginning of a New Society," *Classical Bulletin* 55 (1979): 87–92; and see also Cic. *Off.* 1.17.53 on city and family as creating the greatest bonds among people.

this sky under which I had been born and raised," *cum abessem, quotienscumque patria in mentem ueniret, haec omnia occurrebant, colles campique et Tiberis et adsueta oculis regio et hoc caelum sub quo natus educatusque essem* (5.54.3). He then expresses the hope that these same things will move his audience by "their dearness," *caritate sua* (5.54.3).[41]

Thus he looks forward to Augustus, for Augustus too sought to emphasize his own attachment to the site of Rome's original foundation. Livy has Camillus ask, rhetorically, in the course of his speech: "If in the whole city nothing better or bigger could be built than that well-known hut of our founder, is it not more satisfactory to live in huts in the manner of shepherds and rustic folk among our sacred things and household gods than to go into exile as a people?" *Si tota urbe nullum melius ampliusue tectum fieri possit quam casa illa conditoris est nostri, non in casis ritu pastorum agrestiumque habitare est satius inter sacra penatesque nostros quam exsulatum publice ire?* (5.53.8). A *casa Romuli* had been preserved on the Palatine down to Livy's own day as a national monument.[42] Its postholes are still visible.[43] Augustus' own home, well known for its modesty by the standards of aristocratic residences of that age (Suet. *Aug.* 7), has been identified with reasonable certainty by modern archaeologists.[44] It, too, is on the Palatine, actually within a few steps of Romulus' hut. In 31 B.C.E., perhaps deliberately calling attention to his residence in the very oldest part of town or to his determination to live among his own sacred things, Augustus also vowed to construct a temple to Apollo on the Palatine right next to his own modest residence and Romulus' hut. The temple was formally dedicated on 28 October.[45] Dio Cassius (53.16.5) asserts that Augustus' residence did, in fact, acquire "some reputation," *tina . . . phēmēn,* from being on the Palatine, "in respect to Romulus' having lived there before him," *pros tēn tou Rhomylou proenoikēsin.*

Camillus anticipates Augustus in yet another way. After the Gauls' destruction of Rome, a certain Titus Sicinius attempted to persuade the plebeians to abandon their city for Veii. For this he is characterized, ironically, as a would-be *conditor* whom the Senate refuses to "follow as founder to Veii,

---

41. On this parallel between Camillus and Romulus, see also M. Bonjour, "Les personnages féminines et la terre natale dans l' épisode de Coriolan (Liv. 2, 40)," *Revue des études latines* 53 (1975): 168–69.

42. Dion. Hal. 1.79; Dio 54.29, 53.16.5 (quoted below), 48.43. Other authors, most notably Virgil (*Aen.* 8.654) and Vitruvius (2.1.5) place a *casa Romuli* on the Capitol.

43. Ernest Nash, *Pictorial Dictionary of Ancient Rome,* 2d ed. repr. (New York: Hacker, 1981), vol. 1, pp. 163–65.

44. Ibid., vol. 2, p. 310.

45. Ibid., vol. 1, pp. 31–32.

leaving behind the divine Romulus, son of a god, parent and author of the city of Rome," *conditorem Veios sequantur, relicto deo Romulo, dei filio, parente et auctore urbis Romae* (5.24.11). Camillus stands in sharp contrast to this false *conditor*. In later reminding Romans of their emotional attachments to the site of Rome, he reconfirms his personal loyalty and helps to save the city from abandonment by its own people. His actions shed light on one meaning of Romulus' rivalry with Remus: Romans must be one people, united in loyalty to one city. Concern that dissident Romans might attempt to establish an *altera Roma* to rival or perhaps eclipse the true Rome was also an issue during the late Republic, and it was an element in the propaganda war between Augustus and Mark Antony.[46] Augustus' supporters could claim that by defeating Antony he had prevented the transfer of Roman power to a new capital at Alexandria.[47]

Camillus' *pietas* also forms a conspicuous link between past and future. It makes him an obvious successor to Numa, who, according to Livy, founded Rome anew (1.19.1). Numa's particular contribution to Rome was to complement Romulus' martial *uirtus* with his own *pietas* so that a population hardened to the requirements of warfare might be restrained in peace by fear of the gods (1.19.4). Augustus also sought to complement a return to peace with a call to renewed *pietas*. Just as Livy calls Camillus "the most scrupulous observer of religious practices," *diligentissimus religionum cultor* (5.50.1), so he acknowledges Augustus by name as "founder and restorer of all the temples," *templorum omnium conditorem ac restitutorem* (4.20.7).

Livy never acknowledges explicitly the parallels by which Augustus may be associated with Camillus and, through him, with Romulus. That does not mean that such parallels would not have been apparent to Livy's audience.[48] Livy's reticence is, nonetheless, significant. He may have begun composition of the first pentad sometime before the battle of Actium in 31 B.C.E.; its initial publication was probably no later than 27 B.C.E., certainly no later than 25 B.C.E.[49] Whatever the exact dates, the first pentad must

46. Petre Ceauşescu, "Altera Roma—Histoire d'une folie politique," *Historia* 25 (1976): 79–108, esp. 86–90.

47. Mentioned explicitly in Dio 50.4.1; and see Ceauşescu, pp. 86–90, for related concerns (Cleopatra, *Troia resurgens*) in which contemporary fear of the transfer of Roman power to the East was implicit. It is interesting to note also the first words preserved in Camillus' *elogium* in the Forum of Augustus: "He did not allow migration to Veii after the city was captured," *Veios post urbem captam commigrari passus non est* (*CIL* I², p. 191, no. 7 = *ILS* 52).

48. See the remarks of Ogilvie, pp. 739, 670.

49. T. J. Luce, "The Dating of Livy's First Decade," *Transactions of the American Philological Association* 96 (1965): 209–40, has won broad acceptance for the view that the first pentad of Livy's history was written sometime before 27 B.C.E. and modified by some specific additions

have taken on its essential shape during a period when the main outlines of Augustan policy were being formulated and made public, but before the specific nature of their realization had become clear. The actual fulfillment of Camillus' role by Augustus remained a possibility for which Augustus' propaganda offered promising signs; it was still not a certainty.[50] Livy's presentation of Camillus suggests that Augustan policies can lead to a revitalization of the Roman people and their rededication to essential Roman virtues, but it does not demonstrate that they will necessarily do so.

Indeed, identification of Camillus and Augustus, whether potential or actual, need not preclude a complex attitude toward Augustus on Livy's part. Livy normally eschews simple characterizations of the leading figures in Roman history; this is no less true of Rome's original founder and refounder than it is of others. In contrast to Dionysius of Halicarnassus (1.87.3–4), for example, Livy makes Romulus directly responsible for his brother's murder.[51] He twice calls attention to the hubristic extravagance of Camillus' triumph after Veii (5.23.5, 5.28.1)—a celebration in which the *triumphator's* chariot with four white horses, his quadriga, might suggest comparison with Julius Caesar's triumph of 46 B.C.E. or, more generally,

---

between that year and 25 B.C.E.. As to when Livy actually began and first completed his first pentad, there remains considerable dispute. The evidence and arguments are surveyed by P. G. Walsh, *Livy*, Greece and Rome Surveys in the Classics 8 (Oxford: Clarendon Press, 1974), p. 6; add to his bibliography C. Cichorius, *Römische Studien* (Darmstadt: Wissenschaftliche Buchgesellschaft, 1961), p. 261ff., and Woodman, *Rhetoric*, pp. 128–38. A major reason for scholarly uncertainty and disagreement on this matter is that the language of Livy's preface is vague. In considering potential allusions to Livy's own age in the preface (and, indeed, elsewhere in the first pentad), it is essential to keep in mind that the very same ambiguities that have made it impossible for modern scholars to date Livy's first pentad precisely functioned to extend its potential relevance for his contemporaries. Even if Livy did complete the pentad before 31 B.C.E. (and that is not certain), a Roman reading Livy's preface in, say, 27 B.C.E. could still have found Livy's vague reference to contemporary remedies that are worse than the ills of the age relevant not only to the civil wars before Octavian's victory at Actium in 31 B.C.E. but also to the threat of monarchy that Augustus' subsequent preeminence raised, and to moral legislation that may have been contemplated or enacted in 28 B.C.E.

50. Jürgen Deininger, "Livius und der Prinzipat," *Klio* 67 (1985): 265–72, after a concise and perceptive survey of modern views on Livy's relationship to Augustus, concludes that Livy was simply too close to events to perceive, as later Romans were soon able to do, that Augustus' regime marked a transition from Republican to monarchical government. While I share this view for the early part of Livy's literary career, I am not at all sure that it applies for Livy's entire lifetime.

51. Livy's ambiguous portrayal of Romulus is discussed at greater length in Chapter 4, below.

with the unprecedented splendor of Augustus' own triumph in 29 B.C.E.[52] Such elements in Livy's narrative are consistent with its publication at a time when it could still serve as a guide to the new ruler (rather than as a celebration of him), offering both "what to imitate" and "what to avoid," *quod imitere* and *quod uites.*

IV

Neither the foregoing concept of refoundation nor the concept of recurrent decline that Livy suggests in the first pentad is sufficient by itself to constitute a cyclical sequence. For that, both concepts must be combined, each the necessary complement of the other. Just as Roman decline after the capture of Veii conforms to the pattern that Livy ascribed to his own age in the preface, so the refounding of Rome by Camillus simultaneously recalls the original foundation of the city by Romulus and anticipates a similar achievement by Augustus. Thus while Livy describes explicitly one sequence of foundation, decline, and refoundation from Romulus to Camillus, so he holds out implicitly the prospect of a second sequence from the refoundation by Camillus through the decline of the late Republic described in the preface to a possible new refoundation by Augustus. This potentially recurrent sequence comprises a specific cycle of events in which the acquisition or prospect of wealth distracts Romans from their essential loyalties, traditional religion is neglected, Rome is threatened by foreign enemies, and there is danger that the city of Rome will be abandoned by its own citizens for a more splendid alternative, until a refounder appears who saves the city from its immediate perils, recalls its people to their traditional loyalties to place and to gods, and thus reestablishes the community.[53]

52. For Caesar's triumph, see Suet. *Iul.* 76; Dio 44.4; App. *BC* 2.106. For Augustus' triumph, see Dio 51.21; see also Ogilvie, p. 680, for other reasons why Camillus' excesses might have suggested Augustus to the minds of Livy's contemporaries.

53. Clearly, the duration of individual phases within Livy's cycles was not always the same: the decline after Veii was precipitous, that of the late Republic was conventionally regarded as extending over a century or more. But neither variations in the lengths of phases within a cycle nor of entire cycles are inconsistent with the idea of cyclical history. Unlike some philosophers, who were interested in measurable periods of time (however theoretical), historians of antiquity, as Hunter, pp. 249, 253–54, has argued persuasively, were less concerned with "absolute" than with "relative" chronology, that is, less with the duration of events or episodes than with their place in a predictable sequence.

This pattern has all the more the appearance of a cycle because at 5.54.5 Livy assigns Camillus' refoundation of Rome precisely to the 365th year of the city; that is, to 390 B.C.E. If one reckons inclusively as the Romans did, the period from Rome's founding to its refounding by Camillus is exactly equal to the period from that refounding to 27 B.C.E., the most likely date for Livy's initial publication of the first pentad and the certain date of Augustus' proclaimed restoration of the Republic.[54] This assignment of Camillus' refounding to the 365th year of the city occurs in the context of a chronology that is notoriously confused and with reference to which Livy is at times inconsistent with himself.[55] Explicit designation of the 365th year, then, cannot be understood as the consequence of an unquestioning adherence to some simple chronological tradition. Neither can it represent endorsement of a concept of the "great year" or of some other rigid, cosmological scheme, since Livy elsewhere in book 5 is quite content to assign Camillus' refounding in round numbers to Rome's 360th (5.40.1) or even 400th year (5.45.4).[56] In any event, a system of natural recurrence would be inconsistent with Livy's reticence about the certainty of refounding in his own day and with his emphasis on human initiative. Rather, explicit designation of the figure 365 at this point in the narrative serves a different function: it emphasizes Camillus' position at the virtual midpoint of Roman history down to Livy's own day. The present moment emerges, then, as a singularly fortuitous occasion for the reenactment of Rome's previous refounding by Camillus. The prospect of repeating the specific cycle of Roman history exemplified in the first pentad cannot guarantee Rome's recovery but does provide a reason to be hopeful.

It is this particular cycle also that makes possible Rome's eternal greatness. In book 1 we learn that Tarquinius Superbus planned to make the Capitoline Hill the exclusive sanctuary of Jupiter by removing all other shrines from it. When the auspices were taken preparatory to the deconsecration of each shrine to be removed, they were favorable in every case except one: the shrine of Terminus, god of Rome's boundaries.

54. Augustus *RG* 34.1; Ov. *Fast.* 1.589; Vell. Pat. 2.89; Dio 53.4.

55. Bayet, app. 1 ("Difficultés éponymiques et chronologiques"), vol. 5, pp. 96–107; Ogilvie, p. 749; see also M. Sordi, "Sulla chronologia liviana del IV secolo," *Helikon* 5 (1965): 3–44.

56. For Livy and the "great year," see Hubaux. In general, it is salutary to remember that among adherents of Stoicism contemporary with Livy (the most likely source for models of strict chronological recurrence) the prevailing view seems to have been that events beneath the moon, that is, on earth, did not conform to the precise patterns that ordered events in the higher spheres, but were irregular (see the summary of Stoic beliefs in Cic. *Nat. d.* 2.51–56).

This was taken as a sign of Rome's permanence (1.55.3–5) and is recalled by Camillus in his speech at 5.54.7. In book 4 a tribune of the people named Canuleius argues passionately that plebeians should be allowed to hold the highest offices of the state. He recognizes that what he is demanding is unprecedented, but denies that lack of precedent constitutes a legitimate obstacle. Looking to the past, he points out that the original founders of Rome were necessarily innovators. Then he looks to the future: "In a city that has been founded for eternity and is growing to immense size, who doubts but that new powers, priesthoods, and laws of both peoples and individuals should be instituted?" *Quis dubitat quin in aeternum urbe condita, in immensum crescente nova imperia, sacerdotia, iura gentium hominumque instituantur?* (4.4.4).[57] We have seen that Livy records the gratefulness of the Senate when *equites* and plebeians unexpectedly volunteer their services to help Romans besieged outside of Veii. On that occasion the senators, among other expressions of gratitude, exclaimed that "the city of Rome is blessed and unconquerable, and eternal because of that civic harmony," *beatam urbem Romanam et inuictam et aeternam illa concordia* (5.7.10). These intimations of Rome's immortality are confirmed and explained by the potential for a recurrence of the specific cycle of decline and renewal that is implicit in Livy's narrative of early Roman history.

Interplay between the narrative's explicit emphasis on *pietas* and its implicit emphasis on the subversive influence of wealth suggests a larger, more complex, and somewhat darker dimension to Livy's argument as well. Roman *pietas,* we have seen, has been essential to Roman success, but also to some significant extent vulnerable to the distracting power of wealth: it was the promise of wealth (created by Roman power, the conquest of Veii) that caused Romans to lose sight of and neglect their real responsibilities, those whose performance was essential to their identity. On the other hand, Roman *pietas* was at its height in the early days of their community under Romulus and Numa, when Rome was struggling to define itself and gain a foothold against its powerful neighbors. Roman *pietas* began to reassert itself again only after the Romans had lost virtually everything to the Gauls. Thus *pietas* and *imperium* (which are the conditions for material prosperity) seem to be in competition with each other. This rivalry, implicitly, provides the basis for an endless series of declines and refoundations: as Romans prosper, their *pietas* declines, thus preparing for a subsequent decline in fortune; when Romans are at their weakest, most vulnerable,

57. Livy also has Scipio describe Rome as *in aeternum conditam* (28.28.11).

and most destitute, on the other hand, their *pietas* and with it their moral resolve reassert themselves. Viewed in this context, Augustus has appeared when the time is ripe for Romans to recall their obligations to their gods and reassert their particular excellence. But even if he lives up to the possibilities of his particular moment, Augustus' achievement can be only temporary. He may lead Romans to a resurgence of greatness, but however ambitious his vision or his claims, the peace, power, and prosperity that he may secure for them cannot be lasting. By an ironic but saving paradox Romans are at their very best only when in the most straitened circumstances. Augustus is fortunate to have the opportunity to take advantage of that Roman truth—to do so will be a significant achievement, one that will rank him with Romulus and Camillus, but it will pose its own risks. Understandably, Livy emphasizes the hopeful possibilities before the Roman people after more than a generation of internecine strife, but he does so while suggesting that such possibilities belong to a larger dynamic of Roman history.

V

The concept of this kind of potentially recurring cycle is unprecedented in the historiographic tradition before Livy and attributes to Rome a unique place in the history of peoples. The idea that history is characterized by recurrent patterns of rise and decline is certainly familiar from the Greek historians, most notably Herodotus, Thucydides, and Polybius.[58] Whether or not we regard the patterns of historical recurrence elaborated by those authors as truly cyclical, we must acknowledge that they differ from Livy's view of Roman history in two ways. First, they typically emphasize the fate of successive peoples or rulers, each one fulfilling the pattern of rise and decline once, then replaced by a new people or ruler who will repeat the

---

58. The idea is not to be confused with numerous cosmological theories, such as the Stoic *ekpyrōsis,* the *apokatastasis* of the Chaldean astrologers, the Pythagorean *metakosmēsis,* Platonic theories of the "great year," or the concept of *palingenesia* found in the Sibylline books. The separation of philosophical concepts of cyclical recurrence from the actual practice of ancient historians is generally accepted by recent scholars: see the literature cited above in note 1 and the further development of this view, although in my opinion overstated, by J. de Romilly, *The Rise and Fall of States according to Greek Authors,* Jerome Lectures 11 (Ann Arbor: University of Michigan Press, 1977), esp. chap. 1 ("The Pattern of History"), pp. 1–19.

familiar pattern; they do not call our attention to the repeated rise and decline of a single people.[59]

Related to that initial difference is the second: Livy's predecessors devote their greatest attention to elaborating the course of community decline and perhaps suggesting how it may be averted or delayed; Livy, as we have seen, is also concerned with the reasons for decline, but he emphasizes, in the first pentad at least, the possibility for renewal. Thus Romans, according to Livy, may achieve a distinction not granted to any other people by his Greek and Roman predecessors:[60] Livy's history shows that Rome has the potential not only to survive forever but to be reborn "as though from its roots, more luxuriant and more fruitful [than before]," *uelut ab stirpibus laetius feraciusque*. Refoundation, in the specific sense of restoring strengths embodied in an original foundation, is the key to this renewal. It is through refoundation that Rome can both survive and grow forever without losing its essential identity. How Livy would have viewed the larger course of Roman history at the end of his life is a matter of debate, owing to the fragmentary nature of his later history, but the narrative of the first pentad builds to an unambiguous climax not with Rome's destruction by the Gauls but rather with its dramatic refounding by Camillus and the hopeful possibility of a second refounding under Augustus.

VI

It is clear from the parallels that I have mentioned—between Camillus and Augustus, for example—that allusions to issues important in Livy's own day play a central role in revealing Livy's cyclical view of Roman history. I

59. The closest parallels to Livy in this regard are to be found in a few passages of Plato (*Leg.* 3.676–83; *Ti.* 22d–23a; *Criti.* 111a–112a), Aristotle (esp. *Mete.* 1.351b and *Pol.* 1269aff.), and Polybius (6.5.5–6) that express the hypothesis that in the course of ages individual states might experience successive destructions and reconstructions; but the destructions those philosophers have in mind are cataclysmic natural disasters that wipe out all traces of civilization, and the reconstructions involve not the rededication of a people to the distinctive loyalties embodied in an original foundation, but rather the reinvention of civilization and the civilized arts themselves.

60. The Judaic concept of the chosen people, of course, represents quite a different tradition. The whole question of the role for Livy of the gods, fate, and/or fortune in Roman destiny is complex and remains controversial; see Phillips, "Current Research," for surveys of literature relating to the question. My own sympathies are with those who feel that Livy places the primary responsibility for their destinies on the Romans themselves, not on some providence. See for example, pref. 7, and Chapter 4, below.

would suggest that Livy has not simply incorporated those contemporary preoccupations into some previously existing view of history or of the refounder's role in it. Rather, I believe, the interpretation of Roman history in Livy's first pentad grew out of those preoccupations and represents a particular synthesis of recent ideas, a synthesis that did not exist in the literary tradition before Livy. One aspect of the subject in particular supports this argument: the specific language by which Livy identifies Camillus as a refounder and his particular act of saving Rome as a refounding—that is, Camillus' title as "Romulus and parent of the fatherland, and second founder of the city," *Romulus ac parens patriae conditorque alter urbis* (5.49.7), and the description of the city as "Rome reborn," *Roma renata* (6.1.3). Although this language was beginning to play an important role in honoring saviors of Rome at the end of the Republic, it had not yet been deployed systematically to identify a refounder in Livy's sense. Let us consider the foregoing titles and phrases individually.[61]

Pater patriae or *parens patriae* as a formal title is not to be confused with *pater* or *parens* used as an honorary epithet by itself: the former was a very late development; the latter has a long tradition. The antithesis, for example, between a tyrant and a good ruler who is viewed as a *pater* to his subjects, although first attested in Cicero (*Dom.* 94), may well have been immemorial.[62] The informal honoring of a Roman hero simply as *pater* or *parens* was likewise presumably ancient: Romulus, for example, is addressed as follows in a fragment of Ennius: "O father, O creator, O blood descended from the gods," *o pater, o genitor, o sanguen dis oriundum.*[63] Individuals who saved a Roman army or part of it or who saved the life of a fellow citizen in battle were formally rewarded with special wreaths and honored as *patres* by those whom they had saved.[64] The first occurrence of the actual phrase *parens* or *pater patriae* is in Cicero, who says that we can truly call Marius "father of the fatherland, parent of your . . . liberty and of this Republic," *patrem patriae, parentem . . . vestrae libertatis atque huiusce rei publicae* (*Rab. perd.* 27); but it falls short of an unambiguous assertion that Marius ever received

61. Although I do not agree with all of their conclusions, my discussion here is much indebted to Stefan Weinstock, *Divius Julius* (Oxford: Clarendon Press, 1971), esp. chap. 9 ("The Founder") and chap. 10 ("The Father"), pp. 175–228, and to C. J. Classen, "Romulus in der römischen Republik," *Philologus* 106 (1962): 174–204. See also Jane Evans, *The Art of Persuasion: Political Propaganda from Aeneas to Brutus* (Ann Arbor: University of Michigan Press, 1992), esp. pp. 87–108.

62. See Weinstock, p. 201.

63. *Ann.* frag. 113 Vahlen.

64. The evidence is collected and discussed by Weinstock, pp. 148–52, 163–67, 201.

such titles, and we must consider the likelihood that Cicero is here attempting to find, or create, a precedent in the career of another *novus homo* for an honor that he hoped to receive himself.[65]

There is no doubt that Cicero was awarded that title by the Senate for suppressing the Catilinarian conspiracy. Cicero himself recalls this honor frequently,[66] and Pliny asserts explicitly that Cicero was the first ever to receive the title officially.[67] Julius Caesar was the next to receive the title *pater patriae* officially, in 45 or 44 B.C.E., and after his death a cult to him *parenti patriae* was established in the Forum.[68] Although Augustus refused to accept the title *pater patriae* officially until 2 B.C.E., he was so honored in poetry at least by 23 B.C.E.[69]

It is not surprising to find that the combination of extraordinarily powerful individuals and the disorders of the late Republic should stimulate special interest in the idea of a hero who would protect the state with the kind of authority and beneficence that a *pater* extended over his dependents. The earliest ascriptions of the title *parens* or *pater patriae* to Romulus and to Camillus, all of which postdate the official award of the title to Cicero and all but one of which appear first in Livy, are, therefore, almost certainly deliberate anachronisms that reflect the special concerns of the late Republic and Livy's particular interpretations of the founding and refounding of Rome.[70]

65. Elsewhere Cicero calls Marius "guardian," *custos* (*Cat.* 3.24; *Red. pop.* 9) and "preserver," *conservator* (*Har. resp.* 58; *Sest.* 37); see Weinstock, pp. 202–3, and Classen, "Romulus," p. 186, for further discussion.

66. *Pis.* 6; *Sest.* 121; *Att.* 9.10.3; *Phil.* 2.12; and cf. Plut. *Cic.* 23.6.

67. *HN* 7.117; cf. App. *BC* 2.1.7. Weinstock, p. 202, accepts this evidence; it is rejected by A. Alföldi, "Die Geburt der kaiserlichen Bildsymbolik: Kleine Beiträge zu ihrer Entstehungsgeschichte 3: *Parens Patriae*, 1 (fin)," *Museum Helveticum* 10 (1953): 105, who thinks that Cicero was not the first so honored; Ogilvie, p. 739, following Alföldi, is mistaken in claiming Pliny *HN* 22.10 as evidence that "*parens patriae* was first used loosely" of Fabius Cunctator. Pliny speaks there only of *parens*, not *parens patriae*, and in connection with Fabius' receipt of the grass wreath, *corona obsidionalis*, from soldiers whom he had saved; it would have been they and their leader, not the Senate, who saluted Fabius as *pater*, and he would be their *pater*, not *pater* of the entire *patria*.

68. Julius Caesar as *pater patriae:* App. *BC* 2.106, 144; Dio 44.4.4; Livy *Per.* 116; Suet. *Iul.* 76, 85; Cic. *Fam.* 12.3.1; and see Weinstock, p. 220 n. 3, for further evidence from coins and inscriptions. Cult to Caesar as *pater patriae:* Suet. *Iul.* 85; cf. *ILS* 72; Luc. 9.601.

69. Augustus' refusal: *RG* 3.5.1; Suet. *Aug.* 58.1 f.; Dio 55.10.10; see Weinstock, p. 204 n. 2, for further evidence; honored in poetry: Hor. *Carm.* 3.24.25, 1.2.50.

70. *Pater patriae* applied to Romulus: Cic. *Div.* 1.3; Livy 1.16.3; 16.6; to Camillus: Livy 5.49.7; 7.1.10; Plut. *Cam.* 1.1; Eutropius 1.20.3. On these attributions as anachronisms, see F. Münzer, "Furius" (44), *RE* 1.7.1 (1910), cols. 338–39, who argues the title *parens patriae*,

Likewise, the idea that Rome's survival of a crisis was tantamount to a rebirth could have been appropriate in many periods of its history but seems in fact to have crystallized in response to the repeated upheavals of the late Republic. Although Livy's actual metaphor for Rome after its refounding as a city "reborn," *renata*, is unique not only in his narrative but in all extant literature of the preclassical and classical periods, it has virtual equivalents in the political propaganda of the last forty years of the Republic. These equivalents begin with the *Third Catilinarian*, where Cicero claims to have saved the city from destruction by Catiline and his followers and then goes on to say:

> Et si non minus nobis iucundi atque inlustres sunt ei dies quibus conservamur quam illi quibus nascimur, quod salutis certa laetitia est, nascendi incerta condicio et quod sine sensu nascimur, cum voluptate servamur, profecto, quoniam illum qui hanc urbem condidit ad deos immortalis benevolentia famaque sustulimus, esse apud vos posterosque vestros in honore debebit is qui eandem hanc urbem conditam amplificatamque servavit. (*Cat.* 3.2)

> And if these days in which we are saved are no less pleasing to us and illustrious than those on which we are born—because the joy of salvation is certain, while the condition of birth is uncertain, and because we are born without perception, but it is with pleasure that we are saved—surely then, since we have raised to the immortal gods by our goodwill and good report that person who founded this city, the person who saved this same city after it had been founded and expanded ought to be held in honor among you and your descendants.

Later, Cicero claimed that the day he persuaded the Senate to oppose Catiline, that is, the Nones of December 63 B.C.E., was a "birthday," *dies natalis,* of Rome (*Flac.* 102); and in a line that has given immeasurable pleasure to his detractors throughout the ages, he exclaimed: "O Rome, fortunate to have been born when I was consul," *O fortunatam natam me consule Romam* (quoted at Juv. 10.122 and Quint., *Inst.* 11.1.24).

---

as well as *Romulus* and *conditor alter,* was first assigned to Camillus by the Sullan annalists (accepted by Ogilvie, p. 739); Münzer's argument is based entirely on conjecture (Weinstock, p. 202); for arguments against a traditional association of Romulus and *pater patriae,* and for an attribution of that title to Romulus perhaps as late as Livy (1.16.6), and certainly no earlier than the Sullan annalists, see Classen, "Romulus," pp. 182–83 and 182 nn. 2 and 3.

Stefan Weinstock argues that Caesar's celebration of the *parilia* in 45 B.C.E. was intended to mark the rebirth of Rome.[71] Later, his assassins hoped that the Ides of March would be regarded as Rome's new birthday.[72] It seems reasonable that the idea of the city's rebirth would have been kept alive, at least vaguely, by early Augustan propaganda: by Augustus' claim to have restored the Republic, by his restoration of the city's temples, by his general "urban renewal," by the annual celebration on the date of his first accession to office, and by his plans to inaugurate the beginning of a new age.

The interest of Livy and his contemporaries in the *conditor* both as founder and as refounder is the natural product of a chaotic age when the destiny of the state was in the hands of powerful individuals and there was, simultaneously, a particularly widespread and intense desire to fulfill the timeless hopes implicit in the metaphor of collective rebirth: hopes of a fresh start, and of a return to the good old days and to innocence. The tradition of Rome's founding by Romulus was certainly very old, but exactly how old it was or what roles Romulus played in early legend are impossible to trace.[73] What is certain is that during the first century B.C.E. identification of a Roman leader with Romulus was an ambiguous distinction at best, more often associated with tyrannical aspirations than not.[74] Sallust has M. Aemilius Lepidus attack Sulla as "that misguided Romulus," *scaeuus iste Romulus* (Sall. *Hist.* 1.55.5 [Maurenbrecher]). When Pompey the Great was voted unprecedented powers in 67 B.C.E., C. Piso suggested that he would be assassinated as a tyrant, just as Romulus had been (Plut. *Pomp.* 25.9).

Cicero is the first in this century for whom we can be certain of a favorable identification with Romulus. In describing the rebirth of Rome under his leadership, he compared himself to the original founder, although without actually naming him (*Cat.* 3.2). Critics replied by belittling him as "Romulus of Arpinum," *Romule Arpinas* (Sall. *Invect. in Cic.* 7).[75] Julius Caesar also made efforts to identify himself with Romulus, but primarily with Romulus-Quirinus, the god, not Romulus, the mortal founder.[76] It may

---

71. Pp. 188–91.

72. App. *BC* 2.122, 3.35.

73. See Classen, "Romulus," esp. pp. 174–80, for a survey of the earliest evidence and a conservative assessment of it.

74. See Classen, "Romulus"; Weinstock, p. 85, believes that the tide of opinion turned against Romulus by the second century B.C.E.; Evans, p. 89, dates the change in opinion from the period of Sulla's dictatorship.

75. On the authenticity and dating of Sallust's *Invective* and its relevance to the interpretation of the significance of *Romule Arpinas,* see Classen, "Romulus," p. 183 n. 3.

76. Weinstock, pp. 175–99, esp. 175–84; and Classen, "Romulus," pp. 192–201.

have been those efforts that provoked Catullus to address him as "catamite Romulus," *cinaede Romule* (29.5,9); they certainly were part of the program of self-glorification that made Caesar anathema to traditional Republicans and led to his assassination. Romulus' reputation was still clearly ambiguous when Augustus was supposed to have considered that name as a title but rejected it, probably because of its dangerous associations with tyranny and internecine warfare.[77]

As noted above, Livy acknowledges the ambiguities of Romulus' reputation even as he emphasizes Romulus' role as founder and as model for subsequent refounders: he not only reports the murder of Remus (1.7.2) and gives the story of Romulus' assassination by the senators as a variant (1.16.4);[78] he also expresses ambivalence toward stories of Romulus' divine origin (pref. 7; 1.4.2) and apotheosis (1.16.5–8). Even though Livy's portrayal of Romulus the founder may be connected with an ancient tradition, it reveals the historian deliberately taking a position among the diverse, often conflicting attitudes toward that figure that were current and still being worked out in his own age. It is only in the context of his own, consciously elaborated view of Romulus that Livy could present the identification of Camillus with him as an honor in the eyes of his contemporaries.

In order to make a reasonable conjecture about the origins of the title *conditor alter,* and the concept that it expresses in Livy, it is necessary to have some understanding of the related Hellenistic term, *ktistēs,* and of the Latin term *conditor* by itself.[79] *Ktistēs* can denote the original founder of a commu-

---

77. Associations with tyranny: Suet. *Aug.* 7.2; cf. Dio 53.16.7–8; Florus 4.12.66; Serv. *ad Aen.* 1.292; with internecine warfare: Hor. *Epod.* 7.17–20, echoed in the ironic conclusion of Virg. *G.* 2.532–35 (for the interpretation of which see G. B. Miles, "*Georgics* 3.209–294: *Amor* and Civilization," *California Studies in Classical Antiquity* 8 [1975]: 177–97; and cf. *Aen.* 1.292).

78. Ogilvie, p. 54, contrasts this account of the fratricide, when contradictory attitudes toward Romulus were still unresolved, with later passages, in Ovid and Virgil, that were more favorable to Romulus, presumably because of Augustus' interest in the founder.

79. The concept of *conditor,* or "founder," during the last half of the first century B.C.E. at Rome has received attention chiefly from scholars interested in the official ideologies of Julius Caesar and Augustus; most notably: Classen, "Romulus," esp. pp. 181–83; id., "Gottmenschentum in der römischen Republik," *Gymnasium* 70 (1963): app. 1, pp. 335–36; Chr. Habicht, *Gottmenschentum und griechische Städte,* Zetemata 14 (Munich: C. H. Beck, 1956), pp. 204ff.; Samson Eitrem, "Heros," *RE* 1.8.1 (1912), col. 1136; Münzer, esp. cols. 338–39; Weinstock, pp. 177, 181–83, 202. For *ktistēs,* see Eitrem; and K. Prehn, "Κτίστης," *RE* 1.1.2 (1922), cols. 2083–87. My focus here is on the idea of the *re*founder, the *conditor alter,* as Livy applies it to Camillus. The broader concept and role of *conditor* in Livy's narrative is discussed below, in Chapter 3.

nity (Arist. frag. 484 [Rose]). Romans at the end of the Republic would have been equally or perhaps even more familiar with the term as an honorific title for one who had saved a community from destruction—that is, for a refounder in the general sense of national benefactor or savior.[80] There survive, for example, several inscriptions from Mytilene that honor Pompey the Great as "savior and founder," *sōtēr kai ktistēs* (*IG* 12.2.202), and as "benefactor and savior and founder," *euergetēs kai sōtēr kai ktistēs* (*IG* 12.2.141, 163, 165).[81] In one inscription (*IG* 12.2.163) he is honored as "founder," *ktistēs,* while Theophanes of Mytilene is called "second founder of the fatherland," *ktistēs deuteros tēs patridos,* and Potamon, also of Mytilene, "founder of the fatherland," *ktistēs tēs patridos.* Plutarch later called Cicero "savior and founder," *sōtēr kai ktistēs* (*Cic.* 22). It is very difficult to believe that we would not have heard from contemporary Latin sources if Cicero had ever in fact received the actual title *conditor* or *conditor alter.* The phrase "savior and founder," *sōtēr kai ktistēs,* therefore, must represent Plutarch's own interpretation of other honors paid him—very likely it represents the Greek equivalent for the title that Cicero did receive formally and boasted of in his speeches and writings: *pater patriae.*[82] Insofar as the term suggests some conception of *re*founder, it is simply a recognition, in the conventional and limited Hellenistic sense, of Cicero's having saved Rome from destruction by the Catilinarians. Nothing in Plutarch's context gives it the fuller sense that *conditor alter* acquires in Livy: one who not only saves the city from destruction but also renews specific loyalties that are embodied in the original acts of foundation and remain essential to Romans' distinctive identity and greatness.

This is important to bear in mind when evaluating Plutarch's assertion that Marius had been honored as "third founder," *triton ktistēn* (*Mar.* 27.9), especially since the statement might be interpreted to imply that Camillus was already known as second founder in Marius' age. There is general agreement that Camillus could not have been so honored in his own time, and the Sullan annalists have been suggested as the source of the tradition.[83] My own view is that the source is probably post-Ciceronian. To begin with, there is no evidence to confirm the award of some such title as *conditor* or

---

80. See Eitrem; Habicht, pp. 204f.; on the relevance of *ktistēs* to Latin terminology, see Weinstock, p. 177; and esp. Classen, "Romulus," pp. 181–83.

81. For further references, see Classen, "Romulus," p. 181 n. 5.

82. On *sōtēr kai ktistēs* or *pater kai ktistēs* and *parens et custos* or *conservator et parens* associated as equivalents, see Classen, "Gottmenschentum," pp. 335–36.

83. Weinstock, p. 177, following Münzer, cols. 338ff.; Ogilvie, p. 739.

conditor alter even to Marius. Again, silence is eloquent. I have already noted that Cicero, probably eager to find a precedent in the career of another *nouus homo* for honors he desired himself, claimed only that Marius could be called *pater patriae*, not that he had actually received that title (*Rab. perd.* 27). Given the fact that Cicero also compared himself tacitly to the founder of Rome (*Cat.* 3.2), it is difficult to imagine that he would have missed an opportunity to claim for himself the title *conditor* if there had been a precedent for it, and even more difficult to imagine that he would have been silent about that precedent—especially if it had been associated with Marius. When Plutarch says that Marius was called *ktistēs,* then, we should not take *ktistēs* as a precise translation of the title *conditor* actually awarded to Marius, any more than *ktistēs* represents that title actually awarded to Cicero.

Plutarch's designation of Marius as *third* founder need only reflect the obvious fact that the tradition of Camillus as *conditor alter* was known by the latter half of the first century C.E., when Plutarch wrote. Plutarch might have received his information about Camillus from Sullan annalists, but the evidence of Cicero suggests a later source. Livy, whom we know Plutarch read, is an obvious alternative.[84] In any event, it is clear that Plutarch does not mean by *ktistēs* here what Livy means by *conditor alter.* Plutarch is explicit in saying that Marius was honored as "third founder," *triton ktistēn,* because he had saved Rome from destruction by invading German tribesmen, the Cimbri. In other words, the title as applied to Marius explicitly and to Camillus implicitly means no more than "hero, savior" in accordance with Hellenistic convention; it provides no evidence for a concept of refounder in the fuller and more specific sense that *conditor alter* acquires in Livy.

In fact, it is very likely that the Latin term *conditor* was itself ambiguous until shortly before Livy began writing. Cicero, as we have seen, suggests a comparison between himself and that unnamed hero "who founded this city," *qui hanc urbem condidit* (*Cat.* 3.2), but he nowhere actually describes Romulus as *conditor.* Rather, when he uses a title to identify Romulus as founder, it is the phrase "that first creator of the city," *princeps ille creator urbis* (*Balb.* 32). This is particularly striking because Cicero uses the word *conditor* elsewhere for the organizer of a business (*Clu.* 71) or of a banquet (*Red. sen.* 15) but never for the founder of a city. It has been observed, moreover, that *conditor* in the sense that Livy uses it, of one who first establishes a community or an important public institution, does not occur in extant literature until after the death of Julius Caesar, but then occurs in that

---

84. Plut. *Cam.* 6.2 refers explicitly to Livy 5.22.5.

sense regularly.[85] This pattern of *conditor*'s appearances has been interpreted as indicating that the term was first employed to mean "founder" during or immediately after Caesar's lifetime and as a result of his propaganda.[86] This seems to me to be unlikely, inasmuch as *condere* was the regular verb for the act of founding Rome—from the time of Ennius, at least.[87] Ennius' address to Romulus as *pater* and *genitor* notwithstanding,[88] it is hard to imagine that the regular use of the verb *condere* had not suggested the noun *conditor* well before Livy. There may be another explanation for Cicero's avoidance of *conditor* and his use of "that first creator," *princeps ille creator,* for Romulus. By Cicero's day, members of the Roman aristocracy would have been familiar, as has been observed, with the twin possibilities of *ktistēs.* Cicero's avoidance of *conditor,* his emphasis on Romulus' primacy (*princeps*), and his use of the unambiguous epithet *creator* make good sense as efforts clearly to set apart Romulus, the actual founder of Rome, from other sorts of heroes who might be honored as "founders" in the Hellenistic tradition. Thus the evidence from Cicero suggests that even if *conditor* had been used in the strict sense of "founder" before Cicero, it still may not have been clearly dissociated from the ambiguities in the parallel Hellenistic term.

The regular use of *conditor* for "founder" soon after Cicero would, then, reflect a very recent specialization of the term and differentiation of it from *ktistēs.* That such a process of differentiation and specialization would take place during this period, when Romans were especially interested in the ideas of foundation and the founder, is certainly understandable, and there is some further evidence to support the hypothesis. Virgil does not use *creator* at all; he uses *fundator* and *conditor* once each and distinguishes between the two, using *fundator* for the founder of Praeneste (*Aen.* 7.678), *conditor* for the founder of Rome (*Aen.* 8.313). Livy eschews the synonyms for *conditor* used by Cicero and Virgil. Moreover, he distinguishes in general between *auctores* (especially the senators, who are responsible for guidance of the state) and *conditores* (responsible for creating its important institutions).[89]

---

85. Sall. *Iug.* 89.4; Varro *Rust.* 3.1.6; Nep. *Timol.* 3.2; Virg. *Aen.* 8.313.

86. Weinstock, pp. 183–84.

87. *Ann.* frag. 494 Vahlen = Varro *Rust.* 3.1.3; Suet. *Aug.* 7.

88. *Ann.* frag. 113 Vahlen.

89. Senators as *auctores:* 1.17.9 and passim; others as *auctores:* e.g., Aeneas and Antenor as *auctores* of peace and of the return of Helen at Troy (1.1.1), Aeneas as a "leader of the assembly," *auctor concilii* (1.51.4); Romulus himself as *auctor* of a new rite (1.10.6). In addition to Romulus, Camillus, Augustus, and Titus Sicinius, the false *conditor,* already discussed in this chapter, Livy also characterizes as *conditores* all the kings (excepting Tarquinius Superbus) who increased the size of the city (2.1.2). The only other individuals identified explicitly as *conditores* in the

He distinguishes in particular between *conditor,* the founder of the city ("the city once founded was named for its founder," *condita urbs conditoris nomine appellata,* 1.7.3), and *auctor,* the progenitor of a clan ("the same Iulus whom the Julian clan declares to be the author of its name," *quem Iulum eundem Iulia gens auctorem nominis sui nuncupat,* 1.3.2).[90]

The first actual appearance of the phrase *conditor alter* in extant literature is in Livy. From the foregoing discussion, it is clear that there are good reasons to think that this late appearance of *conditor alter* is not a mere accident of literary survival but the consequence of a very recent consolidation of notions about founding and refounding that preceded Livy and to which he himself made a significant contribution. We have reviewed a number of considerations that militate against locating the origins of the phrase *conditor alter,* especially as Livy uses it, before the Augustan age: the ambiguous character of Romulus, whose role as founder was often subordinated to his role as tyrant; the tentativeness with which Cicero compares himself, tactfully and metaphorically, to Romulus the founder, and his failure to cite any precedent for such a comparison; the certain lateness of the one title that does suggest identification with the founder, *pater patriae*; and the probable lateness with which *conditor* emerged as a quasi-technical term, clearly differentiated from its Hellenistic counterpart.

Even after the last development, obstacles would have remained to the effective use of *conditor alter* to designate a refounder in Livy's sense. Once *conditor* had been accepted as equivalent to *ktistēs* in the restricted meaning of "original founder," it would be natural to take *conditor alter* as a way of expressing the familiar idea of "founder" merely as benefactor or savior. Thus if Livy does not rely on the simple combination of *conditor* and *conditor alter* to define the relationship between Romulus and Camillus, one reasonable explanation is that those titles, especially *conditor alter,* were not adequate by themselves to express the specific kind of relationship that he had in mind. Instead, Livy had recourse to a combination of titles whose meaning in the context of his narrative was clear and unambiguous, just as Cicero a

---

first pentad are Servius Tullius (1.42.4), Appius Claudius (3.58.2), and Brutus (8.34.3). Their roles will be discussed in Chapter 3, sections II and III.

90. The one time that Livy refers to one of Rome's *conditores* as an *auctor* is at 5.24.11 (quoted above), where he contrasts Titus Sicinius, the false *conditor* who urges emigration to Veii, with Romulus, *auctor urbis Romae.* I take it that this identification of Romulus functions both to underscore the ironic characterization of Sicinius and to avoid repetition of the distinctive term, *conditor,* within a brief interval.

generation earlier had had to rely on a combination of epithets in order to identify Romulus unambiguously, not simply as benefactor or savior of his people but specifically as original founder.

As we have seen, Cicero used most, although not all, of the terms under discussion. Always, though, he operated close to the Hellenistic convention according to which one who saved his city from destruction might receive the honorific title of founder. The various hints at the idea of refounding in his speeches and letters were all associated with his suppression of the Catilinarian conspiracy; he never brought them into focus around a well-defined concept of refounding or of a refounder. Julius Caesar, likewise, attempted to associate himself with many, if not all, of the terms under discussion here, even though *parens patriae* was the only one that he ever adopted officially.[91] Under his direction, they became part of an organized program that aimed at his personal glorification, perhaps at his deification.[92] But there is no evidence that they were related to any explicitly articulated concept of Roman history, much less to a specifically cyclical concept of it. Livy, on the other hand, by relating those same terms to central themes in his narrative, underscores the significance of those themes and invests the terminology itself with new meaning.

VII

We have seen, then, that the presentation of Rome's cyclical history in Livy's first pentad depends on a consistent pattern of detail, unique to his narrative—as in the account of the Romans' decline after they captured Veii—and on a specific deployment of terms, also unprecedented—as in Livy's identification of the refounder. Many of the themes central to Livy's cyclical view of Roman history reflect particular concerns, some of which may have recurred throughout Roman history and all of which were especially prominent during the last generation of the Republic, just before Octavian entered upon his startling career. Among these concerns are a strong sense of general decline, a conviction that traditional virtues were being undermined by a new wealth and taste for luxury, a fear that Romans would abandon their city for a rival capital, and a belief that the gods were being neglected and that disorder would continue until the gods once again

91. These terms are surveyed in detail with references to previous scholarship in Weinstock, esp. pp. 175–228; for *parens patriae,* see above, note 68.

92. Weinstock's entire book is devoted to this thesis.

received their due.[93] The terminology that Livy used to identify refounder and refoundation reflects yet another characteristic of the late Republic, the increasing domination of Roman public life by charismatic leaders. One thing that Livy and Augustus have in common is that each was the first in his own sphere to effect a systematic integration of late Republican concerns about decline and renewal, on the one hand, with the emerging role of the charismatic leader in Roman politics, on the other. Precisely because he and Augustus were products of the same age, it is impossible to determine the exact relationship between the development of Livy's ideas and Augustus' policies.[94] What I hope to have demonstrated is that even as Augustus was the first to make such an integration of general concerns and personal leadership the basis for a successful political program, so Livy was the first to make it the basis for a systematic interpretation of Rome's past and its possible meaning for his own age and for Rome's future.

93. A belief familiar from Hor. *Carm.* 3.6.1ff. but expressed before the Augustan age by Varro, who dedicated his *Antiquitates rerum divinarum* to Julius Caesar, pontifex maximus (Lactant. *Div. inst.* 1.6.7), with an exhortation to redress neglect of the gods (*Ant. rer. div.* 1 = frag. 2a in Reinhold Agahd, ed., *M. Terenti Varronis Antiquitatum rerum divinarum libri I, XIV, XV, XVI,* Ancient Religion and Mythology Series [New York: Arno Press, 1975] = August. *De civ. D.* 6.2) on whom Roman greatness depends (frag. 36 Agahd = Tert. *Apol.* 25).

94. Levene's characterization of the relationship between Augustus and the authors of his age on the subject of religion seems to me to express admirably their relationship with respect to many aspects of Augustan ideology: "What then of the question of priority? Was Augustus following Livy, or Livy Augustus? It will be clear from what has been said that the question makes little sense. Augustus is of course setting much of the ideological agenda from Actium onwards; but he alone is not creating its boundaries. Rather we should see him, Livy, and doubtless numerous others, exploiting different aspects of these religious themes and extending their limits in implicit dialogue with one another. This becomes especially clear when we recall that these premises that have been identified as 'Augustan' themselves have roots in the late Republic. . . . Much of the central religious ideology that is shared by Augustus and Livy is not created from nothing, but is rather a distillation or a focussing of previously existing ideas. Those ideas were common currency for numerous individuals; it is to be expected that their 'Augustan' manifestation, although determined in many respects from the centre, should have its boundaries formed by the explorations of many who inherited those ideas" (p. 248).

Chapter 3

Maiores, Conditores, and
Livy's Perspective on the Past

As we have seen, the cycle of historical recurrence implicit in Livy's narrative does not involve exact, mechanical repetition of past events but rather the reenactment of a general pattern of foundation, rise, decline, and refoundation. In addition, the refounder clearly plays a critical role both in the process itself and in making it visible within Livy's narrative. This argument can be further refined. The refounder can be shown to be not just a successor to an original founder but the last of *several* founders. In Livy's narrative these founders displace the *maiores,* the undifferentiated "ancestors" of Roman tradition, as the authors and perpetuators of essential Roman institutions and qualities. Because these founders, and therefore the contributions ascribed to them, are both finite and limited in time, they define a basis for Roman identity that is clearly circumscribed and can exist within a broad and flexible context of historical change. I have already called attention to T. J. Luce's innovative and important emphasis on the "accretion" of institutions and qualities in Livy's view of Roman history. The present interpretation of Livy's narrative adds a significant dimension to that view. It explains how in Livy's historiography Roman identity can accommodate the recurrence of losses as well as gains, decline as well as rise.

It is impossible to write an extended account of the past without making assumptions, whether conscious or unconscious, systematic or arbitrary, consistent or inconsistent, about the relation between past and present. However much or little different authors may say explicitly about them, such assumptions influence their visions of the past and are implicit in their actual analyses and narratives, and, above all, in their rhetoric.[1] Here I would like to focus on the deployment of two terms in Livy's narrative: *maiores* and *conditores.* Each of those terms was highly charged with meaning and had powerful associations for Livy's contemporaries. Livy's use of them helps

---

1. Hayden White, *Metahistory* (Baltimore: Johns Hopkins University Press, 1973), makes this idea the basis for an analysis of the work of nineteenth-century European historians; he explicates the theoretical basis for such analysis in his introduction, pp. 1–43.

define the parameters within which the notion of Rome's potential for rebirth can accommodate both continuity and change.

I

Romans' appeals to the *auctoritas maiorum* are so familiar that it is easy to take them for granted as natural, unreflective elements of Latin discourse. It is noteworthy, then, that in Livy's history, appeals to the *auctoritas maiorum* are infrequent and restricted to well-defined contexts. Within the first pentad, which will be our primary focus, the term *maiores* occurs a total of only thirteen times, and all of those occurrences are in speeches that Livy ascribes, either in direct or in indirect discourse, to others.[2] Of those thirteen references, only two are to the particular *maiores* of the plebeians;[3] five are to the collective *maiores* of the Roman people as a whole;[4] six are to patrician *maiores*.[5] When we turn from the question of which *maiores* are evoked to the related question of who appeals to the *maiores* in the first pentad, the prominence of patricians is even more marked: eleven of the thirteen refer-

2. The occurrences of *maiores* in the first pentad will be discussed in the following text and notes. The relative infrequency of *maiores* holds true throughout the extant portions of Livy's work. Except for books 31–35, where *maiores* occurs twenty-one times, the term occurs even less frequently in later pentads than it does in the first. The restriction of *maiores* to speeches likewise holds true throughout the extant portions of Livy's work. The one exception is a sentence in which Livy describes the Ligurian Apuani as withdrawing to a mountain that was "the ancient home of their ancestors," *antiquam sedem maiorum suorum* (39.32.3); this uncharacteristic use of *maiores* in the narration may be understood as indicating that Livy is thinking of and narrating the Apuani's retreat from their point of view.

3. These two references are an appeal by two unnamed *tribuni plebis* (4.25.11) and another by Appius Claudius Crassus, mil. tr. 403 B.C.E. (5.6.5).

4. These appeals are made by Appius Claudius Inregillensis, cos. 471 B.C.E. (2.56.12); C. Canuleius, tr. pl. 445 (4.3.13); Appius Claudius, mil. tr. 403 (5.6.17); M. Furius Camillus, dictator 390 (5.52.8 and 5.53.9). The one instance in which a plebeian appeals to the collective *maiores* in the first pentad may be regarded as a kind of special pleading. It occurs in the speech in which the tribune of the people, Canuleius, argues for the admission of plebeians to the offices of state on the grounds that the first holders of those offices were, by necessity, like the plebeians of his own day, without a family tradition of office holding to recommend them. By calling upon *maiores nostri,* Canuleius assumes tacitly the essential commonality between plebeian and patrician for which he is arguing explicitly.

5. These appeals are made by P. Valerius, cos. 475 B.C.E. (3.18.6 *bis*); Appius Claudius Inregillensis, cos. 471 (3.56.9); M. Genucius and C. Curiatus Philo, cos. 445 (4.2.9); L. Quinctius Cincinnatus, dictator 439 (4.15.5); unnamed senatorial *patres* (4.54.7).

ences to *maiores* are made by patricians.[6] Of those, it is notable that five concern the Appii Claudii, being either references made by them to their own *maiores* (four) or references to their clan *maiores* made by others (one).[7] Only two references to *maiores* are made by plebeians.[8]

Thus far the pattern of Livy's usage reflects attitudes that are well known to have prevailed at the end of the Roman Republic.[9] Notwithstanding frequent appeals to the *auctoritas maiorum* by new men (not only Cicero, for example, but Cato and Sallust as well), it was the *nobilitas* alone who could claim personal or clan *maiores*.[10] Among the *nobilitas*, the *principes*, the inner circle of those from traditionally prominent families, placed particular emphasis on their own *maiores*.[11] A general tendency to equate the *maiores*

6. 2.56.12; 3.18.6 (*bis*); 3.56.9; 4.2.9, 15.5, 54.7; 5.6.5, 6.17, 52.8, 53.9.

7. References by the Appii Claudii: 2.56.12; 3.56.9; 5.6.5, 6.17; reference by others: 4.15.5. The prominence of the Claudii among those who appeal to the *maiores* in Livy may be understood simply as reflecting the general tendency of the older, more powerful political families to emphasize their own lineage and sense of tradition; it may also reflect the particular visibility of the Appians' clan loyalty in the decades just before Livy began his history. See T. P. Wiseman, *Clio's Cosmetics: Three Studies in Greco-Roman Literature* (Leicester: Leicester University Press, 1979), pp. 121–25.

8. 4.3.13, 25.11.

9. The concepts of the *auctoritas maiorum* and of the *mos maiorum* and their roles both in Latin rhetoric and Roman political thought are surveyed in J. Hellegouarc'h, *Le vocabulaire latin des relations et des partis politiques sous la République* (Paris: Les belles lettres, 1972), esp. pp. 303, 332, 441–42, 475. Hellegouarc'h's survey is based on the three principal studies of those concepts and their roles in late Republican literature: the published dissertations of J. Plumpe, *Auctoritas Maiorum* (Diss., Münster, 1935); H. Rech, *Mos Maiorum* (Diss., Marburg, 1936); and H. Roloff, *Maiores bei Cicero* (Diss., Göttingen, 1938), of which pp. 10–34, 56–82, and 128–31 are reprinted under the same title in *Römische Wertbegriffe*, ed. Hans Oppermann, Wege der Forschung 34 (Darmstadt: Wissenschaftliche Buchgesellschaft, 1967), pp. 274–372.

10. References in Cicero are so numerous and have in any event been so thoroughly discussed in Rech, Roloff, and Plumpe that there is no point in giving examples here. For a list of references to *maiores* in Cato, see Roloff, p. 57 n. 2; for examples of *maiores* in Sallust, see this section, below. On the *nouus homo* as "a man descended from himself," *homo a se ortus*, see Cic. *Planc.* 67; *Phil.* 6.17; and cf. Cicero's praise for Q. Pompeius as an orator who attained the highest honors, even though he was "a man known through himself without the commendation of ancestors," *homo per se cognitus sine ulla commendatione maiorum* (*Brut.* 96). For a general discussion of the *nouus homo* as a man without personal *maiores*, see Hellegouarc'h, *Vocabulaire*, p. 475; and Roloff, pp. 7–10, 134–42, who also points out (p. 56) that this lack did not prevent new men from appealing to the *maiores* of the *nobiles* as their "spiritual" ancestors, and, of course, it did not preclude them from appealing to the generalized *maiores* of the commonwealth. On the *maiores* and the *nobilitas*, see Roloff, pt. 1 ("Maiores und Geschlechteradel"), pp. 3–55.

11. While the term *principes* in Livy may sometimes refer to all senators (26.36.3; 38.10.3), it usually refers clearly just to the most eminent (2.16.5; 3.6.8; 10.45.8). See further Hellegou-

of the state itself with those of its leading families encouraged members of those families to rely heavily on the authority of the collective *maiores* as well.[12] References to the *maiores* of the plebeians, while not unknown, seem to have been unusual.[13]

The conventional role of *maiores* in Livy's speeches makes Livy's avoidance of the term when expressing his views all the more striking, whether speaking in his own person (as in the preface) or as impersonal narrator.[14] One effect of this contrast between Livy and his speakers, who are caught up in the political rivalries of their times, is to suggest that Livy identified appeals to the *auctoritas maiorum* with the rhetoric of partisan politics—a rhetoric that he hoped to transcend.[15]

---

arc'h, *Vocabulaire*, p. 322 n. 12, and on the *principes* as the "final upholders of the *mos maiorum*," pp. 441–42; and A. Gwosdz, *Der Begriff des römischen Princeps* (Diss., Breslau, 1933), pp. 6ff., 93.

12. In Livy four of the five appeals to the collective *maiores* of the Roman people are made by distinguished patricians: Appius Claudius Inregillensis (2.56.12), Appius Claudius Crassus (5.6.17), and M. Furius Camillus (5.52.8 and 5.53.9). Similarly, one of the two appeals to the *maiores* of the plebeians is by Appius Claudius Crassus (5.6.5).

13. For a list of such references, see Roloff, pp. 143–45 ("Anhang 2"). In the first pentad there are only two appeals to plebeian *maiores*. Neither is to the *maiores* of a specific plebeian individual or clan; both are to the collective *maiores* of the plebeians as a class. Of these, one, ascribed to the plebeian tribune Canuleius (4.3.13), is clearly tendentious (see above, note 4). The other appeal to plebeian *maiores* occurs in an address to soldiers at Veii by the patrician Appius Claudius (5.6.5): urging them to accept the unprecedented ardors of continuous year-long service, Appius asserts that they themselves would counter any suggestion of their softness with proud assertion of their own and their *maiores'* toughness.

14. In his preface Livy omits the term even where both sense and diction would otherwise suggest that he is following closely a passage in which Sallust appeals explicitly to the *maiores* (see pref. 9; Ogilvie, ad loc.; and Sall. *Hist.* 1, frag. 16 [Maurenbrecher]). Yet so natural does it seem to equate Livy's general respect for the past with traditional Roman deference to the *maiores* that scholars have sometimes been induced to speak, misleadingly, of Livy's respect for the *maiores* or *mos maiorum*: e.g., T. J. Luce, *Livy: The Composition of His History* (Princeton: Princeton University Press, 1977), p. 246; Stephen Usher, *The Historians of Greece and Rome* (Norman: University of Oklahoma Press, 1985), p. 169. Translations can be similarly misleading. Aubrey de Sélincourt, trans., *Livy: The Early History of Rome* (Baltimore: Penguin, 1971), renders *patres* (1.32.11) as "elders" (p. 70), and "what their way of life, what their customs were," *quae uita, qui mores fuerint* (pref. 9), as "the kind of lives our ancestors lived" (p. 34).

15. The nonpartisan perspective of Livy's narrative is a central concern of Fritz Hellmann, *Livius-Interpretationen* (Berlin: Walter de Gruyter, 1939), p. 4; I do not subscribe to Hellmann's view of Livy's *interpretatio Augustea* as an unqualified endorsement of the spirit of Augustus' program. See also Erich Burck, pp. 373–74 of "Aktuelle Probleme der Livius-Interpretation," in *Vom Menschenbild in der römischen Literatur: Ausgewählte Schriften,* ed. Eckard Lefèvre (Heidelberg: Carl Winter, 1966), vol. 1, pp. 354–75, previously published under the same title in

But the absence of appeals to the *maiores* in Livy's narrative is also consistent with several aspects of his distinctive perspective on the past. Typically, such appeals do not specify a particular ancestor; they do not distinguish among opposing factions of *maiores*; they identify the *maiores*, rather, as exemplars for and creators of the entire commonwealth.[16] They imply a uniformity of judgment. This is the more true because the authority of the *maiores* with reference to any particular situation derives from their authority in general. Specific actions and attitudes of the *maiores* are exemplary not only in their own right, as actions and attitudes whose virtues could be supported by various kinds of logical demonstration; they are exemplary on a more fundamental level because they express the judgment of people whose general management of affairs has shown them to be wise. It was, after all, under the leadership of the *maiores* that Rome grew from obscurity to world dominance, a view epitomized nicely by Sallust in a speech he attributes to Cato: "Undoubtedly courage and wisdom were greater among those men [our ancestors], who out of limited resources made such a great empire, than among us, who scarcely keep our hold on what has been well begun," *profecto uirtus atque sapientia maior illis [maioribus nostris] fuit, qui ex paruis opibus tantum imperium fecere, quam in nobis, qui ea bene parta uix retinemus (Cat.* 51.42).[17] Appeals to the *maiores*, then, suggest a past when all Romans, or at least all leading Romans, lived in accordance with a common body of wisdom.

Although Livy shares the view held by most Romans that the past was better than the present, that does not lead him to envision the past as a

---

Beihefte zum Gymnasium 4 (1964): 220–30, 241–45. In *Die Erzählungskunst des T. Livius* (Berlin and Zürich: Weidmann, 1964), pp. 118–22, Burck's emphasis on Livy's nonpartisan perspective extends to his treatment of Camillus, whom Burck presents as an embodiment of Livy's own values; I regard that view as somewhat overstated: see my remarks on Camillus in section II below.

16. E.g., Cic. *Rep.* 2.21.37. Such passages are based, according to Roloff, p. 58, on a philosophy of history derived from Cato (perhaps via the Stoics and/or Polybius). Rech, p. 79, following F. Altheim, *Epochen der römischen Geschichte,* Frankfurt Studien 9 (Frankfurt am Main: V. Klostermann, 1935), vol. 2, "Abschnitte 1 and 2," argues that Cato was the one who introduced the "proper" (*eigentlich*) appeal to the *mos maiorum* into literature, that before him the *maiores* to whom people appealed were those of the great clans, that after Cato those clan *maiores* were identified as the *Vorbildern* of the commonwealth. Roloff, p. 57 with n. 1, argues that the idea that the *maiores* were responsible for all public institutions was universal at Rome and has Indo-European origins.

17. For the same idea in Cicero, see *Balb.* 39 and *Rosc. Am.* 50–51; and for fuller discussion, see Roloff, pp. 114–15; Rech, p. 88 n. 12. Livy acknowledges this common point of view in a speech that he ascribes to Appius Claudius Crassus, grandson of the decemvir (6.41.8).

utopian age in which the wisdom and virtue of the Roman people or their leaders were uniform. On the contrary, he states explicitly (pref. 10) that the past offers examples to shun as well as to emulate. Both Roman villains and Roman heroes are conspicuous in his narrative; we see depravity as well as virtue among early Romans.

More to the point is that for Livy even villains, such as Tarquinius Superbus, have contributed to Roman greatness, and even heroes have their flaws: Tarquinius added to the size of the city (1.55.7–56.3); Camillus celebrated his triumph over Veii with a splendor more becoming to the gods than to a man (5.23.4–6, 28.1).[18] Often, indeed, it is difficult to decide in which category a leading figure belongs: the violent excesses of Appius Claudius the decemvir were equaled only by those of Tarquinius Superbus; on the other hand, Appius' contribution to Roman law led one of his descendants to include him among the very few Romans who are honored as *conditores* (3.58.2).[19]

This emphasis on variety and complexity over uniformity in Rome's past does not signify complete disregard for the belief that Rome owed its greatness to a ruling aristocracy whose authority derived in part from its collective embodiment of true Roman character. Livy acknowledges that tradition liberally in his treatment of the senatorial *patres*.[20] But there is a distinct difference between the *patres* as he presents them and the kind of idealized ancestral authority suggested by conventional appeals to the *auctoritas maiorum*. One of the important effects of the first pentad is to delimit and qualify the authority of the *patres*. It is true that in Livy's narrative the *patres'* collective virtue and wisdom see Rome through many a crisis and

18. For a more detailed analysis of the way in which Livy could develop the moral ambiguities of individual personality, see Joseph B. Solodow, "Livy and the Story of Horatius, 1.24–26," *Transactions of the American Philological Association* 109 (1979): 251–68.

19. For the others whom Livy identifies as *conditores*, see below, section II.

20. The prevailing view that "Livy regards history as preeminently concerned with individuals" (P. G. Walsh, *Livy: His Historical Aims and Methods* [Cambridge: Cambridge University Press, 1970], p. 82) has been so emphasized by scholars seeking to characterize Livy's distinctive place in ancient historiographic tradition (e.g., R. M. Ogilvie, "Livy," in *The Cambridge History of Classical Literature,* vol. 2, *Latin Literature,* ed. E. J. Kenney and W. V. Clausen [Cambridge: Cambridge University Press, 1982], pp. 461–66, Luce, *Livy,* pp. 230–31) that it may obscure his significant, even if secondary, interest in political groups and classes, and their distinctive characters and roles: e.g., the aristocratic youths, who conspire to bring back the monarchy; the *patres,* whose general conservatism makes them, as a group, leading defenders of Roman tradition; the plebeians, who are fierce in their defense of liberty but also susceptible to the blandishments of demagogues.

are indispensable to the community's survival and greatness.[21] But the *patres* are not *always* united among themselves.[22] Occasionally, their ranks are broken by a group or faction or by an individual,[23] and sometimes we see them falter in their allegiance to traditional standards.[24] More important, we do not see the *patres* in Livy's narrative as representatives of the entire Roman community. They are, rather, a distinct and well-defined class or faction within the community. Even though they often inspire respect for their capacity to perceive the common good and to champion it, we also see them in a narrowly partisan role, defending the exclusive prerogatives of their class against competing interests within the community.[25] Livy's

21. E.g., their statesmanlike concessions to the plebeians prevent abandonment of the city to Lars Porsenna (2.9.5–8); their petitioning of plebeians defeats an initial bill for migration to Veii (5.30.3–7).

22. E.g., 2.23.14. On an occasion of civil crisis Livy says that "the Senate, convened in an uproar, takes counsel in greater uproar," *tumultuose uocatus tumultuosius consulitur* (2.29.5).

23. As for factional divisions, the lesser clans, *minores gentes,* added to the Senate by Servius become "undoubtedly a faction of the king," *factio haud dubia regis* (1.35.6). Sometimes Livy singles out "the younger members of the Senate," *minimus quisque natu patrum* (2.28.9), as particularly rash (their rashness is epitomized in the fierce youth, *ferox iuuenis,* Caeso, 3.11.4–6, who prefers "his own license," *licentiam suam,* to the "freedom of all," *omnium libertatem,* 3.37.8). The elders, *seniores,* are depicted as exercising a moderating influence (e.g., 2.30.4, 55.11), sometimes specifically over younger senators of military age (e.g., 2.14.2–3; 3.41.1, 41.7). For a general discussion of the different roles of *seniores* and *iuniores* see J.-P. Neraudau, *La jeunesse dans la littérature et les institutions de la Rome républicaine* (Paris: Les belles lettres, 1979), and pp. 249–58 in Neraudau for particular reference to the political roles of each group in Livy. As for lone holdouts, a moderate and statesmanlike consensus prevails over the rashness of Appius Claudius in senatorial debate on the right of plebeians to hold their own elections for tribunes (2.57.3–4); but "property owners and a large number of the fathers," *possessores et magna pars patrum,* successfully unite against the consul Aemilius when he proposes an agrarian bill (3.1.3); at 3.40.8–41.6 Livy describes the senators as divided among themselves as a result of family loyalties and personal ambition.

24. E.g., in their treatment of the Fabii, who violated the law of peoples, *ius gentium,* by engaging in hostilities against the Gauls while acting as ambassadors. Livy says that when the Gauls protested to the Roman Senate, the senators recognized the justice of their protest but refused to pass judgment on the Fabii, because "among men of such great nobility interested motives were an obstacle," *in tantae nobilitatis uiris ambitio obstabat* (5.36.9); on another occasion, Livy says of the senators: "Few stand by the Republic; [many] stand by this or that [general] according as interest or favor had privately taken hold of each," *Pauci rei publicae, [plerique] huic atque illi* [rival generals] *ut quosque studium priuatim aut gratia occupauerat adsunt* (5.8.13; cf. 2.30.2).

25. They take advantage of opportunities to suppress the plebeians with "too much joyfulness," *nimis laetitia* (2.21.6; and cf. 2.54.10), and oppose "the freedom of the plebeians," *libertas plebis* (3.55.1). At the opening of book 4 they prefer even an unsuccessful war, *infelix bellum,* to an ignominious peace in which they would be forced to make concessions to the

patres provide a vehicle for the transmission and expression of Roman virtue and wisdom, but their determining influence on Roman history is more limited than that conventionally ascribed to the *maiores,* as transcending partisan loyalties and possessing authority that is properly evoked without questions or qualifications.

The fundamental reason for such appeals to the *auctoritas maiorum,* of course, is not descriptive, an attempt to characterize the past, however attractively; rather, it is persuasive, an attempt to influence judgments not only about the past but about the present and future as well. This kind of appeal to tradition implies that the essential character of society is so unchanged and unchanging that the collective wisdom of the *maiores* not only makes sense in the present but constitutes a standard of judgment that is timeless. In other words, just as reliance on the *auctoritas maiorum* implies uniformity in society of the past, so it implies a historical continuity between past and present, a complex of ideas epitomized in Ennius' famous assertion that "Rome endures because of its ancient customs and its men," *moribus antiquis res stat Romana uirisque.*[26] Such a view is fundamentally conservative.[27] When, for example, the historian Sallust observes that Metellus acted in accordance with the *mos maiorum* by following the advice of a council of senators (*Iug.* 62.5), but that Marius acted contrary to it by enlisting soldiers without regard to their financial qualifications (*Iug.* 86.2), or that Sulla indulged his army "against the custom of the ancestors," *contra morem maiorum* (*Cat.* 11.5), he is not only stating facts. He is also passing judgments, and he is reinforcing a general view in which conformity to tradition is good, and departure from it bad.[28]

But Livy's vision of the past contrasts significantly with the views of those who seek to ignore, to disguise, or to discourage change. Rather, his history is specifically about change: Rome's rise to greatness, the development of Rome's distinctive institutions, and its subsequent decline. His implicit recognition of the partisan nature of appeals to the *maiores* helps to reinforce a concept of Roman history as evolutionary. In Livy the *maiores* are almost

---

plebeians (4.1.4–5); their arguments against admitting plebeians to the consulship on the grounds that they are unqualified to take the auspices (4.2.5) are shown by subsequent history to be invalid.

26. *Ann.* frag. 500 Vahlen. On the ideas of social uniformity and historical continuity implicit in the notion of the *auctoritas maiorum,* see also Rech, pp. 18–19 and 88.

27. For a detailed explication of the relation between the *auctoritas maiorum* and conservatism in Cicero's thought, see Roloff, pp. 72–82.

28. Sallust goes so far as to say explicitly that all of his contemporaries, including *homines noui,* are inferior to their *maiores* in virtue and surpass them only in vice (*Cat.* 4.7–8).

always evoked to support one side in an ongoing struggle between social groups (patricians and plebeians in the first pentad). Livy has Cincinnatus acknowledge that the example of *maiores* may actually be divisive. Cincinnatus contrasts Spurius Maelius, a plebeian suspected of aspiring to *regnum,* with patrician tyrants and demagogues such as Appius Claudius and Spurius Cassius: the latter, he observes, at least had a consciousness of their own distinctions and those of their *maiores* to encourage their ambitions (4.15.5–6). In Livy's history, then, Roman institutions evolve from the progressive resolutions of social and political conflicts, not through the constructive influence of the *maiores* per se.

This evolutionary process anticipates and makes room for significant innovations in the future. I have already cited the passage where Canuleius argues that Rome will continue to grow, adding new commands, new priesthoods, and new people to those already existing (4.4.4).[29] Livy's own history confirms Canuleius' arguments, inasmuch as it has already recorded the examples that Canuleius cites as precedents and will go on to record the ultimate success of the policy that he advocates.[30]

It is important to note, moreover, that the institutional developments that Livy records, while they may all contribute to Rome's gradual evolution as a great power, are not simply cumulative in nature:[31] not all expedients of the Romans' ancestors, not even all constructive ones, constituted lasting models to be preserved or emulated by subsequent generations. Thus at the beginning of book 2 Livy acknowledges the rule of the first kings as a necessary prerequisite to the Republican self-rule that followed, and at the same time makes clear his own view that the freedom of self-governing people is superior to monarchy (2.1.1–6).[32] Monarchy, then, although it has its appropriate time, is not presented as being best for all times. Likewise, even after the principles of Republican government have been established at Rome for almost a half-century, Livy's introduction of the decemvirate

29. See Chapter 2, section IV.

30. A speech attributed to Decius Mus reviews the progressive accessibility of the higher magistracies to plebeians, while arguing successfully for plebeian admission to the colleges of augurs and pontiffs (10.7.2–8.12).

31. The appropriate emphasis in Luce, *Livy,* pp. 239, 241, 245, on "accretion" and "developmental" growth in Livy's narrative should not obscure the fact that Livy does not explain Roman growth solely by the accretion of new institutions. Perhaps better than "developmental" to describe Livy's view of history would be "evolutionary," as encompassing both transient and lasting innovations.

32. For a survey of Livy's thematic preparation for this view of monarchy, see Luce, pp. 243, 244.

acknowledges its "flourishing . . . beginnings," *laeta . . . principia,* as well as its swift decline (3.33.1–2). Again, the substitution of a board of military tribunes for consuls has a temporary value in averting an irreconcilable clash between plebeians and patricians. Livy presents an approach to Roman history that explicitly acknowledges the value of change and that denies to the *maiores* and their institutions a universal and timeless value. In his history the value of institutions is most often judged by the needs of the occasion, not by the more sweeping standard of the *mos maiorum.* Thus the absence of appeals to the *auctoritas maiorum* in Livy's own narrative, made the more apparent by the association of such appeals with partisan interests, complements his emphasis on variety, complexity, and change in Roman history and leaves a wide range for political innovation.

II

The perspective on the Roman past that is suggested by Livy's selective use of the term *maiores* is both complemented and significantly modified by the role that he ascribes to *conditores* in his narrative.[33] In his discussion of traditions that shaped origin stories in antiquity, Elias Bickerman observed that "some twenty-five Greek accounts of the origins of Rome have come down to us. . . . None of them agrees with the accepted Roman tradition" (which Bickerman regards as indigenous).[34] The Roman tradition to which Bickerman refers here is the story of Romulus as we know it from Livy. But Livy's idea of foundation involves considerably more than simply a retailing of Roman tradition, however eloquently presented. Livy conceives of the *conditor* in unusually broad terms. As noted in Chapter 2, he identifies

33. There has been no general discussion of the term *conditor* in Livy's narrative. For a review of the basic scholarship on *conditor,* see above, Chapter 2, note 79.

34. *"Origines Gentium," Classical Philology* 47 (1952): 65. Bickerman's view that the Romulus and Remus story is indigenous to Rome and not the product of Hellenistic influence is generally accepted among modern scholars. For fuller development of it, see C. J. Classen, "Zur Herkunft der Sage von Romulus und Remus," *Historia* 12 (1963): 447, 457; E. Gjerstadt, *Legends and Facts of Early Roman History,* Scripta minora, Regiae societatis humanarum litterarum Ludensis, 1960–61 (Lund: Gleerup, 1962), vol. 2, pp. 38–39; T. J. Cornell, "Aeneas and the Twins: The Development of the Roman Foundation Legend," *Proceedings of the Cambridge Philological Society* 201 (n.s. 21) (1975): 1–32; id., "The Value of the Literary Tradition Concerning Archaic Rome," in *Social Struggles in Archaic Rome: New Perspectives on the Conflict of the Orders,* ed. Kurt Raaflaub (Berkeley: University of California Press, 1986), pp. 52–76.

not just one but several Romans as *conditores*.[35] All together they include Romulus, the original founder of the city;[36] Servius Tullius, who organized the citizens into a formal hierarchy of merit (1.42.4); all the kings (except Tarquinius Superbus), who increased the size of the city (2.1.2); Appius Claudius the decemvir, who presided over the first compilation of written law at Rome (3.58.2); Augustus, honored as "restorer and founder of all our temples," *templorum omnium restitutorem ac conditorem* (4.20.7); Furius Camillus, who saved the city from total conquest by the Gauls, and both the city and its gods from abandonment by disaffected citizens (5.49.7–8); and Brutus, whose expulsion of the last king at Rome initiated a new era of Roman *libertas* (8.34.3). Numa, although not actually named *conditor*, is nonetheless identified as such by the assertion that "the city, recently founded by force of arms, he prepares to found anew on a legal basis with laws and customs," *urbem nouam conditam ui et armis, iure eam legibusque ac moribus de integro condere parat* (1.19.1).[37]

We may better appreciate Livy's originality here by contrast with the three concepts of foundation current in the Hellenistic thought of his age.[38] Foundation might refer to the establishment of a new community by colonists from a mother country. In this case, the founder was the person, the founders the people collectively, who first set out from the mother country. They were the first generation of settlers. Foundation might also involve giving

---

35. The term *conditor* in its various inflections occurs only twenty-two times in Livy's extant work. With one exception, it is used always, whether in the singular or the plural, to refer either to the founder(s) of a city (most often Rome) or to the founder of one or another specifically Roman institution. I include in this category the "false" *conditor*, Titus Sicinius, discussed in Chapter 2, section III, and Romulus and Augustus as *conditores templorum*. The exception is a single use of the term as a rhetorical title of honor: the Capuans promise the Romans that if they spare their city, they, the Capuans, will count the Romans "among their founders, ancestors, immortal gods," *conditorum, parentium, deorum immortalium numero* (7.30.19). This reflects a Hellenistic practice of honoring the savior of a city as its *ktistēs*; for this convention, see below and also the literature cited above, Chapter 2, note 79.

36. At 10.23.12 the phrase "images of the city's infant founders," *simulacra infantium conditorum urbis*, acknowledges Remus as well as Romulus, but Remus has no role as founder beyond sharing his brother's attachment to the site of Rome (1.6.3).

37. The verb *condere* in its various inflections (including participles) occurs seventy-nine times in Livy. Although used most often of founding cities (forty times total), especially Rome (twenty-seven times), it is used also of hiding troops in ambush, confining prisoners, establishing laws, in technical phrases for performing the *lustrum* (or a part of it), and in a small number of miscellaneous contexts where its early senses of gathering together and burying are often prominent. Except for Numa, no Roman is identified as a *conditor* solely by being the subject or agent of the verb *condere*.

38. For a review of basic scholarship on *ktistēs*, see Chapter 2, note 79.

an existing community a new constitution and usually, with it, a new name. This kind of foundation is especially familiar from the exploits of Alexander the Great and his successors in the East. In this case, the founder was the individual under whose authority the community first acquired its new status. Finally, the title *ktistēs* might be assumed as an honorific by a tyrant as representative of the entire race or of the original settlers, and it might, similarly, be offered in thanks to one who saved a city from destruction (physical or political). Thus, as we saw in Chapter 2, Sicilian tyrants represented themselves as founders (Diod. 11.38, 53, 66), and Pompey the Great could be honored as *sōtēr kai ktistēs* of Mytilene (*IG* 12.2.202). Livy is unique, then, in assigning to Rome not one *conditor* but several, each of whom is responsible for a specific aspect of the state's complete foundation.

Except for Augustus, all those whom Livy identifies as *conditores* are figures whose exploits are recorded in the first pentad, and Augustus himself, although he belongs to a much later period of Roman history, is identified as a *conditor* only within the first pentad. Within those books, *conditores* play a conspicuous role: they are leading figures in the portions of the narrative that concern them; their exploits account for a disproportionately large part of the entire narrative—perhaps as much as a third of it. The early prominence of these successive *conditores,* each with an additional contribution to make, reinforces other elements in Livy's narrative that present Rome's history as one of gradual evolution. Similarly, insofar as these *conditores* are innovators, their prominence also calls attention to and dramatizes the importance of change and innovation both as facts of Roman history and as explanations for Rome's rise to greatness. In these ways, the role of the *conditores* confirms the rejection, implicit in Livy's treatment of the *maiores,* of a monolithic and static view of Roman history. Livy not only recognizes change but emphasizes it; and not only does he emphasize it, but, to the extent that he ascribes it to Roman heroes, he honors it.

The important role that Livy ascribes to *conditores* not only qualifies the ideal of collective leadership implicit in the *auctoritas maiorum* but throws into sharp relief his alternative emphasis on the role of the individual leaders, who, as often as not, acted independently, in defiance of popular opinion or of the Roman aristocracy. Both Romulus and Brutus opposed ruling kings. Even after he had risen to power, Romulus alienated the Roman aristocracy (1.15.8). His foundation of the city was entirely his own undertaking—not even shared by the twin with whom he had shared all of his life up to that point. Numa not only took a free hand in elaborating traditional rites but even invented stories about his relations with the gods to place his authority above question (1.19.4–5). Servius Tullius was at the peak of his popularity (1.42.3) but nonetheless acted entirely on his own initiative when he instituted his division of Roman society. Brutus led the entire people against the Tarquins but was himself the catalyst that brought the people together; Camillus pursued his goals even in the face of popular hostility and opposition. Livy did not have to remind his audience that Augustus had come to power through civil war. This is not to deny Livy an appreciation of the Romans' capacity for collective wisdom: we have already noted the importance that he sometimes attributes to the leadership of the *patres*. But it is to say that for Livy such collective leadership is definitely only one aspect of Roman history, an aspect that is often overshadowed by the decisive role of the charismatic leader. This emphasis on the marked independence of Rome's *conditores* also helps to convey a perception of the Romans as a people conscious of being self-made, a people whose success is the expression of native virtues and initiative, a theme that will be developed at greater length in the next chapter.

We have seen, then, that Livy's concept of the *conditor* and his role in history serves to confirm some of the possible attitudes toward the Roman past suggested by his own dissociation from the *auctoritas maiorum*. The *conditor*'s role in Livy's history serves to qualify those implicit attitudes in other ways as well. Livy was not so unconventional a Roman as to view sociopolitical institutions with complete relativism or to endorse unrestrained innovation or to place unqualified trust in powerful individuals. Nor was he so unconventional as not to feel the necessity for some essential continuity between past and present. In all these respects, his treatment of the *conditores* helps to clarify and to define more precisely his perspective on Rome's past and its relation to the present.

Let us take the foregoing topics in order. The very act of ascribing some institutions to the agency of especially distinguished individuals marks those institutions and gives them a special status. Those institutions are the more conspicuous because, in fact, Livy ascribes so few of them to the *conditores*. We can say that for Livy the physical site of Rome, public religion, the formal stratification of society, the rejection of monarchy, rule by law, and the capacity to renew shaken commitments to those foundations are of paramount importance in defining Roman identity and greatness. The special status of the founders' accomplishments is reflected in the thinking that Livy ascribes to the tribune Canuleius. When Canuleius surveys the significant innovations down to his own day, he lists, in order, Numa's creation of priesthoods, Servius' creation of the census and his "division of the centuries and classes," *descriptio centuriarum classiumque,* the creation of consuls (and of the other magistracies to date), and, finally, the creation of the decemvirs, "to write the laws," *legibus scribendis* (4.4.3).

Livy's treatment of the *conditores* allows us to identify further distinctions within that group. Not all of Rome's founders and foundations are equal. Romulus commands the greatest respect. He alone, for example, is often identified simply as "founder," "our founder," and "founder of the city," *conditor, conditor noster,* and *conditor urbis;*[39] to him alone of Rome's founders is attributed the possibility of divine parentage (pref. 7; 1.15.6; 4.15.7); he is the only *conditor* to be honored with a series of titles that endow him with both divine and worldly distinctions: "a god, born of a god, king, parent of the city of Rome," *deum deo natum, regem, parentemque urbis Romanae* (1.16.3; and cf. 1.40.3, 5.24.11). Romulus' preeminence reflects both his primacy and his extraordinary breadth of vision: all of Rome's foundations are adumbrated in Romulus' own actions.[40] Thus Numa, before assuming office, took the auspices—in conscious imitation of Romulus (1.18.6). Numa's subsequent attention to state religion, then, appears as the elaboration of *pietas* first exemplified by Romulus. Similarly, Servius' institution of the census, with its division of the population into classes, developed a concept of political differentiation expressed by Romulus when he created the first council of *patres* and the first *equites* (1.13.8).[41] The kings who added to the size of the city, both in area and in population, reaffirmed Romulus' own choice of site and likewise his policy of recruiting new members for the community. Appius Claudius' codification and publication of the laws formalized a system of social regulation that began when Romulus first gave laws to his subjects (1.8.1).

In this context Brutus, "founder of Roman liberty," *conditor Romanae libertatis* (8.34.4), may seem something of an anomaly. Romulus initially came to power as the closest male descendant of Numitor, the last in a succession of hereditary kings, and was himself a king. That obstacle

39. Pref. 7; 1.7.3, 10.7, 20.3; 3.39.4; 5.53.8; 10.27.9.

40. Luigi Alfonsi, "La figura di Romolo all' inizio delle *Storie* di Livio," in *Livius: Werk und Rezeption: Festschrift für Erich Burck zum 80. Geburtstag,* ed. Eckard Lefèvre and Eckart Olshausen (Munich: C. H. Beck, 1983), pp. 101–6, emphasizes the variety of roles and qualities exhibited by Livy's Romulus, but without distinguishing those that are specifically reaffirmed by subsequent *conditores* in Livy's narrative.

41. At 1.8.7 Livy says that Romulus created the first senators, but equates them at the outset with *patres* and thereafter refers regularly to *patres* throughout book 1, almost never to *senatores* or *senatus. Senator* and *senatus* do not become regular terms until book 2. Tarquinius Priscus' designation of special seats at the circus for *patres* and *equites* (1.35.8) perhaps anticipates Servius' more thoroughgoing development of Romulus' precedent.

notwithstanding, Livy's narrative still makes it appropriate to view Brutus as fulfilling potentialities first prepared for by Romulus. Brutus followed in Romulus' footsteps when he attained authority by leading an insurrection against a tyrannical usurper of the kingship. And Livy implicitly includes Romulus among those kings whose orderly rule was a necessary prerequisite of self-government (2.1.2).

While it is important to recognize Romulus' preeminence among Roman founders, it must be kept in mind that he is still only one of several founders.[42] For all his uncanny anticipation of the institutions that would come to characterize the Roman state, he is not, according to Livy's narrative, solely responsible for Rome's foundation. We have seen that Livy identifies Numa, Servius, Brutus, and Appius as founders in their own right. Comparison with the more conventional representation of the founder in Dionysius of Halicarnassus points up Livy's distinctive emphasis on a succession of leaders who may not all be of equal stature but who are all founders, nonetheless. Dionysius mentions either Romulus as the founder of Rome or "those who founded Rome," *hoi oikisantes,* who turn out to be "those who left their ancestral homes," *hoitines . . . tas patrious oikēseis exelipon* (Dion. Hal. 1.5.1). He names no other founders of Rome. Inasmuch as Dionysius equates Rome's founders with a single generation of settlers and in particular with their leader, he tends also to attribute as many important institutions as possible to that initial stage in the nation's history.[43]

Consequently, in Dionysius' narrative we find institutions that Livy ascribes to later generations, such as the first written laws, ascribed instead to Romulus (Dion. Hal. 2.24.1). While Livy says that Numa, for example,

---

42. In this respect, Livy may be understood as giving particular embodiment to a historio-graphic position articulated by the elder Cato who, according to Cicero, "used to say that the constitution of our state surpasses those of other states because in the latter single individuals generally had each established his own state according to their own laws and institutions, . . . but our Republic was established by the genius not of a single individual but of many, not during a single lifetime but over several ages and generations," *dicere solebat ob hanc causam praestare nostrae ciuitatis statum ceteris civitatibus, quod in illis singuli fuissent fere, qui suam quisque rem publicam constituissent legibus atque institutis suis, . . . nostra autem res publica non unius esset ingenio, sed multorum, nec una hominis uita, sed aliquot constituta saeculis et aetatibus (Rep.* 2.1).

43. Georges Dumézil, *Horace et les curiaces,* 5th ed. (New York: Arno, 1978), p. 116, regards this concentration of responsibility for the nation's foundations in the person of its original founder as an expression of Dionysius' particularly Hellenistic point of view. By contrast, E. Gabba, *Dionysius and the History of Archaic Rome,* Sather Classical Lectures 56 (Berkeley: University of California Press, 1991), pp. 162–63, sees Dionysius' depiction of Romulus as reflecting "an historical source with a political bias in favor of the Senate," one originating most likely, in his view, with the Sullan annalists.

founded anew, Dionysius says merely that Numa did things "worthy of memory and note," *mnēmēs axia kai logou*, but that Romulus was responsible for their "seeds and beginnings," *ta spermata kai tas archas*, and that it was Romulus who established "the most authoritative," *ta kyriōtata*, religious customs (2.23.6). Similarly, where Livy has Numa call for the auspices in conscious emulation of Romulus, Dionysius says that Romulus not only established the precedent of sanctifying accession to office by the taking of auspices, but that he laid down the taking of auspices as a custom incumbent upon all would-be kings and magistrates.[44] Despite his suggestion that Rome's political institutions evolved gradually (1.9.4), Dionysius names only Romulus as *ktistēs*; his narrative suggests that Rome was largely the creation of a single individual and that its foundation certainly did not extend beyond the first generation of Rome's settlers: Dionysius can speak of the virtues that appeared "right from the first after [Rome's] founding," *euthys ex archēs meta ton oikismon* (1.5.3).

In addition to emphasizing Romulus' personal preeminence among Rome's founders, Livy's narrative, through its representation of Augustus and Camillus, calls special attention to the principle of *re*foundation. I have already noted that Livy calls Augustus "restorer and founder of all our temples," *templorum omnium conditorem ac restitutorem* (4.20.7). The phrase recalls an earlier description of Romulus as *conditor* of the temple of Jupiter Feretrius, the first temple built at Rome (1.10.5–7). But, of course, Augustus was not the first to formalize or extend Romulus' precedent of founding temples (although he may have been Romulus' most energetic successor in this regard). Livy's description of Augustus here clearly refers to his "rebuilding" of the city of Rome, particularly the temples that had been left in neglect during the civil wars. In their narrowest application, the terms *restitutor* and *conditor* presumably refer to two separate categories, temples that Augustus restored and new temples that he had built, respectively. In a broader sense, the reconstruction and building of temples referred to here should be understood in the context of appeals during the late Republic for a general renaissance of *pietas* after generations of "neglect of the gods," *neglegentia deum*.[45] Augustus, then, is less a founder in the sense that Numa,

---

44. Dion. Hal. 2.6.1; and cf. 2.60.3, where the augurs report on Numa's accession independent of his initiative.

45. On Augustus' rebuilding program, see *RG* 4.17; Dio 53.2; Suet. *Aug.* 29. For *neglegentia deum*, see above, Chapter 2, note 93; Livy himself uses the expression more than once (see Ogilvie *ad* 3.20.5); the interrelation of *pietas* and Roman fortunes, a major theme throughout Livy, is elaborated explicitly in Camillus' speech, 5.51–54.

Servius, Brutus, and Appius are founders, the first to sanction formally one of Romulus' precedents, than he is a *re*founder, one who assures the continuity of a Roman foundation when it has been threatened with extinction.[46]

We observed in Chapter 2 how the role of the refounder and his significance is developed fully and dramatically in the character of Camillus. Here it will be useful to recall only that Camillus neither formalizes nor adds to any of Romulus' precedents. Rather, in saving Rome from destruction by foreign enemies and in saving the city and its traditional gods from abandonment by disaffected citizens, he reaffirms principles that have already been established both in the initial precedents of Romulus and in their formalization and elaboration by subsequent *conditores.* In particular, he reaffirms the allegiance to the physical site of Rome and to the gods attached to that site. More generally, he establishes the principle of refoundation, for which he is accorded the title that places him second only to Romulus: "Romulus and parent of the fatherland and second founder of the city," *Romulus ac parens patriae conditorque alter urbis* (5.49.7). This title and the sheer length and drama of the narrative devoted to his accomplishments confer a special status upon them.

Such use of titles is but one of several complementary, rhetorical strategies by which Livy distinguishes and emphasizes Rome's different foundations. Just as distinctive titles mark Romulus and Camillus, so also does their dramatic positioning at the beginning and conclusion of the narrative unit comprised by the first pentad. Another form of emphasis in narrative is length: a subject may assume importance in proportion to the amount of narrative devoted to it. By this standard, *libertas,* and with it the organization of Romans for voting and the rule of law, gains prominence through the recurrent and extended attention to the struggle of the orders that is a central concern of books 2–4. In addition, the narrative positioning of the political and social struggle for *libertas* matches the historical context that Livy ascribes to it. Just as the narrative of the struggle for *libertas* is framed by attention to place and religion, so the actual struggle is itself circumscribed and limited by those foundations. The idea that loyalty to the city in the

---

46. In this sense, of course, there are many Romans whom Livy might have titled *conditores.* His restriction of the honor lends particular distinction to those few to whom he does accord the title. His choice of Augustus here is consistent with the great importance that he attaches to *pietas* throughout his history and may also reflect his sense of Augustus as a potential refounder on the pattern of Camillus, whose role he is to elaborate in book 5. See above, Chapter 2.

face of a foreign enemy takes precedence over domestic rivalries recurs prominently throughout the first pentad.[47]

The idea that religious scruple is also necessary to contain civil discord is articulated explicitly by Numa, who cites it as the rationale for his religious innovations (1.19.4). It is well illustrated also in the story of Appius Herdonius' slave uprising and its aftermath (3.15–20). Even after Herdonius and his followers had captured the Capitol, the plebeians were so disaffected by their own failure to achieve *libertas* that they refused to defend the city either against Herdonius or against external enemies who later plan to attack the divided, and therefore virtually helpless, city. After all other attempts to rouse the plebeians to the common defense have failed, the patricians successfully call upon their sense of *pietas*. Valerius Publicola cries: "If no care for the city, no care for yourselves touches you, fellow citizens, at least fear your gods who have been captured by the enemy," *Si uos urbis, Quirites, si uestri nulla cura tangit, at uos ueremini deos uestros ab hostibus captos* (3.17.3). Unnamed patricians urge the plebeians that "the conflict is not between the fathers and the plebeians; but at one and the same time fathers and plebeians, the citadel of the city, the temples of the gods, the tutelary gods of the city, and those of ourselves are being surrendered to the enemy," *non inter patres ac plebem certamen esse, sed simul patres plebemque, arcem urbis, templa deorum, penates publicos priuatosque hostibus dedi* (3.17.11). While the issue remains undecided at Rome, the leader of Tusculum argues that not only the present crisis but their own oaths of alliance require the Tusculans to assist Rome: "The danger itself, the crisis, the allied gods, and the good faith of our treaties demand this," *periculum ipsum discrimenque ac sociales deos fidemque foederum id poscere* (3.18.3). After Herdonius has been overcome, a new consul compels unwilling plebeians to march against the Volscians and Aequians by holding them to their previous oath of obedience; he is able to overcome the quibbles of the tribunes, because, Livy editorializes, "this neglect of the gods that now possesses our age had not yet come about," *nondum haec quae nunc tenet saeculum neglegentia deum uenerat* (3.20.5). Here, where not even the fear of common enemies both inside and beyond the city's walls can move disaffected Romans to defend their city, it is religious scruple, finally, that saves the day. Together, then, loyalty to place and *pietas* contain civil discord at Rome, just as emphasis on them early in book 1 and late in book 5 frames the longer story of the struggle for *libertas* that is the dominant theme of books 2–4. In this way one kind of rhetorical emphasis balances another in Livy's narrative, not only distributing emphasis

---

47. E.g., 1.9.4; 2.32.6, 39.7, 54.2; 3.9.1, and passim.

among Rome's several foundations but figuratively replicating and thus reemphasizing the historical interrelations among foundations that the narrative purports to describe.

The importance that Livy attached to those foundations would have been reinforced for his immediate audience by the fact that the institutions he marked as foundations were focuses of Roman concern and self-perception among his contemporaries. They would still have identified Rome the state with Rome the physical city, the *urbs,* traditionally the geographical, social, political, and cultural center of the Empire.[48] Similarly, Livy wrote at a time when expiation for generations of *neglegentia deum* was receiving conspicuous expression in Augustus' building program (as noted above), when the traditional *ordines* of Roman society were being demarcated more sharply than ever before,[49] when the self-styled *liberatores* and the Brutus of early history who was evoked on their behalf were fresh in memory, when the value of rule by law had been vividly impressed upon the minds of Livy's contemporaries by recent civil wars and by the proscriptions of 43–42 B.C.E., and when Augustus' vaunted "transferral" of the Republic from his own power to that of the Senate in 27 B.C.E. (*RG* 34.1) had made refoundation, perhaps hinted at in Cicero's political thought and Julius Caesar's propaganda, a matter of the highest politics.[50] The prominence of such institutions in Livy's account of early Roman history and especially the emphasis placed on refoundation at the end of the first pentad call attention to them and suggest their importance as lasting sources of collective identity and strength. But again it must be remembered that the extent of such continuity is very narrowly and sharply defined and that it is presented within Rome's larger history of change and innovation. It is precisely delimited in a way that a vague appeal to *auctoritas maiorum* is not, and leaves open the possibility for acceptable change in other areas.

The elements of institutional continuity that Livy singles out, despite their small number, nonetheless have a considerable influence on the shape and character of Roman history as he presents it. Within the first pentad, they constitute a growing set of standards by which action and policy come

---

48. Repeated scares that Rome might be displaced as the center of empire by "another Rome," an *altera Roma,* would have kept the importance of the city's position in the forefront of people's minds during the last decades of the Republic; see Petre Ceauşescu, "*Altera Roma*—Histoire d'une folie politique," *Historia* 25 (1976): 79–108.

49. See Claude Nicolet, "Augustus, Government, and the Propertied Classes," in *Caesar Augustus,* ed. Fergus Millar and Erich Segal (New York: Clarendon Press, 1984), pp. 90–96.

50. On Cicero and Caesar, see Stefan Weinstock, *Divus Julius* (Oxford: Clarendon Press, 1971), chap. 9 ("The Founder"), pp. 175–99; and see above, Chapter 2, section VI.

to be judged. As their number increases, so the scope for individual initiative decreases. This is revealed clearly in the way that the *conditor's* role changes in the course of the first pentad. In a new community, with no institutions or only rudimentary ones, Rome's first three founders acted essentially by fiat, as observed above. Brutus was supported by virtually the entire Roman people in his coup d'état, but it was his charismatic leadership alone that galvanized the people into action (1.59 and 60).

The position of subsequent founders is more complex. They must operate within the limits of a constitutional apparatus. Although Appius Claudius is granted extraordinary powers, those powers are nonetheless a grant of the people; he is not a completely free agent but rather the leading member of a commission of ten; his task is a limited one, and the length of time when he can hold his special powers is accordingly restricted. While Appius Claudius clearly conforms to the model of the tyrant first exemplified by Tarquinius Superbus, his particular history of achievement and excess may also be seen as expressing a tension between the previous, unfettered role of the founder and a new situation in which the founder is constrained by a growing body of traditional institutions. Thus, within the confines of his official mandate, he enjoys unrestricted authority; it is only when he attempts to extend his authority beyond the time allotted to him and for private ends not sanctioned in his mandate from the people that Appius arouses universal enmity and brings about his own downfall.[51]

With Camillus any tension between founder as free agent and as public magistrate is resolved: Camillus is conspicuous for the extent to which he respects tradition and subordinates himself to established institutions. As already noted, his claim to be a *conditor* is, to begin with, not based on innovation. His greatest achievement is not to create something new but to preserve essential Roman traditions. He is able to do this in part because he can look back over a record of achievements by the Roman people and argue on the basis of past experience for the efficacy of those traditions and for the dependence of Roman greatness upon them. His speech in book 5 (51–54) is a plea to preserve essential continuity with the past.

Camillus' decisive role is prepared for by a whole lifetime of scrupulous deference to traditional values and institutions. In his dealings with foreign peoples he is a perfect embodiment of Roman *fides*;[52] he is meticulous in

51. It is perhaps indicative of Appius' ambiguous standing that Livy does not himself name him as a *conditor* but rather puts ascription of that honor in the mouth of one of Appius' descendants.

52. On Camillus' *fides* and *iustitia* see Burck, *Erzählungskunst*, pp. 120–21.

his observance of the religious responsibilities of a commander, from his employment of *euocatio* to his determination to fulfill his promise of a share of the spoils to Apollo (5.25.4–8, 12; 32.8). Similarly, he submits to the authority of the Roman courts, even as he protests their injustice, when he goes into self-imposed exile (5.32.8–9)—an act that later Romans recalled as exemplary (25.4.2). Above all, he recognizes the prerogatives of the Senate, even to the point of complicating his own affairs: he consults the Senate about distribution of booty from Veii;[53] he leaves the pontiffs to determine how his vow to Apollo shall be fulfilled (5.23.10–11); Livy goes out of his way to express his own conviction that Camillus, although eager to defend Rome from the Gauls, would not have left his place of exile until he had received formal authorization from the Senate (5.46.10–11). Even after his dramatic rescue of the city from the Gauls, Camillus is presented as still acting within the confines of tradition. As powerful as his argument for staying in Rome is, it is not accepted as a matter of policy until the Senate grants its enthusiastic endorsement, and the Senate itself, although sympathetic to Camillus, does not extend that endorsement until the centurion's famous pronouncement "Here will be best for us to stay," *hic manebimus optime* (5.55.1), seems to signal divine sanction.

It is significant that Camillus figures so prominently at the end of the first pentad, that is, at what we have noted was the very midpoint of Roman history between the city's founding and Livy's own day, for Camillus quite clearly marks the end of one distinctive phase in Roman development and the beginning of a new one. With him, the role of the charismatic leader who imposes his own imprint on the character of Roman civilization comes to an end or at least is radically redefined. Henceforth, charisma is linked closely to Rome's foundations. Manlius Capitolinus is a case in point. He is regarded as a hero for his defense of the city (5.47.4–8); when his personal jealousy and ambition threaten another of Rome's foundations (*libertas*), he loses his charisma (even though he trades on it for as long as he can) and comes to a disgraceful end (6.11 and 14–20).[54]

Excepting the two refounders, Augustus and Camillus, the last five *"conditores"* in Livy's extant narrative are presented clearly as false *conditores*. They

---

53. Livy 5.20.2–3, where Ogilvie, ad loc., has noted: "Camillus is careful to frame his request in the punctiliously correct language of official dispatches (8.13.11; 31.31.20; 45.23.1)."

54. See also Christina S. Kraus, "Initium Turbandi Omnium A Femina Ortum Est: Fabia Minor and the Election of 367 B.C.," *Phoenix* 45 (1991) who sees the stories of Manlius and Fabia "as part of a pattern in Book 6, which describes a noticeable trend away from the heroic" (p. 323).

are demagogues who attempt unsuccessfully to usurp the role of *conditor* with their own spurious innovations. I have already discussed Titus Sicinius, leader in the abortive movement for emigration to Veii.[55] The remaining four false *conditores* were, Livy reports, punished as the "heads of a conspiracy," *capita coniurationis,* to introduce Bacchic rites to Rome (39.17.6–7, 19.2). The conclusion of Rome's period of foundation, however, does not mean an end to all constructive change and innovation. Livy's concept of foundation identifies only a very few, well-defined institutions as essential to Roman identity. Since they do not constitute a list of what can be changed but rather a very restricted list of what cannot be changed, they leave a wide scope for innovation.

III

As the preceding discussion indicates, the roles of the *maiores* and of the *conditores* in Livy's narrative are complementary. By refusing to evoke the *maiores* in his search for historical meaning and guidance, Livy departed from the general practice of his Roman contemporaries. That departure was of considerable historiographic moment, for it freed the historian from a perspective that was diachronically and synchronically monolithic: it made possible the exploration of variety and change in Roman historical experience, the perception of the dynamic interaction among groups and individuals as a creative force in Roman history, and the appreciation of short-term expedients as well as of lasting accomplishments. At the same time, Livy's conception of the founder's role assures that his narrative does not present all innovations as equally significant. Association with founders sets certain institutions apart from the rest as central to Roman identity and as sources of vital continuity between past and present. They can be compromised only at risk to the very survival of the Roman people; they call attention to the important role of the individual, and they help to emphasize the self-made character of the Roman people. At the same time, however, these institutions are specific in nature, finite in number, and their establishment confined to a particular phase in Rome's development.[56]

55. See above, Chapter 2, section III.

56. The principle of discriminating between institutions that are essential and must therefore remain unchanged and others whose value is transitory is articulated explicitly, although in a somewhat more restricted context, later in Livy's narrative. There Lucius Valerius argues against the elder Cato for repeal of the *lex Oppia*. Passed during the war with Hannibal, when Rome's finances were stretched to their limits, this law forbade women to display their personal wealth in public. In the course of his argument, Valerius makes the following distinction: "I acknowledge that none of the laws passed, not for some particular circumstance, but rather

Since Livy's perspective on history comprehends specific threads of continuity within a larger field of potential change, it can be complex yet coherent. Thus Livy's perspective simultaneously empowers and constrains the charismatic leader. Because so much value is attached to the acts of the founders, those acts help to emphasize the importance of strong leadership. At the same time, they restrict the scope of the leader's initiative, inasmuch as he is obligated to respect the integrity of the founders, and his own status comes increasingly to derive from allegiance to them. Similarly, Livy can claim that the past was better than the present without representing it as utopian or its leaders as one-dimensional paragons of Roman virtue: what determines the excellence of an age is not its approximation to idealized standards of perfection, but the security of the community's foundations. Finally, Livy does not have to perceive all change as decline: after the refounding by Camillus, Livy describes the city reborn "as though from its roots, more fruitful and more flourishing [than before]," *uelut ab stirpibus laetius feraciusque* (6.1.3). So long as the foundations laid during the formative stage of Rome's development remain secure, there is ample scope for change, for growth as well as for decline, without the community's losing its identity or its potential for renewal. This perspective on Roman history had a particular relevance for a generation that had lived through a succession of civil wars and was confronted by a still ambiguous and problematic program of "renewal" under a leader whose influence had not been equaled since the days of Rome's first kings.

For the same reasons, Livy's sense of the importance but also of the limits of the charismatic leader's role was especially timely. As argued in Chapter 2, it is not difficult to see in Livy's portrayal of Camillus an endorsement of Augustus' proposal to restore the Republic and especially of his call for an end to *neglegentia deum* and for a renewed commitment to the actual city

---

with the aim of lasting usefulness, for eternity, ought to be repealed—unless experience has discredited it or some circumstance of the Republic has rendered it useless. Just so, I see that laws required by particular circumstances are, so to speak, mortal and changeable with the circumstances themselves," *Ego enim quem ad modum ex iis legibus, quae non in tempus aliquod sed perpetuae utilitatis causa in aeternum latae sunt, nullam abrogari debere fateor, nisi quam aut usus coarguit aut status aliquis rei publicae inutilem fecit, sic quas tempora aliqua desiderarunt leges, mortales, ut ita dicam, et temporibus ipsis mutabiles esse uideo* (34.6.4–6). Valerius illustrates this general principle by distinguishing between those laws made during peacetime and those made during war—two classes of laws, he argues, that are "different by nature," *natura distincta* (34.4.7). On the complementarity between Valerius' speech and that in which Canuleius anticipates the perpetual development of Roman institutions (4.4.4), see Jane D. Chaplin, *Livy's Use of Exempla and the Lessons of the Past* (Ph.D. diss., Princeton University, 1993), p. 150, and, on the relation of precedent, exempla, and innovation more generally, pp. 145–154.

of Rome. This last was not a purely academic issue. Augustus' propaganda had encouraged the fear that Mark Antony would establish his capital at Alexandria, leaving Rome a backwater. As champion of the gods and the city of Rome, Augustus was acting within the tradition of refoundation established by Camillus. Livy's narrative encourages the reader to welcome those initiatives and to look upon them with favor.

But even though the narrative makes *pietas* and loyalty to place preeminent among the acts of foundation, and even though it grants to Camillus, the refounder, a place second only to that of Romulus, we have seen that it also places substantial constraints upon Camillus' successors. Like Camillus, they belong to an age of *re*foundation, not to an age of radical innovation. Camillus' strict respect for constitutional formalities offers a tacit standard for the leader who would claim the status of refounder.[57] In addition, there were the other foundations that must be honored: the stratification of society, the rule of law, and, finally, *libertas*. It was this last, of course, that was the most problematic, and, as I suggested in Chapter 1, there were good reasons for Livy to see danger in pushing the claims of *libertas* too vigorously at the time when he published his first pentad. The act for which Livy honors Brutus as a founder, the expulsion of Tarquinius Superbus and the permanent overthrow of tyranny at Rome, is recorded in the first pentad. However, it is not until book 8, which would have been published some time after the first pentad had been available for inspection by the public, and more particularly by Augustus himself, that Livy actually called Brutus *conditor Romanae libertatis*. I take it, then, that Livy was encouraged by the course of events following 25 B.C.E. Encouraged in what way is not so clear. It may be that he felt Augustus' regime really was proving to be consistent with the ideal of *libertas* or that the memory of the *liberatores* whom Octavian had pursued in the name of Mars Ultor was safely fading or simply that the response to Livy's first pentad had made him a little more confident about what he might get away with. Whatever the explanation, I think that his apparent hesitation over the title *conditor Romanae libertatis* points to what Livy, as he composed the first pentad, regarded as the critical question about Augustus' role.[58] And it also suggests that Livy was very much aware of the

57. In addition to my observations above on Camillus' strict deference to authority, see J. Hellegouarc'h, "Le principat de Camille," *Revue des études latines* 48 (1970): 112–32, who also finds reasons for regarding Livy's Camillus as a model for a constitutional principate in aspects of Livy's narrative in book 6.

58. The assertion at 2.1.9 that Brutus "had been no keener a champion of liberty than he then was its guardian," *non uindex acrior libertatis fuerat quam deinde custos fuit,* is not inconsistent with my argument here. The term *uindex* is even less a substitute for *conditor* than is *auctor.* It

political implications of his ideas about Roman history and, in particular, about the foundations of Rome.

IV

Thus Livy's rhetorical stance and his actual perspective on the past are at least partly in conflict with each other. As observed earlier in this chapter, the contrast between the conventional appeal to the *auctoritas maiorum* in Livy's speeches and the unconventional absence of such appeals in the author's own narrative suggests the narrator's fastidious transcendence of partisan rhetoric. This contrast is consistent, also, with my argument in Chapter 1 that Livy was reluctant to join in the political appropriation of the past that was such a prominent feature of his own age. The rhetoric of Livy's narrative, in other words, reinforces his explicit claim in the preface (5) to offer a disinterested interpretation of the past.

Examination of Livy's history has shown, however, that his interpretation of the past, whether we judge it finally as partisan or nonpartisan, nonetheless confers special status upon certain aspects of Rome's political history. To the extent that such status is conferred not by analysis or demonstration but by the attribution of an institution to a "founder," it is an expression of the author's own political judgments. This is even clearer when we note the distinctive selection of institutions that Livy identifies as foundations. We might imagine, though we probably need not do so, that virtually any history of Rome's early development would attach significance to the choice of its site, the formation of its priesthood, the introduction of the census, and so on. But other historians might not, and did not, make a formal distinction between those institutions and, say, the formation of the Senate, the right of appeal, the introduction of the tribunate. Livy certainly acknowledges the importance of such other institutions. Inasmuch as he does not elevate them above the rest, however, as he does with those institutions that he singles out as the acts of "founders," he does not put them on a par with Rome's "foundations." His selection of foundations is, so far as I can determine, unique: it expresses not a traditional consensus but rather the historian's own political values. Through it he claims

---

is one thing to claim or champion *libertas,* another to "found" it. At 6.14.10 the people are described as following the demagogic Marcus Manlius (Capitolinus) as their *uindicem libertatis*; at 23.10.13 the Capuan Decius Magius, when offered freedom to return either to Capua or to Rome, elects rather to have King Ptolemy as his "champion and author . . . of liberty," *uindicem atque auctorem . . . libertatis,* and asks him for asylum.

special historical significance for those institutions that he has judged to be of particular value. In other words, Livy's "objective" designation of certain Romans as "founders" is a vehicle by which he appropriates the past in the service of his own political ideals.[59]

There is yet another, more indirect way in which Livy effectively appropriates the past even while dissociating himself from those who commonly did so through appeal to the *auctoritas maiorum*. This is, paradoxically, through the appeals to the *maiores* in the speeches that he attributes to historical figures. We may well recognize in these appeals to the *maiores* the author's attempts to capture the typical language of political speeches at Rome or to underscore the speaker's (as opposed to the narrator's) overtly political use of the past. This acknowledgment need not negate the emotional force of such appeals. This is especially true when the speaker is calling upon his audience to acknowledge a historical precedent that Livy's own narrative has confirmed for us, the readers. Canuleius, for example, points out that *maiores nostri* accepted foreigners as kings (4.3.13); Camillus evokes the *maiores'* exemplary religious scruple (5.52.8) and their energetic building of the city (5.53.9). In each case, the speaker's evocation of the *maiores* confers on those past events a special authority that we are prepared to accept: Livy's narrative has already shown the truth of the events in question and has placed them in a historical context that reveals their value.[60] Livy, then, is sometimes not above borrowing the trenchant support of the *maiores* to reinforce his own interpretation of history, although he never does this in his own narrative voice but always obliquely, through another speaker.

Both Livy's personal dissociation from appeals to the *auctoritas maiorum* and his own appropriation of the past are essential elements in a complex historical perspective. The former allowed him the opportunity to emphasize aspects of Roman history whose significance might have been obscured or diminished by a monolithic conception of the past, and it conferred on him the authority of political disinterest; the latter allowed him, in turn, to claim a special historical authority for those political institutions to which he attached special value. Whether the rhetorical duplicity that lies behind this strategy was intentional or unwitting—the product of a powerful cultural

59. For a full and well-documented example of how far-reaching the ideological implications of foundation myths may be, see Hugh A. MacDougall, *Racial Myth in English History: Trojans, Teutons, and Anglo-Saxons* (Hanover, N.H.: University Press of New England, 1982).

60. Camillus' argument for *pietas*, for example, has already been borne out in the vicissitudes of Rome's fortunes; Canuleius' insistence on the value of accepting foreigners as kings has been anticipated in the introduction to book 2, where Livy acknowledged the important contributions of Rome's kings explicitly and without regard to their different origins (2.1.2).

predisposition to appropriate the past even when he sought to transcend such appropriation—that is a question we cannot answer and is, in any event, a matter for the biographer, not for the student of historiography. This duplicity nonetheless demands recognition as a significant aspect of Livy's narrative stance. It is at least in part an unavoidable consequence of the fact that the author continues, inescapably, to work within a rhetorical tradition that he is attempting to reshape but cannot hope to displace. The next chapter will show how Livy engages a similar dilemma and its consequences on the thematic level.

Chapter 4

Foundation and Ideology in Livy's Narrative of Romulus and Remus

But the social placement of myth as charter and its social functions are not all there is to context. . . . [P]recisely because myth is charter it is going to provoke a debate between groups. . . . [I]t also embodies the sedimentation of past debates, a dialogue if you will with the tradition's perception of its past. . . . [T]he existence of a myth of any significance is a provocation.

Gananath Obeyesekere
The Work of Culture

Elias Bickerman noted at least twenty-five different Greek accounts of Rome's foundation known in antiquity, not one of which agrees with the accepted Roman tradition.[1] In fact, if one were to distinguish among significant variants of different versions (both Greek and Roman), one could increase the total still further. The version most familiar to moderns is that based on the birth of the twins, Romulus and Remus, the vicissitudes of their early lives, and Romulus' eventual foundation of Rome.[2] Livy's narrative is one of several variants of this story. As far as we can tell by comparison with the only other sustained narratives of Romulus' foundation that survive, those of Dionysius of Halicarnassus and Plutarch, Livy's is distinct in its

---

1. "*Origines Gentium,*" *Classical Philology* 47 (1952): 65.
2. Dionysius of Halicarnassus (1.73) seems to indicate that Latin authors uniformly favored accounts centering on Romulus and Remus, and himself chooses as "the most believable," *ta pithanōtata* (1.75.4), a version that is consistent in its main lines with those of Livy and Plutarch. Modern scholars are now in general agreement that the story of the twins was essentially indigenous and predated other (imported, Greek) versions, although various elements may have been added at different times; see above, Chapter 3, note 34.

emphasis on Romulus as a hero who is characterized by self-sufficiency and whose essential character reflects the formative influence of his austere rustic upbringing. This emphasis is at odds with several traditional elements of the Romulus story and with other interpretations of it that focus rather on Romulus' inherited qualifications as the son of a god and the representative of a line of heroic kings. The distinctive emphasis that we find in Livy is intelligible as a response (whether conscious or intuitive) to questions of Roman ideology that were of particularly immediate concern to his Roman contemporaries. The tension apparent within Livy's narrative between a dominant emphasis on Romulus' human self-sufficiency and the traces of alternative representations that insist rather on his distinctive heritage in some cases creates, in others reveals, contradictions in contemporary ideologies of Roman self-representation.

I

The narrative that concerns Romulus and his foundation of Rome is framed by editorial comments making clear that his achievements and those of his Romans are to be understood not within the Hellenistic tradition of divine or semidivine founding heroes but rather as the consequences of purely human endeavor. Livy introduces the topic of Romulus' ancestry and its significance as a specific example of the unreliability of the traditions surrounding early Rome generally (pref. 6–7).[3] He then proceeds directly to make the distinction, already discussed in Chapter 1, between the validity of the tradition that made Mars the parent of Romulus and of Rome and the validity of the Romans' *right to claim* descent from Mars (pref. 7): the *claim* of divine ancestry is justified here not because of its literal truth but rather because it appropriately symbolizes the martial accomplishments of

---

3. J. Poucet, "Temps mythique et temps historique: Les origines et les premiers siècles de Rome," *Gerion* 5 (1987): 76–78 and 85, locates Livy's skepticism here in relation to larger traditions of Roman and Greek historiography. For the more general argument that Livy did not support the notion of divine intervention in human affairs, and in Roman destiny in particular, see I. Kajanto, *God and Fate in Livy*, Annales Universitatis Turkensis 64 (Turku: Turun Yliopiston Kustantama, 1957), esp. pp. 42–53. To his survey of opposing views (esp. p. 10) should be added M. Rambaud, "Une défaillance du rationalisme chez Tite-Live?" *Information littéraire* 7 (1975): 21–30.

the Romans, who, whatever the reality of their origins, have the ability to compel others to accede to that claim.[4]

The care with which the author here distinguishes between literal and symbolic interpretations of Romulus' ancestry is echoed in the narrator's summation at the end of Romulus' life:

> Haec ferme Romulo regnante domi militiaeque gesta, quorum nihil absonum fidei diuinae originis diuinitatisque post mortem creditae fuit, non animus in regno auito reciperando, non condendae urbis consilium, non bello ac pace firmandae. . . . Multitudini tamen gratior fuit quam patribus, longe ante alios acceptissimus militum animis; trecentosque armatos ad custodiam corporis quos Celeres appellauit non in bello solum sed etiam in pace habuit. (1.15.6–8)

> These were the better part of Romulus' accomplishments as king, both in peace and at war. None of them is inconsistent with confidence in his divine origin and in the divinity that was ascribed to him after his death: neither his courage in regaining his ancestral kingdom, nor his wisdom in founding the city and in consolidating it in war and peace. . . . Nonetheless, he was more popular with the multitude than with the fathers, way beyond others most welcome to the spirits of the soldiers; he kept three hundred armed men, whom he called Celeres, as a bodyguard not only in war but also in peace.

Here, the focus on Romulus' deeds (*gesta*) and the understatement "not inconsistent" (*nihil absonum*) together call attention conspicuously to the narrator's reserve about Romulus' actual divinity, even as they acknowledge the distinction of his deeds.[5] The subsequent report that Romulus' popularity was mixed and that he felt the need of a bodyguard further underscores his human limitations. It is within this context that Romulus' troops, his most loyal supporters, lead an initiative to proclaim him "god, son of a god, king, and parent of the city," *deum, deo natum, regem parentemque urbis* (1.16.3), and a distinguished senator counters popular suspicion that senators had

---

4. See Chapter 1, section 2. This emphasis on the symbolic rather than the literal meaning of Romulus' ancestry is the exact opposite of what we find in Plutarch's *Life of Romulus.* Writing, as was Livy, within a historiographic tradition that eschewed or rationalized the fabulous and supernatural, Plutarch nonetheless seeks to accommodate those elements of the tradition, arguing that we should suspend our normal disbelief, since those elements alone were adequate to explain Romulus' and Rome's greatness (*Rom.* 8.9).

5. According to Kajanto, *Fate,* p. 31, this passage "does not at all show that Livy himself believes in Romulus' divinity. What Livy here wants to say is that Romulus' exploits were such as to give grounds for what his contemporaries believed of him."

murdered Romulus by claiming to have witnessed his apotheosis (1.16.5–8). Thus in reporting the circumstances surrounding Romulus' deification, Livy acknowledges Romulus' extraordinary popularity with the Roman army and masses but stops conspicuously short of himself endorsing claims of his divinity. Those claims reflect intense partisan rivalry; Romulus' deeds remain wholly intelligible as those of a mortal human. The story of Romulus, then, and of the people whom he represents, is framed as a story of human achievement—however exalted—rather than of superhuman agency.

In framing the story in this way, however, Livy inevitably runs counter to received tradition; for the fabulous and supernatural elements in Romulus' story are not only particularly dramatic and memorable by their very nature; they also play an essential role in the narrative chain of events, accounting both for the twins' birth and for their rescue from exposure. The ideological implications of these aspects of the story are quite inconsistent with a representation of Romulus' achievements as distinctively human. The rape of Rhea Silvia by Mars explains how the twins' birth from a vestal virgin could be in some sense legitimate or at least socially and religiously acceptable; it also explains and justifies Rome's unique success in war. More than that, of course, by providing divine ancestry for Romulus and, through him, for the community that he founds, the story also provides divine sanction for them. In this context the rescue of the twins by a wolf reconfirms the qualities of fierceness and aggressiveness implicit in Romulus' descent from Mars; it also reconfirms that his destiny and that of his community are guided by a special providence.[6]

Livy's narrative itself acknowledges this tradition, but, in keeping with the orientation established by the frame of the Romulus story, it treats the fabulous and divine elements of the tradition with pointed caution and skepticism. In relating that a flood of the Tiber had provided the circumstances for the twins' survival, Livy as narrator does acknowledge the view that Rome's rise from obscurity to preeminence was extraordinary, but his language is conspicuously ambiguous: "By a certain chance, divinely, the Tiber had overflowed its banks in calm pools. It was impossible to go all the way to the course of the river proper, and this raised the hope among those bearing the infants that they could be drowned in the water, no matter how sluggish," *Forte quadam diuinitus super ripas Tiberis effusus lenibus stagnis nec adiri usquam ad iusti cursum poterat amnis et posse quamuis languida mergi aqua infantes spem ferentibus dabat* (1.4.4). When it comes to the unambiguously

---

6. On the wolf as Mars' animal see Livy 10.27.8 and 9; Virg. *Aen.* 9.566; Hor. *Carm.* 1.17.9; Prop. 4.1.55.

supernatural elements of the story, however, the narrator consistently distances himself from the tradition. He reports with skepticism Rhea Silvia's
allegation that Mars raped her (1.4.2). He disavows responsibility for the
story of the wolf's suckling the twins by reminding the reader repeatedly
that this part of his narrative represents only uncritical tradition (*fama*),
repeats what "some people think" (*sunt qui . . . putent*), and is a mere "story"
(*fabula*) (1.4.6–7).[7]

The actual story of Romulus' life can be divided into two distinct
phases in Livy's narrative. The first begins with the circumstances of his
birth and concludes with his establishment as undisputed ruler of the
new city of Rome. The second concerns his monarchy. The first phase,
which will be our initial focus here, establishes Romulus' self-sufficiency
by emphasizing both his isolation from his family of birth and his social
marginality. It begins with the rivalry between Numitor and Amulius
(Romulus' maternal grandfather and maternal great uncle, respectively)
for control of the kingdom bequeathed by their father. It ends with the
murder of Remus. The conditions of Romulus' birth are determined
when Amulius kills Numitor's son and makes his daughter, Rhea Silvia,
a vestal virgin in order to deprive Numitor of male successors. Although
Amulius' machinations fail to prevent Rhea Silvia from producing a
child, they do effectively deprive her son Romulus of all family save his
twin Remus. Inasmuch as Rhea Silvia is a vestal, Romulus cannot be a
legitimate child. In fact, he is not only illegitimate; the identity of his
father is, in Livy's narrative, utterly beyond speculation. We are told that
Rhea Silvia claimed Mars as the father, either because "she believed that
to be the case," *seu ita rata,* or "because she felt that a god was a more
respectable cause of her transgression," *seu quia deus auctor culpae honestior
erat* (1.4.2). It is notable that these alternatives concern only the mother's
motives for saying that the twins were fathered by Mars. What the actual
truth of the matter may have been the narrator does not attempt to say:
Rhea Silvia claims Mars as the parent, but for the narrator the twins

7. Erich Burck, *Die Erzählungskunst des T. Livius* (Berlin and Zürich: Weidmann, 1964),
p. 137, notes these expressions as examples of Livy's general distrust of the traditions about
pre-foundation Rome. He does not observe that they are associated particularly with elements
of the tradition that support the idea of Romulus' divinity, although Burck does affirm
elsewhere (p. 138) that "to be sure, Livy by no means speaks categorically of Romulus' and
Remus' divine origin." Similarly, Kajanto, *Fate,* pp. 30–31, notes that Livy's treatment of
Rome's foundation story is consistent with the ancient tradition of rationalizing the *fabulosum,*
but does not discuss particular implications of this tradition for the characterization of Romulus
in Livy's narrative.

themselves remain "offspring of uncertain paternity," *incertae stirpis* (1.4.2).[8]
The twins thus are linked to the Latin kings and the dynasty of Aeneas, but
the link is a weak one at best, through their unmarried mother to a ruler
who has been deposed. The priority given to descent through the male
line and the requirements of legitimacy at Rome mean that Romulus and
Remus have no formal claim to a place in the line of kings descended
from Aeneas.[9]

But even their tenuous link to royal ancestry is broken when the twins
are separated from their mother and exposed on the banks of the Tiber
River. Their complete isolation from relatives who could support them and
from ties that could legitimize claims to power is emphasized by the uncertainty and confusion surrounding their rescue and the identity of their foster
mother. According to tradition, Romulus and Remus are first rescued by a
she-wolf, a *lupa,* and then by the herdsman Faustulus, who brings the boys
home to be reared by his wife, Laurentia. To this tradition Livy, as others,
added a rationalizing explanation: Laurentia was a whore, and whores were
known as *lupae* in colloquial parlance; the story of the she-wolf is to be
understood as resulting from a literal interpretation of what had been a
colloquial usage of the term *lupa.*[10] According to this narrative, then, either
the twins really were first suckled by a she-wolf, a literal *lupa,* or Laurentia
was a whore, a figurative *lupa,* since only so could the story of the she-wolf
have arisen. Such a presentation leaves the reader only with alternatives that
emphasize Romulus' and Remus' complete separation both from family and
from ordinary society. On the one hand, we see them virtually as the
products of nature, and this, as R. M. Ogilvie has pointed out, "is an age-
old explanation, like siring by the fire-god . . . , to account for the emergence
of a new force without background or pedigree."[11] On the other hand,
Romulus and Remus owe their upbringing to a simple shepherd and a

8. Contrast Dionysius (1.77.1), who reports variant traditions according to which
Ilia's suitors or Amulius himself, disguised in armor, may have raped her, in the latter
case giving the twins a claim to royal descent through their father, albeit a claim that
would not be sanctioned by the legitimacy of marriage. Dionysius also reports that Ilia's
attacker identified himself as a god and predicted that she would bear twins, a prediction
whose eventual fulfillment was subsequently advanced by Numitor as proof that the twins
were the product not of adultery but of a divine parent (1.78.3–4).

9. As Ogilvie, p. 537, *ad* Livy 4.4.12, observes, "It is only children born in *iustae nuptae*
(i.e., marriages sanctioned by *conubium*) that take the status of their father (Gaius 1.76–96)";
and see also Gai. *Inst.* 1.6.

10. Ogilvie, pp. 46–47, *ad* Livy 1.3.10–4, offers a reconstruction of how this tradition
might have evolved.

11. Ogilvie, p. 46.

whore, that is, to individuals at the very bottom of the social hierarchy.[12] In either case, what is emphasized is that the founder-to-be of Rome began life entirely without the resources of family and social position.

In a striking paradox, Livy's narrative identifies this relegation to the margins of society as the very condition for the twins' distinctive excellence: "Such was their birth and upbringing. When they reached maturity, although sluggish neither at the stables nor with their flocks, they roamed the woodlands hunting. From this they acquired strength in body and spirit," *Ita geniti itaque educati, cum primum adoleuit aetas, nec in stabulis nec ad pecora segnes uenando peragrare saltus. Hinc robore corporibus animisque sumpto* (1.4.8–9).[13] It is from this position on the margins of society that Romulus and Remus eventually restore Numitor to his rightful inheritance and achieve recognition as his grandsons.

Thus far I have been concerned to demonstrate how Livy's narrative emphasizes the human self-sufficiency of Romulus and Remus. A second, closely related theme is that the twins, and Romulus in particular, not only are self-sufficient but are essentially self-created. That is, recognition of their true identity comes as the result entirely of their own achievements. At this point, extended comparison with the narratives of Dionysius of Halicarnassus and Plutarch will help to make the characteristic emphasis of Livy's narrative particularly clear. In each of the former authors the recognition of Romulus and Remus is prepared for by visible evidence of their divine natures and is clinched by tangible proofs. In Plutarch's narrative, for example, we are told that upon Remus' arrest, Numitor,

θαυμάζων μὲν ἀπὸ τοῦ σώματος τὸν νεανίσκον ὑπερφέροντα μεγέθει καὶ ῥώμῃ πάντας, ἐνορῶν δὲ τῷ προσώπῳ τὸ θαρραλέον καὶ ἰταμὸν τῆς ψυχῆς ἀδούλωτον καὶ ἀπαθὲς ὑπὸ τῶν παρόντων, ἔργα δ' αὐτοῦ καὶ πράξεις ὅμοια τοῖς βλεπομένοις ἀκούων, τὸ δὲ μέγιστον, ὡς ἔοικε, θεοῦ συμπαρόντος καὶ συνεπευθύνοντος ἀρχὰς μεγάλων πραγμάτων, ἁπτόμενος ἐπινοίᾳ καὶ τύχῃ τῆς ἀληθείας, ἀνέκρινεν ὅστις εἴη καὶ ὅθεν γένοιτο. (*Rom.* 7.5)

marveling at the youth's body, which surpassed everyone's in stature and strength, and seeing in his visage that the courage and daring of his spirit

---

12. Faustulus' status is not improved much even by versions of the story that identify him as Amulius' steward (Dion. Hal. 1.84.3) or one of his swineherds (Dion. Hal. 1.79.9), since in either case he would likely have been a slave.

13. The word *stabulis* underlines the twins' lowly position in society, since it not only can mean "stables" (the home of shepherds) but also was a familiar term for "brothel" (see, for example, Cic. *Phil.* 2.69)—a reminder of Laurentia's uncertain background.

were unbowed and unmoved under the present circumstances, and hearing that his deeds and actions were consistent with what he had seen, and— most important, it seems—with the presence of a god who helped to guide the beginnings of great things, grasped the truth by reflection and chance and asked him who he was and what his origins were.[14]

Numitor's strong suspicions of the twins' identities are reinforced by Remus, who reports that although he had until recently believed himself to be the son of Faustulus, he and his brother now hear "great things about themselves," *megala peri heautōn* (*Rom.* 7.6). He adds: "The present danger is likely to decide if these things are reliable," *ei de pista, krinein eoike nun ho kindunos* (7.6).

In fact, in Plutarch's narrative it is not the twins' own behavior that proves decisive in establishing their identity. It turns out rather that the "trough," *skaphē,* in which the twins were exposed survives. Remus mentions it to Numitor as a proof of their identity. In the meantime, Faustulus, the twins' rescuer, prepares to introduce his evidence. This Faustulus may also, according to Plutarch's narrative, have been the servant originally charged with exposing the twins (*Rom.* 3.5). In any event, Faustulus, the rescuer and nurturer of Romulus and Remus, is under no uncertainty as to the twins' identity. On hearing of Remus' arrest, he goes to Romulus, "clearly informing him about his birth," *saphōs didaxas peri tēs geneseōs* (8.1). He then takes the trough, which he had evidently been saving for such a contingency, to show to Numitor as proof of the twins' identity. As if Faustulus' own testimony were not enough, it is confirmed by a guard who happened to have been among those who first exposed the twins and recognizes the trough that Faustulus attempts to smuggle in to Numitor (8.1–3). Thus the twins' identity is established through no act on their own part, and not only on the basis of implausible coincidences but on the basis of compelling material evidence as well. The significance of that evidence is confirmed by two independent witnesses whose testimony is further validated because they represent quite different interests—Faustulus, those of Numitor and the twins; the guard, those of Amulius.

The exact details of Dionysius' narrative differ somewhat from those of Plutarch's, but the two overlap in essentials and make the same point: Romulus' descent from the royal dynasty that had controlled Latium since the arrival of Aeneas and his Trojans is established for all to see by clear and irrefutable proofs. According to Dionysius, Faustulus, the rescuer and nurturer of Romulus and Remus, is not certain of their identity with the

---

14. Cf. Plut. *Rom.* 6.3; Dion. Hal. 1.79.10, 81.3.

twins who were exposed by Amulius' orders, although he does suspect it (Dion. Hal. 1.80.3). Similarly, Numitor is led by Remus' account of his exposure and upbringing only to suspect the truth of his identity, although he is sufficiently confident in his suspicions (or sufficiently opportunistic) to engage Remus' assistance as though he were in fact his grandson (1.81.4–82.1). Subsequently, Remus' story of his exposure and upbringing is confirmed by Romulus, whose words, we are told, "were received gladly by those who wished to believe and did not need many proofs in order to trust," τοῖς δὲ βουλομένοις τε καὶ οὐ πολλῶν ἵνα πιστεύσειαν τεκμηρίων δεομένοις καθ' ἡδονὰς τὸ λεγόμενον (1.82.2). Nonetheless, proofs are forthcoming. As in Plutarch's narrative, so here Faustulus appears with the trough in which the royal twins had been exposed, and he is discovered by the guard who had been among those who exposed the twins and who now recognizes this token of their identity (1.82.5).

All this is quite different from what we find in Livy's narrative. References to inherited qualities are only faintly echoed. There, after Numitor's attention has been called to the parallels between Romulus and Remus and the twins whom Amulius had exposed, he is struck also by Remus' "far from servile character itself," *ipsam minime seruilem indolem* (1.5.6), but, as the narrative has already informed us, the twins got their "strength of body and spirit" from their hard work tending their flocks at home and in the fields and by hunting (1.4.8–9). Similarly, Livy mentions no token that might prove the twins' identity beyond a doubt. Nor is there any certain witness of the twins' exposure to confirm their identities. There is no question (as there is in Plutarch's narrative) that the Faustulus who rescued the twins might also have been the servant who exposed them. Faustulus himself suspects the twins' identities, but the narrative makes clear that his suspicions are not certainties. They are motivated by "hope," *spes* (1.5.5), and based only on his knowledge that royal twins had been exposed at the time when he discovered Romulus and Remus.

For his part, Numitor, as we have seen, is struck by the appearance and bearing of the captured Remus and, on hearing that he is one of twins, by the similarity of his age with that of the twins who had been exposed. By further questioning, "he reached the point, finally, that he was not at all far from acknowledging [or recognizing—the ambiguity of *agnoscere* cannot be resolved in this context] Remus," *eo demum peruenit ut haud procul esset quin Remum agnosceret* (1.5.6). Significantly, however, Numitor does not actually reach the point of acknowledging or recognizing Remus. Does that mean that he guesses Remus' identity but is not certain of it? Readers are left to guess. The certainty is that Numitor does *not* acknowledge or recognize

Remus and that, at this point in the narrative, the identity of the twins has not been established.

How, then, in Livy's narrative does Romulus come to be accepted as Numitor's true grandson? Not through any external confirmation or recognition. Rather, his identity is accepted only *after* and *because* of his own successful self-assertion. Romulus attacks Amulius apparently on his own initiative. Numitor's support is implicit in a notice that Remus comes to Romulus' aid with "another band of men gathered from Numitor's house," *a domo Numitoris alia comparata manu adiuuat Remus* (1.5.7), and Numitor certainly joins in by summoning the Alban youth to take the citadel "during the first confusion," *inter primum tumultum* (1.6.1). Still, it is only *after* Amulius has been assassinated and *after* Numitor sees the twins approach him with congratulations (*postquam iuuenes perpetrata caede pergere ad se gratulantes uidit*) that anyone for the first time actually affirms the identity of Romulus and Remus as Numitor's grandsons: "[Numitor] at once convened an assembly and revealed his brother's crimes against himself, the origin of his grandsons, the circumstances of their birth and upbringing, how they were identified, and, finally, the murder of the tyrant and that he himself was responsible for it," *extemplo aduocato concilio scelera in se fratris, originem nepotum, ut geniti, ut educati, ut cogniti essent, caedem deinceps tyranni seque eius auctorem ostendit* (1.6.1). All this is quite extraordinary in light of the foregoing narrative, for, as we have seen, the initiative for the assassination of Amulius lay with Romulus, and at no time prior to the appearance of the successful assassins was Numitor reported to have come to a certain recognition of the twins. If Numitor now accepts responsibility for the assassination of Amulius and acknowledges the twins as his grandsons, it is both because it suits his own interests to do so and because the twins have themselves laid claim to their ancestry by acknowledging Numitor's position and by presenting themselves—as they approach him with congratulations—as supporters of his rule rather than as contenders for it. But this is only possible because the resourceful attack on Amulius initiated by Romulus has been successful. It is Romulus' own actions rather than the testimony of witnesses or the proof of evidence that establish his place in the royal line descended from Aeneas.

Even after their acknowledgment, however, Livy's narrative minimizes the twins' dependence on Numitor and continues to emphasize their own initiative and resourcefulness. Livy reports the decision to leave Alba Longa and found a new city as the twins' own (1.6.3). Romulus' choice of site reflects a determination to return to the source of his strength, the environment that formed him: "He fortified the Palatine first of all, where he had himself been brought up," *Palatium primum, in quo ipse erat educatus, muniit*

(1.7.3). Numitor provides the twins with no special assistance on their venture.[15] The narrative accounts for their followers only obliquely with the assertion that "there was an excess multitude of Albans and Latins," *supererat multitudo Albanorum Latinorumque* (1.6.3). This account of the twins' followers tacitly anticipates explicit descriptions of them as a motley crowd— like their leader himself, refugees from the margins of society.[16]

But Romulus' isolation, his self-sufficiency, and his self-creation are most clearly marked in the initial acts of founding his city and the accompanying dispute with his twin. What began as a joint venture becomes a rivalry: competition for divine sanction, the right to give his own name to his city, and the right to rule with *imperium* lead to the famous augury in which Remus is the first to sight birds of omen, but Romulus soon afterwards sees more (1.7.1). The result is a dilemma. The twins' claims are evenly matched; there is no way to decide between them. Neither Romulus nor Remus appeals to any religious authority. Each can appeal only to his own followers, and they, predictably, support their respective leaders (1.7.1–3). In the end, the question is settled only by the murder of Remus and by the success of Romulus and his city. Like the story of Romulus' ancestry, the omens acquire their meaning only in retrospect, as a consequence of Romulus' determination: divine will is ambiguous; it is human action that is decisive. Within the context of the previous narrative this episode confirms the characterization of Romulus as one who makes his own destiny.

---

15. Contrast Dion. Hal. 1.85.1–3, where Numitor first conceives the idea that the twins should found a new city as a way of ridding his own of potentially troublesome elements, assigns the twins the territory for their city, and outfits them with money, arms, and supplies.

16. Livy 1.8.1, 8.6; 2.1.4; and contrast Dionysius (1.85.3), who acknowledges that Romulus' and Remus' followers were a mixed bunch, but insists that they included men prominent among the most powerful members of Alba and descendants of the noblest Trojans; contrast also his extended argument (1.89.1–2.2.4) that Rome was from the first a Greek city (1.89.1) and the people who first settled there were descended from the Greeks, a barbarian admixture coming only later (1.89.3). On Dionysius' ideology, see Emilio Gabba, *Dionysius and the History of Archaic Rome,* Sather Classical Lectures 56 (Berkeley: University of California Press, 1991); id., "Political and Cultural Aspects of the Classicistic Revival in the Augustan Age," *Classical Antiquity* 1 (1982): 43–65; id., "La 'storia di Roma arcaica' di Dionigi d'Alicarnasso," *ANRW* 2.30.1 (1982), pp. 799–816, with references to numerous other related articles by Gabba; François Hartog, "Rome et la Grèce: Les choix de Denys d'Halicarnasse," in Έλλη-νισμος, *Quelques jalons pour une histoire de l'identité grecque,* ed. S. Said, Université des sciences humaines de Strasbourg, Travaux du centre de recherche sur le proche-orient et la Grèce antiques 11 (Leiden: E. J. Brill, 1991), pp. 149–67; C. Schultze, "Dionysius of Halicarnassus and His Audience," in *Past Perspectives,* ed. I. S. Moxon, J. D. Smart, and A. J. Woodman (Cambridge: Cambridge University Press, 1986), pp. 121–41.

The murder of Remus is the final affirmation of Romulus' legitimacy. It completes Romulus' movement toward self-sufficiency, establishes his capacity to defend his city, and marks complete personal identification with the city as a particular source of Rome's strength. Livy's narrative briefly acknowledges uncertainty about the exact circumstances of Remus' death but explicitly identifies his murder by Romulus as the "more common version," *uolgatior fama* (1.7.2), and elaborates that version by attributing to Romulus a telling exclamation.[17] As Remus leaps over Rome's unfinished walls in mockery, Romulus, according to Livy, strikes him dead with the words "So perish, then, whoever else will jump over my walls," *Sic deinde, quicumque alius transiliet moenia mea* (1.7.2). In the face of Remus' provocation, the same Romulus who had once rescued his brother now denies any special status to kinship. To challenge Romulus' city is to challenge Romulus himself, "whoever," *quicumque*, one is. Romulus is the rightful founder of this city, then, because he has shown beyond dispute both the unqualified determination and the ability to make his claims prevail.

One of Romulus' first acts as ruler of his new city will be to affirm his own allegiance to the principle that heroism should be understood not as the source but rather as the product of virtue. As already noted, the only Greek ritual that Romulus incorporates into his city is the cult of the hero Hercules (all other rites introduced by Romulus are in accordance with native, Alban ritual; see 1.7.3, 15).[18] This anomalous decision is attributed not to Hercules' divinity but rather to the fact that Romulus was "even then a promoter of the immortality begotten of virtue to which his own destiny was leading him," *iam tum immortalitatis uirtute partae ad quam eum sua fata ducebant fautor* (1.7.15).

II

Thus far I have sought to establish two main points. First, Livy's representation of Romulus as a self-sufficient, human hero whose particular source of excellence lies in the austerity of his rustic origins is systematic. Second—a

---

17. Dionysius suppresses altogether the story that Romulus himself murdered Remus, and, indeed, insists upon Romulus' inconsolable grief at Remus' death by an unknown hand (1.87.2–3; see also 1.88.1). Plutarch acknowledges this version of Remus' death but also offers the alternative that one Celer was the murderer and implies further that the scuffle in which Remus died was so confused that the identification of his slayer could never have been certain (*Rom.* 10.2, 34.1 = *Comparison of Theseus and Romulus* 5.1).

18. See Chapter 1, section 8.

more tacit suggestion—the characteristic emphasis of Livy's account of Romulus is distinctive, if not unique: it was achieved by discounting or minimizing some traditional elements and stressing others. Comparisons with the only other sustained narratives of Romulus' life that are extant, those of Dionysius of Halicarnassus and Plutarch, helped to clarify further the nature and extent of Livy's distinctiveness. At this juncture I would like to point out that the distinguishing emphasis of Livy's account was especially pertinent to at least three prominent themes in the ideology of his Roman contemporaries. The first is the notion that the Romans were a self-made people who surpassed Hellenistic peoples in morality, practical wisdom, and warfare.[19] Closely related to this idea is a second notion, that the Romans were superior not in spite of but precisely because of their apparent cultural backwardness: the simple austerity of their rustic traditions fostered a strength of character that the literary sophistication of the Hellenes could not equal. A further variation of these two themes, constituting a third, arose as the consequence of the appropriation of the first two themes by *noui homines,* who argued that precisely because they were self-made they were closer to the traditional source of Roman excellence than contemporary *nobiles* were, and in fact embodied the very qualities on which the ancestors of the Roman *nobilitas* had based their original claims to distinction and privilege.[20]

These three closely related themes, engaged implicitly in Livy's representation of Romulus, are developed explicitly elsewhere in his work. I have already, for example, called attention to the passage in the preface where the author insists that whatever the truth of Romulus' paternity, it was the Romans' own achievements that justified their claim to divine ancestry. The connection between Roman virtue and the austere simplicity of rustic life is reaffirmed in the well-known critique of a tradition that attributed Numa's wisdom to Pythagorean teaching (1.18.1–4).[21] After an uncharacteristically

---

19. I survey the first two themes in *Virgil's "Georgics": A New Interpretation* (Berkeley: University of California Press, 1980), pp. 1–63. For a more extensive survey of Roman attitudes toward the Greeks, see Nikos Petrocheilos, *Roman Attitudes to the Greeks,* Vivliotheke Sophias N. Saripolou 25 (Athens: National and Capodistrian University of Athens, Faculty of Arts, 1974).

20. D. C. Earl, *The Political Thought of Sallust* (Amsterdam: Adolf M. Hakkert, 1966), pp. 34–35; T. P. Wiseman, *New Men in the Roman Senate* (London: Oxford University Press, 1971), chap. 5, pt. 3 ("The Ideology of *Novitas*"), pp. 107–16.

21. Livy's critique is closely paralleled in Cic. *Rep.* 2.15.28, which characterizes the belief that Numa was a disciple of Pythagoras as one heard "often," *saepe,* from elders and as "generally believed," *uulgo existimari* (and cf. *Tusc.* 1.16.38). Dionysius acknowledges the question about a relationship between Numa and Pythagoras and professes himself unable to reach a conclusion on the matter, although his presentation of the issues seems to favor the

polemical argument demonstrating that Numa and Pythagoras could not possibly have been contemporaries, Livy concludes: "Therefore I think rather that his mind was governed by virtues because of his own disposition and was educated not so much by foreign arts as by the stern and austere discipline of the old Sabines; no race has ever been more uncorrupted," *Suopte igitur ingenio temperatum animum uirtutibus fuisse opinor magis instructumque non tam peregrinis artibus quam disciplina tetrica ac tristi ueterum Sabinorum, quo genere nullum quondam incorruptius fuit* (1.18.4).

Similarly, the idea that the kings of Rome provided a precedent for recognizing the qualifications of "new men" is developed explicitly in Livy's narrative of the struggle of the orders. There, in a striking anachronism, the plebeian tribune, Canuleius, protests the exclusion of plebeians from political office by a general appeal to the example of "the best of the kings, new men," *optimis regum, nouis hominibus* (4.3.17). Canuleius goes on to evoke the example of Servius Tullius in language that is particularly notewor-thy because it applies almost exactly to the earlier representation of Romulus as well: "Don't you believe what you've heard people say, that . . . Servius Tullius, . . . born of a captive woman from Corniculum, with no father, his mother a slave, held the kingship through his natural abilities, his excellence?" *Enunquam creditis fando auditum esse . . . Ser. Tullium . . . captiua Corniculana natum, patre nullo, matre serua, ingenio, uirtute regnum tenuisse?* (4.3.10–12).[22] The references here to *ingenium* and *uirtus* recall the arguments of *noui homines* such as Cicero that they were no different from the founders of the *nobilitas* who had won their positions of respect at Rome on the basis of

---

negative view (2.59.1–4). Plutarch likewise acknowledges the difficulty of the question but in the end gives the impression of favoring the view that Numa and Pythagoras were acquainted (*Num.* 1; 8.5–10; 14.4; 22.2–5). For a review of the ancient traditions about Numa and his relationship (or nonrelationship) with Pythagoras and a reconstruction of how the story of their relationship came about, see Emilio Gabba, "Considerazioni sulla tradizione letteraria sulle origini della repubblica," in *Les origines de la République romaine,* Entretiens sur l'antiquité classique 13 (Vandoeuvres-Genève: Fondation Hardt, 1966), pp. 154–64.

22. Compare Servius' lack of ancestry with that of Republican *noui homines* such as Cicero, who characterized himself as a *homo se ortus,* "a man risen from himself," in contrast to the *nobiles,* whose entrance halls displayed prominently the busts of their distinguished ancestors (Cic. *Planc.* 67; *Phil.* 6.17), and who regarded Pompey's political success as all the more laudable because he was "a man known only for himself, without any commendation of ancestors," *homo se cognitus sine ulla commendatione maiorum* (*Brut.* 96). Ogilvie, p. 535, *ad* Livy 4.3.17, observes: "The whole passage with its emphasis on the virtues of the *novus homo* might easily have been penned by Cicero."

their own talent and virtue, not birth.[23] The characterization of Rome's "best kings" as *noui homines,* then, provides the strongest kind of sanction for the new men's arguments. Such explicit evocations of language and themes from contemporary ideology reinforce the implicit ideological pertinence of Livy's narrative about the life and achievements of Romulus.

III

The interpretation of Romulus and Rome that I have surveyed in Livy's narrative, however, is in many ways problematic. It contains unresolved tensions and contradictions that call into question the coherence not only of the narrative but, more important, of the values and attitudes that underlie it. In what follows I argue that problematic aspects of Livy's foundation narrative are sometimes created, at other times exacerbated, by his systematic emphasis on Romulus as radically self-created. Of course, any claim must necessarily be problematic on at least one level, inasmuch as it implies alternative possibilities:[24] one cannot argue, for example, that Romulus was distinguished for the human qualities nurtured by his rigorous upbringing—in any event it would make no sense to do so—without some awareness that alternative representations of his character are possible. To make that argument, therefore, is to acknowledge, if only tacitly, the existence of opposing claims.

As we have seen, some of those alternatives are acknowledged within Livy's own narrative on those occasions when the narrator explicitly distances himself from traditional elements that would credit Romulus with divine parentage or would attribute his survival to supernatural interventions. To assert that we need not accept Mars' role in the story or need not take it literally, or to attribute the story of the twins' suckling by a she-wolf to anonymous (and implicitly unreliable) *fama* is inevitably to call attention to those alternative ways of explaining Romulus' extraordinary destiny. In fact, to do so calls attention to the paradox that Romulus' human self-sufficiency is credited with results so extraordinary that they have been popularly con-

---

23. The ideological positions of *nobiles* and *noui homines* vis-à-vis each other are summarized in Wiseman, *New Men,* pp. 107–16. See also Earl, esp. pp. 34–35.

24. On the problematic nature of all assertions, deconstructionists have simply claimed as a central and universal principle what students of history and literature have regularly accepted in specific contexts. See, for example, Barbara Levick: "Indeed, the fragility of the Tiberian claim is exposed by the very themes used to advance it: to proclaim *concordia* was to acknowledge that opposition existed" (*Tiberius the Politician* [London: Croom Helm, 1976], p. 86).

ceived as the consequences of superhuman agency. The narrator himself exploits precisely this kind of ambiguity when he develops and dramatizes the *uolgatior fama* of Remus' murder, even though he has just acknowledged the uncertainty about what actually happened in a brief and colorless notice: the rhetorical strategy that has been put forward to this point as a justification for omitting alternative versions here serves to introduce a favored version.

In Livy's narrative, then, alternative constructions are never far from the surface. Their existence becomes problematic and threatens the logical consistency of the narrative with the author's own assertion that Romulus, self-made in every other respect, nonetheless is seized by a desire for tyranny that is explicitly identified as an ancestral, an inherited, failing: "Then these plans [for Rome's future] were interrupted by an ancestral evil, the desire for tyranny. As a result, a shameful conflict arose out of a mild enough beginning," *Interuenit deinde his cogitationibus auitum malum, regni cupido atque inde foedum certamen coortum a satis miti principio* (1.6.4). In some other contexts the editorial *auitum malum* might be limited to some rather vague sense of "timeless," or "age-old," but Romulus' own family history—the efforts of Amulius, Romulus' maternal uncle, to seize *regnum* from his own brother and to kill Romulus and Remus in order to preserve it—militate against such a vague reading of *auitum malum* here. The desire that seizes Romulus may be the particular expression of a phenomenon that has recurred throughout time, but it is also the very same desire, emanating first from his maternal uncle, then from his brother and himself, that has shaped his life from the very moment of his birth.

To describe the desire of Romulus and Remus for *regnum* as an *auitum malum,* therefore, is to remind us that Romulus does after all have an ancestry, that he is not just a lowly shepherd whose character was forged by the circumstances of his upbringing. He is, we are here reminded, the descendant of kings. Even if his paternity is obscure or disputed, he nonetheless can trace his ancestry back to the hero Aeneas and ultimately to the goddess Venus. In founding their own cities, he and Remus are claiming for themselves the kingdom that should have been theirs through the natural right of succession. But the *auitum malum* that denied him his rightful kingdom is also a part of his heritage. Awareness of this raises difficult questions: Does the murder of Remus represent the enactment of a final, radical discontinuity with the past, the ultimate separation of Romulus from his family that affirms Romulus' self-creation and creates a necessary *tabula rasa* from which a new and unified community can arise? Or is it rather the reenactment and thus perpetuation of an ancestral propensity to internecine strife? Or does it represent an irresoluble dilemma, that the only way to escape *auitum malum* is to reenact it? These uncertainties call into play the ambiguity of the term *regnum* itself: will Rome, Romulus' *regnum,* be a kingdom or a tyranny?[25]

This question is sustained and developed on two distinct registers in the subsequent, second phase of the narrative, which concerns Romulus' monarchy. The first register is that of characterization. On the one hand, Livy insists upon the excellence of Romulus' acts as king and concludes, as I have already noted, that they are not inconsistent with belief in his divinity (1.15.6–7).[26] On the other hand, the narrative presents Romulus in the typical role of the tyrant, admired by the masses, resented by the aristocracy. Livy explicitly endorses the favorable assessment of Romulus' rule that "admiration for the man and the immediate terror made well known," *admiratio uiri et pauor praesens nobilitauit,* at the time of his death (1.16.4). Nonetheless he also acknowledges the following: "I suppose that there were also at the time some who alleged secretly that the king had been torn apart at the hands of the senatorial fathers; for this rumor too, although obscure, has leaked out," *Fuisse credo tum quoque aliquos qui descerptum regem patrum manibus taciti arguerent; manauit enim haec quoque sed perobscura fama* (1.16.4).[27] This report would have been very suggestive to Livy's contemporaries. For them the memory of Julius Caesar's controversial reputation, his assassination by senators, and the outpouring of popular affection at his funeral would not yet have been distant memories.

Indeed, the narrative of Romulus' death contains other elements that would have reinforced the parallel between him and Caesar. Romulus' deification is confirmed in much the same way as Julius Caesar's: the Senate interprets a celestial vision as evidence of apotheosis—an occurrence otherwise unparalleled in Roman history before Julius Caesar.[28] Indeed, parallels

25. For these two meanings of *regnum* see the *Oxford Latin Dictionary,* s.v. On *regnum* as a term of political invective during the late Republic, see Ch. Wirszubski, *Libertas as a Political Idea at Rome* (Cambridge: Cambridge University Press, 1968), pp. 23, 62–64.

26. For discussion of this passage, see section 1 above. For passages where Livy editorializes about the value of Romulus' achievements, see, for example, 1.8.6; 10.5–7. See also 1.16.1 where Livy summarizes Romulus' accomplishments as "these immortal deeds," *his immortalibus,* a phrase that Ogilvie prints *his mortalibus,* against manuscript authority.

27. Cf. 1.16.8.

28. On the unprecedented nature of Julius Caesar's apotheosis and its importance in defining the role of the Senate in the apotheoses of subsequent emperors, see pp. 71–76 of Simon Price, "From Noble Funerals to Divine Cult: The Consecration of Roman Emperors," in *Rituals of Royalty: Power and Ceremonial in Traditional Societies,* ed. David Cannadine and Simon Price (Cambridge: Cambridge University Press, 1987), pp. 56–105. See also Jane Evans, *The Art of Persuasion: Political Propaganda from Aeneas to Brutus* (Ann Arbor: University

with Caesar aside, Romulus had been a controversial figure in the late Republic, evoked more often, apparently, as the type of the tyrant than of the benign despot.[29] By acknowledging that alternative representation of Romulus, if only to deny it, Livy keeps alive the questions raised earlier by Romulus' susceptibility to *auitum malum regni cupido* and by his murder of Remus. In particular, he keeps alive the question of whether Romulus' foundation represents a radical departure from the tyranny of Amulius or its reenactment.

At this point one might argue that Livy is simply taking an honest approach to his sources, acknowledging alternatives in the tradition and then making clear his own judgment. This biographical approach, even aside from being purely speculative, cannot resolve the ambiguous nature of the narrative for several reasons. First, as already noted above, the author himself insists upon the problematic nature of the traditions about early Rome in his preface (pref. 6–7): the truth of the foundation story, he tells us there, is beyond confirmation or denial. By his own standards, therefore, the narrator's expressed preferences can have no better basis in fact than the alternatives that he rejects. Second, the ambiguities are there. As William Empson and certain reader-response critics have observed, it is impossible to reject an alternative without first having considered it; once raised, it remains part of our experience of the text.[30] Third, the narrator himself introduces judgments (that Romulus and Remus were motivated by *regni cupido* and that that desire is an *auitum malum*) that actually support the alternative tradition.

Finally, the questions raised about the nature of Romulus' foundation (that is, about the nature of Rome itself) are played out on another, less tractable register of the narrative, one that is concerned less with personal characterization of the founder than with competing representations of what constitutes the best kind of human community. The characterization of Romulus suggests judgments about the nature of Rome figuratively, through the trope of synecdoche: Romulus is especially significant inasmuch as he represents in himself the collective character of Rome. This personalization

---

of Michigan Press, 1992), pp. 91–94.

29. C. J. Classen, "Romulus in der römischen Republik," *Philologus* 106 (1962): 174–204; Evans, pp. 91–93, 102, argues that the rehabilitation of Romulus' reputation began with Julius Caesar's personal propaganda and continued under Augustus.

30. William Empson, *Seven Types of Ambiguity,* 3d ed. (London: Hogarth, 1984); Stanley Fish, "Interpreting the *Variorum,*" *Critical Inquiry* 2 (1976): 465–85, repr. in *Reader-Response Criticism,* ed. Jane P. Tompkins (Baltimore: Johns Hopkins University Press, 1980), pp. 164–84.

of ideological issues is characteristic, of course, a way in which Romans were particularly disposed to think.[31] But in Livy's narrative uncertainty about the nature of Roman civilization rests on more than simply the problematic identity of its founder. It is rooted in a fundamental uncertainty about the very nature and value of urban civilization, an uncertainty that makes itself felt in ambivalence toward the founder but also in the juxtaposition of competing and incompatible models of ideal community.

This ambivalence may be more apparent if we think of the narrative about Romulus' foundation of Rome as an example of what Hayden White, developing the literary typologies of Northrop Frye, has identified as the "Romantic mode of emplotment."[32] This mode of emplotment, in the most general terms, relates the reassertion of a utopian order over a subsequent age of corruption. This change may appear as the triumph of a timeless innocence embodied in a youthful new order over degenerate old age. From this perspective the story of Rome's foundation may be analyzed in terms of a series of oppositions:

Amulius and Numitor	*Romulus and Remus*
old order	young order
urban	rustic
central	marginal
civilized	natural
hierarchical	communal
authoritarian	egalitarian
impious	pious

31. This disposition is particularly well summarized and located in its cultural context by Daniel Selden, "*Ceveat lector:* Catullus and the Rhetoric of Performance," in *Innovations of Antiquity,* ed. Ralph Hexter and Daniel Selden (New York: Routledge, 1992), pp. 461–512: "This intense interest of writers of the later Republic in problems of characterization was part and parcel of the cult of personality that saturated Roman social thinking at every level. Other Indo-European peoples . . . tended to encode traditional politico-religious values in fantastic narratives about the cosmos, heroes, and the gods. In Italy, however, the Latin tribes projected this common heritage onto the plane of human history, which transpired largely as a sequence of exemplary individuals," pp. 493–94, n. 192; Selden refers to Georges Dumézil, *Servius et la fortune* (Paris: Gallimard, 1943), pp. 116–17; and id., *L'heritage indo-européen à Rome* (Paris: Gallimard, 1949), chap. 3 ("Maiores nostri"), pp. 115–82.

32. "The Romance is fundamentally a drama of self-identification symbolized by the hero's transcendence of the world of experience, his victory over it, and his final liberation from it. . . . It is a drama of the triumph of good over evil, of virtue over vice, of light over darkness, and of the ultimate transcendence of man over the world in which he was imprisoned by the Fall" (Hayden White, *Metahistory* [Baltimore: Johns Hopkins University Press, 1973], pp. 8–9). Although White here uses the specifically Christian imagery of the Fall, his essential

The narrative pits the older generation of Amulius and Numitor against the younger generation of Romulus and Remus. The corruption of the older generation is marked both by the misuse of power and by the weakness that makes such misuse possible: Amulius violates the respect due both to a father's authority and to seniority by usurping Numitor's rightful position (1.3.10); he compounds this act of filial impiety and injustice by the murder of Numitor's son and the sequestration of his daughter as a vestal virgin. Standing in opposition to Amulius' injustice and Numitor's weakness are the twins, who, with strength of body and spirit derived from their way of life, maintain good order in their pastoral world, hunting down wild beasts and robbers alike. While their band of rustic confederates grows, the robbers become increasingly hard-pressed and ultimately must turn to treachery and to the city for help (1.5.3). Numitor himself is helpless to oppose Amulius until he wins the support of the youthful twins; they avenge the injustice done to him and restore him to his rightful place. In the world of this story, then, violence and disorder originate at the seat of authority in the civilized center, the city (to which even the rustic robbers turn for support and revenge, when they are hard-pressed by the twins); order, the rectification of injustice, comes from the social and physical margins, from the twins, who, having been brought up by a herdsman (and probable slave) and his wife (a possible prostitute), make their livelihood in the countryside by the primitive and borderland occupations of hunting and herding.

This general contrast between the two worlds of city and country is marked by several specific contrasts as well. A particular sign of Amulius' corruption is his cynical manipulation of religious institutions, his appointment of Numitor's daughter as a vestal virgin in order to prevent her from continuing Numitor's line. Similarly, the robbers who capture Remus and turn him over for punishment do so by ambushing him while he is (piously) engaged in celebrating the Lupercalia. In contrast to these cynical exploitations of religious institutions and occasions, the countryside offers the Lupercalia and the twins' participation in it. Similarly, in contrast to the city, where authority is centralized and hierarchical, there is no sign of social or political hierarchy in the countryside; Livy's narrative does not even identify

---

point concerns the opposition between utopian innocence and degeneration—an opposition, I shall argue below, that is developed in Livy's narrative by the characterization of the twins' shepherd community in terms that Livy's readers would have associated with Golden Age and Stoic idealism. For further elaborations of the Romantic mode and its analytic possibilities, see Fredric Jameson, *The Political Unconscious: Narrative as a Socially Symbolic Act* (Ithaca, N.Y.: Cornell University Press, 1981), esp. pp. 68–74 and 107–13.

the twins as leaders of their rustic companions.[33] Rather there is sharing and a concern for the common welfare that suggest the social ideal of the Stoics and evoke an important aspect of Golden Age society as it had been characterized in the literature familiar to Livy's contemporaries.[34] The band of youths with whom Romulus and Remus associate divide among the shepherds the booty that they recover from the robbers and come together as a growing "herd," *grex,* to share both the serious and the trivial aspects of their lives: "they shared their booty with them and as the herd of youths

33. As a kind of corollary of this, the narrative does not present the robbers who capture Remus at the Lupercalia as singling out the twins for attack. Rather the robbers plan their attack simply against those who are engaged in the celebration (*huic deditis ludicro,* 1.5.3): Remus happens to get captured; Romulus is able to fight his way free. Contrast Plutarch (*Rom.* 6.3–4), who depicts a hierarchy in which the twins are superior to the other rustics, and Romulus is superior to Remus.

34. For communalism in Stoic thought, see Cicero: "But since, . . . as it pleases the Stoics, what grows on the earth is created for the use of humans, and humans have been generated for the sake of humans so that they can benefit each other mutually among themselves, we ought to follow nature's lead in this, to contribute common advantages to the common good through the exchange of services and obligations," *Sed quoniam . . . ut placet Stoicis, quae in terris gignantur, ad usum hominum omnia creari, homines autem hominum causa esse generatos, ut ipsi inter se aliis alii prodesse possent, in hoc naturam debemus ducem sequi, communes utilitates in medium afferre mutatione officiorum* (*Off.* 1.22). For communalism as a feature of the Golden Age, see Virgil:

> ante Iouem nulli subigebant arua coloni:
> ne signari quidem aut partiri limite campum
> fas erat; in medium quaerebant, ipsaque tellus
> omnia liberius nullo poscente ferebat.
>
> (G. 1.125–28)

> Before Jupiter no farmers worked ploughlands:
> It was against religion even to mark or divide the field;
> they sought for the common good, and the earth itself
> bore all more freely without being asked.

See also Virgil's description of the bees' utopian society:

> uenturaeque hiemis memores aestate laborem
> experiuntur et in medium quaesita reponunt.
> (G. 4.156–57)

> Mindful of the coming winter, they expend effort in summer,
> and return what they have sought to the common store.

Nothing in Dionysius or Plutarch suggests the kind of communal egalitarianism that characterizes the society of young herdsmen to which Romulus and Remus belong in Livy.

grew day by day joined with them in their activities, both serious and trivial," *pastoribusque rapta diuidere et cum his crescente in dies grege iuuenum seria ac iocos celebrare* (1.4.9). This undifferentiated, unorganized society is in turn part of a more general contrast between a world that is not only primitive but "natural" and the civilization that is implicit in the political organization of the city, with its central meeting places, its social institutions, its rulers with their retinues, and its history. The twins' story, then, celebrates the triumph of a kind of primitive innocence over civilized corruption.

But it is a paradoxical triumph at best, for its culmination, the act that finally valorizes the twins and their pastoral innocence, is not the displacement of civilization by the morally superior society in which they grew up. Rather, the admirable way of life that shapes the twins is valued, is in fact the subject of the narrator's attention, not for its own sake but only because it serves as a means to renew and perpetuate the old order. Romulus' *auitum malum*, his *regni cupido*, is, then, expressed not just in the reenactment of fraternal strife but more broadly and more fundamentally in the re-creation of civilization. He forsakes the way of life that made him strong, leaves the countryside, and founds a city of which he is king. His city, like Amulius' Alba Longa, becomes a locus of power and authority: among Romulus' first acts is the walling of his city. To this center he draws "a whole crowd without distinction, whether free or slave," *turba omnis sine discrimine, liber an seruus esset* (1.8.6), but he immediately organizes this undifferentiated mass into an increasingly differentiated social and political hierarchy. This process begins with his own assumption of the symbols and instruments of authority (designed to awe the "rustic class of men," *generi hominum agresti*, 1.8.1, who inhabited Rome), continues with the creation of the politically privileged *patres* (1.8.7), and ends after the union of Roman and Sabine peoples with division of the Quirites into *curiae* and the creation of three centuries of knights (1.13.6–8).

And just as Amulius manipulated state religion in order to secure his rule, so also does Romulus. He founds his city on the basis of an augural interpretation for which the only authority is his own subsequent success; he feigns divine communion to rally his troops when he encourages them, "as though he perceived that his prayers had been answered," *ueluti si sensisset auditas preces* (1.12.7); he creates a religious celebration as an occasion to abduct the Sabine women (1.9.6–10). All this is consistent with a view of Romulus' *regnum* as tyranny. Seen in narrative context, then, Romulus was reestablishing the older order of Amulius and Numitor. Viewed from the perspective of Livy's contemporaries, he could also be understood as establishing the old order of the monarchy, one whose eventual abolition and replacement by elected officials was to mark the beginning of *libertas* at Rome.[35] Romulus' monarchy appears, after all, to be not the triumph of the new over the old but rather a reaffirmation of the old and a betrayal of the new, as the analysis below shows:

Amulius and Numitor	*Romulus and Remus*	*Romulus*
old order	young order	old order (regal period)
urban	rustic	urban
central	marginal	central
civilized	natural	civilized
hierarchical	communal	hierarchical
authoritarian	egalitarian	authoritarian
impious	pious	impious

This interpretation of Romulus' rule is suppressed in Livy's narrative. The narrator intervenes on several occasions to call attention explicitly to the efficacy of Romulus' policies, most notably but not only in the passage where he concludes that Romulus' achievements were consistent with divine origin and the divinity ascribed to him after his death.[36] In fact, given the initial contrast between the twins and Amulius and Numitor, such editorial interventions are essential if the reader is to judge Romulus' acts of foundation favorably. Without them, the logic of the preference for rustic or primitive culture over civilization (implicit in the foregoing contrast between the corrupt monarchy of Amulius and Numitor and the innocent life of the twins) suggests the very different interpretation of Romulus' rule sketched above.

The authorial interventions—with their assurances that what might otherwise have seemed to be negative qualities or conditions according to the preceding narrative must now be perceived as positive—require, then, that the reader reassess his or her interpretation of the preceding narrative. In other words, accepting the narrator's explicit valuation of Romulus' achievements as king requires the reader to reassess the immediately preceding characterization of primitive life. If civilization as embodied in an urban monarchy is now a good thing (in fact, the essential basis of Rome's future greatness), then the primitive existence of the twins must be lacking in some essential respects. We still understand the narrative in terms of a

35. See Livy 2.1.1.
36. See section 1 and n. 26 above.

progression from an old order that is flawed to a new, more vital order, but the substance of those orders has been reversed. Instead of the displacement of an older corrupt urban monarchy by a younger, vital communalism, the reader is unexpectedly confronted by the displacement of what now must appear to be an older anarchy by a younger, more vital monarchy. The following schema shows how the movement from the world of the twins to Romulus' urban monarchy involves the reevaluation and reinterpretation of the two political and cultural models that are proposed in the narrative:

Amulius and Numitor	Twins	Twins	Romulus
	(from the perspective of Amulius' kingdom)	(from the perspective of Romulus' kingdom)	
old order	young order	old order	new order
central	marginal	marginal	central
urban	rustic	rustic	urban
civilized	natural	primitive	civilized
hierarchical	communal	anarchic	hierarchical
authoritarian	egalitarian	anarchic	authoritarian
impious	pious	barbaric[37]	pious

37. The attitude of Livy's contemporaries toward the Lupercalia seems to have been ambiguous, so that their view of it as barbaric or venerable would depend largely on the context in which it was viewed. In the *Fasti,* for example, Ovid gives two explanations for the Luperci's nakedness. One (*Fast.* 3.303-58) is based on a comic opposition between civilization and primitive naïveté. In this version Faunus is attracted by the finery and elegance of a young woman as she travels through the countryside with Hercules, but mistakenly attempts to seduce Hercules when he sneaks up on the couple during their sleep, since the young woman and Hercules had exchanged clothes; in anger, embarrassment, and frustration, Faunus decrees that his worshippers shall henceforth go naked. Ovid follows this account with another (*Fast.* 3.359-80) that attributes the Luperci's nakedness rather to the primitive vigor of the first celebrants: Romulus and his companions were exercising naked while priests prepared a sacrifice to Faunus; when they heard that robbers were driving off their flocks, the young men rushed off without taking time to dress. The nakedness of the Luperci commemorates their subsequent victory. A similar ambivalence is expressed rather differently by Cicero at *Cael.* 11.26. There he casts scorn on the behavior of a contemporary Lupercus by supposing that it reflects the brotherhood's primitive origins: "Nor indeed does it disturb me that he [Caelius' accuser] said that Caelius was a fellow member with him in the brotherhood of the Luperci—a savage brotherhood indeed, that of the true Luperci, one obviously of herdsmen and rustics whose wilderness association was formed before civilization and laws. Indeed, members of the brotherhood not only inform on each other but even call attention

The ambiguity that is created in Livy's narrative, the ambivalence that is implied by the narrator's shift of perspectives, is confirmed in the author's introduction to book 2. There he apologizes for the monarchical tradition begun by Romulus on the grounds that it was a necessary stage in the socialization that prepared Rome's motley population for the responsibilities of *libertas*:

> Quid enim futurum fuit, si illa pastorum conuenarumque plebs, transfuga ex suis populis, sub tutela inuiolati templi aut libertatem aut certe impunitatem adepta, soluta regio metu agitari coepta esset tribuniciis procellis, et in aliena urbe cum patribus serere certamina, priusquam pignera coniugum ac liberorum caritasque ipsius soli, cui longo tempore adsuescitur, animos eorum consociasset? (2.1.4–5)

> For what would have happened if that plebeian population, shepherds and immigrants, refugees from their own peoples, had attained freedom, or at least impunity, under the protection of inviolable sanctuary, and, released from fear of a king, had begun to be stirred up by tribunes' stormings and, in a city not their own, had begun to sow conflicts with the fathers before the guarantees of wives and children and affection for the soil itself (to which one becomes accustomed by the long passage of time) had joined their minds?

This is a particularly revealing passage in the context of the present discussion. Not only does it confirm the author's ambivalence toward the monarchy. It also confirms that judgments of the monarchy and of primitive society are interrelated and that the revaluation of one necessarily requires revaluation of the other: justification of the monarchy here depends on a reconception of preurban society not as communal and egalitarian but rather as anarchic and unstable. But this, as we have seen, is not the picture of it that was evoked in the description of the twins' early life in the countryside.

---

to the brotherhood in making their accusations, as though afraid that anyone would not know about it," *Neque vero illud me commovet quod sibi in Lupercis sodalem esse Caelium dixit. Fera quaedam sodalitas et plane pastoricia atque agrestis germanorum Lupercorum, quorum coitio illa silvestris ante est instituta quam humanitas atque leges, si quidem non modo nomina deferunt inter se sodales sed etiam commemorant sodalitatem in accusando, ut ne quis id forte nesciat timere videantur!* In Livy's own narrative ambivalence is expressed in juxtaposed references to the Lupercalia either as a frivolous or a sacred event: "[Evander] had instituted the ceremony . . . so that naked young men ran playfully and wantonly worshipping Lycaean Pan," *sollemne . . . instituisse . . . ut nudi iuuenes Lycaeum Pan uenerantes per lusum atque lasciuiam currerent*; "while they were engaged in this diversion, the robbers ambushed them, since the ceremony was well known," *huic dediti ludicro cum sollemne notum esset insidiatos . . . latrones* (1.5.2–3).

The kinds of contradictions generated by Livy's narrative hardly arise in the narratives of Dionysius and Plutarch, because in each, and in similar ways, the contrast between the world of the twins and that of the city is qualified and mediated in such a way that the city retains a formative role throughout the twins' lives. Plutarch says that he favors a version of the tradition according to which Numitor knew about the twins' rescue from the first, and he follows this assertion by acknowledging the views of those who believed that the twins were sent to Gabii for a formal education befitting "ones who were wellborn," *tous eu gegonotas* (*Rom.* 6.2). Even the twins' rustic activities are recast to fit an aristocratic mold. Having called attention to the signs of "noble birth," *eugeneia,* in the twins' stature and bearing (6.3), Plutarch then reports that

ἐχρῶντο δὲ διαίταις καὶ διατριβαῖς ἐλευθερίοις, οὐ τὴν σχολὴν ἐλευθέριον ἡγούμενοι καὶ τὴν ἀπονίαν, ἀλλὰ γυμνάσια καὶ θήρας καὶ δρόμους καὶ τὸ λῃστὰς ἀλέξασθαι καὶ κλῶπας ἑλεῖν καὶ βίας ἐξελέσθαι τοὺς ἀδικουμένους. (*Rom.* 6.5)

they occupied themselves in the way of life and the pastimes of free men, not regarding leisure and ease as the occupation of a free man but rather gymnastics and hunting and footraces and repelling robbers and catching thieves and rescuing the victims of injustice from violence.

I have translated *gymnasia* "gymnastics" here to capture the associations of the Greek, which might be translated in the present context simply as "physical exercise" but can also refer to "gymnasia" and therefore has strong associations with an institution that was the very center of Greek culture in the Hellenistic world.[38] One can easily imagine hunting and footraces as natural occupations of the countryside, but they also, of course, epitomized the life of the aristocrat.[39] In context, the entire passage, then, suggests that

---

38. The most forceful accounts of the gymnasium's central role in Hellenistic culture with which I am familiar are studies of the conflict between Judaism and Hellenism, since the role of the gymnasium as a center for the perpetuation and acquisition of Hellenic or Hellenistic culture made it a particular focus of controversy. See Edouard Will and Claude Orrieux, *Ioudaïsmos-Hellènismos: Essai sur le judaïsme judéen à l'époque hellénistique* (Nancy: Presses universitaires de Nancy, 1986), pp. 97–175 and esp. pp. 120–24. See also Alexander Tscherikover, *Hellenistic Civilization and the Jews* (New York: Atheneum, 1970), pp. 161–74.

39. J. Aymard, *Essai sur les chasses romaines,* Bibliothèque des écoles française d'Athènes et de Rome 171 (Paris: E. de Boccard, 1951). For the hunt as a debased, but no less aristocratic, pastime in the late Republic, see also Ronald Syme, *Sallust,* Sather Classical Lectures 33 (Berkeley: University of California, 1964), p. 44.

the twins' life in the countryside represented a spontaneous and, perhaps, untutored expression of their aristocratic heritage as much as or more than it did rustic simplicity. From this perspective their suppression of robbers and thieves takes on the character of a kind of noblesse oblige.

The overshadowing of the twins' independence and of the country by the city is even more marked in Dionysius' narrative. In the rationalizing account reported there, Numitor is responsible for replacing the twins with substitutes even before they are exposed, for sending the twins to Gabii to receive a thoroughly Greek education, and even for initiating the arrest of Remus as part of a plot to avenge himself on Amulius (Dion. Hal. 1.84.1–8). Even the version that is not rationalized and that Dionysius favors places Numitor and the city (or town) of Alba Longa at the center of the action and makes Numitor's initiative, not Romulus', the decisive motivating force. When Remus is presented to Numitor in person, Numitor recognizes him but does not let on the full extent of his knowledge (1.81.4–82.1). Thereafter, he directs the entire operation that leads to the overthrow of Amulius: he gets Remus to swear to support his claim to the throne, saying: "I will be in charge of the right time for action," *tēs men praxeōs . . . ton kairon egō tamieusomai* (1.82.1); he summons Romulus to town by messenger; he exhorts the twins to bravery; and he brings along "a band, and not a small one," *cheira ouk oligēn* (1.83.3) of his own followers. Only then are the conspirators joined by men from the country. Even the idea that the twins should found a city of their own comes from Numitor, after he has been restored to his own kingdom (1.85.1–3). In fact, as François Hartog has shown, their project has all the characteristics of a traditional Greek colonization (*apoikia*).[40] So, here too, no significant contrast between city and country is established, because the twins' rustic upbringing (if it existed at all) never emerges as an independent, let alone decisive, influence on the course of events.

In Livy, as we have seen, the contrast between city and country, civilized and pastoral life, is essentially unmediated, inasmuch as the links that tie the twins to the city and to their ancestry have been radically broken. The initiative that leads to the vindication of Numitor and of the twins comes not from Numitor but from Romulus himself. The prowess and resourcefulness that Romulus displays in planning and carrying out the attack against Amulius are not presented as expressions of a divine nature. Insofar as they are made intelligible by the narrative, it is implicitly, but clearly, as an extension of the qualities that the twins had developed in their rugged life

40. See Hartog, pp. 149–67, esp. p. 162.

of herding, hunting, and self-defense in the countryside. Thus the contrast between city and country is sharply defined, and the dependence of the former on the latter is unambiguous. As a consequence, questions raised by the necessity of redefining their relationship in light of Romulus' monarchy are also sharply defined: we are left with two contradictory ideals of community. This unresolved conflict of ideals provides a perspective from which to understand the contradictions and ambiguities in Livy's representation of the founder: if the narrative is unclear whether we should regard Romulus as a champion of self-sufficiency or of a heroic inheritance, as perpetuator of rustic innocence or of urban corruption, as king or tyrant, it is in part because the narrative is informed by a more basic confusion about the nature and value of civilization itself.

IV

Just as Livy's representation of Romulus engages important aspects of Roman collective self-representation, so the kinds of questions that emerge from his narrative have strikingly close parallels in the ideological questions that arose in the political lives of his contemporaries. Many of the questions that Livy's narrative raises about Romulus as founder and leader, for example, are analogous to those raised by Augustus' ambiguous position as both destroyer and restorer of the Republic. Just as Romulus' murder of Remus raised the question whether internecine violence and the elimination of equals were unavoidable and necessary conditions for the foundation of Rome, so one could reasonably debate whether Augustus' role in the proscriptions of the forties and in the civil wars was or was not essential for the restoration or survival of the state.

Similarly, just as Romulus might be evoked as a precedent either for the "new man" or for aristocratic tradition, so a closely related ambiguity was embodied in Augustus' own self-representation. On the one hand, Augustus insisted that his political powers and honors were legitimate, because they had been bestowed upon him by the people (or their representatives, the Senate) in willing recognition of actual achievements. In his *Res gestae,* although it was produced late in his life, Augustus develops this theme systematically. The only reference in that document to his distinguished ancestry and its divine origins is oblique at best, in his identification of himself as the avenger of his "parent," *parentem* (*RG* 2). Rather his focus is aggressively constitutional. He enumerates extensively and with great specificity his impressive record of political achievements, military victories, and public benefactions. These form the context for understanding the numerous offices and honors that were bestowed upon him. Together this record of achievement and public recognition serve to explain the exceptional *auctoritas* that Augustus identifies as the real basis of his political power and influence in the concluding sections of the document (*RG* 34.3). Such a justification of Augustus' position in terms of traditional Republican constitutionality tended naturally to represent Augustus as embodying the virtues of self-sufficiency and self-creation that characterized the *nouus homo.*

On the other hand, even as Augustus insisted that he was no more than the *princeps,* the first among political equals, he identified himself in art, architecture, and coinage as *diui filius,* "son of the divine Julius," and he aggressively propagated the tradition of an aristocratic ancestry that could be traced back not only to Aeneas, father of the Roman people, but, through Aeneas, to the goddess Venus. He accepted cult worship as a god everywhere in the Roman Empire except in Rome itself.[41]

Augustus attempted persistently to reconcile the essential contradiction between such representations of himself as self-made statesman and as divinity. This effort to achieve a harmonious blend of opposites is perhaps most readily illustrated in the famous Augustus of the Prima Porta. That statue brings together the accoutrements and gestural vocabulary of a Roman general (the cloak, spear, and the extended arm of a general commanding his followers' attention) with elements that call attention to Augustus' divinity (a cupid, who recalls his own and Augustus' common descent from Venus; bare feet, evocative of heroic nudity; a contrapposto stance, familiar from classical Greek representations of gods and heroes).[42] The neoclassical serenity of this statue and its aesthetic success have encouraged interpreters to regard

41. Simon Price, *Rituals and Power: The Roman Imperial Cult in Asia Minor* (Cambridge: Cambridge University Press, 1984), p. 84.

42. Augustus' extended arm may have its origins in Hellenistic representations of Alexander the Great; see, for example, the bronze statue of Alexander with radiate crown at the Glyptothek, Munich, illustrated in Klaus Vierneisel and Paul Zanker, eds., *Die Bildnisse des Augustus: Herrscherbild und Politik im kaiserlichen Rom* (Munich: Glyptothek und Museums für Abgüsse klassischer Bildwerke, 1979), p. 76. It had become a regular part of Roman gestural vocabulary long before Augustus; see, for example, the headless marble statue of a Roman general whose cuirass shows Medusa, trophies, and victory figures, dated about 70 B.C.E., at the Glyptothek, Munich, and the "Arringatore" bronze, dated to the early first century B.C.E., no. 249 Museo archeologico, Florence, illustrated in George M. A. Hanfmann, *Roman Art* (New York: W. W. Norton, 1975), pl. 48 and descriptive text on pp. 81–82. The iconographic value of this gesture as a sign for Roman generalship is attested clearly by a *sestertius* that presents Caligula in the Prima Porta pose accompanied by the legend *ADLOCUT*[io] *COH*[ortium] or *COH*[ortis]; see *BMCRE*, no. 33, p. 151, and pl. 28.3.

its message as unproblematic.[43] Another interpretation might be that it combines elements whose interrelationship was always precarious and frequently in danger of slipping out of balance.[44] The essential precariousness and instability of the balance that Augustus sought is well illustrated in the contrasting failures of his first two successors: the unsuccessful efforts of Tiberius to respect the Senate's Republican prerogatives during the earlier part of his reign and the hostility provoked by belief that Caligula wanted to be worshipped as a living god at Rome.[45] It is not unreasonable, in fact, to suspect that different elements of the Prima Porta statue must have evoked widely divergent responses from different classes and individuals, just as Augustus' person evoked both adulation and attempts at assassination—the very same ambivalence that marks the characterization of Romulus in Livy's narrative.

Just as the self-representation of Augustus is characterized by many of the same ambiguities and inconsistencies that arose in Livy's representation of Romulus, so the problems of Augustan self-presentation take place within and are entangled with larger uncertainties and contradictions about the nature of civilization. Rome of the late Republic and early Augustan age was undergoing radical changes, some of which invited comparison with

43. For an appreciation of the statue's harmony, see Paul J. Zanker, *The Power of Images in the Age of Augustus,* trans. Alan Shapiro (Ann Arbor: University of Michigan Press, 1989), pp. 98–99 for the face, pp. 245–52 for the stance as a successful and "typical compromise between Hellenistic/Late Republican traditions and the values of the new Rome."

44. Andrew Wallace-Hadrill, "Rome's Cultural Revolution," review of *The Power of Images in the Age of Augustus,* by Paul J. Zanker, *Journal of Roman Studies* 79 (1989): 157–64, does not comment specifically on Zanker's appreciation of the Prima Porta statue, but two of his general criticisms of Zanker's argument are relevant, I believe, to that appreciation. On pp. 162–63 ("3. The Reception of the Image"), Wallace-Hadrill suggests that the reception of Augustus' program of self-presentation must have been more varied and complex than Zanker acknowledges; on pp. 163–64 ("4. Hellenization") he argues that Zanker overstates the extent to which the Augustan age saw the resolution of conflicts between Greek and Roman aesthetics that were apparent in the styles and values of the late Republic.

45. For Tiberius, see Levick, p. 114: "We have seen that Tiberius inherited a political paradox from his predecessor, and that he tried to deal with it by educating his masters [the Senate] into independence. His failure to do so was due to faults on both sides"; and more generally, see chaps. 6 and 7 ("The Policy of the Princeps" and "Policy in Practice: The Senate and Its Members," respectively), pp. 82–115. For Caligula, see Price, "Noble Funerals," p. 85. He observes that "emperors such as Gaius, Domitian, and Commodus who tried [or were suspected of trying] to get divine honors for themselves in the city of Rome itself met with hostility and death." For a recent, conservative review of the question of how to interpret reports of Caligula's efforts to have himself worshipped as a god at Rome, see Anthony A. Barrett, *Caligula* (New Haven: Yale University Press, 1989), pp. 140–53.

the transition from pastoral primitivism to urban sophistication that Livy ascribed to the earliest period of Rome's foundation. The late Republic and early Augustan age was a period of intense development of the city of Rome. Augustus is supposed to have boasted that he had found Rome a city of brick and left it a city of marble (Suet. *Aug.* 28). In fact, the previous generation had already seen the beginnings of what was to constitute a virtual transformation of the city. The elder Pliny recalled that the house of Lucullus was the most luxurious of its day (78 B.C.E.), but that thirty-five years later there were a hundred even grander at Rome (*HN* 36.109).

This kind of change in the private sphere was paralleled in the public. It amounted to more than just an increase in the scale and quantity of building. The last years of the Republic and the first of the Augustan age saw the introduction of major innovations in city planning and architecture.[46] In 55 B.C.E. Pompey the Great dedicated the first permanent theater at Rome, a monumental structure modeled on the theater of Mytilene and dedicated as a temple to his patron divinity, Venus Victrix. Attached to it were lavish gardens where Pompey displayed statues taken from the fourteen states that he had conquered during his campaigns in the East.[47] In 46 B.C.E. Julius Caesar dedicated his Forum Julium, the first of what was to be a succession of imperial fora. The year 29 B.C.E. saw the dedication of a temple to the Divine Julius in the Forum Romanum and next to it what was most likely the first marble arch in the city, celebrating Octavian's victory at Actium.[48] These structures were part of a general reorganization of the Forum Romanum as a "showplace of the *gens Julia*."[49] That same year the amphitheater of Statilius Taurus was completed, the first permanent amphitheater at Rome. By 25 B.C.E. Agrippa had completed the first major public bathing facilities in the city, a complex that eventually included not only the baths proper but also public gardens and a large artificial lake whose water was supplied by a new aqueduct, the Aqua Virgo (completed in 19 B.C.E.).

46. For the dates and basic information about the examples cited, see S. B. Platner and T. Ashby, *A Topographical Dictionary of Ancient Rome* (Oxford: Oxford University Press, 1929) s.vv.

47. By 17 B.C.E. the second major theater in Rome, the theater of Marcellus, was ready to use (although not yet formally dedicated). It was located in a space that Julius Caesar had cleared for a theater that he had planned but did not live to build.

48. On the character of previous arches in Rome, see Axel Boëthius, *Etruscan and Early Roman Architecture,* 2d ed. (New York: Penguin, 1978), p. 149.

49. This characterization is Zanker's, p. 79; see also pp. 80–82 in Zanker.

This surge of development in both the private and the public sectors amounted to more than a simple refurbishing of the city. It constituted a fundamental reconception of what the city was and meant inasmuch as the most conspicuous building activity, both private and public, was largely the responsibility of the political "dynasts" of the age and was, in fact, an expression of their competition for political preeminence. The political leaders who were most conspicuously responsible for the transformation of the city in this period were the leading men, who, it was widely feared, might make themselves kings. Thus the development of Rome into not just an important civic center but rather the center of empire and one of the great monuments of the known world was directly connected with the destabilization of the Republic and the ever more clearly emerging possibility of monarchy or tyranny.[50]

This transformation of the *urbs* set the stage for a new conceptualization of the countryside and rustic life as well. As Rome itself became more distinctly urban, more clearly the locus not only of imperial but also of personal power, the Italian countryside became more clearly and persistently imagined as the repository of alternative possibilities. Two prominent contrasts between city and country recur in the literature of this period. First, country life was portrayed as relatively simple and innocent, by comparison with city life, although rustic simplicity and innocence might be conceived of in many different forms and might also be evoked only to be criticized.[51] Second, the country was conceived of as the locus for egalitarian community, in contrast to the city as a locus of power focused on a single individual.[52]

---

50. In a recent review of the city's development during the late Republic and Augustan age, Diane Favro, "*Pater urbis:* Augustus as City Father of Rome," *Journal of the Society of Architectural Historians* 50 (1992): 61–84, reaches a very similar conclusion from a somewhat different perspective: "By the late 40s B.C., the city on the Tiber was undergoing several simultaneous transformations. As individuals gained unprecedented political power, they began to see themselves as synonymous with the state. Rome became their personal charge. . . . As the Romans forged an empire, Rome was transformed from one city among a confederation into a capital" (p. 71).

51. On idealization of the countryside in late Republican and early Augustan literature, see Eleanor Winsor Leach, *Vergil's "Eclogues": Landscapes of Experience* (Ithaca, N.Y.: Cornell University Press, 1974), pp. 25–69; on the multiplicity of attitudes toward the countryside and rustic life and their political implications in this period, see Miles, *Virgil's "Georgics,"* pp. 1–63.

52. Such a conception of the countryside was not a timeless element of Roman *mentalité*. Contrast, for example, Pliny's enthusiasm not for the conviviality but rather for the solitude of his country estate at Laurentum: "I converse only with myself and with my little books," *mecum tantum et cum libellis loquor* (*Ep.* 1.9).

We have seen both of these themes in the contrast between the imagined world of the twins' upbringing and the conceptualizations of urban culture that precede and follow it in Livy's narrative.

Examples of the contrast between rustic egalitarianism and urban autocracy are common in the literature of Livy's near contemporaries. One has only to think of Virgil's first *Eclogue,* where the city is identified as the source of violence that disrupts the order and stability of the country and also is the home of the young savior on whose power and beneficence the country shepherds depend. By contrast, the countryside is the locus for song that celebrates and creates community.[53] Or one can turn to the poetry of Horace, where the companionable and unassuming egalitarianism that prevails in the countryside contrasts sharply with the pervasive magnetism of personal power that is dramatized in Horace's vignettes of city life. Contrast, for example, Horace's evocation of the congenial society at his Sabine farm (*Sat.* 2.6) with his caricature of the boor who wants an introduction to the powerful Maecenas (*Sat.* 1.9) or of the curious who pester him for news of the *princeps* and his policies (*Sat.* 2.6.47–58).[54] From this perspective, as Michael O'Loughlin has pointed out, Horace is able in *Satire* 1.5.1–2 to transform even a significant political mission (the embassy of statesmen that issued in the Treaty of Brundisium) into an occasion for fellowship that is made possible by "departure from the great world of the city [*Egressum magna me . . . Roma*] to the limitations of rural simplicity [*Aricia . . . hospito modica*]." [55] I am well aware that for Horace place is less important than state of mind (e.g., *Epist.* 1.7). Nonetheless, his poems consistently convey a sense of the city as subversive, the country as supportive of peace of mind: "Small things become a small person: royal Rome does not please me now, / but rather Tibur, free from distraction, or peaceful Tarentum," *paruum parua decent: mihi iam non regia Roma, / sed uacuum Tibur placet aut imbelle Tarentum* (*Epist.* 1.7.44–45).[56]

---

53. Paul J. Alpers, *The Singer of the "Eclogues"* (Berkeley: University of California Press, 1979).

54. For his most general and sustained contrast between city and country, see *Sat.* 2.6.

55. *The Garlands of Repose: The Literary Celebration of Civic and Retired Leisure* (Chicago: University of Chicago Press, 1978), p. 90; and for fuller discussion see pp. 76–154. M. J. McGann, "The Three Worlds of Horace's 'Satires,' " in *Horace,* ed. C. D. N. Costa (London: Routledge and Kegan Paul, 1973), pp. 59–93, argues for a hierarchy of sociability in Horace's *Satires* that extends from "the mundane world of opportunism and competition," up to the circle of Maecenas, and finally to the society exemplified at Horace's Sabine farm (pp. 66–71).

56. As O'Loughlin, p. 118, elegantly puts it, "Nothing is more important in a consideration of Horace than to see that the importance of the rural scene was not the special charm of a particularly picturesque location but its effect on the poet's inner reality—its faculty, as he

Cicero's dialogues on philosophical and rhetorical subjects are invariably presented as a congenial exchange of views among speakers who engage each other with mutual respect and graciousness, even though their views may differ sharply. Most often these dialogues are set unambiguously at a country villa.[57] In his *De republica,* for example, Cicero makes a country villa the setting for discussion among statesmen of an earlier age who exemplify the spirit of Republicanism in the combination of *gravitas* and cordiality with which they exchange views.[58] But the exigencies of their subject, the ideal state, lead to increasing focus on the idea of a statesman whose central role and personal influence strain the limits of Republican *libertas* (*Rep.* 5). The circumstances in which Cicero composed most of his dialogues form an ironic parallel to their congenial villa settings: most were written while Cicero himself was in imposed or voluntary exile from a city and politics that were dominated by Julius Caesar.[59]

Such exploitation of the country as a repository for Republican values helped to create or reinforce a sense that the opposition between Republic and monarchy was not just a constitutional issue but one that also involved competing models of civilization itself, as it might be exemplified variously in the city and in one or another model of rustic life. That is, opposition between city and country helped to define the choice between Republic and monarchy as an issue not just of constitutional formalities but of life-style and of cultural values as well. It further complicated that choice by identifying the city as the locus of power, the country as the locus of virtue. The statesman, therefore, had somehow to combine two contrary modes of life, city sophistication with country simplicity. Implicit in the contrasts

---

said in an epistle to the keeper of his farm, of returning him to himself, *mihi me reddentis* (*Epistles* 1.14.1)."

57. E.g., *Tusculanae disputationes, De fato, Academica, De divinatione, De legibus, De oratore.*

58. I base my claim that the dialogue is presented as taking place at a rural villa on the reference to the interlocutors' seating themselves in the sunniest part of a "small meadow," *pratuli* (*Rep.* 1.12.18), a setting that seems inconsistent with an urban *domus.* Similarly, the *Brutus* should probably be understood as having a rural setting because of Cicero's reference there to himself as strolling in his *xystus,* an open-air space used for walks and exercise (*Brut.* 10).

59. Cicero wrote his *De republica* and *De legibus* in 54 and 51 B.C.E., respectively, while Roman politics was controlled by the "Triumvirate" of Caesar, Pompey, and (until his death in 53 B.C.E.) Crassus. During this time Cicero's political appearances were very limited, and chiefly in reluctant response to pressure from the triumvirs. The great majority of Cicero's philosophical works were written during an extraordinarily brief period, that of his complete withdrawal from politics after the death of his daughter Tullia in February of 45 B.C.E. to the delivery of his *First Philippic* before the Senate in September of 44 B.C.E. This period began during Julius Caesar's extended dictatorship and ended six months after his assassination.

between urban and country virtues are competing models of community, and of civilization itself. To be a true Roman, to combine power and virtue, sophistication and simplicity, urbanity and rusticity, had come to imply simultaneously endorsing divergent notions of civilization.

We can get some glimpse of the consequent pressures, I believe, in the contrast between Augustus' extravagant self-advertisement in such monuments as his mausoleum and the ostentatious simplicity of his personal lifestyle: the modesty of his home on the Palatine, his insistence that his daughter and granddaughter be taught the traditional women's tasks of spinning and weaving; his diligent attention to the education of his grandsons in fulfillment of a father's traditional responsibilities.[60]

The contrast between rustic and urban was problematic in another way as well. The wealth, power, and values of the city had penetrated the countryside to such an extent that extremes in the hierarchy of power were perhaps even more marked there than in the city, ranging from the proprietors of large luxury villas to the chain gangs imprisoned in *ergastula*. Varro's advice to hire neighboring farmers for agricultural work that might be unhealthy or overburdensome for one's own slaves is a telling commentary on the debasement of the Italian peasantry (*Rust.* 1.17.3), as is Sallust's characterization of farming and hunting as "servile occupations," *servilibus officiis* (*Cat.* 4.1). In the larger course of Roman history, as in Augustus' own personal career, the balance was loaded in favor of monarchy, the city, urban sophistication; the experiments in imagining pastoral and rustic alternatives that characterized the literature of the late Republic and early Augustan age soon passed. But the composition of Livy's first pentad (however we date it) falls within the period when such experiments were at their height, when Roman identity comprised virtues and attributes that contemporary thought derived from competing ideals of urban and rustic community.[61]

V

The foregoing discussion invites several general conclusions. The first is that the kinds of contradictions to which I have called attention in Livy's narrative

60. Augustus' mausoleum: Zanker figs. 58 and 59, p. 74; Zanker offers a dramatic measure of its scale in comparison with other mausolea in antiquity; the modesty of Augustus' Palatine home: Suet. *Aug.* 72.1; the education of his daughter and granddaughter: Suet. *Aug.* 64.2; the education of his grandsons: Suet. *Aug.* 64.3.

61. For the dating of the first pentad, see above, Chapter 2, note 49.

are not the consequence of mindlessness, of the arbitrary and unthinking use of sources that Quellenforschung, for example, has so often ascribed to Livy. Quite the reverse. They can be related directly to Livy's systematic emphasis on the theme of a radical self-sufficiency that is not based on inherited qualities and is developed not in spite of but rather because of the harsh requirements for survival on the social and economic margins of civilization. Contradictions accompany the development of this theme, as we have seen, in part because it does not fit well with certain essential aspects of received tradition about Romulus and his foundation of Rome. This incompatibility brings us back to Gananath Obeyesekere's claim, quoted at the opening of this chapter, that myth provokes debate and embodies the sedimentation of past debates,[62] for Livy's emphasis on radical self-sufficiency does not import an entirely new theme into the story of Rome's foundation; rather it is achieved, as we have seen, through selective suppression or elaboration of elements that already existed.

Furthermore, Livy's systematic emphasis on radical self-sufficiency itself represents a specific position in a debate among his Roman contemporaries about the distinctive nature and origin of Rome's greatness and about the conditions that should determine membership among Rome's ruling aristocracy. We may better appreciate the very particular kinds of interests served by Livy's narrative by noting briefly how the different narrative emphases of Dionysius and Plutarch correspond to these authors' respective circumstances. The narrative of Livy's Greek contemporary Dionysius is addressed in Greek to an audience of Hellenistic aristocrats. Its tone throughout is apologetic: it presents Rome and Romans as worthy to rule.[63] As we have seen, it readily accepts the idea of the semidivine founding hero that Livy's narrative so persistently seeks to undercut but that was well established in the Hellenistic world. Rather than emphasizing differences between Rome

---

62. Obeyesekere goes on to observe: "Not all myths have this character, though. For example, myths that are intimately tied to the ethnic identity of a group may resist debate, as do myths that constitute the axiomatic bases of a religious or political order" (*The Work of Culture,* The Lewis Henry Morgan Lectures, 1982 [Chicago: University of Chicago Press, 1990] p. 133), but he later qualifies that assertion, as follows: "I pointed out that myths that centrally define the origin and ethnic identity of a group permit little debate, *unless people face serious problems pertaining to their origin and identity as a consequence of historical vicissitudes"* (p. 147; my emphasis). Obeyesekere's qualification obviously applies to Romans of the late Republic and early Augustan age, who were in the process of (re)defining their relation to Hellenistic culture and at the same time were having to come to terms with the demise of one political order and the emergence of a new one.

63. On Dionysius' audience and his bias, see above, note 16.

and the world of the Hellenistic aristocracies, Dionysius' narrative stresses similarities—above all, the urban rather than rustic character of Rome and its founder.

Plutarch, a century and a half later, wrote in an age when not only the city but the government of Rome was becoming cosmopolitan, when the cultural distinction between Italians and Romans had ceased to be significant and Italians' access to political office was no longer a pressing issue, when urbanity was accepted unequivocally as the hallmark of Roman civilization, when debate about the nature and role of rustic life had ceased to be a central concern, when monarchy was firmly established as the form of Roman government, and the emperor's divinity was accepted in cult every-where in the Empire outside of the city itself. Plutarch himself came from a Greek aristocracy whose members had long been accustomed to trace their origins to gods and heroes, and many of whom, like himself, had by now become fully integrated into the highest levels of Roman society and government.

Plutarch's position as an insider in a Greco-Roman aristocracy, generally disposed to favor positive over hostile traditions about the subjects of his biographies, is reflected in his narrative.[64] Plutarch acknowledges some hostile elements in the tradition about Romulus (his murder of Remus), but he does not favor them. In his comparison between Theseus and Romulus, he insists upon Romulus' superiority, insofar as "he rose to power from the smallest beginnings. For [Romulus and Remus], although known as slaves and children of swineherds, freed almost all the Latins before becoming free themselves," τὸ μικροτάτας λαβεῖν ἀρχὰς ἐπὶ τὰ πράγματα. Δοῦλοι γὰρ δὴ καὶ συφορβῶν παῖδες ὀνομαζόμενοι, πρὶν ἐλεύθεροι γενέ-σθαι, πάντας ὀλίγου δεῖν ἠλευθέρωσαν Λατίνους (*Rom.* 33.1–2). In the *Life* itself, however, while acknowledging that some authors regard the prevailing version of Romulus' early life with skepticism, Plutarch himself explicitly endorses the "fabulous and fictitious," *to dramatikon kai plasmatōdes,* in it on the grounds that "there is no need to be distrustful, seeing of what great works chance is the demiurge and reflecting that the affairs of the Romans would not have reached such a degree of power if their origin,

64. On Plutarch's social position and its relation to his narrative, see C. P. Jones, *Plutarch and Rome* (Oxford: Clarendon Press, 1971), esp. chaps. 5, 6, 10, 11, and 13; on Plutarch's general tendency to favor positive traditions, see p. 94. Plutarch's lack of interest in the issues surrounding Italian new men may have been further reinforced by a general tendency to reduce Roman politics to conflicts between the Senate and the people: C. B. R. Pelling, "Plutarch and Roman Politics," in *Past Perspectives,* ed. I. S. Moxon, J. D. Smart, and A. J. Woodman (Cambridge: Cambridge University Press, 1986), pp. 159–87.

instead of being divine, was neither great nor exceptional," οὐ δεῖ δ᾽ ἀπιστεῖν, τὴν τύχην ὁρῶντας οἵων ποιημάτων δημιουργός ἐστι, καὶ τὰ ῾Ρωμαίων πράγματα λογιζομένους, ὡς οὐκ ἂν ἐνταῦθα προΰβη δυνάμεως, μὴ θείαν τιν᾽ ἀρχὴν λαβόντα καὶ μηδὲν μέγα μηδὲ παράδοξον ἔχουσαν (*Rom.* 8.9). He emphasizes Romulus' inherited excellence (his *eugeneia*) and (as observed above) identifies the city rather than the country as the formative influence in the development of Rome and its founder. By contrast, then, the kinds of tensions and inconsistencies that I have noted in Livy's narrative can be understood as a consequence of adapting to the interests of a particular political and ideological situation, a tradition that was itself already complex. These tensions are the more apparent because Livy's narrative explicitly acknowledges divergent elements within the tradition of Rome's foundation, even as it privileges some of them over others.[65] From this complex relation between narrative theme and traditional material, there arise, I have argued, kinds of problems that have much in common with those implicit in Augustus' self-presentation.

The tensions and inconsistencies that characterize Livy's narrative may also be understood as a problem of rhetorical figuration. As founder, Romulus functions synecdochically: the Romans' collective identity is embodied and dramatized in Romulus' individual character. It may well be that it was useful to understand the Roman state as distinctively self-sufficient and self-created in its relation to other communities. But modern scholarship has concluded, rightly I believe, that a state is by its very definition complex and hierarchical.[66] To identify such a collectivity with an individual whose unique source of strength comes from the margins of society outside the

---

65. Such explicit acknowledgment of diversity within tradition is common to the legendary/historical narratives that I have been considering. However, it is not to be taken for granted. Rambaud, pp. 21–30, points out that Cicero had established a clear precedent for suppressing aspects of tradition that were not consistent with his own aggressively rationalizing analysis of Rome's foundation in *Rep.* 2.1–40. It should be clear, however, that I do not agree that Rambaud's contrast between Cicero and Livy, particularly in their respective inclusion or exclusion of the *fabulosa*, constitutes evidence that Livy "wanted to demonstrate in Rome's growth the accomplishment of a providential design . . . of an historical fatality established from the outset by the gods" (p. 29).

66. Paul Wheatley, *Pivot of the Four Quarters: A Preliminary Inquiry into the Origins and Character of the Ancient Chinese City* (Chicago: University of Chicago Press, 1971), p. xviii, concludes from a comparative study of early cities that urbanism is in each case characterized by "a particular set of functionally integrated institutions . . . devised . . . to mediate the transformation of relatively egalitarian, ascriptive, kin-structured groups into socially stratified, politically organized, territorially based societies."

city involves a paradox at best, since the state, then, is associated with an individual whose presence within a political hierarchy must be problematic. The distinctive virtues of the state come to be identified with qualities that originate outside the state and that are themselves dependent on conditions to which the state is antithetical. Thus to the extent that Romulus succeeds with his foundation, he destroys the very conditions that explain his extraordinary powers; to the extent that his state grows and concentrates power within itself, it leaves behind its distinctive source of excellence.[67]

This process, as we have seen, happens very rapidly in Livy's narrative, and our perception of it is sharpened by the idealization of the twins' life before it is marred by *regni cupido*. The preceding discussion suggests at least two ways to understand this idealization of pre-Roman country life. It may be understood, in part, as a response by the Roman aristocracy to dramatic changes for which they were themselves responsible, that is, as an expression of what has recently been characterized as "imperialist nostalgia."[68] Such nostalgia is a means of denying responsibility for the destruction of previous values and ways of life by asserting sorrow and respect for what has been lost. It is familiar today not just as the longing of colonialists for the native ways that their own colonization has destroyed but also as the longing of Americans for the "simple" life of Native Americans or of the European pioneers. Inasmuch as such nostalgia is not disinterested but is motivated rather by a need to explain, justify, and demonstrate respect for the past, it encourages exaggeration of the virtues of the past.

The kind of idealization of the past that we find in Livy's narrative may also be understood as part of a larger Roman strategy to find a place for traditional values—or for values that some Romans attempted to sanction by the claim of tradition—during a period of rapid change. In this regard, idealization of the past and the idealization of country life that we find in the literature of Livy's contemporaries are complementary: the one is a temporal, the other a spatial projection of the same ideals and issues.[69] Each

67. E. Dutoit, "Thème de 'La force qui se détruit elle-même' (Hor., *Epod.* 16.2) et ses variations chez quelques auteurs latins," *Revue des études latines* 17 (1939): 365–73, surveys explicit expressions of this idea in classical Latin literature, including Livy pref. 4 (with reference also to 7.29.2), which he sees as a response specifically to the civil wars of the late Republic.

68. For this concept and a review of some recent discussions of it, see the chapter entitled "Imperialist Nostalgia," in Renato Rosaldo, *Culture and Truth* (Boston: Beacon Press, 1989), pp. 68–87.

69. On the potential complementarity of spatial and temporal projection, I am particularly indebted to Jonathan Z. Smith, *To Take Place: Toward Theory in Ritual* (Chicago: University of Chicago Press, 1987), although he develops their complementarity in a different context than I do here.

acknowledges the overpowering of "traditional" values and ways of life. Spatially, this is expressed in the representation of the city as center of power, the countryside as victim of urban exploitation or as the locus of the retired life.[70] Temporally, it is expressed in the representation of the displacement of an earlier innocence by a suspect sophistication. Thus the movement from the life shared by Romulus and Remus before they were overcome by *regni cupido* to the foundation of Romulus' city looks forward to the later development from Republic to decline that is anticipated in the author's preface.

Similarly, both temporal and spatial projection acknowledge ambivalence toward the alternatives that they embrace. Spatially, this ambivalence is expressed in the professed longing of city dwellers for country life and their simultaneous exportation of urban tastes and life-styles into country villas. Temporally, it is expressed in the shifting of perspectives over time. In Livy's narrative, as we have seen, we move from rustic primitivism as the model for society to Romulus' city, then to a retrospective assessment of Romulus' monarchy as a compromise necessitated by rustic anarchy.

Even though we can understand these two modes, the one spatial, the other temporal, as two different ways of projecting the same ambiguous and conflicting values, we should also recognize that they have somewhat different consequences. The spatial projection of ideological conflicts offers choice, or at least the illusion of choice, even if each choice has its own limitations: Horace, as I have noted, sets the power of the city against the serenity and virtue of the countryside. Temporal projection invites different responses. Displacement of one alternative by another creates pressure for judgment: are things getting better or worse? It encourages location of the present on a continuum of change. It postpones choice among alternatives to the future, and, in so doing, it also admits the question of whether choice, in fact, will be possible.

In Livy this question is implicit in the studied ambiguity of the author's preface. There the author observes:

> Ceterum aut me amor negotii suscepti fallit, aut nulla umquam res publica nec maior nec sanctior nec bonis exemplis ditior fuit, nec in quam ciuitatem tam serae auaritia luxuriaque immigrauerint, nec ubi tantus ac tam diu paupertati ac parsimoniae honos fuerit. . . . nuper diuitiae auaritiam et

---

70. Note especially O'Loughlin, p. 90, and for fuller discussion see pp. 76–154.

abundantes uoluptates desiderium per luxum atque libidinem pereundi perdendique omnia inuexere. (pref. 11–12)

> For the rest, either my love for the task that I have undertaken deceives me, or no state has ever been greater or more upright or richer in good examples; nor have greed and luxury moved into any state so late; nor have poverty and parsimony enjoyed such great respect anywhere and for so long. . . . Recently, wealth has brought in greed, and abundant pleasures have brought a longing for self-destruction and the destruction of everything through wanton overindulgence.

These statements indicate clearly that, in the author's view, Rome has, or at least may have, lost the sources of its unique preeminence and succumbed at last to the vices that have sapped the integrity and vitality of all previous powers, leading to the successive displacement of old powers by new. But that is a matter yet to be decided finally. The invasion of wealth and pleasures is a recent phenomenon. The use of perfect tenses for the duration of Rome's exemplary character (*nec sanctior nec bonis exemplis ditior fuit*, . . . *nec ubi tantus . . . honos fuerit*), as well as for the more recent invasion of vices (*nuper . . . inuexere*), holds open the possibility that the old virtues may continue to persist alongside the new, destructive conditions. How the situation will ultimately be resolved is uncertain.

This uncertainty is further reflected in a tension between escapist and pragmatic perspectives expressed in the preface. On the one hand, the author contrasts the impatience of those interested only in contemporary affairs with the pleasure that he takes from immersing himself in a better past:

> Ego contra hoc quoque laboris praemium petam, ut me a conspectu malorum, quae nostra tot per annos uidit aetas, tantisper certe dum prisca illa tota mente repeto, auertam, omnis expers curae, quae scribentis animum, etsi non flectere a uero, sollicitum tamen efficere posset. (pref. 5)

> I, on the other hand, will also seek the following reward for my efforts, that at least so long as I devote my entire attention to those ancient matters I may turn myself from the sight of those ills that our age has witnessed for so many years and be free from every care that may cause distress, even if it could not divert the writer's attention from the truth.

This despairing attitude toward Rome's present difficulties notwithstanding, the author calls attention to his subject as one "from which you may choose for yourself and your state what to imitate and what, disgraceful both in its inception and outcome, to avoid," *inde tibi tuaeque rei publicae quod imitere capias, inde foedum inceptu, foedum exitu, quod uites* (pref. 10)—a perspective that holds out the possibility, at least, that if one is willing to learn from the past, then the ills of the present may not after all be irremediable. The concurrence of these two attitudes toward the past (as escape or as model), implying as they do two different attitudes toward the future (as irremediable or hopeful), reinforces a sense that the final questions of Roman identity are as yet fundamentally unresolved.[71] This conclusion, I hope to have shown, is the consequence of a sustained effort to develop contemporary ideological themes in a narrative of Rome's foundation and it reflects certain unavoidable contradictions inherent in the effort to adapt traditional material to contemporary ideology: for example, tensions between the ideal of the new man, with its emphasis on self-sufficiency, and associations with divine ancestry and supernatural interventions in the traditional story of Romulus. This uncertainty about Roman identity is also reflected by Livy's inclusion of elements that seem to express a willful acknowledgment of ambiguities, uncertainties, and contradictions inherent in the play among contemporary Roman ideologies: for example, Livy's references to the possibility that Romulus' rule may have been a kind of tyranny or to the twin's desire for *regnum* as an *auitum malum*. Together, then, ambiguity, uncertainty, and contradiction reflect less on Livy's failings as a thinker than they do on the depth and candor of his engagement with the prevailing ideologies of his age.

71. For a different sort of argument for narrative indeterminacy in Livy, see John Henderson, "Livy and the Invention of History," in *History as Text,* ed. Averil Cameron (Trowbridge: Duckworth, 1989), pp. 66–85.

Chapter 5

The First Roman Marriage and the Theft of the Sabine Women

Thus far I have focused exclusively on Livy. Although I have drawn comparisons with other ancient authors, I have not been concerned with alternative narratives in their own right, nor have I used other narratives to identify any of the underlying qualities that distinguish Livy's narrative. Rather, such comparisons have been in a sense incidental to my larger argument, serving primarily to clarify specific points of interpretation relating to one or another particular passage in Livy. Thus they have called attention to many individual examples of Livy's distinctiveness and originality. Their cumulative effect, however, suggests something more, that Livy's narrative is exceptional for the extent to which it engages (sometimes directly, sometimes implicitly) issues of methodology and ideology inherent in Livy's material. We have seen already, for example, how Livy grapples unsuccessfully but openly with the problem of evaluating the relation between material and oral evidence, or how within his story of Romulus he includes elements, often suppressed in other narratives, that problematize his own argument about Roman self-sufficiency and the larger contemporary ideologies that inform it.

In this chapter comparisons between Livy and other ancient authors will be our principal focus and will be developed fully. The basis of comparison will be extended still further through models from anthropology that help isolate essential cruxes in the narratives that I have chosen. This exercise will give some sense of the range of ancient responses to an ideological issue that was particularly significant for Livy and his contemporaries, the nature and function of marriage. This range of alternatives in turn provides a context within which to argue not only that Livy's narrative is complex and rich but that it is exceptionally so by the standards of other authors who concerned themselves with the same traditional material as he. This is not necessarily to argue that Livy was more radical in his vision than others. My point here is rather to show how Livy's characteristic efforts to integrate all aspects of his material into a coherent narrative, to avoid loose ends, to fill in gaps in conventional ideology, to make connections, and to offer explanations raise issues that other less ambitious narratives do not engage.

I

The story of the theft of the Sabine women occupies an important position in Roman ideology. It was closely associated with the foundation of Rome, as one expression of the daring and resourcefulness that characterized Romulus, the city's legendary founder. The story, moreover, figures prominently not only in Livy but also in the ambitious works of other major authors of antiquity who sought to provide a comprehensive interpretation of Roman character. Thus, for example, the story is included in Cicero's *De republica,* written between 54 and 51 B.C.E., during the turbulent last years of the Roman Republic. Cicero's adaptation of Plato's *Republic* locates the potentiality for an ideal state not in theoretical speculation but in specifically Roman traditions and institutions. During the following decades, under Rome's first emperor, Augustus, the story was included both in Dionysius of Halicarnassus' *Antiquitates Romanae,* an encyclopedic review of early Roman history that attempts to reveal the essence of Rome to Greek readers, and in Ovid's *Fasti,* a poetic survey of Roman religious festivals as expressions of traditional Roman values. A century and a half later, the Greek Plutarch included the story of the Sabine women in a biography of Romulus, which he paired with that of Theseus, the legendary founder of Athens. These works, spanning the critical period from the collapse of Republican government at Rome through the consolidation of the Empire, offer different versions of the theft of the Sabine women and present it as a cornerstone of Roman society.[1]

The ancient narratives associate the theft of the Sabine women explicitly with the origins, and thus with the essence, of Roman marriage.[2] Livy and Plutarch, for example, trace the origin of a specific element of traditional Roman wedding festivities, the cry "for Thalassius" (*Thalassius* in Livy's spelling, *Talasios* in Plutarch's), to the occasion of the Sabines' abduction (Livy 1.9.12; Plut. *Rom.* 15). In Cicero's *De republica* the abduction is followed by a formal marriage supervised by Romulus, although Cicero says nothing

---

1. Other, briefer mentions of the story are cited in T. P. Wiseman, "The Wife and Children of Romulus," *Classical Quarterly* 33 (1983): 445–52.

2. The passages with which the following argument is primarily concerned are Cic. *Rep.* 2.12–14; Dion. Hal. 2.30–47; Livy 1.9–1.13.8; Ov. *Fast.* 3.167–258; Plut. *Rom.* 14–19. I have chosen not to include Ovid's version of the theft in *Ars am.* 1.101ff. among my primary passages, because, even though narrated from a different perspective, it seems to me to offer essentially the same interpretation of the theft as Ovid presents in the *Fasti.* Julie Hemker, "Rape and the Founding of Rome," *Helios* n.s. 12 (1985): 41–47, has contrasted the narrative of the Sabine women in the *Ars* with that of Livy in terms that adumbrate the fuller contrast that I draw below between Livy's narrative and that of Ovid's *Fasti.*

about the nature of the ceremony in his spare narrative (*Rep.* 2.6.12). Dionysius of Halicarnassus identifies that marriage as the basis for subsequent ceremonial. He says that after the abduction, but before consummation of the marriage, Romulus assembled the Sabine women and their husbands-to-be and formally married them "according to the ancestral customs of each woman, solemnizing the marriages with a sharing of fire and water, just as they are performed down to our times" (Dion. Hal. 2.30.5–6; cf. 2.24.4–25.6).

The narratives of Livy, Ovid, and Plutarch do not report a formal wedding after the abduction.[3] Nonetheless, even though the relationship between Sabine women and Roman men begins with abduction, it ends in these narratives with a legitimate marriage. According to Livy, when the abducted women intervene between Romans and Sabines as they confront each other in the Roman Forum, the women describe their fathers as fathers-in-law (*soceri*), their abductors as sons-in-law (*generi*), their own offspring as the grandchildren of their fathers (*nepotes*) and the legitimate children (*liberi*) of their abductors (1.13.2).[4] In appealing to their fathers and abductors to cease hostilities, the women claim, successfully, that kinship and marriage ties exist between them: "if you regret the ties of marriage among you, if you regret our marriage," *si adfinitatis inter uos, si conubii piget* (1.13.3). The terminology of Livy's narrative is echoed in Plutarch (*Rom.* 19.6–7), where the Sabine women make their appeal in the name of "fathers-in-law" (*pentheroi*), "grandfathers" (*pappoi*), "kin" (*oikeioi*), and "in-laws" (*gambroi*), as well as with the ambiguous "men/husbands" (*andres*). In Ovid's narrative, moreover, the conflict between the Romans and the Sabines who seek to avenge their women's abduction is seen from the very first as one between kin; it is a prototype, in fact, for civil war. Immediately after reporting the women's abduction, Ovid continues: "The [people of] Cures swelled [with rage], as did the others who experienced the same grief. Then for the first time father-in-law bore arms against son-in-law," *Intumuere Cures et quos dolor attigit idem / tum primum generis intulit arma socer* (*Fast.* 3.201–2). The absence of any mention of a formal wedding ceremony in these narratives makes such language all the more striking and calls attention dramatically to the fact that somehow Roman abductors and their Sabine captives have

---

3. In Livy's narrative, Romulus does, however, promise the newly abducted women that they will be married (1.9.14).

4. For *liberi* not just as "children" but as originating with the more particular sense of "freeborn, legitimate children," see Émile Benveniste, *Le vocabulaire des institutions indo-européennes* (Paris: Les éditions de Minuit, 1969), vol. 1, pp. 324–25.

succeeded in constituting an actual marriage without taking part in a formal wedding ceremony.

In his analysis of Indo-European myths about marriage, Georges Dumézil understands the theft of the Sabine women as incorporating each of several types of Indo-European marriage and as epitomizing an imagined evolution in Roman tradition from abduction to *confarreatio* (a religious ceremony in which the bride was formally transferred from the authority, or *manus*, of her father to that of her husband) to *usus* (a kind of common-law marriage that nonetheless assured the husband the power of *manus* over his wife) to *coemptio* (a fictional sale of the bride to the groom, who thereby acquired legal authority over her).[5] Of these, Romulus is represented as formally instituting *confarreatio; usus* and *coemptio* are represented as evolving out of the initial theft—*usus* through the conversion of the abducted women, *coemptio* through the indemnification of the women's fathers.[6] In Dumézil's reading (based primarily on the narrative of Livy and secondarily on that of Dionysius of Halicarnassus) the theft itself represents no more than the first, but otherwise essentially incidental, element in the succession of developments that characterize the evolution of Roman marriage in the story of the Sabine women: "It is useless to insist upon the rape: . . . it conforms in all points to the *rakṣasa* mode. But it evolves rapidly."[7]

These forms of wedding also help to define the social context within which the story of the theft of the Sabine women would have been understood by Romans. Each of these three types of Roman marriage involves arrangements between male-headed households in which the bride is trans-

---

5. *Mariages indo-européens suivi de quinze questions romaines* (Paris: Payot, 1979), pp. 73–76. On the question of whether the story of the Sabine women should be understood as the vestige of an actual marriage theft, see the survey of literature in J. Poucet, *Recherches sur la légende sabine des origines de Rome*, Recueil de travaux d'histoire et de philologie ser. 4, fasc. 37 (Kinshasa: Éditions de l'Université Lovanium, 1967), pp. 171–72 n. 134.

6. Dumézil, *Mariages*, p. 76.

7. Ibid., p. 73. R. Köstler, "Raub–und Kaufehe bei den Römern," *Zeitschrift der Savigny-Stiftung für Rechtsgeschichte: Romanistische Abteilung* 65 (1947): 53–54, sees in the story of the Sabine women the memory of a time when bride theft was actually practiced in early Rome. Whether there was an original theft of Sabine women and it was preserved in Roman lore because of its cultural suggestiveness or, to the contrary, the story gradually evolved as a way of expressing values and attitudes deeply embedded in Roman society seems to me to be beyond clear resolution, and in any event to be more of antiquarian than of cultural interest. For an excellent discussion of the practice of bride theft, its functions, and attitudes toward it during the later Roman Empire, see Judith Evans-Grubbs, "Abduction Marriage in Antiquity: A Law of Constantine (*CTh* IX.24.1) and Its Social Context," *Journal of Roman Studies* 79 (1989): 59–82. I know of no study of bride theft for earlier, historical periods of Roman history.

ferred from the *manus*, "hand," or formal authority of her *pater familias* to that of her husband.[8] The most elaborate of the wedding ceremonies, *confarreatio*, reveals that, in addition to its economic and political functions (assuring the husband control of his wife, her property, and their offspring), the transfer of *manus* had a religious aspect. As Numa Denis Fustel de Coulanges long ago demonstrated, the ceremony of *confarreatio* took place in the context of a family religion that was organized around worship of ancestors in the male line.[9] The ceremony provided for the deconsecration of the bride from the religious unit comprised by her father and his agnates and her consecration into the religious unit comprised by her husband and his agnates, thus assuring that both religious units remained pure and that there would be no danger of divided loyalties within the husband's household to threaten the fullfilment of his religious responsibilities to his ancestors. In the most general terms, then, these traditional wedding ceremonies may be understood as strategies to domesticate a potentially disruptive outsider upon her incorporation into a new household.

These formalities gradually became obsolete during the last two centuries B.C.E. Nonetheless, to the extent that Roman marriages continued to be arranged among males with political, economic, or social ends primarily in mind, the general pattern of relationships expressed in the older forms of wedding persisted, even when marriages did not entail actual abduction or a formal transfer of legal guardianship from father to husband.[10] Émile Benveniste has pointed out that the perception of women's essential passivity in marriage was perpetuated in Latin idiom. In marriage, men characteristically acted upon women, while women changed their condition: a father "gives his daughter into marriage" (*filiam dare in matrimonium*); a man "leads

8. Jane F. Gardner, *Women in Roman Law and Society* (Bloomington: Indiana University Press, 1986), p. 152.

9. *The Ancient City* (Garden City, N.Y.: Doubleday, 1956), pp. 46–48; and, more recently, Gardner, p. 152.

10. See Susan Treggiari, *Roman Marriage* (Oxford: Oxford University Press, 1991), on the motives for marriage, esp. pp. 83–160; for the conditions under which women might play a part in or even initiate marriage negotiations see Susan Treggiari, "*Iam Proterva Fronte*: Matrimonial Advances by Roman Women," in *The Craft of the Ancient Historian: Essays in Honor of Chester G. Starr*, ed. J. W. Eadie and J. Ober (Lanham, Md.: University Press of America, 1985), pp. 331–52; and Jane E. Phillips, "Roman Mothers and the Lives of Their Adult Daughters," *Helios* n.s. 6 (1978): 68–80. See A. S. Gratwick, "Free or Not So Free? Wives and Daughters in the Late Roman Republic," in *Marriage and Property*, ed. Elizabeth M. Craik (Aberdeen: Aberdeen University Press, 1984), pp. 38–53, for a valuable caution against misconstruing the motivation behind the practice of marrying women *sine manu* and also against overestimating the consequences of that practice.

someone's daughter into marriage" (*alicuius filiam ducere in matrimonium*), but a woman "enters into marriage" (*ire in matrimonium*).[11]

Roman marriage as it is epitomized in the theft of the Sabine women, then, is framed by larger social and political relationships among men, and it is in terms of those male relationships that the relationship between man and woman is defined and takes on its full meaning. Accordingly, all of the major Roman sources identify social and political considerations, not personal or private, as the primary motive forces behind the theft of the Sabine women.[12] Cicero in his brief account says that the theft was motivated by the Romans' desire to "safeguard resources," *ad muniendas opes* (*Rep.* 2.12), but the other major sources are more specific. Plutarch considers two explanations: first, that Romulus planned the theft in order to provoke war with the Sabines; second, that he planned it because he regarded theft of the Sabine women as an opportunity to stabilize Roman society, both by assuring that all Romans (rich and poor) would be able to have wives and by providing an occasion for intermingling and political union (*synkraseōs kai koinōniās archēn*) between Roman and Sabine peoples (*Rom.* 14.2). Of these explanations, Plutarch favors the latter, in which the acquisition of women for unmarried Roman men is understood as a means for effecting social and political alliances. Later in his narrative, when the Sabines demand return of their daughters, Plutarch reports that the Romans not only expressed their determination to keep the Sabine women but demanded in addition that the Sabines grant them *koinōniā*, which can denote both "partnership" in a general sense and, in a specific usage, "community of marriage."[13] Dionysius of Halicarnassus acknowledges three possible motives for the theft: to make up for a shortage of women at Rome, as a pretext for war with the Sabines, as an excuse to make an alliance with the Sabines. Of these, he, like Plutarch, explicitly favors the last (Dion. Hal. 2.30.1–2, 31.1).

Livy and Ovid, too, consider multiple reasons for the theft of the Sabine women and likewise give primary emphasis to the Romans' desire to establish alliances with their neighbors. According to Livy, shortly after Romulus has succeeded not only in fortifying his city but also in attracting to it a substantial population of settlers, the otherwise flourishing community faces an unexpected crisis: "due to a dearth of women, the greatness of Rome was only going to last one generation," *penuria mulierum hominis aetatem duratura*

---

11. Benveniste, vol. 1, pp. 239–44.

12. For a slightly different analysis of the motives ascribed to the Romans by different ancient authors who narrate the theft of the Sabine women, see Poucet, *Recherches*, pp. 164–67.

13. See LSJ[9], s.v.

magnitudo erat (1.9.1). The obvious interpretation of this statement might be that the existing population could not survive without women simply because it would not be able to procreate new members. However, Livy's narrative glosses this assertion with a somewhat more complicated explanation: "inasmuch as they had neither expectation of offspring at home nor the possibility of establishing marriage rights with neighboring peoples," *quippe quibus nec domi spes prolis nec cum finitimis conubia essent* (1.9.1). Of course, it is possible to take the second part of that compound clause as a further explanation of the Romans' inability to produce offspring: "there was no hope for children at home [since there were no women there] and [no hope for children from abroad since] there was no possibility for marriage relations with neighbors." This is surely one meaning of the clause but not its only meaning. The actual expression here identifies *conubium* itself, "intermarriage between two groups of people or . . . the right to intermarry," as essential to the Romans' continued existence.[14] The Romans' subsequent plan to steal wives is attributed to their neighbors' rejection of Roman offers to establish relations of alliance and marriage, *societatem conubiumque* (1.9.3).

Ovid's narrative, similarly, understands the Romans' desire for wives in relation to their need to populate Rome and to secure effective alliances with neighbors. After sketching the modest scale of early Rome, Ovid sums up:

> iamque loco maius nomen Romanus habebat,
>   nec coniunx illi nec socer ullus erat.
> > (*Fast.* 3.187–88)

Already the Roman had a reputation greater than his territory, and he had neither wife nor any father-in-law.

In fact, in Ovid the Romans are motivated as much by wounded male pride as by practical necessity.[15] His narrator, the god Mars, continues:

> spernebant generos inopes vicinia dives,
>   et male credebar sanguinis auctor ego.
> in stabulis habitasse et oves pavisse nocebat

14. *Oxford Latin Dictionary*, s.v.

15. This aspect of their behavior is underscored by Ovid's introduction to the story. There, Mars attributes the course of events to rivalry between himself and Minerva: he claims responsibility for the events of the following narrative and offers them as a demonstration that he, the god of war, can serve the interests of peace just as well as Minerva can (*Fast.* 3.173–76).

iugeraque inculti pauca tenere soli.

. . . .

extremis dantur conubia gentibus, at quae
Romano vellet nubere, nulla fuit.

(*Fast.* 3.189–96)

Neighboring wealth spurned destitute sons-in-laws, and I was scarcely
credited as the founder of the race. It counted against the Romans that
they had lived in stables and grazed sheep, and that they possessed a few
acres of uncultivated soil. . . . Marriage rights are extended to the most
remote peoples, but there was none that wanted to marry a Roman.

From the first, then, all versions of the story are in essential agreement.
Women or wives are not objects of value in and of themselves for the
Romans, but as means to three other closely related but separate necessities:
the propagation of offspring, the contraction of alliances through marriage,
and the acknowledgment of Roman worth by neighboring peoples. Of
these, the last two consistently receive the most emphasis.

Paradoxical as it may seem, abduction of brides is not inconsistent with
these goals. Study of contemporary Cretan communities, for example, has
documented a perception that bride theft is analogous to the theft of live-
stock.[16] In both cases the immediate object of the theft is not the primary
goal but rather the means for establishing an alliance between the thief and the
relatives/owners of the stolen object.[17] In particular, such theft is perceived as
a way in which the thief may display his manhood, his resourcefulness,

16. Michael Herzfeld, *The Poetics of Manhood: Contest and Identity in a Cretan Mountain
Village* (Princeton: Princeton University Press, 1985), pp. 25, 162, 252.

17. Ibid., pp. 174–75, 180. On bride theft alone, see Michael Herzfeld, "Gender Pragmatics: Agency, Speech, and Bride-Theft in a Cretan Mountain Village," *Anthropology* 9 (1985):
25–44; and id., *Anthropology through the Looking-Glass* (Cambridge: Cambridge University
Press, 1987), p. 179. Other studies of Mediterranean societies demonstrate that bride theft
can be motivated by quite other considerations than establishment of the thief's manhood as
a means to alliance with the bride's family. It can, for example, be a means for a romantically
attracted couple to circumvent parental disapproval (i.e., a kind of elopement) or a means for
families to sanction a marriage alliance without the groom's family having to incur the expense
of a bride-price. For alternative motives for bride theft, see D. G. Bates, "Normative and
Alternative Systems of Marriage among the Yoruk of Southeastern Turkey," *Anthropological
Quarterly* 47 (1974): 270–87; M.-E. Handman, *La violence et la ruse: Hommes et femmes dans
un village grec* (La Calade: Édisud, 1983), p. 85; W. G. Lockwood, "Bride-Theft and Social
Maneuverability in Western Bosnia," *Anthropological Quarterly* 47 (1974): 288–303; P. J. Magnarella, *Tradition and Change in a Turkish Town* (New York: John Wiley and Sons, 1974),
pp. 112–18.

establish that he is someone to be reckoned with, and in this way command the recognition of individuals or family groups who might otherwise be indifferent or hostile to him.[18] When practiced against lowland farmers, it provides a means of self-assertion against the higher status enjoyed by farmers over pastoralists "in rural Greek mixed-economy communities" and serves to recast "the economic and social margin . . . as the moral center."[19] A recent proliferation of animal theft for purely monetary reasons is perceived by traditionalists in these shepherd communities as a disturbing and disgraceful perversion of values.[20]

The theft of the Sabine women clearly functions much as the bride theft and animal theft analyzed in contemporary Crete. It not only leads, in fact, to eventual alliance between Romans and the more established neighbors who formerly spurned them; in particular it is used as an opportunity by the Romans to demonstrate their claims to be taken seriously. This is most clear, of course, in the wars provoked by the theft in which the Romans convincingly demonstrate their manliness and military prowess in an impressive succession of victories. It is further emphasized in Livy's narrative, where the religious festival that gives the Romans their opportunity to abduct the Sabine women also serves as a means of continuing negotiations with their neighbors indirectly, after the neighbors have refused the Romans a formal hearing: it is an occasion for the Romans to demonstrate their qualifications as prospective husbands and allies. They use their imagination and their resources lavishly to make the festivities both "distinguished and anticipated," *claram exspectatemque* (1.9.8). Once their guests arrive, they invite them "hospitably," *hospitaliter,* to view their homes, the site of the city, its walls, and its populous civic center—efforts by which they succeed not only in distracting but also in impressing their guests (1.9.9).

The element of theft also emphasizes the passive role of women in the traditional Roman wedding: they are objects transferred from the ownership

18. Animal theft as a means of displaying manhood and of making alliances is a central theme of Herzfeld, *Poetics,* but see especially chap. 5 ("Stealing to Befriend"), pp. 163–205. The fact that bride theft rarely, if ever, takes place today in the communities that Herzfeld studies does not diminish the force of the perceived analogy with animal theft. In the context of the villagers' own concept of *simasia* ("significance" or "meaning") "any distinction between 'how the Glendiots [Herzfeld's name for the villagers of his study] tell stories' and 'what actually happened' is entirely artificial. Both the event and the narration of event are social constructions, each reinforcing the other. . . . Glendiot theory recognizes this in the conflation . . . of the concepts of *exciting event* and *story* in a single term, *istoria,* which also significantly happens to be the official term for 'history' " (p. 207).

19. Herzfeld, *Poetics,* p. 228.

20. Ibid., pp. 267–69, 224.

of one male to another. This, of course, was their formal religiolegal role in the traditional wedding ceremonies by which women were transferred from the *manus*, "hand," of their *pater familias* to that of their husband. According to Plutarch, the custom that a husband carried his bride over the threshold of her new home was a survival from this first marriage in which brides were acquired by abduction (*Rom.* 15.6), would not willingly enter a building where they were about to lose their virginity, and could only be kept in their new homes under constraint (Plut. *Quaest. Rom.* 271D). The perpetuation of such explanations for a Roman wedding custom suggests that abduction continued to express one aspect of the marriage relationship as Romans perceived it. Plutarch reinforces this point of view by including in his account of the theft a reference also to the traditional practice of parting the bride's hair with the point of a spear, an act that he interprets, again, as reflecting the first marriages, when brides were captives, won by the spear (*Rom.* 15.7).

The dominant role played by men in Roman marriage is further underscored by the explanations that both Livy and Plutarch give for the origin of the traditional wedding cry "Thalassio/Talasio." Plutarch offers three explanations (*Rom.* 15.1–5). One is that it refers to spinning and to the fact that the women will enjoy a privileged status in their new marriages, their only responsibility being to spin wool. Another explanation is that "Talasio" (for whatever reason) was the signal given by Romulus to begin the theft. But the first explanation offered by Plutarch and the one developed at greatest length by him is that the cry originated when some abductors of low status attempted, successfully, to protect their claim to a particularly attractive Sabine by calling out that they were taking her to Talasios, a young man, but one of good reputation and worth (Plut. *Rom.* 15.1–2). The marriage, Plutarch adds, was a particularly happy one. For Plutarch, then, the cry "Talasio" constitutes a good omen. Livy's narrative, on the other hand, reports only the last explanation for "Thalassio," with some modifications. His Thalassius is a young man of position; the abductors of the beautiful Sabine, his agents; Livy says nothing about the success of the resulting marriage (1.9.12). All of these etiological stories locate the origins of distinctive aspects of the marriage ceremony in the theft of the Sabine women and interpret them as recalling the original condition of Roman brides as captives. More specifically, they call attention to the women's role as prizes in male competition, to their passivity, and to their good fortune. According to the version favored by Livy and Plutarch, the repetition of the cry "Thalassio/Talasio" at Roman marriage ceremonies perpetuates a view in which every Roman bride is a prize chosen for her beauty; every groom, a distinguished young man whose good standing in the community is a shield of protection for his bride and promises a happy marriage.[21]

Thus the fact and circumstances of the Sabines' abduction exaggerate elements typical of Roman marriage, and by doing so throw them into relief. Claude Lévi-Strauss has observed that "when an exotic custom fascinates us in spite of (or on account of) its apparent singularity, it is generally because it presents us with a distorted reflection of a familiar image."[22] The story of the theft of the Sabine women does the reverse of this: it introduces an anomalous element into a familiar custom. That is, bride theft and warfare between neighboring communities function here as metaphors that offer "perspective by incongruity" through "purposive nonconventionality."[23] They make the familiar strange, making it possible to see the familiar with new eyes. The rivalry between Rome and its neighbors, for example, can be understood as a magnification of rivalry, or the potential for it, between families that are not bound by ties of kinship; the comparative youthfulness of grooms and their need to prove themselves to prospective in-laws are exaggerated in the youthfulness of the Roman community and the contempt its neighbors hold toward it; the passivity of the brides and the trauma of their separation from their families are exaggerated in the forcible abduction experienced by the Sabine women; at the same time, the resourcefulness and youthful manliness of the grooms are magnified by the Romans' abduction of the Sabines and in their success in the wars against the women's vengeful relatives; the groom's social respectability and the bride's beauty, in the story of Thalassius/Talasios.

The final reconciliation effected by marriage is similarly exaggerated by the theft of the Sabine women. In the historical period (within which our accounts of the theft of the Sabine women fall), a marriage survived at the pleasure of the respective partners' fathers: thus a woman's father could

---

21. The same idea is suggested by Cicero's assertion that Romulus "placed [the Sabine women] in marriages with the best households," *in familiarum amplissimarum matrimoniis collocavit* (*Rep.* 2.6.12).

22. *The Savage Mind* (Chicago: University of Chicago Press, 1966), pp. 238–39.

23. On "perspective by incongruity," see Kenneth Burke, *Permanence and Change: An Anatomy of Purpose,* 3d ed. (Berkeley: University of California Press, 1984), pp. 89–96; and id., *Perspectives by Incongruity,* ed. Stanley Edgar Hyman (Bloomington: Indiana University Press, 1964), pp. 94–99. For a review of theories of metaphor and their usefulness in anthropological interpretation, see Michael Herzfeld, "Exploring a Metaphor of Exposure," *Journal of American Folklore* 92 (1979): 285–87. On "purposive nonconventionality," see Malcolm Crick, *Explorations in Language and Meaning: Towards a Semiotic Anthropology* (New York: John Wiley/Halsted, 1976), p. 135.

legally dissolve his daughter's marriage, even against the will of the married couple.[24] The potential hostility and interference of the wife's father in a conventional marriage, then, is magnified and made patent in the actual warfare initiated by the Sabines. In response to their challenge, the Sabine women not only affirm willingly their status as Roman wives; they risk their lives in order to reconcile warring peoples. In doing this, they fulfill the original purpose of the abduction and their original function in it. Only then do they finally win the full measure of their husbands' and their relatives' affections: "After such a sorrowful war, joyous and unexpected peace made the Sabine women dearer to their husbands and relatives and above all to Romulus himself," *ex bello tam tristi laeta repente pax cariores Sabinas uiris ac parentibus et ante omnes Romulo ipsi fecit* (Livy 1.13.6). From separation, rivalry, and hostility comes a legitimate marriage of husband and wife, not just a reconciliation but a willing union of peoples.

The foregoing representation of the first Roman marriage as an institution subordinated to male purposes, and of women, consequently, as subordinate to men, is closely related to the Romans' perception of themselves not as an autochthonous people but as a self-made community of immigrants. It is noteworthy that the ancient narratives present the story of the Sabine women in close association with passages describing the motley character of Rome's early population and Romulus' efforts to attract immigrants to his new city from throughout Italy.[25] The Romans' perception of themselves

24. For a father's right to effect a divorce between his son and daughter-in-law, see Alan Watson, *Rome of the XII Tables: Persons and Property* (Princeton: Princeton University Press, 1975), pp. 32–33, who observes: "Nothing could better illustrate the fact that marriage was an arrangement between families, not just between individuals." Sarah Pomeroy, "The Relationship of the Married Woman to Her Blood Relatives in Rome," *Ancient Society* 7 (1976): 221 (and also p. 220), calls attention to the evidence of Cic. *Att.* 13.3 that Cicero "even considered breaking up Tullia's marriage to Dolabella when she was expecting a child [because of] political rivalry and the difficulties involved in paying the installments on Tullia's dowry." It should be noted, however, that the formal prerogatives of the father with regard to a daughter's marriage were often exercised in fact by the mother. See Phillips, "Roman Mothers," pp. 69–80.

25. Livy's description of Romulus' sanctuary and the indiscriminate band of men that it attracted (1.8.4–5) is separated from the story of the Sabine women by only a brief few lines on Romulus' organization of the city's population. Plutarch (*Rom.* 14.5) notes in his introduction to the story of the Sabine women that the new city was filling with aliens, most of whom were "a rabble of the needy and obscure," *migades ex aporōn kai aphanōn*. Dionysius makes it a point to deny that Rome, being a Greek settlement, was a refuge of barbarians, fugitives, and vagabonds (1.89.1). He acknowledges the tradition that Romulus welcomed numerous immigrants from other communities, although he sanitizes it by asserting that Romulus accepted only free men (2.15.3). Romulus' immigration policy is not mentioned

as a community of immigrants may be related, in turn, to their immemorial policy of controlling neighboring populations through assimilation. This was achieved in large part by extending various degrees of citizen status to allied and subject peoples.[26] While the rights to participate in Roman voting assemblies (*suffragium*) and to hold public office at Rome (*per magistratum*) were among those extended relatively late and very selectively to non-Romans, *conubium,* the right of intermarriage, was among the earliest citizen rights that non-Romans might receive.[27] The particular function of *conubium* was not so much to assure the availability of marriage partners as it was to assure that the union formed by a Roman and a non-Roman would be legally recognized at Rome, so that their children would be regarded as legitimate and would, with their parents, enjoy the protection of Roman laws, particularly those governing inheritance. This, as A. N. Sherwin-White observes, "is no small exception to the exclusiveness of local politics in fourth-century Latium."[28] Thus the story of the Sabine women is in part about one of the most important ways in which the Romans had, in historical reality, extended their community and their *imperium.* It constitutes a partial explanation of how and why that process worked.

The Sabine women are themselves central to this explanation in two ways. First, they produce children in whom the family lines of both mother and father are united and who, therefore, provide a basis for common interest between separate peoples. However, in every narrative in which the children are introduced as mediators between Sabines and Romans (that is, in all of the narratives except for Cicero's very spare account), it is the Sabine women themselves who call attention to the children, and, in several versions, they even carry them onto the field of battle between Sabines and Romans and present them to their fathers and grandfathers for acknowledgment.[29] The role of the children, therefore, is subordinate to that of their mothers. Their presence on the field of battle reflects the Sabine women's own initiative, their own desire to put an end to the hostilities between Sabine and Roman men, and their own affirmation of attachment and loyalty both to Sabine fathers and to Roman husbands. It is this initiative, this desire, and this

---

either in the very brief narrative of Cicero or in Ovid's narratives in the *Ars amatoria* and *Fasti,* neither of which is organized as a chronological history of Rome.

26. The standard treatment of this practice from earliest times through the Principate is A. N. Sherwin-White, *The Roman Citizenship,* 2d ed. (Oxford: Clarendon Press, 1973).

27. On *suffragium* and *per magistratum,* see Sherwin-White, pp. 35–36; on *conubium,* see p. 34.

28. P. 34.

29. Dion. Hal. 2.45.4–5; Livy 1.13.2; Ov. *Fast.* 3.213–24; Plut. *Rom.* 19.1–6.

affirmation that are decisive in uniting Sabine and Roman peoples and in fulfilling Romulus' original purpose.

Viewed from this perspective, the story of the Sabine women displays the essential elements of a rite of passage as it was first characterized by Arnold Van Gennep, inasmuch as its subjects move from separation through a transitional, liminal period to final incorporation into society in their new roles.[30] Moreover, as Loring Danforth, for example, has documented in *The Death Rituals of Rural Greece,* a rite of passage may operate on several interlocking planes simultaneously. In the customs that he describes, death separates from society both the deceased and the female relative who survives him or her. The survivor then passes through a period of mourning before being reincorporated into more normal social relations, while the deceased is regarded as going through a period of purification until his or her bones, cleansed of decomposed flesh, are removed from the earth and placed in an ossuary above ground, a sign that the spirit, too, has been cleansed and received into the afterlife.[31]

These models from anthropology help both to clarify the essential structure of the story of the Sabine women and to illuminate the value of specific details as they may be related to that structure. In the story of the Sabine women, it is the progress of community and that of individuals that parallel each other and are interdependent. As we have seen, the narratives begin with hostilities between Romans and Sabine neighbors, who are disdainful of the young community growing up in their vicinity. They end with a reconciliation of Roman and Sabine peoples. The versions of Cicero, Dionysius, Plutarch, and Livy record not just the cessation of hostilities, as does the version of Ovid, but the formal union of the two peoples, who share citizenship, religious rites, and a common name, although they maintain their separate centers of habitation.[32] At the same time, the story moves

---

30. *The Rites of Passage* (Chicago: University of Chicago Press, 1960). The three stages characterizing rites of passage are represented schematically in Edmund Leach's summary discussion of the subject, *Culture and Communication* (Cambridge: Cambridge University Press, 1976), chap. 17, pp. 77–79; Leach's schema is on p. 78. Both M. Torelli, *Lavinio e Roma: Riti iniziatici e matrimonio tra archeologia e storia* (Rome: Edizioni Quasar, 1984), p. 75, and Jean Gagé, *Matronalia,* Collection Latomus 60 (Brussels: Revue d'études latines, 1963), pp. 273–76, see the historical accounts of the theft of the Sabine women as preserving the memory of an archaic rite of passage based on a perception of marriage as entailing the forcible separation of the bride from her parents. See also Köstler, p. 53.

31. Loring M. Danforth, *The Death Rituals of Rural Greece* (Princeton: Princeton University Press, 1982), p. 43.

32. Cic. *Rep.* 2.13; Dion. Hal. 2.46.3; Plut. *Rom.* 19.9; 20.1–3, 5; 21.1; Livy 1.13.4–5.

from the abduction of the Sabine women and their separation from their homes and families of birth to their reunion, when Sabines and Romans join as one people, and many parents of the abducted women (abducted Antemnates and Crustumini as well as Sabines) move to Rome to be close to their daughters.[33] This, in turn, is related to a change in the women's status from victims of male violation to objects of male respect.[34]

Finally, as rites of passage often begin with elements that are inverted at their conclusion to mark formally that the transition from one state to another has been completed, so the story of the Sabine women is marked by contrasting festivals near its beginning and at its conclusion. Before their abduction, the Sabine women observe the Consualia as outsiders.[35] Indeed, this festival is the lure that is used to attract them and their families to Rome from their native towns. At the completion of their transformation into wives, the Sabine women, now Roman *matronae,* participate in another Roman festival, the Matronalia.[36] Specific characteristics of the two festivals make their contrast in this context particularly striking. The Consualia seems to have been an agricultural celebration featuring contests among men.[37] Ancient authors associated it with secrecy and the making of plans, both because of apparent etymological connections between *condere* (to store, bury, or hide), Consus (a god associated with stored harvests), and *consilium* (plan), and because the Consualia was associated with Romulus' plot to abduct the Sabine women.[38]

By contrast, although exact details of the Matronalia are imperfectly known to us, such evidence as there is indicates clearly that women not

33. Livy 1.11.2 and 4.

34. Livy 1.13.6–7; Dion. Hal. 2.47.2–4; Ov. *Fast.* 3.227–28; Plut. *Rom.* 19.9; 20.3–4; 21.1.

35. On inversions in rites of passage, see Leach, *Culture,* p. 78.

36. For the Sabines as observers of the Consualia, see Cic. *Rep.* 2.12; Dion. Hal. 2.31.2; Livy 1.9.6; Ov. *Fast.* 3.199–200; Plut. *Rom.* 14.2–6. For the Sabine women as celebrants of the Matronalia, see Ov. *Fast.* 3.167–70, 229–58; Plut. *Rom.* 21.1

37. The evidence is summarized by James George Frazer, ed., *Publii Ovidii Nasonis Fastorum libri sex: The "Fasti" of Ovid* (London: Macmillan, 1929), vol. 3, pp. 50–57, ad *Fast.* 3.189, and by Franz Bömer, ed., *P. Ovidius Naso: Die Fasten* (Heidelberg: Carl Winter, 1957), vol. 2, p. 156, ad *Fast.* 3.199. Of particular relevance to the present discussion are Ov. *Fast.* 1.345; Plut. *Quaest. Rom.* 48; Dion. Hal. 2.31.2; Wallace M. Lindsay, ed., *Nonii Marcelli De compendiosa doctrina libros XX* (Hildesheim: G. Olms, 1964), vol. 1, p. 31, quoting Varro *De vita populi Romani* s.v. *"cernui": ibi pastores ludos faciunt coriis Consualia;* Festus s.v. *"Mules,"* in *Sextus Pompeius Festus,* ed. Wallace M. Lindsay (Hildesheim: G. Olms, 1965), p. 135.

38. See Dion. Hal. 2.31.3; Plut. *Rom.* 14.3; Tert. *De spect.* 5; Lindsay, *Festus,* s.v. "Consualia," p. 36; Serv. *ad Aen.* 8.636; Bömer, vol. 2, p. 156, ad *Fast.* 3.199, citing Alios Walde and J. B. Hofmann, *Lateinisches etymologisches Wörterbuch,* 3d ed. (Heidelberg: Carl Winter, 1938–56), vol. 1, p. 266.

only participated in this festival but were its principal and honored celebrants. Aspects of the Matronalia that have parallels in the Saturnalia are of particular relevance to interpreting narratives about the theft of the Sabine women. The Matronalia seems to have been an occasion when women entertained slaves, just as men did at the Saturnalia.[39] Similarly, it was an occasion when men gave presents to women, just as presents were given to men at the Saturnalia.[40] These parallels have led to speculation that the Matronalia should be understood as a kind of Saturnalia in honor of women; and, indeed, the most striking feature of both festivals is that for one day at least they give preeminent status to a part of the population that is normally more or less marginal. Inasmuch as the Matronalia is associated with Juno Lucina, goddess of childbirth, and its origins are traced to the theft of the Sabine women, it identifies women's claim to status in the community with their role as intermediaries between male kinship groups, a role that derives in large part from their ability to produce offspring that are common to both kin by marriage and kin by blood.[41] As a virtual mirror image of the male-oriented Consualia, from which women were excluded, the Matronalia signals the transformation of the Sabine women from outsiders to insiders and completes their incorporation into Roman society.

The conditions just summarized represent the extreme points of the rite of passage, the beginning and end, respectively. Between them occur the critical liminal experiences that make transition from one extreme to the other possible. Here in the liminal zone the Roman men prove themselves to the Sabines in warfare, and there is a change in the women's behavior from passivity, as largely incidental objects caught up in a conflict between males, to action, as agents in the reconciliation among men, when, on their own initiative, they intervene between warring communities and affirm their married status. Between the two extremes one or several of the following help to establish affective bonds between Roman men and Sabine women: formal

---

39. Evidence for the Matronalia is summarized by Bömer, vol. 2, p. 154, *ad Fast.* 3.167, and by Frazer, vol. 3, pp. 48–49, *ad Fast.* 3.169. The following are particularly relevant to the present discussion: Macrob. *Sat.* 1.12.7; Lydus *Mens.* 4.42, in the edition of Ricardus Wünsch (Stuttgart: Teubner, 1967), p. 99.

40. See Suet. *Vesp.* 19.1; *Corpus Tibullanum* 3.1.1–4 and 4.2.1; Plaut. *Miles gloriosus* 691–93; Tert. *De idololatria* 14; *Digesta* XXIV 1.31.8.

41. On the Matronalia as a women's Saturnalia, see Frazer, vol. 3, pp. 48–49, *ad Fast.* 3.169; on the role of Juno Lucina in the Matronalia, see *Fast.* 2.425–52, where Juno Lucina is credited with fostering the childbirths without which Romulus would have regarded the theft of the Sabine women as futile; on the origins of the Matronalia, see Ov. *Fast.* 3.167–70, 229–58; Plut. *Rom.* 21.1.

weddings, informal courtship of the abducted women by the Roman men, and the sharing of common offspring. Stages in the rite of passage are outlined in the following chart.

Beginning	Liminal Period	End
Romans and Sabines separate peoples	War between Romans and Sabines	Romans and Sabines one people[a]
Sabine women as Sabine daughters	Sabine women won over by Romans (through marriage[b], courtship[c], children[d])	Sabine women as Roman wives
Sabine women objects of dispute		Sabine women agents of reconciliation
Sabine women abducted from families		Sabine women reunited with families[e]
Sabine women objects of violence		Sabine women honored for their intervention[f]
Sabine women observers of a Roman festival		Sabine women celebrants of a Roman festival[g]

Unless specifically noted below, each of the elements listed above occurs in all of the narratives discussed here.

a. Cic. *Rep.* 2.13; Dion. Hal. 2.46.3; Livy 1.13.4–5; Plut. *Rom.* 19.9; 20.1–3, 5; 21.1.

b. Cic. *Rep.* 2.6.12; Dion. Hal. 2.30.5–6 (cf. 2.24.4–25.6).

c. Livy 1.9.16.

d. Livy 1.9.14.

e. Reunion is implicit in all the narratives that record the joining of Roman and Sabine peoples; it is explicit only in Livy 1.11.2 and 4, where it is asserted that many Antemnates and Crustumini moved to Rome after their defeat in order to be with their daughters.

f. Livy 1.13.6–7; Dion. Hal. 2.47.2–4; Ov. *Fast.* 3.227–28 (by fathers only); Plut. *Rom.* 19.9; 20.3–4; 21.1.

g. Ov. *Fast.* 3.169–70, 229–34; Plut. *Rom.* 21.1.

One advantage of looking at the narratives of the Sabine women as narratives of a rite of passage is that the logical centrality of the role played by the Sabine women themselves becomes clear. Their spontaneous and decisive intervention between warring Roman and Sabine men identifies their own transformation from passive objects to active agents as essential to the resolution of conflict. The movement from extreme to extreme that characterizes this story emphasizes the importance of the critical liminal stage in which the women's transformation is effected, and underscores the fact that it is their transformation, their successful initiation as Roman wives, upon which the final incorporation of male and female, Roman and Sabine, into a single community depends. As I have already emphasized, however, the Sabine women's initiation is framed by a story about the fulfillment of male goals and the realization of Roman masculine prowess. According to this story, all of the first Romans are men. The action of the story is set in motion by their needs (the Romans' need for children to populate their city, for allies to secure Rome's greatness, and for recognition of their own manliness). The story reaches its natural conclusion, accordingly, when the Roman men have achieved those goals by fathering children, winning allies, and demonstrating their prowess. Although the role of the Sabine women in this process is both central and essential, their story is subordinated to that of male achievement and is told from an exclusively male point of view. Thus there is a tension between the logical requirements of the story, which point to the women's role as central, and the male perspective from which the story is told and which treats the women's experience as irrelevant or at best of secondary interest.

II

While all of the narratives have this much in common, they nonetheless differ considerably in how they negotiate the distance between the two perspectives noted above. In the process they offer widely divergent responses to the ideological foundations of Roman marriage and gender relations. These differences of perspective emerge most clearly, in fact, in the different ways in which the individual narratives deal with what their exclusively male perspective makes most problematic, the nature of women and the manner in which women come to play an active role in the events surrounding them. In this regard, the narratives under consideration may be divided into three distinct categories. The first embraces the narratives of Cicero, Dionysius of Halicarnassus, and Plutarch. The second is represented by Ovid, and the third by Livy.

The narratives of Cicero, Dionysius, and Plutarch are characterized by an essential lack of interest in the process by which the Sabine women are initiated into their roles as Roman *matronae* and by a tacit assumption that there is nothing problematic about their initiation. Cicero essentially bypasses description of this process: he reports that Romulus organized a formal wedding between the Sabine women and their Roman abductors (*Rep.* 2.6.12), but he offers no details that might suggest why and how the formalities of a wedding ceremony transform captives into active and willing marriage partners. The narrative of Dionysius of Halicarnassus expands only superficially on Cicero's stark reference to marriage. Dionysius presents the wedding arranged by Romulus as a concession to the Sabine women's sensibilities: the men refrain from actual intercourse until after the wedding, and the wedding ceremony itself is based on the women's own traditions (Dion. Hal. 2.30.6; cf. 2.24.4–25.6). But Dionysius does not reveal what makes the Sabines' traditional wedding ceremony an effective vehicle for initiating Sabine women into Roman society. To call attention to the Romans' deference to Sabine formalities is to offer the illusion of an explanation, but at the expense of trivializing the Sabine women, who, it is suggested, could be won over by the merest gesture of consideration on the men's part.

Plutarch approaches the problem somewhat differently. In his narrative, the Sabine women vaguely justify intervention on behalf of their Roman abductors by reference to the neglect of their own families and to the necessities imposed by time:

ἁρπασθεῖσαι δ' ἠμελήθεμεν ὑπ' ἀδελφῶν καὶ πατέρων καὶ οἰκείων χρόνον τοσοῦτον ὅσος ἡμᾶς πρὸς τὰ ἔχθιστα κεράσας ταῖς μεγίσταις ἀνάγκαις πεποίηκε νῦν ὑπὲρ τῶν βιασαμένων καὶ παρανομησάντων δεδιέναι μαχομένων καὶ κλαίειν θνησκόντων. (*Rom.* 19.4)

After we were abducted, we were neglected by our brothers, our fathers, and relatives for such a long time that we have become mixed up in the most hateful circumstances by the greatest necessities and have been made to fear on behalf of those who criminally took us by force when they engage in battle and to weep for them when they die.

Thus the narrative of Plutarch, just as those of Cicero and Dionysius, rather than describing or explaining the Sabine women's transformation, proceeds as though there were nothing problematic about it. To the extent that they do no more than refer to formalities, to the Romans' limited gestures of goodwill, or to the healing effects of time, these narratives offer an illusion of explanation that is persuasive only insofar as their readers are uncritical.

If the narratives of Cicero, Dionysius of Halicarnassus, and Plutarch proceed as though the details of the Sabine women's initiation were of no interest because there is nothing problematic about it, Ovid's narrative takes a radically different approach. It makes explicit and emphatic the male perspective that is implicit in all the other narratives. Even though Ovid is male, he marks the particular maleness of this portion of his narrative by identifying its narrator as the god of war. Mars takes a proprietary interest in this story, because the festival that Romulus created to entice the Sabines to Rome was presented in his honor. Mars himself is represented as perceiving the theft of the Sabine women in terms of his own rivalry with the female divinity of peace, Minerva. He offers the story as proof that he can outdo the goddess in her own special sphere, inasmuch as the theft of the Sabine women issued in peace between hostile peoples.[42] The god introduces his story belligerently: "I do not regret this undertaking; it is a pleasure to linger over this part also, that Minerva may not think that she alone can do this [i.e., excel in the arts of peace]," *nec piget incepti, iuvat hac quoque parte morari, / hoc solam ne se posse Minerva putet* (*Fast.* 3.175–76).

Just as Ovid's narrative emphasizes the male appropriation of the story of the Sabine women, it minimizes deliberately the role of the women. It says nothing of any Roman overtures to the abducted women; there is no wedding or promise of one, no Roman efforts at courtship (such as we will find in Livy's narrative). Rather, after promising a later description of the actual abduction and of the festival at which it took place—a promise that is not in fact fulfilled—Mars moves on directly to note the anger of the women's relatives and the consequent wars between son-in-law and father-in-law (*Fast.* 3.199–202). The abrupt transition from plans for abduction to the outbreak of war ignores the women so conspicuously that it calls attention to their absence from the narrative and to the paradoxical assumption that the theft alone, the mere possession of Sabine daughters, is sufficient to make the fathers fathers-in-law, the abductors sons-in-law.

The women's own status is left ambiguous, and this ambiguity is sustained in the subsequent narrative, where they are referred to with seeming indifference once as *nuptae* (*Fast.* 3.205), but other times as *raptae* (*Fast.* 3.203, 208, 217). The very next couplet offers a comparably stark and brutal report of the unions' fruitfulness: "Already the abducted women generally had the name 'mother' also; the wars between relatives had been protracted by long delay," *iamque fere raptae matrum quoque nomen habebant, / tractaque erant longa bella propinqua mora* (*Fast.* 3.203–4). No mention here, as we will find in Livy's narrative, of mutuality, of fortunes that are shared or are the source of *caritas*, "dearness," or of any other binding sentiment. The women's new

---

42. Hemker, p. 44, emphasizes the inconsistencies that discredit the anonymous narrator of Ovid's account in the *Ars amatoria*.

status reflects only the physical consequences of their abduction and rape and the length of time that has passed. It is significant, too, that there is absolutely no mention of or even allusion to the Sabine women themselves up to this point in Ovid's narrative: they exist, insofar as they exist here and throughout the narrative, only by virtue of their relations to others. They first get a title, "mothers," only when they have produced children, and it is only after that that they are identified as brides: "the brides gather in the shrine known as Juno's," *conueniunt nuptae dictam Junonis in aedem* (*Fast*. 3.205). Even Romulus' wife, Hersilia, identified by name in the accounts of Livy (1.11.2), Dionysius (2.45.6), and Plutarch (*Rom*. 14.7–8), is referred to by Mars anonymously as *nurus*, "daughter-in-law" (*Fast*. 3.206). When the abducted women are at last identified as the celebrants of Mars' rites by a proper name, that name, Oebaliae, identifies them as the descendants of a man, Oebalus, Spartan ancestor of the Sabine peoples (*Fast*. 3.230).

The persistent refusal to acknowledge the Sabine women, their effacement in the narrative, and the practice of referring to them only indirectly—in terms of their relationships to others—are factors contributing to the relative denseness and economy of Ovid's narrative, but the significance of those factors cannot be exhausted by stylistic considerations. It is precisely the fact that these women are allowed no identity apart from their fathers, husbands, and children—apart from others—that motivates their intervention between husbands and fathers and also determines the manner of that intervention. When Mars' daughter-in-law summons the women to meet, it is in response to a crisis:

> o pariter raptae, quoniam hoc commune tenemus,
> 	non ultra lente possumus esse piae.
> stant acies, sed utra di sint pro parte rogandi,
> 	eligite! hinc coniunx, hinc pater arma tenet.
> quaerendum est, viduae fieri malimus an orbae:
> 	consilium vobis forte piumque dabo.
> 							(*Fast*. 3.207–12)

> O fellow victims of abduction—for we have this in common—we cannot be calmly dutiful any longer. The battle lines are drawn. On which side to evoke the gods, choose. On one side your husband, on the other your father is in arms. We must consider whether we would rather become widows or orphans. I will give you strong and responsible advice.

Unless they intervene in the imminent battle, they will become "widows" and "orphans"; they will be diminished by the loss of their men and by the loss of identity and protection that goes with it.[43] It is for this reason that piety is presented to these women not as an expression of loyalty or even of obligation but of necessity.[44]

Even when the abducted women do intervene in the battle between fathers and husbands, their own role is minimized, barely transcending their original passive anonymity. The women assume the appearance of mourning and take to the field of battle, but once there virtually their only act is to assume a posture of submission (*Fast.* 3.213–20). In contrast to Livy's narrative, in which the women call on their men in the name of their children (1.13.2), here the women actually bring the children onto the field with them—a critical difference, since in Ovid's narrative the children, not the women, are the only ones actually to speak. Insofar as the women speak,

43. The idea that the Sabine women fear that they will be made widows or orphans occurs in Livy's narrative, and that is very likely Ovid's source for it. However, the significance of this fear is quite different in the two narratives. In Ovid it is presented as the reason for the Sabine women's intervention and as the only reason for it. In Livy's narrative it is part of the women's appeal to their fathers and husbands. It concludes their appeal to the men to recognize the relationships by which they are bound to each other through the Sabine women, and it is presented as an expression of the women's concern on their behalf (1.13.3).

44. This passage echoes the appeal of the Sabine women in Livy: "better that we perish than that we live without either of you, widows or orphans," *melius peribimus quam sine alteris uestrum uiduae aut orbae uiuemus* (1.13.3). Women's dependence on men for their identity is vividly expressed in India when a widow casts herself—or is coerced—onto her husband's funeral pyre in the ritual act of sati. This behavior has been attributed to, among other things, a perception that "because of the very close identification between a man and his wife [among certain Hindu castes], indeed to the point where she is subsumed under his identity, she is considered, at his death, to be socially dead" (Elizabeth Leigh Struchbury, "Blood Fire and Mediation: Sacrificing and Widow Burning in the Nineteenth Century," in *Women in Nepal and India,* ed. Michael Allen and S. N. Mukherjee, Australian National University Monographs on South Asia 8 [Canberra: Australian National University Press, 1982], p. 36; see also p. 43). V. N. Datta, *Sati: A Historical, Social, and Philosophical Enquiry into the Hindu Rite of Widow Burning* (Riverdale, Md.: Riverdale, 1988), pp. 207–21, calls attention to this and to other complementary motives for widow burning. In general, "it has been observed that the more the bereaved defined themselves in terms of their relationship to the deceased, the more the death threatens their socially constructed world" (Danforth, p. 138, citing Jack Bynum, "Social Status and Rites of Passage: The Social Context of Death," *Omega* 4 [1973]: 323–32, and Robert Blauner, "Death and Social Structure," in *Passing,* ed. Charles O. Jackson [London: Greenwood Press, 1977], pp. 174–209). At Rome women's dependence on men for their identities is expressed literally in the naming of women by the feminine form of their father's clan name and in the traditional formula by which a woman accepted her role as wife: *ubi tu Gaius ego Gaia.* A woman is first her father's daughter and then her husband's wife. These are precisely the claims to identity that the Sabine women find threatened. For other implications of the naming conventions noted above, see Judith P. Hallett, *Fathers and Daughters in Roman Society* (Princeton: Princeton University Press, 1984), pp. 76–83.

it is only through their children. The children wave to their mothers' fathers; those who can, call out to their grandfathers. Even when their children cannot speak their grandfathers' names, the mothers assert themselves only so far as to coach the children:

> et, quasi sentirent, blando clamore nepotes
> > tendebant ad avos bracchia parva suos:
> qui poterat, clamabat avum tunc denique visum,
> > et, qui vix poterat, posse coactus erat.
> > > (*Fast.* 3.221–24)

And, as though they understood, with ingratiating clamor the grandchildren were holding out their small arms to their own grandfathers. He who could was calling out to his grandfather, then seen for the first time, and he who was hardly able to had been forced to be able.

The women of Livy's narrative make their appeal themselves and in the name of their own marriage (*conubium*) as well as in the name of their children. Where it is the women in Livy's narrative who become *cariores* because of their initiative (1.13.6), here it is the children who are "dear guarantees" or "tokens," *pignora cara* (*Fast.* 3.218). In Ovid's narrative, the women are voiceless, (almost) entirely passive, never more than vehicles for children: they bear children and then literally carry them onto the field of battle.

By implication the women are of little or no value themselves. This view is confirmed even in Ovid's subtle recasting of significant elements in Livy's narrative. In Livy the Roman men appealed to their Sabine captives with "blandishments," *blanditiae* (1.9.16). In Ovid, the women are the objects of no such attention: *blanditiae* here are associated instead with the childishly inarticulate appeals (*blando clamore*) that the children address to their grandfathers (*Fast.* 3.221). In Livy's narrative the children were the basis for a shared relationship between mother and father, "than which nothing is dearer to the human race," *quo nihil carius humano generi,* and the Sabine women become *cariores* to husbands and parents alike because of their intervention (1.9.14; 1.13.6). As a mark of honor the tribal divisions, *curiae,* into which the newly unified people were divided took their names from Sabine women—even if names were perhaps chosen for this honor on the basis of the husband's status (1.13.6–7). In Ovid, however, we hear only that the women were honored by their fathers: "fathers-in-law . . . / embrace their honored children," *soceri . . . / laudatas tenent natas* (*Fast.* 3.226–27). The contrasts noted here between Ovid and Livy are the more telling inasmuch as Livy's text was available to Ovid, and so departures from it are likely to reflect conscious revision of the story on Ovid's part.

At the end of the story, Mars observes that from the day of their intervention, the Sabine women have had the weighty obligation of celebrating his day, the Kalends of March. But whether this obligation reflects upon their heroism or Mars' own masculine prowess is unclear even to the god himself:

> inde diem, quae prima mea est, celebrare kalendas
>   Oebaliae matres non leve munus habent.
> aut quia committi strictis mucronibus ausae
>   finierant lacrimis Martia bella suis,
> vel quod erat de me feliciter Ilia mater,
>   rite colunt matres sacra diemque meum.
>   (*Fast.* 3.229–34)

From that time, mothers descended from Oebalus have this obligation, not a light one, to celebrate the day that is my first, the Kalends of my month. Either because they had dared to confront drawn sword points and through their tears had brought the wars of Mars to an end or because Ilia [whose rape by Mars produced Romulus] was a mother with good results because of me, mothers formally observe my rites and day.

This reflection upon the god's own prowess brings us back to the introduction of the story and to the assertion there that the theft of the Sabine women and their subsequent intervention between fathers and husbands were the consequence of Mars' desire to prove himself superior to Minerva in her own arts of peace.

For Ovid, then, the Sabine women are responsible (indirectly) for bringing an end (or at least a temporary halt) to internecine hostilities, but the incorporation that they effect is conspicuously incomplete, and it is incomplete specifically because of the kind of recognition that is given (or not given) to women. As mere vehicles for children, they have no direct power to engage the affections and loyalties of their husbands. It is to their maternal grandfathers alone that the children make their appeal. It is the Sabine fathers-in-law who take the initiative of offering their hands to the Roman sons-in-law; and it is the Sabine fathers alone who honor the women. Save for the vague assertion that "the men's weapons and their spirits drop," *tela viris animique cadunt* (*Fast.* 3.225), the narrative makes no mention, offers no suggestion, of concessions on the part of the Romans. There is no mention of the formal reconciliation between Roman and Sabine that is the capstone of all the other narratives. The narrator's earlier assertion that "then for the *first* time father-in-law bore arms against son-in-law," *tum primum generis intulit arma socer* (*Fast.* 3.202), is allowed to echo ominously through this conclusion.

Livy's narrative falls somewhere in between those of Cicero, Dionysius of Halicarnassus, and Plutarch, on the one hand, and that of Ovid, on the other. Like the former narratives but unlike Ovid's, it presents the story of the Sabine women in an essentially positive light, emphasizing the achievement of harmony between men and women, Sabines and Romans. But unlike the narratives of Cicero, Dionysius of Halicarnassus, and Plutarch, it does not take for granted the process by which the theft leads, paradoxically, to harmony. In Livy's narrative, as in Dionysius', Romulus plays a mediating role, but within a more complex and ambiguous pattern of circumstances. The women are abducted, some (as the woman intended for Thalassius) taken off to the homes of their prospective husbands, "their hope for themselves no better, their indignation no less [than those of their relatives who fled Rome]," *nec raptis aut spes de se melior aut indignatio est minor* (1.9.13); Romulus himself goes among the women justifying their abduction by reference to the intransigence of the Sabine men, promising the women marriage and a partnership of fortunes with their Roman husbands, and counseling them to give their affections (*animos*) to those to whom fate had given their bodies (1.9.14–15), but the exact sequence of events is unclear. There is no mention of Roman restraint, only the promise of marriage ceremonies, and Romulus' tone here seems to be as much admonitory as conciliatory.

Nonetheless, his admonitions do identify one basis for accommodation between the Sabine women and their abductors:

> illas tamen in matrimonio, in societate fortunarum omnium ciuitatisque et quo nihil carius humano generi sit liberum fore; . . . adnisurus pro se quisque [Romanus] sit ut, cum suam uicem functus officio sit, parentium etiam patriaeque expleat desiderium. (1.9.14–15)

> they nonetheless will be married and will share in all the fortunes and in the state, and, what is dearest to the human race, in legitimate children; . . . each Roman will strive on his own behalf not only to perform his responsibilities in his turn but also to satisfy the [women's] desire for parents and fatherland.

Romulus here views marriage between husband and wife as a kind of microcosm of the political alliance between families and peoples that it is supposed to effect. It is an "alliance," a *societas,* just like that which the

Romans sought unsuccessfully with the Sabines.[45] It offers the same sharing of fortunes and above all sharing of community that the Romans and Sabines will ultimately agree to. It is precisely because marriage constitutes a kind of substitute for (as well as a means to) an alliance between states that Roman husbands can promise to satisfy their wives' desire for parents and for fatherland. In marriage as Romulus views it, children will perform the same function in relation to mother and father that the Sabine women will perform in relation to husband and blood relations: they will be the mutually valuable object that will bring parties together. In fact, their role as catalysts extends beyond mother and father to grandparents. When the Sabine women intervene between their husbands and their fathers, they appeal to them to think of their children and grandchildren, respectively, as evidence of a shared relationship and as reasons to cease hostilities (1.13.2).

Similarly, the most important basis for the couples' own alliance is the *caritas* of their children. As we have seen, Romulus qualifies his promise of shared offspring with the assertion that nothing is more dear to the human race: *quo nihil carius humano generi sit* (1.9.14).[46] *Caritas* in Livy is the quality possessed by things, people, and relationships of exceptional value. It is used, for example, in the sense of "very expensive" to describe grain supplies during times of famine.[47] It is the source of the power that both children and the Roman homeland have to evoke strong sentimental attachments.[48] The *caritas* of children to their parents and of Rome to its inhabitants are very similar—*caritas liberum* and *caritas patriae* are the only two kinds of *caritas* described as "innate" (*ingenita:* 1.34.5; 8.7.8)—and, in fact, are closely associated. At 2.1.5 the narrator observes that the motley assemblage of immigrants to Rome only became a coherent community capable of self-government "after the guarantees of wives and legitimate children and after dearness of the soil itself . . . had allied their minds," *pignera coniugum ac liberorum caritasque ipsius soli . . . animos eorum consociasset. Caritas,* then, is an important constitutive element of community. Conversely, *caritas* may be

---

45. Columella *Rust.*, pref. 12.1, citing Xenophon's *Economicus*, characterizes marriage as "life's most useful alliance," *utilissima uitae societas*, which serves to preserve the race and to provide for the couple's old age, but for the husband it is an alliance based on an essentially economic division of labor in which male and female natures each make their distinctive contributions—the man farming and fighting abroad, the more timid woman charged with stewardship of the household (pref. 12.2–6).

46. This sentiment is expressed somewhat differently and more fully in Dio 56.3.4.

47. E.g., 2.12.1, 34.2; 10.11.9; 44.7.10.

48. See, for example, for children 1.34.5; 5.42.1, 54.2, 3; 3.49.3; and 8.7.18, 34.2; 40.9.3, 15.15 for homeland.

attained by contributing to the community: the Sabine women will be described as "dearer," *cariores*, to both fathers and husbands for bringing an end to their hostilities (1.13.6). Romulus' reference to the *caritas* of shared children adds to our understanding of why and how Sabine women are transformed from passive and incidental tokens of male rivalry into active and valued participants in Roman society, but it does not provide a full explanation. It moves from a political perspective that is by definition in this society essentially male (*societas fortunarum omnium ciuitatisque*) to a sentimental perspective that can include both men and women (*caritas liberum*). But it acknowledges no distinctively female point of view, no particular stake for women that corresponds to men's political stake in *societas*.

While Romulus appeals to the Sabine women with the voice of male authority, in the name of formal alliances undertaken for mutual interest, and in the name of sentiments associated with kinship and community, the women's abductors appeal to them in quite different terms: "There were in addition the blandishments of the men, who excused their deed by desire and love, prayers that have the greatest effect on woman's nature," *Accedebant blanditiae uirorum, factum purgantium cupiditate atque amore, quae maxime ad muliebre ingenium efficaces preces sunt* (1.9.16). The term *blanditiae* and its cognates are uncommon in Livy; they occur only thirteen times in the extant narrative. They are associated especially with women (24.4.4; 27.15.11; 29.23.7; 30.7.8; 32.40.11), more generally with the immature and the weak, both as their own characteristic manner of appeal or as a means of appealing to them: the young Hannibal begged his father to take him on campaign "with boyish blandishments," *pueriliter blandientem* (21.1.4); the Senate attempts to manipulate the plebeians with *blanditiae* (2.9.1).

Blanditiae are also associated with irrational behavior or emotions: threats, pity, fickleness (32.40.11; 30.12.18; 27.15.11), and, in particular, with the powerful irrationality of love. Hasdrubal manipulates the Numidian king Syphax—a man personally "inflamed with desire" (*accensum cupiditate*) and belonging to a people "beyond all [other] barbarians unrestrainedly given to lust" (*ante omnes barbaros . . . effusi in Venerem*)—through "the blandishments of his young wife" (*blanditiis . . . puellae*) (29.23.7).[49] Needless to say, *blanditiae* are associated with the very antithesis of male, public virtue. At Capua the insidious influence of sleep, drink, banquets, whores, baths, and leisure was made "daily more seductive by virtue of habit" (*consuetudine in*

---

49. On *Venus* as simply "lust" in contrast to the broader semantic range of *amor*, see Hirta Klepl, *Lucrez und Virgil in ihren Lehrgedichten* (Darmstadt: Wissenschaftliche Buchgesellschaft, 1967), p. 21 nn. 28 and 29.

dies blandius), until it completely enervated battle-hardened troops (23.18.11). Thus the Romans' recourse to *blanditiae* to win over their new wives is in keeping with their evocation of desire and love and implies a particular perception of female nature (its characterization by passion rather than by reason) and a concession to its weakness. The concession is a critical one, for it is immediately after reporting it that Livy observes: "Already the feelings of the abducted women had been greatly softened," *iam admodum mitigati animi raptis erant* (1.10.1).

Thus while Livy's narrative presents women as subordinate to male goals and relationships, it nonetheless presents women's contributions to those goals as justifying or necessitating concessions to the distinctive nature that is ascribed to them. The liminal period between the initial abduction of Sabine women and their final incorporation in marriage consequently entails a double accommodation. Women are, first of all, invited to join in an alliance, a *societas,* and to enjoy the benefits of shared fortunes and citizenship that follow from such an alliance, as well as to join in the ties of shared children—ties that are not unique to husbands and wives but extend to fathers, fathers-in-law, grandfathers, and others as well. That such *societas* is conceived of in an essentially, if not exclusively, male context is revealed by the absence of reference in the narrative to any women other than the abducted Sabines: when the Sabine women appeal to the ties embodied in their children, they do so only in terms of male relationships—fathers, grandfathers, sons, sons-in-law, grandsons, and so forth; they say nothing, for example, of sisters, mothers-in-law, or grandmothers. Participation in such an alliance entails primarily an accommodation of women to masculine values and society. The second accommodation is that made by men to women's nature as they perceive it: their acknowledgment of women's weakness and susceptibility to strong emotions. The accommodation reached between Roman men and Sabine women comes about because each party—man and woman, husband and wife—to some extent enters into the world of the other, at least as those worlds are perceived by men. It is noteworthy that the narrator himself affirms the perception of women held by Roman men in his narrative, when he observes that appeals to desire and love are especially suited to woman's nature.

As a practical solution to the problems of how to achieve stable marriages and lasting alliances among families joined by marriage at Rome, Livy's story of the Sabine women is scarcely realistic. This is most evident both in its failure to acknowledge any separate identity for women and in its exaggeration of the distances that must be bridged in more normal relationships: instead of the distance between bride and groom, one between captive and captor; instead of that between separate families, one between warring communities. As Lévi-Strauss has observed, such exaggerations serve "to justify the shortcomings of reality, since the extreme positions are only *imagined* in order to show that they are *untenable*."[50] In Livy's narrative this tacit acknowledgment of the dissonance between ideal and reality is borne out in specific detail. There, even though the union of Romans and Sabines seems complete—even though the two communities are finally bound by ties of kinship, are joined as one *civitas,* recognize a dual kingship, accept Rome as the common capital, and share a common name, Quirites, after the Sabine town of Cures (1.13.4–5)—peace between them is not lasting. In fact, tensions between the two communities surface even during Romulus' lifetime. When disgruntled Laurentians murder Tatius, the Sabine king, in a riot at Lavinium, Livy notes: "They say that Romulus was less distressed by this than was becoming, whether because the alliance of kingship was unreliable or because Romulus thought that [Tatius] had not been killed at all unjustly," *Eam rem minus aegre quam dignum erat tulisse Romulum ferunt, seu ob infidam societatem regni seu quia haud iniuria caesum credebat* (1.14.3). Romulus not only declines to avenge the murder of Tatius but actually renews a treaty with Lavinium.[51] Thereafter, both Livy and Dionysius record a succession of conflicts between Rome and Sabine communities until Rome won a decisive victory over the Sabines in 449 B.C.E.; Livy even records a subsequent Roman conquest of the Sabines as late as 229 B.C.E. (*Epit.* 11).[52]

This imperfect political union between Sabine and Roman communities has a parallel in the relations between male and female in Livy's narrative. As noted above, a decisive step in the reconciliation of the abducted Sabines to their Roman husbands was taken when the Romans appealed to their individual brides through *cupiditas* and *amor,* the Roman men seeking to justify their deed (*purgantium*), according to the narrative, "by desire and love," *cupiditate atque amore* (1.9.16). This statement might mean that the men sought to win their brides over by the expression of actual desire and love for the women, but the context suggests a different reading. The participial phrase *factum purgantium cupiditate atque amore* explains *blanditiae* and is followed by the relative clause *quae maxime ad muliebre ingenium efficaces*

50. "The Story of Asdiwal," in *The Structural Study of Myth and Totemism,* ed. E. Leach (London: Tavistock, 1967), p. 30; and see p. 28.

51. Dion. Hal. 2.51–53.1 offers a similar but more detailed account of the circumstances leading up to the murder of Tatius and the murderers' acquittal by Romulus.

52. Livy 2.16ff.; 3.38.3ff.; Dion. Hal. 5.37ff.; Plut. *Val. Publ.* 20–23.

preces sunt, "which prayers have the greatest effect on woman's nature" (1.9.16). In other words, the men's self-justification is depicted as essentially rhetorical; it entails primarily, if not exclusively, words or external show, "blandishments" and "prayers." The narrative is pointedly silent about the nature of the men's actual feelings. Thus while it records the Romans' response to woman's nature as they perceive it, the narrative also suggests a distance between the Roman men and that nature. The men accommodate it, but they do not share it. Just as the alliance between Sabine and Roman communities attempts to create a single community from two, while preserving the separate identity of each, so Roman marriage aims to achieve a union that seeks to accommodate but cannot completely harmonize two distinct natures. At the most private, most intimate level of the relationship between Sabine bride and Roman groom there remains a note of reserve—at least on the part of the men—and distance.

This distance, viewed as a consequence of the inherent nature of women, calls attention to the existence of potentially disruptive elements that can never be totally expunged at the very heart of Roman society. Marriage and thus the alliances based on it remain dependent in part on notoriously unpredictable and uncontrollable passions, "desire and love," *cupiditas atque amor.* The precariousness of loyalties that are based, even in part, on these emotions is exemplified in the story of Tarpeia, a story of betrayal that occurs within and complements the story of the Sabine women's loyalty. The story of Tarpeia has several versions, which support a variety of interpretations. In one version Tarpeia betrayed the Roman citadel in exchange for the gold bracelets that the Sabine attackers wore on their left arms. This story is reported by Livy (1.11.6–9), Plutarch (*Rom.* 17.2), and Dionysius, in whose version Tarpeia's betrayal is attributed specifically to *erōs . . . tōn psellion,* "lust for bracelets" (Dion. Hal. 2.38.3). According to another version, Tarpeia betrayed the citadel not to the Sabines but to the Gauls and was motivated by her love for the enemy general, a version reported but rejected by Plutarch (*Rom.* 17.6–7; see also Prop. 4.4). In a third version, reported by Livy (1.11.9) and Dionysius (2.38.3; 39.1–40.1), Tarpeia did not in fact intend to betray Rome but rather sought to trick the Sabines into giving her the shields that they wore on their left arms, thus leaving them defenseless. This version, rejected by Livy, is favored by Dionysius, although in the end he disclaims any certainty in the matter and leaves a final judgment up to the reader (2.50.3).

The ancient authors record disagreement also as to why the Sabine attackers murdered Tarpeia by burying her under their shields: they hoped by so doing to hide the fact that they had taken Rome by treachery rather than by force (Livy 1.11.7); they despised her as a traitor to her country, even though she was aiding them (Livy 1.11.7; Plut. *Rom*. 17.3–4); they killed her in anger at her attempt to trick them out of their armor (Livy 1.11.9; Dion. Hal. 2.40.1); they killed her out of anger at the size of the reward that she claimed (Dion. Hal. 2.40.2). Plutarch even reports, if only to reject, the possibility that Tarpeia was herself a Sabine woman (daughter of the Sabine king, Tatius), who betrayed Rome because she had been forced to live with Romulus against her will (Plut. *Rom*. 17.5).

In this context it is particularly significant that Livy's narrative also acknowledges contradictory versions of the tradition about Tarpeia, even if it favors one version over the others in the end. The point of the story, then, is not so much that women are inherently disloyal, but that, being perceived by men as constitutionally susceptible to emotions of desire and love, their motives are regarded as inherently suspect, difficult to predict (the Sabine attackers are either deceived or not, according to different versions), and difficult even after the fact to determine with confidence. Thus, in contrast to the Sabine women, whose susceptibility to *cupiditas* and *amor* contributes to their identification with Rome, stands Tarpeia, in whom those same emotions might just as well have led to betrayal.[53]

Livy's account of Tarpeia and her motives creates still further complications for the narrative, for it raises questions about the behavior and nature of the Roman men who appealed to the Sabine women in terms of the very passions for which Tarpeia is subsequently held suspect. If the men were actually motivated by the feelings of *cupiditas* and *amor* on the grounds of which they excused themselves to their captives, then the implicit moral of Tarpeia's story, that the qualities that make women malleable to men's purposes also make them unreliable members of community, must apply to Roman men as well. This reading is supported within the immediate narrative context, which contrasts the initial resolve of the avenging Sabines with

---

53. This ambivalence toward Tarpeia in the literary tradition is reflected in the lack of consensus among modern scholars on how to interpret pictorial representations of Tarpeia; see Jane Evans, *The Art of Persuasion: Political Propaganda from Aeneas to Brutus* (Ann Arbor: University of Michigan Press, 1992), pp. 122–23. This ambivalence may derive ultimately from a widespread mythological type associated with the foundation of cities. Joseph Rykwert, *The Idea of a Town* (Princeton: Princeton University Press, 1976), p. 160, noting that Tarpeia was the recipient of the state sacrifice that opened the *dies parentales* (public holidays in honor of the dead) at Rome, identifies her as a particular type of heroine who figures in many foundation stories from around the world. She is, according to Rykwert, "the virgin at the sacred hearth [through whose] guilty or substitute intercourse with god or hero, as well as its punishment, a new city, a new alliance, a new nation, a new state are founded."

that of the Romans. Of the wars provoked by the theft of the Sabine women, according to Livy, that with the Sabines was the greatest (*maximum*), because by them "nothing . . . was done with anger or desire," *nihil . . . per iram aut cupiditatem actum est* (1.11.5). After capturing Rome's citadel, the Sabines did not leave that stronghold until "the Romans came up to meet them, anger and desire to recapture the citadel arousing their spirits," *ira et cupiditate reciperandae arcis stimulante animos in aduersum Romani subiere* (1.12.1). The danger of the Romans' irrationality is underscored both by their putting themselves in a tactically disadvantageous position (coming up from the flat plain below to meet the Sabines) and by the rout that occurs when the Roman's audacious leader, Hostius Hostilius, is killed early in the fighting (1.12.1–3).

The problem of passions and of the Romans' susceptibility to them takes on even wider implications in light of the preface to Livy's narrative. There, Livy ascribed the decline of contemporary Rome to a general, undifferentiated desire for wealth and to the play of passions that excessive wealth makes possible: "In fact, the more modest its affairs, the less greed there was. Recently wealth has introduced avarice, and abundant pleasures have introduced a longing to perish and to destroy all things through extravagance and passionate desire," *Adeo quanto rerum minus, tanto minus cupiditatis erat: nuper diuitiae auaritiam et abundantes uoluptates desiderium per luxum atque libidinem pereundi perdendique omnia inuexere* (pref. 11–12). If we are to understand that men as well as women are motivated by *cupiditas* and *amor*, then the whole distinction between stronger, more rational men and weaker, more passionate women that justifies the abduction and accounts for the women's transformation from captives into wives dissolves. Men are revealed to be no more competent to govern rationally than are women. The implicit justification for their exploitation of women is exposed as spurious; the singling out of women in the figure of Tarpeia as a particular source of danger to the community, as disingenuous.

The men, however, may only have been feigning *cupiditas* and *amor*, and their appeals may have been merely rhetorical. There is, as we have seen, much to support this view. The phrase "excusing their deed by *cupiditas* and *amor*" is ambiguous: it could mean excusing themselves by the *cupiditas* and *amor* that they actually felt, but it could equally well mean excusing themselves simply by *claiming* to have been motivated by *cupiditas* and *amor*. The placement of that phrase between characterizations of the men's appeals as *blanditiae* and *preces* favors the latter interpretation. In this case, we must recognize that the men are compounding their original act of violence by an act of bad faith—they are, in fact, increasing the distance between themselves and their captives even as they seem to be bridging it, and they are evoking and fostering the very passions that threaten the integrity of their community. Thus they become implicated in Tarpeia's crime.

III

The narratives of the theft of the Sabine women in Cicero, Dionysius of Halicarnassus, Livy, Ovid, and Plutarch begin with assumptions about the nature and function of marriage that were widely held and were the basis for actual practice among those authors' contemporaries.[54] For members of the Roman aristocracy, marriage typically entailed the union of young men of perhaps age twenty-four and girls of fifteen or so. Half of these girls would still have been under the legal authority of their fathers at the time of marriage, an even greater proportion at the time of their betrothal.[55] Among these Romans, marriage was regularly employed as a means of securing social, economic, and/or political advantage through alliances

54. I am aware that ideology and practice did not necessarily or always coincide. See, for example, Suzanne Dixon, *The Roman Family* (Baltimore: Johns Hopkins University Press, 1992), p. 50, and her "Family Finances: Terentia and Tullia," in *The Family in Ancient Rome,* ed. Beryl Rawson (Ithaca, N.Y.: Cornell University Press, 1986), p. 95. See also Mireille Corbier, trans. Ann Cremin, "Family Behavior of the Roman Aristocracy, Second Century B.C.—Third Century A.D.," in *Women's History and Ancient History,* ed. Sarah B. Pomeroy (Chapel Hill: University of North Carolina Press, 1991), p. 190, who concludes: "The most surprising feature [of aristocratic family behavior] remains the coexistence of ideals and of practices which were to a high degree mutually contradictory, as if the supreme achievement . . . lay in *not* [original emphasis] using all the resources of 'law.'"

55. See K. Hopkins, "The Age of Roman Girls at Marriage," *Population Studies* 18 (1965): 309–27, who argues persuasively for a "typical" married couple composed of a pagan female of fifteen and a pagan male of twenty-four (the ages are somewhat different for Christian couples) (p. 325); and, more recently, Bernard D. Shaw, "The Age of Roman Girls at Marriage: Some Reconsiderations," *Journal of Roman Studies* 77 (1987): 30–46, who argues for some variations in age at marriage according to region and to social class but confirms, nonetheless, that it was the general practice in first marriages among all Romans for women to marry men several years older than themselves. As Richard P. Saller, "Men's Age at Marriage and Its Consequences in the Roman Family," *Classical Philology* 82 (1987): 21–34, has argued, ancient life expectancy rates suggest that at the age of first marriage perhaps half of senatorial women and one third of senatorial men were still *in potestate,* legally subject to the *potestas* of their fathers (p. 32); see also Saller's "*Patria potestas* and the Stereotype of the Roman Family," *Continuity and Change* 1 (1986): 7–22. For the age of women at betrothal, see Treggiari, *Roman Marriage,* pp. 153–54.

between male-headed households.[56] In this process women were the necessary vehicles through which marriage alliances were made. The political history of the late Republic and early Empire provides numerous examples that illustrate the subordination of women to this end—Cicero's daughter, Tullia, and Augustus' Julia are only among the most notable.[57] In its broad outlines the story of the Sabine women provides a precedent and a sanction for such marriages of convenience. It does this by asserting, at least on its most explicit level, the extraordinary efficacy of an institution that can unite not only separate families but even hostile peoples in a mutually beneficial relationship.

This kind of marriage functioned within a society that was explicitly divided into a formal hierarchy: senatorials, knights, undifferentiated plebeians, freedmen (former slaves formally manumitted by their owners), slaves, and noncitizens, whose relationship to Rome might be defined in a variety of ways. The most influential segment of Rome's senatorial leadership, the *nobiles,* came from a long-established aristocracy and justified their privileged position in part on the basis of a tradition of family distinction and service that was inherited. Although the strata of the Roman social and political hierarchy were not castes (that is, they were not defined exclusively by birth), and movement from one to another was possible, marriage alliances, by cementing family relationships within ranks, had traditionally served more often to consolidate the integrity of the separate ranks, especially the senatorial rank, than to bridge them.[58]

---

56. It is in this context that we may understand Watson's observation: "The *lex* [*Julia* of Augustus] shows that the idea persisted—right from the time of the kings—that a woman's adultery was even more of an insult to her blood relatives, especially her father, than to her husband" (p. 37).

57. Pomeroy, pp. 215–27, provides a good discussion of this well-known aspect of Roman social relations.

58. Treggiari, *Roman Marriage,* surveys several criteria for choosing a marriage partner (birth, rank, wealth, personal qualities, character, *pudicitia, affinitas,* affection) and concludes that the calculations involved in selecting a marriage partner were intricate (pp. 83–124), but asserts, nonetheless, that "disparity of birth in husband or wife was something to be avoided by all classes" (p. 83); in addition, see her remarks on p. 107. See also Suzanne Dixon, "The Marriage Alliance in the Roman Elite," *Journal of Family History* 10 (1985): 353–78; Gardner, p. 35, indicates that reliance on marriage alliances to consolidate the highest ranks of Rome's sociopolitical hierarchy may in fact have been increasing during the late Republic: "In classical Rome, however, there is by the second century B.C. an observable tendency to endogamy within or between certain aristocratic *gentes,* and by the first century B.C. marriage between first cousins was permitted."

Under the influence of broad social and political changes brought about by Rome's acquisition of an empire and more directly by the violent political disorders of the late Republic, the traditional role and character of Roman marriage experienced a variety of strains. Rapidly shifting political alliances during the civil wars led to a high incidence of divorce and remarriage, which perhaps in turn accounts for the apparently large number of extramarital liaisons that characterize aristocratic society of the late Republic. At the same time, Roman wives were attaining an unprecedented degree of legal and economic independence, and there is good evidence to suggest that the legal dominance of men in the control of marriages had been compromised in practice, now, if not before, by mothers who played an active and often leading role in both arranging and dissolving their daughters' marriages.[59] In addition, the lines dividing the separate ranks in the Roman social hierarchy became somewhat blurred and more permeable than before: the range of possible marriage alliances became broader and more flexible. This new flexibility had special relevance for Rome's senatorial aristocracy, the *nobiles,* whose ranks had been thinned by the civil wars of the late Republic. "The outbreak of the war between Caesar and Pompey [49 B.C.E.] ended the dominance of the nobility."[60] Amid these developments—each of which in one way or another must have complicated the traditional function of marriage as a vehicle for creating family alliances—it appears that the ideal of sentimental attachment between husband and wife gained currency at Rome.[61]

Under the emperor Augustus, changing attitudes toward the role and nature of Roman marriage provoked an official reaction. Augustus ruled according to the fiction that he had not created a monarchy but rather had restored Republican government, that the traditional social and political

59. Treggiari, "Matrimonial Advances"; id., *Roman Marriage,* pp. 125–38, 445–46, 460–61; Phillips, "Roman Mothers," pp. 69–80. Study of other cultures indicates that it should not be surprising to find women taking an active role in arranging marriages even within societies that give formal control of such matters to men. Pierre Bourdieu, *Outline of a Theory of Practice,* trans. Richard Nice, Cambridge Studies in Social Anthropology 16 (Cambridge: Cambridge University Press, 1977), pp. 52–68, observes a distinction that may be applicable to ancient Rome between "ordinary marriages, generally set up by the women, within their own network of relationships" and "marriages within the close kin or extraordinary marriages (arranged by men, outside the usual area, for purposes of alliance)."

60. P. A. Brunt, *"Nobilitas* and *Novitas," Journal of Roman Studies* 72 (1982): 6.

61. See Dixon, "The Marriage Alliance," pp. 353–78. The argument presented there is further developed in the same author's *Roman Mothers* (London: Croom Helm, 1988); Treggiari, *Roman Marriage,* p. 120, suggests that an apparent change in attitude may reflect rather a greater abundance of sources for this period of Roman history.

hierarchy of Rome was intact, and that the state was ruled by the same aristocracy that had ruled it for centuries. A central goal of his political program was to reassert clear divisions between the principal ranks or "orders" of Roman society.[62] In part Augustus pursued this policy by exhortation and example. He berated senators, for example, who wore informal dress rather than the traditional Roman toga on public occasions.[63] But, above all, he was responsible for new laws that sought to stabilize marriage, especially among the political aristocracy.[64] He made it illegal for a husband to ignore adultery on the part of his wife. He passed other laws aimed at discouraging the marriage of senatorial men to women outside of their political order, and still others that provided political incentives for the production of legitimate children by members of the aristocracy. While the nature of Augustus' domination discouraged overt opposition to such legislation, the laws were not widely popular and were often circumvented.[65]

The particular character of Augustus' legislation concerning marriage makes patently clear that what was perceived as at stake in the issues surrounding Roman marriage was not simply the welfare of the individual or of the family or even of the clan; it was nothing less than the sociopolitical organization of the Roman state. The narratives of the theft of the Sabine women, though not directly addressing the issue of class and rank, nonetheless acknowledge the political relevance of their subject in more general terms: the theft/marriage is explicitly presented in each narrative as essential to the welfare of the state, to the perpetuation of Rome's greatness. These

62. See S. Demougin, "Uterque ordo: Les rapports entre l'ordre sénatorial et l'ordre équestre sous les Julio-Claudiens," in *Epigrafia e ordine senatorio,* Atti del Colloquio internazionale AIEGL su epigrafia e ordine senatorio, Roma, 14–20 maggio 1981, vol. 4 (Rome: Edizione de storia e letteratura, 1982); Claude Nicolet, "Augustus, Government, and the Propertied Classes," in *Caesar Augustus,* ed. Fergus Millar and Erich Segal (Oxford: Oxford University Press, 1984), pp. 90–96.

63. Suet. *Aug.* 40.

64. Augustan marriage legislation is clearly summarized by Treggiari, *Roman Marriage,* pp. 60–80; see also p. 61 nn. 93, 94, for a survey of modern views about its motivation. In addition, see Gardner, esp. pp. 32–33, 77–78, 127–33, and passim; Pál Csillag, *The Augustan Laws on Family Relations* (Budapest: Akadémiai Kiadó, 1976); and Leo Ferrero Raditsa, "Augustus' Legislation Concerning Marriage, Procreation, Love Affairs, and Adultery," *ANRW* 2.13 (1980), pp. 278–339. Andrew Wallace-Hadrill, "Family and Inheritance in the Augustan Marriage Laws," *Proceedings of the Cambridge Philological Society* 27 (1981): 58–80, sees these laws, or at least some of them, as designed more specifically to "stabilize the transmission of property and consequently of status" within the Roman aristocracy, p. 59.

65. See, for example, Suet. *Aug.* 34.1; Prop. 2.7; Tac. *Ann.* 3.25, 54.2; Dio 56.1.2; Gordon Williams, "Poetry in the Moral Climate of Augustan Rome," *Journal of Roman Studies* 52 (1962): 28–46.

narratives also make it clear that Roman marriage and therefore the sociopolitical edifice that it supports depend in turn on roles for men and women
that were constructed both by social practice and by legend. The traditional
use of Roman marriages to consolidate alliances among male-headed households was based upon and perpetuated distinct notions about the respective
natures of men and of women. Roman men, as we have seen, were perceived
as ambitious, energetic, resourceful, aggressive, and successful. In claiming
their brides they demonstrate their manhood and give evidence of their
ability to maintain a secure and prosperous household in the future. Women,
on the other hand, were represented as weak, passive bearers of children
whose active allegiance is evoked principally through their children, by
appeal to the passions (*cupiditas* and *amor*), and by their own awareness of
their helpless dependence on men.[66] One of the particular interests of the
story of the theft of the Sabine women is that it reveals so clearly how the
entire organization of the Roman state rests upon specific perceived differences between, and the inequality of, men and women.

All the narratives that we have been considering operate within the
prevailing ideology of their time. That is, they accept traditional ideas about
the nature and function of marriage and about the respective natures of
men and women—they could hardly do otherwise.[67] But we have also
seen that these same narratives express quite different attitudes toward the

66. For a cautious assessment of the different meanings of Roman assertions about the
weakness of women, see S. Dixon, "*Infirmitas Sexus:* Womanly Weakness in Roman Law,"
Tijdschrift voor Rechtsgeschiedenis 52 (1984): 343–71. In particular, she distinguishes between a
retrospective and artificial notion of women as incapable, too "weak" to engage in business
(a notion perhaps imported from Hellenistic philosophers), and an indigenous Roman association of "feminine infirmity" with "emotional areas" (see esp. pp. 369–71). But even as regards
the emotional weakness of women, Roman views might be fluid and not altogether consistent.
Contrast, for example, Sen. *Consolationes ad Marciam* 1.1 and 11.1 with 16.1. On unchastity
and the love of riches as typical female vices, see, for example, Sen. *Consolationes ad Helviam* 16.3.

67. As Jacques Derrida has observed, "We cannot utter a single destructive proposition
which has not already slipped into the form, the logic, and the implicit postulations of precisely
what it seeks to contest" ("Structure, Sign, and Play in the Discourse of the Human Sciences,"
in *The Structuralist Controversy,* ed. R. Macksey and E. Donato [Baltimore: Johns Hopkins
University Press, 1977], p. 250). Jean-Luc Comolli and Jean Narboni argued the same point
in a rather different context in their editorial in *Cahiers du cinéma* 216 (1969): 11–15, trans.
and repr. in *Movies and Methods,* ed. Bill Nichols (Berkeley: University of California Press,
1976–85), vol. 1, pp. 22–30. My choice of categories in which to group the narratives
discussed in this essay—(1) Cicero, Dionysius of Halicarnassus, and Plutarch; (2) Ovid; (3)
Livy—has been influenced by the categories defined by Comolli and Narboni to distinguish
the different orientations of movies toward the ideology of the society and culture in which
they are produced.

construction of sexual identities and roles that was recorded in tradition and implicit in contemporary political policy. These differences of perspective inevitably imply substantially different attitudes toward and relationships to the prevailing ideology under which the understanding of Roman marriage was subsumed. The narratives of Cicero, Dionysius of Halicarnassus, and Plutarch represent an uncritical acceptance of that ideology—uncritical both in the sense that they find no fault with it and, more important, in the sense that they regard it as completely unproblematic, requiring neither explanation nor justification. These narratives perpetuate a fiction that the official ideology is utopian, that the existing social order is one in which everyone is fulfilled and satisfied—everybody is happily reconciled at the end of the story—and in which unity and reconciliation are achieved without noteworthy cost.

It is perhaps not coincidental that the two most critical and ideologically complex narratives, those of Livy and Ovid, were composed very close to the time when Augustus' controversial marriage legislation brought questions about the nature and function of marriage—and by implication about the nature and roles of men and women—to the surface of Roman consciousness.[68] Ovid's narrative clearly challenges the prevailing ideology. It does not imagine an alternative way of ordering society, nor does it suggest a radically different nature for women from the one implied by the other narratives: women are still conceived of as weak and essentially passive. But it does acknowledge some of the implications of exploiting women's assumed weakness both for the women and for society as a whole. It strips away any

---

68. On the dating of Livy's first pentad, see above, Chapter 2, note 49. Ovid interrupted work on his *Fasti* in C.E. 8, making only revisions to the incomplete text during his exile thereafter. Major parts of Augustus' legislation on marriage and morals can be dated with certainty to 18 B.C.E. and C.E. 9, but such legislation seems to have occupied Augustus throughout his reign and probably began as early as 28 B.C.E.; see Raditsa, pp. 295–97. The need for such legislation was suggested explicitly at least as early as 46 B.C.E., when Cicero advised Julius Caesar as follows: "You alone, Gaius Caesar, must revive all those things that you see lying overwhelmed and prostrate—as was inevitable—due to the shock of war itself: courts must be constituted, good faith restored, license checked, offspring produced; everything that has already dissolved and melted away must be brought under control by strict laws," *omnia sunt excitanda tibi, C. Caesar, uni quae iacere sentis belli ipsius impetu, quod necesse fuit, perculsa atque prostrata: constituenda iudicia, reuocanda fides, comprimendae libidines, propaganda suboles, omnia quae dilapsa iam diffluxerunt seueris legibus uincenda sunt (Marcell. 23).* On the ages of the Second Triumvirate and Augustus as a period of crisis and reform in ideas about Roman marriage, see Treggiari, *Roman Marriage,* pp. 211–15. Controversy surrounding Augustus' marriage laws and legislative adjustments to them continued intermittently for generations; see Csillag, pp. 199–211.

pretense that the abduction and rape of the women was anything other than an act of violence, that it could somehow be mitigated by formalities, by promises of shared fortunes, or by the calculated rhetoric of endearment. It gives voice to the women's own desperation in the brief speech attributed to Hersilia, and it suggests the incompleteness of the social union that their violent treatment helps to achieve.[69] Ovid's narrative, then, is subversive in that it suggests a connection between the precariousness of the sociopolitical order and the brutality by which it is sustained at the most fundamental level. His narrative insists that order at Rome is built ultimately on brute force.[70]

Livy's narrative is, as we have seen, in some ways the most complex and interesting of all. Although it endorses the prevailing ideology—it emphasizes reconciliation and the effective fulfillment of social and civic needs accomplished by the theft—it does not take it for granted. Its attempt to rationalize the tradition, however, to explain a process that Cicero, Dionysius, and Plutarch take for granted, leads to the elaboration of assumptions that become problematic when they are integrated into a larger narrative. As perceived inferiors, the Sabine women can never exercise enough influence to outweigh the public concerns by which men in this world define themselves.

69. Sympathic representation of the victims of rape may be a general characteristic of Ovid's narratives. According to Leo C. Curran, "Rape and Rape Victims in the *Metamorphoses,*" *Arethusa* 11 (1978): 232, "Perhaps the most impressive element of Ovid's treatment of rape is his understanding of the sheer horror of the experience for the woman and his ability to empathize with her and thereby to portray her terror with compelling authenticity." For a survey of different interpretations of Ovid's attitudes toward women, see Phyllis Culham, "Decentering the Text: The Case of Ovid," *Helios* n.s. 17 (1990): 161–70, esp. p. 163 and the notes there; and, more recently, Amy Richlin, "Reading Ovid's Rapes," in *Pornography and Representation in Greece and Rome,* ed. Amy Richlin (New York: Oxford University Press, 1992), pp. 158–79.

70. For an interpretation of Ovid's *Metamorphoses* that emphasizes the narrative as exposing the reality of force underlying the facade of Augustan constitutionality, I am indebted to the unpublished manuscript of Mary-Kay Gamel entitled "Ovid Imitating Vergil: *Aeneid* I and *Metamorphoses* I." Leslie Cahoon, "The Bed as Battlefield," *Transactions of the American Philological Association* 118 (1988) notes a parallel with "the *libido dominandi* deplored by Sallust (*In Catilinam* 2.2)" which "becomes in the *Amores* a kind of internal moral rot pervading the lives and loves of individuals," p. 307. For a more general discussion of Ovid as "out of tune with the harmony that Augustus wanted to hear from Rome's cultured classes," see Culham, p. 163 n. 28. According to Hemker's assessment of Ovid's narrative of the Sabine women in the *Ars amatoria,* "Ovid exposes the tragedy inherent in any philosophy which espouses domination as a means of gratifying one's own desires" (p. 46). See, however, Richlin's rather different assessment of this passage, which emphasizes its essentially male-centered orientation (pp. 158–79). Richlin does not discuss the version of the Sabines' story that Ovid presents in the *Fasti.*

Even though affection for the Sabine women and for the offspring they produce enables them to interrupt hostilities between men, in time latent rivalries between groups of men reassert themselves, and hostilities break out anew. Similarly, women's perceived susceptibility to *cupiditas* and *amor* means that they must remain always a potential threat to domestic order. Tarpeia (whether guilty of treachery or innocent) embodies possibilities that are inherent in the nature ascribed to women. But we have also seen that the ascription of this nature to women raises further questions about the nature and integrity of Roman men as well. Thus even as it constructs images of men and women to fit the conventional character and function of Roman marriage, Livy's narrative exposes limitations inherent in the Roman practice of trying to base ideal social and political unions on a relationship of inequality between men and women.

Taken together and in their historical context, the foregoing narratives about the theft of the Sabine women demonstrate how ideas about the nature and function of marriage necessarily imply ideas about the nature and roles of men and women, and how conceptions both of marriage and of the sexes are integrally bound up with the larger organization of society and its supporting ideology. More particularly, these narratives demonstrate a suggestive parallelism between the social and political inequality imbedded in political institutions and inequality within the institution of marriage: they raise the question of whether it is possible to have equality on one level if there is inequality on the other.[71] They demonstrate how stories that we tell about marriage may contain their own critiques, both of marriage and of the broader ideologies within which the institution of marriage is subsumed, and how they may do this not just in the overt criticism of an Ovid but also in the rationalizations of a Livy and even in the silences of a Cicero, a Dionysius, or a Plutarch.

The narratives of those last three authors reveal, further, how silences, while they cannot resolve ideological contradictions, may function to obscure them. They also suggest, by contrast, how striking and original are those authors such as Livy and Ovid, who recognize and confront the assumptions that underlie contemporary ideologies. Finally, they suggest,

71. As argued by Gayle Rubin, "The Traffic in Women," in *Toward an Anthropology of Women,* ed. Rayna R. Reiter (New York: Monthly Review Press, 1975), p. 207: "Kinship and marriage are always parts of total social systems, and are always tied into economic and political arrangements." My argument may be read in part as a modest response to Rubin's exhortation that a search be "undertaken for data which might demonstrate how marriage systems intersect with large-scale political processes like state-making" (p. 209). See also Edmund Leach, *Rethinking Anthropology* (New York: Humanities Press, 1971), p. 90.

perhaps paradoxically, how efforts such as Livy's to rationalize ideological assumptions may in the end expose contradictions implicit in them more fully than more radical, but ultimately less reflective critiques such as Ovid's: Ovid's narrative calls attention dramatically to the forcible exploitation of women by men in Roman society; Livy's narrative, while seeking to minimize the role of force, reveals contradictions inherent in the tacit assumptions by which such exploitation was justified.

Conclusion

The argument I have presented has, I hope, reconfirmed the position that Livy's narrative is more than just a series of episodes culled more or less arbitrarily from legend and literary sources, more than a string of morality tales (although it is that, too), and more than a succession of stories linked by common interest in traditional values and attitudes. I have sought, rather, to demonstrate that Livy's narrative is informed by significant historiographic principles, principles that are both coherent and, in fact, highly original. Often, they are based on theories and ideas that were well established in Hellenic and Hellenistic literature. Among those that I have discussed are the concept of the heroic founder, the idea of a city's savior as its refounder, the notion of historical recurrence, and the principle that the most important distinction among evidence is that between what has been heard and what has been seen. Within the narrative these established ideas contribute to the framework within which Roman legend and tradition is organized and retold. In this respect, then, the narrative reflects the adaptation of Hellenistic and Roman elements to each other.

The character and role of the heroic founder and refounder figure prominently in this adaptation. As we have seen, the concept of the founder as a semidivinity who is responsible for establishing virtually the entire apparatus of a community is significantly modified in Livy's narrative. Tension between the reality of dominant individuals in Roman politics and the general hostility of Republican Romans to despotism is reflected in the marked ambivalence with which Livy portrays Romulus, Rome's initial and most autocratic ruler. The figure of Romulus is further accommodated to Republican ideology (or, rather, to one ideological position within Roman Republicanism) in Livy's emphasis on those aspects of Romulus' character that define him as a prototype and sanction for the political inclusiveness sought by the "new men" of the late Republic. The Republican ideal of *libertas* is central to the role of Camillus, Rome's refounder and last in its succession of founders. He not only saves the physical community from conquest and restores control of the city to its native population; he relies on his personal *auctoritas* to recall his fellow citizens to their own traditional *pietas* and identity as a community—a role for which he is prepared by his own compelling memories of Rome and which he fulfills through his own example of *pietas* and of strict personal subordination to the city's constitution.

Finally, the accommodation of *libertas* is manifest in a simultaneous contraction and expansion of the role and definition of the founder. On the one hand, the role of Romulus, Rome's first founder, is significantly restricted. He is identified above all with a particular founding act, the choice of Rome's site and the establishment of a community there. On the other hand, the definition of founder is expanded to include a succession of leaders— including Brutus, *conditor libertatis*. While Romulus anticipates many (but not all) subsequent acts of foundation, he is not the unambiguously divine and authoritative figure that we find, for example, in the narrative of Dionysius of Halicarnassus. He is one among several founders and is himself chiefly identified with only one aspect of the city's complete foundation.[1]

This distribution of the task of foundation among a succession of founders serves to qualify and diminish somewhat the role of the initial founder. It is in keeping with an early Roman historiographic tradition that insisted on viewing Roman development as the product of a collective effort to which many individuals and all social orders contributed over time.[2] It also reflects the influence of Polybius, but with characteristically Roman modifications. Polybius, in accordance with Greek political philosophy, focused on the progressive introduction, degeneration, and displacement of distinct constitutional forms, each representing the interests of a particular stratum of society, until a final compromise was attained in a tripartite constitution that combined monarchy, aristocracy, and democracy.[3] There

---

1. And, indeed, as T. J. Luce, *Livy: The Composition of His History* (Princeton: Princeton University Press, 1977), p. 239, points out, none of the kings (and this applies equally well to *conditores*) is the exclusive originator of the institution for which he is particularly responsible.

2. The evidence for this early historiographic tradition is cited and summarized by A. J. Woodman, *Velleius Paterculus: The Tiberian Narrative (2.94–131)* (Cambridge: Cambridge University Press, 1977), pp. 30–31; see also Cic. *Rep.* 2.1, quoted above, Chapter 3, note 42.

3. Kurt Von Fritz, *The Theory of the Mixed Constitution in Antiquity* (New York: Arno Press, 1975), remains the basic work on this subject.

are prominent traces of that argument in Livy, but his narrative is much more personal in its focus and·does not present the Roman constitution as having its own dynamics, which operate in isolation from other institutions and values of equal centrality. Livy identifies founders and their specific contributions as the essential basis for Roman identity: Servius Tullius' organization of the state into orders each with its distinct privileges takes its place as only one among several foundations that include also the site of Rome, religious piety, the replacement of kings by consuls, the rule of law, and the act of refounding.

This focus on a succession of founding acts overlaps with another area in which Livy makes significant modifications to Hellenic and Hellenistic thought: the idea of historical recurrence. Before Livy this idea had become well established in both philosophical and historical literature, although taking somewhat different forms in each. Philosophers focused on large-scale patterns, often mechanically exact: the recurrence of all civilization or even of the entire universe. Historians were more concerned with the recurrence of approximate patterns, particularly of rise and decline, as enacted in successive states. Polybius evokes both perspectives, although he does not integrate them. In what is effectively a digression, he praises the natural evolution of the Roman constitution for its unique capacity to stop the endless progression from monarchy to tyranny to aristocracy to oligarchy to democracy to ochlocracy back to monarchy and so forth indefinitely that underlies the constitutional instability of other states. On the other hand, in his actual narrative of Roman political history, he seems more attracted to the idea that individual states each rise and decline in their turn.[4]

In Livy, however, the philosophical idea of universal reenactment and the historical tradition of the rise and decline of successive states are joined

---

4. This perspective is epitomized in Polybius' report of Scipio's unexpected reaction to the destruction of Carthage, which he had himself ordered. Scipio is said to have wept as he watched the city being burned and said: "O Polybius, . . . it is a good thing, but somehow as I look ahead I am afraid that someone else will give this same order about my fatherland," ὦ Πολύβιε . . . καλὸν μέν, ἀλλ' οὐκ οἶδ' ὅπως ἐγὼ δέδια καὶ προορῶμαι, μήποτέ τις ἄλλος τοῦτο τὸ παράγγελμα δώσει περὶ τῆς ἡμετέρας πατρίδος (38.21.3). He is reported also (Polyb. 38.22, quoted in App. *Pun.* 132) to have repeated the following lines from the *Iliad*: "There will come a day when sacred Ilium shall perish / along with Priam and the people of Priam of the good ashen spear," ἔσσεται ἦμαρ ὅταν ποτ' ὀλώλῃ Ἴλιος ἱρὴ / καὶ Πρίαμος καὶ λαὸς ἐυμμελίω Πριάμοιο (6.448–49). Both the text and its interpretation have been the subject of considerable discussion, which is well summarized by A. E. Astin, *Scipio Aemilianus* (Oxford: Clarendon Press, 1967), who quotes the relevant texts on pp. 251–52 and discusses them in app. 4, pp. 281–87, and by F. W. Walbank, *A Historical Commentary on Polybius* (Oxford: Clarendon Press, 1979), vol. 3, pp. 722–25.

for the first time: Rome is depicted as having, like other states, progressed through the cycle of rise and decline, but it is also presented as having already once recovered and renewed itself, after reaching the nadir of decline with the military defeat by the Gauls and the public demoralization that followed. Conspicuous parallels between that early decline and recovery and events in Livy's own day further suggest that Roman recovery after defeat by the Gauls may serve as a model for the new recovery proposed by Augustus.

This provocative parallelism between past and present in Livy's narrative calls attention to yet another factor that is critical to the union of Hellenistic and Roman elements in Livy, a factor that provided a particular impetus for their union and that often helps to explain its specific shape and character: the pressures and challenges faced by a historian writing during the turbulent transition from Republic to Empire at Rome. Foremost among these was the necessity to define (or perhaps redefine) the relation between Roman past, present, and future and, more specifically, to identify the relationship between continuity and change. However cynical, manipulative, or superficial we may judge it, Augustus' program of reform was centrally concerned with that relationship and lent to any contemporary reflection upon it a particular point and urgency that were inescapable. Any attempt to understand Roman tradition and the Augustan program for renewal in relation to each other necessarily involved mediating between tradition and change in a tremendously complex ideological and political context, in which change meant decline, collapse, and perhaps the promise of renewal, while "restoration" was highly selective and included radical innovation. Consequently, the task of mediating between past and present entailed mediating between continuity and change and raised the difficult question of where a collective identity might reside in the relationship between them.

Livy addresses that problem, as we have seen, in part through his elaboration of the role of Rome's founders. Limited in number and time, they serve to identify a specific, formative period in Roman history. Limited in the specific institutions and values with which they are associated, they serve to identify core aspects of Roman character around which change may take place without compromising Rome's essential identity and continuing potential for greatness. Livy's critique of established standards for evaluation of historical evidence adds a further dimension to his understanding of the relationship between continuity and change in Roman history. In his narrative Roman identity derives less from a substratum of "facts" or events than from the collective memory of the Roman people. Inasmuch as Roman memory is itself not the result of uncritical accumulation but rather reflects an ongoing process of deliberate elaboration and revision, it is a dynamic creation. Livy locates himself and his narrative within the tradition of elaboration and revision from which Roman memory and identity emerge. Thus his role as historian is analogous to that of the founders and other heroes whom his narrative celebrates.

The complexities of the Augustan program, characterized by paradoxes and outright inconsistencies, created uncertainties that put other pressures on the historian. It was not known, for example, to what extent Augustus' program of renewal would embrace traditional Republican freedom of expression, or whether the new regime would be totalitarian and oppressive. In addition, the program incorporated divergent, sometimes conflicting, ideological positions. Such uncertainties and complexities would have posed problems for a historian such as Livy, on the margins of Rome's powerful and traditionally exclusive ruling aristocracy, and, we might expect, would have pressured the historian to reaffirm certain traditional values and attitudes even as the ill-defined power of a new ruler pressed in other directions. Consequently, the task of mediating between past and present was not only conceptually complex and difficult; it was further complicated by the necessity for political tact. From this perspective, one of the most striking aspects of Livy's work is his willingness (in contrast to other authors who dealt with the same material) to address and try to resolve ideological problems raised by his new interpretations of tradition. We have seen, for example, how he not only relates that Roman marriage facilitated alliances but seeks to explain how and why it did so, that he not only dramatizes Roman self-sufficiency but tries to work out its relation to Roman power and growth. The fact that these efforts often reveal contradictions in Roman ideology makes them all the more significant.

In many ways Livy was a product of his age and personal circumstances. He used the materials available to him: Roman tradition, Hellenistic thought, Roman Republican and Augustan ideologies. He combined them in ways that are consistent with his particular position on the margins of the Roman aristocracy and under the influence of a new ruler whose effective power and will to exercise it were (especially during the early, formative stages of Livy's work) as yet not fully tested. Given all of this it does not seem possible that the specific ideas found in his narrative could have been predicted. They are the product of a unique mind. They reflect a determination to reveal rather than take for granted the ideological underpinnings of Roman behavior and to do so while acknowledging and integrating rather than excluding troublesome elements in Roman tradition. They are manifest in the unique ways in which Hellenistic concepts and Roman traditions are adapted to each other, but also in formulations that are sometimes tentative, guarded, and occasionally inconsistent. Together they contribute to a narrative that is many-layered, complex, subtle, often original, and genuinely illuminating.

Works Cited

Agahd, Reinhold, ed. *M. Terenti Varronis Antiquitatum rerum divinarum libri I, XIV, XV, XVI.* Ancient Religion and Mythology Series. New York: Arno Press, 1975.

Alföldi, A. "Die Geburt der kaiserlichen Bildsymbolik: Kleine Beiträge zu ihrer Entstehungsgeschicht 3: *Parens Patriae,* 1 (fin). *Museum Helveticum* 10 (1953): 103–24.

Alfonsi, Luigi. "La figura di Romolo all' inizio delle *Storie* di Livio." In *Livius: Werk und Rezeption: Festschrift für Erich Burck zum 80. Geburtstag,* ed. Eckard Lefèvre and Eckart Olshausen, pp. 101–6. Munich: C. H. Beck, 1983.

Alpers, Paul J. *The Singer of the "Eclogues."* Berkeley: University of California Press, 1979.

Altheim, F. *Epochen der römischen Geschichte.* 2 vols. Frankfurt Studien 9. Frankfurt am Main: V. Klostermann, 1933–35.

Astin, A. E. *Scipio Aemilianus.* Oxford: Clarendon Press, 1967.

Aymard, J. *Essai sur les chasses romaines.* Bibliothèque des écoles françaises d'Athènes et de Rome 171. Paris: E. de Boccard, 1951.

Badian, E. "The Early Historians." In *Latin Historians,* ed. T. A. Dorey, pp. 1–38. New York: Basic Books, 1966.

Barrett, Anthony A. *Caligula.* New Haven: Yale University Press, 1989.

Barthes, Roland. "Le discours de l'histoire." *Social Science Information* 6 (1967): 65–75.

———. *The Rustle of Language.* Translated by R. Howard. New York: Hill and Wang, 1986.

Bates, D. G. "Normative and Alternative Systems of Marriage among the Yoruk of Southeastern Turkey." *Anthropological Quarterly* 47 (1974): 270–87.

Bayet, Jean, ed. *Tite-Live: Histoire romaine.* Vol. 4. Budé series. Paris: Les belles lettres, 1965.

———, ed. *Tite-Live: Histoire romaine.* Vol. 5. Budé series. Paris: Les belles lettres, 1959.

Benveniste, Émile. *Le vocabulaire des institutions indo-européennes.* 2 vols. Paris: Les éditions de Minuit, 1969.

Bickerman, Elias J. "*Origines Gentium.*" *Classical Philology* 47 (1952): 65–81.

227

Boëthius, Axel. *Etruscan and Early Roman Architecture.* 2d ed. New York: Penguin, 1978.

Bömer, Franz, ed. *P. Ovidius Naso Die Fasten.* 2 vols. Heidelberg: Carl Winter, 1957.

Bonjour, M. "Les personnages féminins et la terre natale dans l'épisode de Coriolan (Liv. 2, 40)." *Revue des études latines* 53 (1975): 157–81.

Bourdieu, Pierre. *Outline of a Theory of Practice.* Translated by Richard Nice. Cambridge Studies in Social Anthropology 16. Cambridge: Cambridge University Press, 1977.

Briscoe, John. Review of *Livy: The Composition of His History,* by T. J. Luce. *Journal of Roman Studies* 68 (1978): 227–28.

Brunt, P. A. "*Nobilitas* and *Novitas.*" *Journal of Roman Studies* 72 (1982): 1–17.

Burck, Erich. "Aktuelle Probleme der Livius-Interpretation." *Beihefte zum Gymnasium* 4 (1964): 220–30, 241–45.

———. *Das Geschichtswerk des Titus Livius.* Bibliothek der klassischen Altertumswissenschaften, n.s. 2, vol. 87. Heidelberg: Carl Winter, 1992.

———. *Die Erzählungskunst des T. Livius.* Berlin and Zürich: Weidmann, 1964.

———. *Vom Menschenbild in der römischen Literatur: Ausgewählte Schriften,* 2 vols. edited by Eckard Lefèvre. Heidelberg: Carl Winter, 1966 and 1981.

———. "Zum Rombild des Livius." *Der altsprachliche Unterricht* 3 (1957): 34–75.

———, ed. *Wege zu Livius.* Darmstadt: Wissenschaftliche Buchgesellschaft, 1967.

Burke, Kenneth. *Permanence and Change: An Anatomy of Purpose.* 3d ed. Berkeley: University of California Press, 1984.

———. *Perspectives by Incongruity.* Edited by Stanley Edgar Hyman. Bloomington: Indiana University Press, 1964.

Cahoon, Leslie. "The Bed as Battlefield." *Transactions of the American Philological Association* 118 (1988): 293–307.

Ceauşescu, Petre. "Altera Roma—Histoire d'une folie politique." *Historia* 25 (1976): 79–108.

Chaplin, Jane D. *Livy's Use of Exempla and the Lessons of the Past.* Diss., Princeton University, 1993.

Cichorius, C. *Römische Studien.* 2d ed. Darmstadt: Wissenschaftliches Buchgesellschaft, 1961.

Classen, C. J. "Gottmenschentum in der römischen Republik." *Gymnasium* 70 (1963): 312–38.

———. "Romulus in der römischen Republik." *Philologus* 106 (1962): 174–204.

———. "Zur Herkunft der Sage von Romulus und Remus." *Historia* 12 (1963): 447–57.

Collingwood, R. G. *The Idea of History.* Oxford: Clarendon Press, 1946.

Comolli, Jean-Luc, and Jean Narboni. *Cahiers du cinéma* 216 (1969): 11–15. Translated and reprinted in *Movies and Methods,* ed. Bill Nichols, vol. 1, pp. 22–30. Berkeley: University of California Press, 1976–85.

Corbier, Mireille. "Family Behavior of the Roman Aristocracy, Second Century B.C.–First Century A.D." Translated by Ann Cremin. In *Women's History and*

Ancient History, ed. Sarah B. Pomeroy, pp. 173–96. Chapel Hill: University of North Carolina Press, 1991.

Cornell, T. J. "Aeneas and the Twins: The Development of the Roman Foundation Legend." *Proceedings of the Cambridge Philological Society* 201 (n.s. 21) (1975): 1–32.

———. "The Formation of the Historical Tradition of Early Rome." In *Past Perspectives: Studies in Greek and Roman Historical Writing*, ed. I. S. Moxon, J. D. Smart, and A. J. Woodman, pp. 67–86. Cambridge: Cambridge University Press, 1986.

———. "The Value of the Literary Tradition Concerning Archaic Rome." In *Social Struggles in Archaic Rome: New Perspectives on the Conflict of the Orders*, ed. Kurt A. Raaflaub, pp. 52–76. Berkeley: University of California Press, 1986.

Crick, Malcolm. *Explorations in Language and Meaning: Towards a Semiotic Anthropology*. New York: John Wiley/Halsted, 1976.

Csillag, Pál. *The Augustan Laws on Family Relations*. Budapest: Akadémiai Kiadó, 1976.

Culham, Phyllis. "Decentering the Text: The Case of Ovid." *Helios* n.s. 17 (1990): 161–70.

Curran, Leo C. "Rape and Rape Victims in the *Metamorphoses.*" *Arethusa* 11 (1978): 213–41.

Danforth, Loring M. *The Death Rituals of Rural Greece*. Princeton: Princeton University Press, 1982.

Datta, V. N. *Sati: A Historical, Social, and Philosophical Enquiry into the Hindu Rite of Widow Burning*. Riverdale, Md.: Riverdale, 1988.

Delia, Diana. "Fulvia Reconsidered." In *Women's History and Ancient History*, ed. Sarah B. Pomeroy, pp. 197–217. Chapel Hill: University of North Carolina Press, 1991.

Deininger, Jürgen. "Livius und der Prinzipat." *Klio* 67 (1985): 265–72.

Demougin, S. "Uterque ordo: Les rapports entre l'ordre sénatorial et l'ordre équestre sous les Julio-Claudiens." In *Epigrafia e ordine senatorio*. Atti del Colloquio internazionale AIEGL su epigrafia e ordine senatorio, Roma, 14–20 maggio 1981, vol. 4. Rome: Edizione de storia e letteratura, 1982.

de Romilly, J. *The Rise and Fall of States according to Greek Authors*. Jerome Lectures 11. Ann Arbor: University of Michigan Press, 1977.

Derrida, Jacques. "Structure, Sign, and Play in the Discourse of the Human Sciences." In *The Structuralist Controversy*, ed. R. Macksey and E. Donato, pp. 250–69. Baltimore: Johns Hopkins University Press, 1977.

de Sélincourt, Aubrey, trans. *Livy: The Early History of Rome*. Baltimore: Penguin, 1973.

Dessau, H. "Livius und Augustus." *Hermes* 41 (1906): 142–51.

Dewald, Carolyn. "Narrative Surface and Authorial Voice in Herodotus' *Histories.*" *Arethusa* 20 (1987): 147–74.

Dixon, Suzanne. "Family Finances: Terentia and Tullia." In *The Family in Ancient Rome: New Perspectives*, ed. Beryl Rawson, pp. 93–120. Ithaca, N.Y.: Cornell University Press, 1986.

———. *"Infirmitas Sexus:* Womanly Weakness in Roman Law." *Tijdschrift voor Rechtsgeschiedenis* 52 (1984): 343–71.

———. "The Marriage Alliance in the Roman Elite." *Journal of Family History* 10 (1985): 353–78.

———. *The Roman Family.* Baltimore: Johns Hopkins University Press, 1992.

———. *Roman Mothers.* London: Croom Helm, 1988.

Dumézil, Georges. *Horace et les curiaces.* 5th ed. New York: Arno, 1978.

———. *L'héritage indo-européen à Rome.* Paris: Gallimard, 1949.

———. *Mariages indo-européens suivi de quinze questions romaines.* Paris: Payot, 1979.

———. *Servius et la fortune.* Paris: Gallimard, 1943.

Dutoit, E. "Thème de 'La force qui se détruit elle-même' (Hor., *Epod.* 16, 2) et ses variations chez quelques auteurs latins." *Revue des études latines* 17 (1939): 365–73.

Earl, D. C. *The Political Thought of Sallust.* Amsterdam: Adolf M. Hakkert, 1966.

Eitrem, Samson. "Heros." *RE* 1.8.1 (1912), col. 1136.

Empson, William. *Seven Types of Ambiguity.* 3d ed. London: Hogarth, 1984.

Evans, Jane. *The Art of Persuasion: Political Propaganda from Aeneas to Brutus.* Ann Arbor: University of Michigan Press, 1992.

Evans-Grubbs, Judith. "Abduction Marriage in Antiquity: A Law of Constantine (*CTh* IX.24.1) and Its Social Context." *Journal of Roman Studies* 79 (1989): 59–82.

Favro, Diane. *"Pater urbis:* Augustus as City Father of Rome." *Journal of the Society of Architectural Historians* 50 (1992): 61–84.

Feichtinger, B. *"Ad Maiorem Gloriam Romae:* Ideologie und Fiktion in der Historiographie des Livius." *Latomus* 51 (1992): 3–33.

Fish, Stanley. "Interpreting the *Variorum.*" *Critical Inquiry* 2 (1976): 465–85. Reprinted in *Reader-Response Criticism,* ed. Jane P. Tompkins, pp. 164–84. Baltimore: Johns Hopkins University Press, 1980.

———. "Literature in the Reader: Affective Stylistics." *New Literary History* 2 (1970): 123–62. Reprinted in *Reader-Response Criticism,* ed. Jane P. Tompkins, pp. 70–100. Baltimore: Johns Hopkins University Press, 1980.

Fornara, Charles. *The Nature of History in Ancient Greece and Rome.* Berkeley: University of California Press, 1983.

Frazer, James George, ed. *Publii Ovidii Nasonis Fastorum libri sex: The "Fasti" of Ovid.* 5 vols. London: Macmillan, 1929.

Frisk, H. *Griechisches etymologisches Wörterbuch.* 3 vols. Heidelberg: Carl Winter, 1973.

Fustel de Coulanges, Numa Denis. *The Ancient City.* Garden City, N.Y.: Doubleday, 1956.

Gabba, Emilio. "Considerazioni sulla tradizione letteraria sulle origini della repubblica." In *Les origines de la République romaine.* Entretiens sur l'antiquité classique 13. Vandoeuvres-Genève: Fondation Hardt, 1966.

———. *Dionysius and the History of Archaic Rome.* Sather Classical Lectures 56. Berkeley: University of California Press, 1991.

———. "La 'storia di Roma arcaica' di Dionigi d' Alicarnasso." *ANRW* 2.30.1 (1982): 799–816.

———. "Political and Cultural Aspects of the Classicistic Revival in the Augustan Age." *Classical Antiquity* 1 (1982): 43–65.

Gagé, Jean. *Matronalia.* Collection Latomus 60. Brussels: Revue des études latines, 1963.

Gamel, Mary-Kay. "Ovid Imitating Vergil: *Aeneid* I and *Metamorphoses* I." Unpublished manuscript.

Gardner, Jane F. *Women in Roman Law and Society.* Bloomington: Indiana University Press, 1986.

Gelzer, M. "Nasicas Widerspruch gegen die Zerstörung Karthagos." *Philologus* 40 (1931): 261–99.

Gillis, John R. Introduction to *Commemorations: The Politics of National Identity,* ed. John R. Gillis, pp. 3–24. Princeton: Princeton University Press, 1994.

Gjerstadt, E. *Legends and Facts of Early Roman History.* Scripta minora, Regiae societatis humaniarum litterarum Ludensis, 1960–61, vol. 2. Lund: Gleerup, 1962.

Gratwick, A. S. "Free or Not So Free? Wives and Daughters in the Late Roman Republic." In *Marriage and Property,* ed. Elizabeth M. Craik, pp. 38–53. Aberdeen: Aberdeen University Press, 1984.

Gries, Konrad. "Livy's Use of Dramatic Speech." *American Journal of Philology* 70 (1949): 118–41.

Gwosdz, A. *Der Begriff des römischen Princeps.* Diss., Breslau, 1933.

Habicht, Chr. *Gottmenschentum und griechische Städte.* Zetemata 14. Munich: C. H. Beck, 1956.

Hallett, Judith P. *Fathers and Daughters in Roman Society.* Princeton: Princeton University Press, 1984.

Handman, M.-E. *La violence et la ruse: Hommes et femmes dans un village grec.* La Calade: Édisud, 1983.

Hanfmann, George M. A. *Roman Art.* New York: W. W. Norton, 1975.

Hartog, François. "Rome et la Grèce: Les choix de Denys d' Halicarnasse." In Ἑλληνισμος: *Quelques jalons pour une histoire de l'identité grecque,* ed. S. Said, pp. 149–67. Université des sciences humaines de Strasbourg, Travaux du centre de recherche sur le proche-orient et la Grèce antiques 11. Leiden: E. J. Brill, 1991.

Hedrick, Charles. "The Meaning of Material Culture: Herodotus, Thucydides, and Their Sources." In *Nomodeiktes: Greek Studies in Honor of Martin Ostwald,* ed. Ralph R. Rosen and J. Farrell, pp. 17–37. Ann Arbor: University of Michigan Press, 1993.

Hellegouarc'h, J. "Le principat de Camille." *Revue des études latines* 48 (1970): 112–32.

———. *Le vocabulaire latin des relations et des partis politiques sous la République.* Paris: Les belles lettres, 1972.

Hellmann, Fritz. *Livius-Interpretationen.* Berlin: Walter de Gruyter, 1939.

Hemker, Julie. "Rape and the Founding of Rome." *Helios* n.s. 12 (1985): 41–47.

Henderson, John. "Livy and the Invention of History." In *History as Text,* ed. Averil Cameron, pp. 66–85. Trowbridge: Duckworth, 1989.

Herzfeld, Michael. *Anthropology through the Looking-Glass.* Cambridge: Cambridge University Press, 1987.

———. "Exploring a Metaphor of Exposure." *Journal of American Folklore* 92 (1979): 285–301.

———. "Gender Pragmatics: Agency, Speech, and Bride-Theft in a Cretan Mountain Village." *Anthropology* 9 (1985): 25–44.

———. *The Poetics of Manhood: Contest and Identity in a Cretan Mountain Village.* Princeton: Princeton University Press, 1985.

Heurgon, Jacques, ed. *Tite-Live: Ab urbe condita liber primus.* 2d ed. Budé series. Paris: Les belles lettres, 1970.

Hickson, Frances V. "Augustus *Triumphator:* Manipulation of the Triumphal Theme in the Political Program of Augustus." *Latomus* 50 (1992): 124–38.

History and the Concept of Time. History and Theory 6. Middletown, Conn.: Wesleyan University Press, 1966.

Hopkins, K. "The Age of Roman Girls at Marriage." *Population Studies* 18 (1965): 309–27.

Houston, George W. Review of *Livy: The Composition of His History,* by T. J. Luce. *Classical Philology* 75 (1980): 73–77.

Hubaux, Jean. *Rome et Véies: Recherches sur la chronologie légendaire du moyen age romain.* Paris: Les belles lettres, 1958.

Hunter, Virginia. *Past and Process in Herodotus and Thucydides.* Princeton: Princeton University Press, 1982.

Jaeger, M. K. "*Custodia Fidelis Memoriae:* Livy's Story of M. Manlius Capitolinus." *Latomus* 52 (1993): 350–63.

Jal, Paul. Review of *Livy: The Composition of His History,* by T. J. Luce. *Latomus* 39 (1980): 230–34.

Jameson, Fredric. *The Political Unconscious: Narrative as a Socially Symbolic Act.* Ithaca, N.Y.: Cornell University Press, 1981.

Jones, C. P. *Plutarch and Rome.* Oxford: Clarendon Press, 1971.

Joplin, Patricia Klindienst. "Ritual Work on Human Flesh: Livy's Lucretia and the Rape of the Body Politic." *Helios* 17 (1990): 51–70.

Kajanto, I. *God and Fate in Livy.* Annales Universitatis Turkensis 64. Turku: Turun Yliopiston Kustantamo, 1957.

———. "Notes on Livy's Conception of History." *Arctos* 2 (1958): 55–63.

Klepl, Hirta. *Lucrez und Virgil in ihren Lehrgedichten.* Darmstadt: Wissenschaftliche Buchgesellschaft, 1967.

Klingner, F. Review of *Die Erzählungskunst des T. Livius,* by Erich Burck. *Gnomon* 11 (1939): 583–86.

Koestermann, E., ed. *Cornelius Tacitus: Annalen.* 2 vols. Heidelberg: Carl Winter, 1965.

Köstler, R. "Raub- und Kaufehe bei den Römern." *Zeitschrift der Savigny-Stiftung für Rechtsgeschichte: Romanistische Abteilung* 65 (1947): 43–68.

Kraus, Christina S. "Initium Turbandi Omnium A Femina Ortum Est: Fabia Minor and the Election of 367 B.C." *Phoenix* 45 (1991): 314–25.

Lambert, André. *Die indirekte Rede als künstlerisches Stilmittel des Livius.* Diss., Zürich, 1946.

Leach, Edmund. *Culture and Communication.* Cambridge: Cambridge University Press, 1976.

——. *Rethinking Anthropology.* New York: Humanities Press, 1971.

Leach, Eleanor Winsor. *Vergil's "Eclogues": Landscapes of Experience.* Ithaca, N.Y.: Cornell University Press, 1974.

Leeman, A. D. *Orationis Ratio.* 2 vols. Amsterdam: Adolf M. Hakkert, 1963.

Lefèvre, Eckard, and Eckard Olshausen, eds. *Livius: Werk und Rezeption: Festschrift für Erich Burck zum 80. Geburtstag.* Munich: C. H. Beck, 1983.

Levene, D. S. *Religion in Livy.* Mnemosyne Supplement 127. Leiden and New York: E. J. Brill, 1993.

Levick, Barbara. *Tiberius the Politician.* London: Croom Helm, 1976.

Lévi-Strauss, Claude. *The Savage Mind.* Chicago: University of Chicago Press, 1966.

——. "The Story of Asdiwal." In *The Structural Study of Myth and Totemism,* ed. E. Leach, pp. 1–47. London: Tavistock, 1967.

Lindsay, Wallace M., ed. *Nonii Marcelli De compendiosa doctrina libros XX.* 3 vols. Hildesheim: G. Olms, 1964.

——, ed. *Sextus Pompeius Festus.* Hildesheim: G. Olms, 1965.

Lintott, A. W. "Imperial Expansion and Moral Decline in the Roman Republic." *Historia* 21 (1972): 626–38.

Lockwood, W. G. "Bride-Theft and Social Maneuverability in Western Bosnia." *Anthropological Quarterly* 47 (1974): 288–303.

Luce, T. J. "Ancient Views on the Causes of Bias in Historical Writing." *Classical Philology* 84 (1989): 16–31.

——. "The Dating of Livy's First Decade." *Transactions of the American Philological Association* 96 (1965): 209–40.

——. "Design and Structure in Livy 5.32–55." *Transactions of the American Philological Association* 102 (1971): 265–302.

——. *Livy: The Composition of His History.* Princeton: Princeton University Press, 1977.

MacDougall, Hugh A. *Racial Myth in English History: Trojans, Teutons, and Anglo-Saxons.* Hanover, N.H.: University Press of New England, 1982.

Magnarella, P. J. *Tradition and Change in a Turkish Town.* New York: John Wiley and Sons, 1974.

Marincola, John. "Herodotian Narrative and the Narrator's Presence." *Arethusa* 20 (1987): 121–45.

Mazza, Mario. *Storia e ideologia in Tito Livio.* Catania: Bonanno, 1966.

McGann, M. J. "The Three Worlds of Horace's 'Satires.' " In *Horace,* ed. C. D. N. Costa, pp. 59–93. London: Routledge and Kegan Paul, 1973.

Mensching, E. "Livius, Cossus und Augustus." *Museum Helveticum* 24 (1967): 12–32.

Mette, H. J. "Livius und Augustus." *Gymnasium* 68 (1961): 269–85. Reprinted in *Wege zu Livius,* ed. E. Burck, pp. 156–66. Darmstadt: Wissenschaftliche Buchgesellschaft, 1967.

Miles, G. B. "*Georgics* 3.209–294: *Amor* and Civilization." *California Studies in Classical Antiquity* 8 (1975): 177–97.

———. *Virgil's "Georgics": A New Interpretation.* Berkeley: University of California Press, 1980.

Moles, John. "Livy's Preface." *Proceedings of the Cambridge Philological Society* 39 (1993): 141–68.

Momigliano, A. "Camillus and Concord." *Classical Quarterly* 36 (1942): 111–20.

Münzer, F. "Furius" (44). *RE* 1.7.1 (1910), cols. 324–48.

Nagy, Gregory. *Pindar's Homer.* Baltimore: Johns Hopkins University Press, 1990.

Nash, Ernest. *Pictorial Dictionary of Ancient Rome.* 2 vols. 2d ed. repr. New York: Hacker, 1981.

Neraudau, J.-P. *La jeunesse dans la littérature et les institutions de la Rome républicaine.* Paris: Les belles lettres, 1979.

Nicolet, Claude. "Augustus, Government, and the Propertied Classes." In *Caesar Augustus,* ed. Fergus Millar and Erich Segal, pp. 89–128. Oxford: Clarendon Press, 1984.

Obeyesekere, Gananath. *The Work of Culture.* The Lewis Henry Morgan Lectures, 1982. Chicago: University of Chicago Press, 1990.

Ogilvie, R. M. *A Commentary on Livy: Books 1–5.* Oxford: Oxford University Press, 1970.

———. "Livy." In *The Cambridge History of Classical Literature,* vol. 2, *Latin Literature,* ed. A. J. Kenney and W. V. Clausen, pp. 458–466. Cambridge: Cambridge University Press, 1982.

———. "Livy, Licinius Macer, and the *Libri Lintei.*" *Journal of Roman Studies* 48 (1958): 41–46.

———, ed. *Titi Livi Ab urbe condita.* Vol. 1. Oxford: Clarendon Press, 1979.

O'Loughlin, Michael. *The Garlands of Repose: The Literary Celebration of Civic and Retired Leisure.* Chicago: University of Chicago Press, 1978.

Packard, David W. *A Concordance to Livy.* Cambridge, Mass.: Harvard University Press, 1968.

Parry, A. M. "The Language of Thucydides' Description of the Plague." *Bulletin of the Institute of Classical Studies* 16 (1969): 106–8.

———. " 'Thucydides' Historical Perspective." *Yale Classical Studies* 72 (1972): 47–61.

Pelling, C. B. R. "Plutarch and Roman Politics." In *Past Perspectives,* ed. I. S. Moxon, J. D. Smart, and A. J. Woodman, pp. 159–87. Cambridge: Cambridge University Press, 1986.

Peterson, Hans. "Livy and Augustus." *Transactions of the American Philological Association* 92 (1961): 440–52.

Petrocheilos, Nikos. *Roman Attitudes to the Greeks.* Vivliotheke Sophias N. Saripolou 25. Athens: National and Capodistrian University of Athens, Faculty of Arts, 1974.

Phillips, Jane E. "Current Research in Livy's First Decade: 1959–1979." *ANRW* 2.30.2 (1982), pp. 998–1057.

———. "Livy and the Beginning of a New Society." *Classical Bulletin* 55 (1979): 87–92.

———. "Roman Mothers and the Lives of Their Adult Daughters." *Helios* n.s. 6 (1978): 69–80.

Platner, S. B., and T. Ashby. *A Topographical Dictionary of Ancient Rome.* Oxford: Oxford University Press, 1929.

Plumpe, J. *Auctoritas Maiorum.* Diss., Münster, 1935.

Pomeroy, Sarah. "The Relationship of the Married Woman to Her Blood Relatives in Rome." *Ancient Society* 7 (1976): 215–27.

Poucet, J. *Recherches sur la légende sabine des origines de Rome.* Recueil de travaux d'histoire et de philologie, ser. 4, fasc. 37. Kinshasa: Éditions de l'Université Lovanium, 1967.

———. "Temps mythique et temps historique: Les origines et les premiers siècles de Rome." *Gerion* 5 (1987): 69–85.

Prehn, K. "Κτίστης." *RE* 1.11.2 (1922), cols. 2083–87.

Press, Gerald A. *The Development of the Idea of History in Antiquity.* Montreal: McGill-Queens University Press, 1982.

Price, Simon. "From Noble Funerals to Divine Cult: The Consecration of Roman Emperors." In *Rituals of Royalty: Power and Ceremonial in Traditional Societies,* ed. David Cannadine and Simon Price, pp. 56–105. Cambridge: Cambridge University Press, 1987.

———. *Rituals and Power: The Roman Imperial Cult in Asia Minor.* Cambridge: Cambridge University Press, 1984.

Pritchett, Kendrick W. *Dionysius of Halicarnassus: On Thucydides.* Berkeley: University of California Press, 1975.

Raaflaub, Kurt A., and L. J. Samons II. "Opposition to Augustus." In *Between Republic and Empire: Interpretations of Augustus and His Principate,* ed. Kurt A. Raaflaub and Mark Toher, pp. 417–54. Berkeley: University of California Press, 1990.

Raditsa, Leo Ferrero. "Augustus' Legislation Concerning Marriage, Procreation, Love Affairs, and Adultery." *ANRW* 2.13 (1980), pp. 278–339.

Rambaud, M. "Une défaillance du rationalisme chez Tite-Live?" *Information littéraire* 7 (1975): 21–30.

Rech, H. *Mos Maiorum.* Diss., Marburg, 1936.

Reinhold, Meyer. *From Republic to Principate: An Historical Commentary on Cassius Dio's "Roman History," Books 49–52 (39–29 B.C.).* Atlanta: Scholars Press, 1988.

Richlin, Amy. "Reading Ovid's Rapes." In *Pornography and Representation in Greece and Rome,* ed. Amy Richlin, pp. 158–79. New York: Oxford University Press, 1992.

Roloff, H. *Maiores bei Cicero.* Diss., Göttingen, 1938. Pp. 10–34, 56–82, and 128–31 are reprinted under the same title in *Römische Wertbegriffe,* ed. Hans Oppermann, Wege der Forschung 34 (Darmstadt: Wissenschaftliche Buchgesellschaft, 1967), pp. 274–372.

Rosaldo, Renato. *Culture and Truth.* Boston: Beacon Press, 1989.

Rubin, Gayle. "The Traffic in Women." In *Toward an Anthropology of Women,* ed. Rayna R. Reiter, pp. 157–210. New York: Monthly Review Press, 1975.

Runchina, Giovanni. "Letteratura e ideologia nell' Età Augustea." *Annali della Facoltà di Magistro dell' Università di Cagliari* n.s. 3 (1978–79): 15–87.

Rykwert, Joseph. *The Idea of a Town.* Princeton: Princeton University Press, 1976.

Sacks, Kenneth. *Polybius on the Writing of History.* Classical Studies 24. Berkeley: University of California Press, 1981.

Sage, Evan T., trans. *Livy.* Vol. 11. Loeb Classical Library, no. 313. Cambridge, Mass.: Harvard University Press, 1965.

Saller, Richard P. "Men's Age at Marriage and Its Consequences in the Roman Family." *Classical Philology* 82 (1987): 21–34.

———. "*Patria potestas* and the Stereotype of the Roman Family," *Continuity and Change* 1(1986): 7–22.

Schultze, Cl. "Dionysius of Halicarnassus and His Audience." In *Past Perspectives,* ed. I. S. Moxon, J. D. Smart, and A. J. Woodman, pp. 121–41. Cambridge: Cambridge University Press, 1986.

Schur, W. *Sallust als Historiker.* Stuttgart: W. Kohlhammer, 1934.

Scott, Kenneth. "The Political Propaganda of 44–30 B.C." *Memoirs of the American Academy in Rome* 11 (1933): 7–49.

Selden, Daniel. "*Ceveat lector:* Catullus and the Rhetoric of Performance." In *Innovations of Antiquity,* ed. Ralph Hexter and Daniel Selden, pp. 461–512. New York: Routledge, 1992.

Serres, Michel. *Rome: Le livre des fondations.* Paris: Éditions Grasset & Fasquelle, 1983. Translated by Felicia McCarren under the title *Rome: The Book of Foundations* (Stanford: Stanford University Press, 1991).

Shaw, Bernard D. "The Age of Roman Girls at Marriage: Some Reconsiderations." *Journal of Roman Studies* 77 (1987): 30–46.

Sherwin-White, A. N. *The Roman Citizenship.* 2d ed. Oxford: Clarendon Press, 1973.

Smith, Jonathan Z. *To Take Place: Toward Theory in Ritual.* Chicago: University of Chicago Press, 1987.

Snell, Bruno. *The Discovery of the Mind.* Translated by T. G. Rosenmeyer. New York: Dover, 1982.

Solodow, Joseph B. "Livy and the Story of Horatius, 1:24–26." *Transactions of the American Philological Association* 109 (1979): 251–68.

Sordi, M. "Sulla chronologia liviana del IV secolo." *Helikon* 5 (1965): 3–44.

Struchbury, Elizabeth Leigh. "Blood Fire and Mediation: Sacrificing and Widow Burning in the Nineteenth Century." In *Women in Nepal and India,* ed. Michael Allen and S. N. Mukherjee. Australian National University Monographs on South Asia 8. Canberra: Australian National University Press, 1982.

Stübler, G. *Die Religiosität des Livius.* Tübinger Beiträges zur Altertumswissenschaft 35. Stuttgart: W. Kohlhammer, 1941.

Syme, Ronald. "Livy and Augustus." *Harvard Studies in Classical Philology* 64 (1959): 27–87.

———. *The Roman Revolution.* Oxford: Oxford University Press, 1967.

———. *Sallust.* Sather Classical Lectures 33. Berkeley: University of California Press, 1964.

Toher, Mark. "Augustus and the Evolution of Roman Historiography." In *Between Republic and Empire: Interpretations of Augustus and His Principate,* ed. Kurt A. Raaflaub and Mark Toher, pp. 139–54. Berkeley: University of California Press, 1990.

Torelli, M. *Lavinio e Roma: Riti iniziatici e matrimonio tra archeologia e storia.* Rome: Edizioni Quasar, 1984.

Treggiari, Susan. "*Iam Proterva Fronte:* Matrimonial Advances by Roman Women." In *The Craft of the Ancient Historian: Essays in Honor of Chester G. Starr,* ed. J. W. Eadie and J. Ober, pp. 331–52. Lanham, Md.: University Press of America, 1985.

———. *Roman Marriage.* Oxford: Oxford University Press, 1991.

Trompf, Garry. *The Idea of Historical Recurrence in Western Thought.* Berkeley: University of California Press, 1979.

Tscherikover, Alexander. *Hellenistic Civilization and the Jews.* New York: Atheneum, 1970.

Usher, Stephen. *The Historians of Greece and Rome.* Norman: University of Oklahoma Press, 1985.

Van Gennep, Arnold. *The Rites of Passage.* Chicago: University of Chicago Press, 1960.

Vierneisel, Klaus, and Paul Zanker, eds. *Die Bildnisse des Augustus: Herrscherbild und Politik im kaiserlichen Rom.* Munich: Glyptothek und Museums für Abgüsse klassischer Bildwerke, 1979.

Von Fritz, Kurt. *The Theory of the Mixed Constitution in Antiquity.* New York: Arno Press, 1975.

Walbank, F. W. *A Historical Commentary on Polybius.* 3 vols. Oxford: Clarendon Press, 1979.

———. *Polybius.* Berkeley: University of California Press, 1972.

Walde, Alios, and J. B. Hofmann. *Lateinisches etymologisches Wörterbuch.* 3 vols. 3d ed. Heidelberg: Carl Winter, 1938–56.

Wallace-Hadrill, Andrew. "Family and Inheritance in the Augustan Marriage Laws." *Proceedings of the Cambridge Philological Society* 27 (1981): 58–80.

———. "Rome's Cultural Revolution." Review of *The Power of Images in the Age of Augustus,* by Paul J. Zanker. *Journal of Roman Studies* 79 (1989): 157–64.

Walsh, P. G. *Livy.* Greece and Rome Surveys in the Classics 8. Oxford: Clarendon Press, 1974.

———. *Livy: His Historical Aims and Methods.* Cambridge: Cambridge University Press, 1961; repr., 1970.

———. "Livy and Augustus." *Proceedings of the African Classical Association* 4 (1961): 26–37.

———. Review of *Livy: The Composition of His History,* by T. J. Luce. *Phoenix* 32 (1978): 171–74.

Watson, Alan. *Rome of the XII Tables: Persons and Property.* Princeton: Princeton University Press, 1975.

Weinstock, Stefan. *Divus Julius.* Oxford: Clarendon Press, 1971.

Whatmough, Joshua. *The Foundations of Roman Italy.* New York: Haskell House, 1971.

Wheatley, Paul. *Pivot of the Four Quarters: A Preliminary Inquiry into the Origins and Character of the Ancient Chinese City.* Chicago: University of Chicago Press, 1971.

White, Hayden. *Metahistory.* Baltimore: Johns Hopkins University Press, 1973.

Will, Edouard, and Claude Orrieux. *Ioudaïsmos-Hellènismos: Essai sur le judaïsme judéen à l'époque hellénistique.* Nancy: Presses universitaires de Nancy, 1986.

Williams, Gordon. "Poetry in the Moral Climate of Augustan Rome." *Journal of Roman Studies* 52 (1962): 28–46.

Wirszubski, Ch. *Libertas as a Political Idea at Rome.* Cambridge: Cambridge University Press, 1968.

Wiseman, T. P. *Clio's Cosmetics: Three Studies in Greco-Roman Literature.* Leicester: Leicester University Press, 1979.

———. "Monuments and the Roman Annalists." In *Past Perspectives: Studies in Greek and Roman Historical Writing,* ed. I. S. Moxon, J. D. Smart, and A. J. Woodman, pp. 87–100. Cambridge: Cambridge University Press, 1986.

———. *New Men in the Roman Senate.* London: Oxford University Press, 1971.

———. "The Wife and Children of Romulus." *Classical Quarterly* 33 (1983): 445–52.

Witte, Kurt. "Über die Form der Darstellung in Livius' Geschichtswerk." *Rheinisches Museum* 65 (1910): 270–305, 359–419. Reprinted separately (Darmstadt: Wissenschaftliche Buchgesellschaft, 1969).

Woodman, A. J. *Rhetoric in Classical Historiography.* Portland, Oreg.: Areopagitica Press, 1988.

———. *Velleius Paterculus: The Tiberian Narrative (2.94–131).* Cambridge: Cambridge University Press, 1977.

Wünsch, Ricardus, ed. *Johannes Lydus: De Mensibus.* Stuttgart: Teubner, 1967.

Zanker, Paul J. *The Power of Images in the Age of Augustus.* Translated by Alan Shapiro. Ann Arbor: University of Michigan Press, 1988.

Index of Ancient
Passages Cited

General Index